The 1967
American League
Pennant Race

The 1967 American League Pennant Race

Four Teams, Six Weeks, One Winner

CAMERON BRIGHT

McFarland & Company, Inc., Publishers
Jefferson, North Carolina

LIBRARY OF CONGRESS CATALOGUING-IN-PUBLICATION DATA

Names: Bright, Cameron, 1960– author.
Title: The 1967 American League pennant race : four teams, six weeks, one winner / Cameron Bright.
Description: Jefferson : McFarland & Company, Inc., Publishers, 2018 | Includes bibliographical references and index.
Identifiers: LCCN 2018004770 | ISBN 9781476672960 (softcover : acid free paper) ∞
Subjects: LCSH: American League of Professional Baseball Clubs—History. | Baseball—United States—History.
Classification: LCC GV875.A15 B75 2018 | DDC 796.357/64097309046—dc23
LC record available at https://lccn.loc.gov/2018004770

BRITISH LIBRARY CATALOGUING DATA ARE AVAILABLE

ISBN (print) 978-1-4766-7296-0
ISBN (ebook) 978-1-4766-3297-1

© 2018 Cameron Bright. All rights reserved

No part of this book may be reproduced or transmitted in any form or by any means, electronic or mechanical, including photocopying or recording, or by any information storage and retrieval system, without permission in writing from the publisher.

Front cover illustration © 2018 CSA Images

Printed in the United States of America

McFarland & Company, Inc., Publishers
  Box 611, Jefferson, North Carolina 28640
  www.mcfarlandpub.com

For my father and mother
Alec and Clarita
Athletes and sports fans

Table of Contents

Acknowledgments ix
Preface 1
Introduction 3
Prologue 7

1—"A bastard every day" 15
2—"Hairy-chested home run hitters" 23
3—"A bucket of warm spit" 30
4—"Watch where you are going, Bush" 39
5—"What are you crying for?" 46
6—"A great manager from the ankles down" 53
7—"I can win in the big leagues" 62
8—"Hope like hell it goes somewhere" 69
9—"The dry side of a fastball" 78
10—"Getting an alligator to play the piano" 86
11—"155,000 rounds of ammunition" 95
12—"The dumbest pitcher I ever caught" 103
13—"Sometimes you wonder what these kids are thinking" 112
14—"Die right here in the dirt" 121
15—"A menace to baseball" 126
16—"That runt" 136

17—Four-Way Tie	147
18—"That friggin' skinny, shallow body"	154
19—"A well-mannered colored boy"	164
20—"Too big for us"	176
21—"Short-winded"	186
22—"$10,000"	196
23—"We are now out of tomorrows"	204
24—"Black Wednesday"	212
25—"I'll make sure I hit one for you"	225
26—"It was a dumb play"	236
27—"Surprised the hell out of me"	243
28—The Last Game	256
The 1967 World Series	263
Epilogue: After 1967	275
Chapter Notes	287
Bibliography	303
Index	309

Acknowledgments

Both my parents were athletes—members of the Olympic ski team—and then sports fans. While I was a child, my father took me to all manner of sporting contests: professional baseball, hockey, basketball and tennis, all levels of track and field, college football, baseball, and especially hockey, high school sports, and even sports that he had little interest in like soccer, curling and lacrosse. I owe my passion as a sports fan to him.

I don't remember the first time I visited Fenway Park, but I was familiar with it when a classmate and I were allowed to go to a night game in the late spring of 1967 with our first grade teacher. I had never been to a night game. As we emerged from the runway in the stands beyond third base, the bright green field under the lights dazzled me. It remains one of the most awesome sights that I have ever seen.

In New England, the 1967 season remains very much alive. As I first contemplated this book, I was driving with the radio on. The DJ unexpectedly referenced Billy Rohr. Although almost 45 years had elapsed since Rohr's short career ended, the announcer felt no need to identify Rohr for his audience. I was not listening to a sports talk station, but one with an all-music format.

When a librarian who fielded my many requests for obscure and long out-of-print baseball tomes found out why I wanted these books, she brought to the library and showed me her 8 × 10 autographed glossy of Tony Conigliaro. She is not alone. The number of people who have mementos from the 1967 season or can instantly, and excitedly, recall details like Dean Chance's throwing motion or Walt Williams backing up first base constantly surprises me. Their enthusiasm kept me inspired.

While writing this book, I have benefited from a lot of support. Researching from a small town in the corner of the country would not be possible without the tremendous resources of public libraries. In addition to Joanne Libby and her colleagues at Freeport Public Library, I am particularly grateful to Eileen, the interlibrary loan librarian at Portland Public Library, for her persistence in sourcing and borrowing reels of newspaper microfilm. Even institutions officially willing to lend microfilm are often reluctant, have other short-term priorities, or are understaffed. Without her tenacity, I would not have had access to the material to write this book. My thanks are also due to Abraham Schechter and Gabrielle Danielo at the Portland Public Library's Portland Room.

Another valuable resource was the Giamatti Research Center in Cooperstown, New York. Reference librarian Cassidy Lent pulled and assembled a wide-ranging list of player files, reference books and bound periodicals to make my visits there as efficient as possible. She was also a valuable resource for prioritizing my research time. Thanks to her, my days were productive beyond reasonable expectation.

Denny Ryus bailed me out at a critical moment with much needed image support.

Statistics are vitally important to any conversation about baseball. There are two websites that I consulted constantly at every stage of the process. The voluminous information on retrosheet.org and baseball-reference.com was invaluable for corroborating statistics and game summaries from other sources.

I read hundreds of newspapers from the 1967 season on microfilm. The beat reporters' game stories included revealing interviews and eyewitness perspectives that cannot be gleaned from objective game summaries. Their passion for the game, the teams, and the players was an incredible source of insight. Opinions of sports columnists helped me identify and focus on the important issues of the pennant race during 1967.

David Weld and Pete Collins each read an early version of this manuscript. I am thankful for their best efforts. All the remaining mistakes and oversights are my responsibility.

This book would not have been possible without the love and support of my wife Patty, who is the biggest baseball fan in the family. I am grateful to my now grown children Wesley and Acacia who patiently listened with apparent interest to countless stories that began, "You won't believe what happened in 1967."

Preface

On September 6, 1967, four teams tied for the lead of the American League. It was not a quirky coincidence. All four teams would spend the season's final six exhausting weeks locked in the biggest, closest pennant race in major league history. During the final month, each team led at some point and none led by more than one game.

The Red Sox won the pennant on the season's last day, with help from the California Angels. Only four days before, the Red Sox were loudly booed off their home field and believed they had lost their last chance at the pennant.

Any of the teams could have, or should have, won. The Tigers, Twins and White Sox were not merely worthy foils, but just as exciting and frustrating for their fans as the Red Sox. All four teams supplied stars, goats and characters. Each figures equally in this great story of playing under pressure.

A critical part of understanding this pennant race is its context. The 1967 season was at or near the end of one of baseball's eras. There were no playoffs, no free agents, no long-term player contracts, no designated hitter, no closers, and no weightlifting. Pitchers still threw from a high mound; starters often completed nine innings; and the spitball, while officially banned, seemed ubiquitous. Some players did not wear batting helmets and catchers had only cloth caps under their masks.

Players and their skills were not viewed as rare assets to be preserved. Instead, they were paid and deployed like perishable commodities. Even correcting for inflation, salaries of the day seem small. The major-league minimum of $7,000 adjusted for inflation would be about $50,000 50 years later. The highest paid stars made $100,000—about three quarters of a million dollars. Baseball was such a small business that one owner left his office door at the stadium open to the public.

Although that seems quaint, these were not simpler times somehow innocent and carefree. The season featured thousands of war fatalities in Vietnam, large-scale urban rioting and massive industrial strikes. This upheaval forced players to frequently miss games and games to be postponed and moved.

This book chronologically covers the entire 1967 season, although the focus is on the tensions and drama of the pennant race. The early season provides context to introduce the characters, their times and the game they played.

The emphasis is on human beings striving to succeed in different ways as the pennant race took each team through one pivotal crisis after another. Fairly conventional statistics are used as shorthand for describing player performance. There are no groundbreaking analytics. Players' personal lives are examined only in the rare cases where they have an impact on this pennant race.

Baseball biographies and team histories covering the 1960s provide the skeleton of information around which the book is organized and from which many of its main themes are drawn. The majority of the research, though, was taken from contemporary periodicals, primarily the daily newspapers from the contending cities. These yield the flesh of the story—player anecdotes, detail of individual games, the public's mood and players' emotional reactions.

Baseball is a game of statistics. Game summaries and statistics from retrosheet.org and baseball-reference.com were used to corroborate or correct recollections, impressions and accounts from other sources. These bestow a backbone of fact to the excited reportage during the season's closing month.

Introduction

The tension of a pennant race is now a lost emotion. In 1967 there was no second chance for the runners-up. No playoff series existed to salvage the season. Only the regular-season winner continued and that team went to the World Series. Pressure was bad enough when two teams battled, but in the American League race that year four teams were tied for first on September 6. The four clubs had been tightly packed since mid–August and would remain stubbornly bunched during the season's remaining weeks.

It was thrilling for fans, who set attendance records. For players, the stress became oppressive. Photos show players and managers becoming increasingly gaunt and haggard. Many complained of excessive weight loss and inability to sleep. Beyond the emotional pressure to win, there was the fear of losing a substantial payday. For some, their winning World Series share would more than double their annual salary.

The 1967 pennant race is typically remembered for its dramatic final weekend or the improbable rise of the Red Sox from ninth place to pennant winners, but these were just the climaxes to six weeks of an unrelentingly close contest between five and then four teams. The four—Red Sox, Tigers, Twins and White Sox—figure equally in this account. All had notable weaknesses as well as strengths, providing a wide range of contrasts.

The White Sox had excellent pitching including the league's only effective bullpen, tempered by poor infield defense. Woeful at the plate, they hit for neither average nor power. Their manager offset that with elaborate base-running stratagems and by demanding physical aggression.

Complementing their power hitters, team speed and strong starting pitching, the Twins embraced risk-taking aggressiveness. On good days, it amplified all of their skills. When it failed, the team seemed to specialize in careless fundamentals. Their team chemistry was an unstable if not volatile mixture.

Oddly for a veteran team, the Tigers did not seem to have the will, or understanding of what it took, to win. Except for the bullpen, they were fundamentally sound at every position with strong hitting, an excellent catcher and talented but mercurial starters. On defense, they had possibly the best outfielder in the game and a consistently above average infield. They lacked speed, playing conservatively.

An excitable young team with a young manager, the Red Sox were built as they had been for decades of futility: lots of hitting and little pitching. Their powerful lineup produced by far the most runs in the league. Except for an ace, their pitching staff garnered little respect. This shortcoming was ameliorated by a generally superior defense.

Outside of the pennant race, the season was memorable. Tony Conigliaro's beaning was one of the two most infamous in baseball history. The prevalence of outlawed spitball pitches reached a zenith in 1967. Pitchers were dominant; never before had a season produced more shutouts. The firing of a player and its recriminations remained newsworthy for the season's final five weeks and led to a major turning point in the ascent of the Players' Association. Most interestingly, there was a wide selection of emotionally charged feuds spread through and among the contending teams.

Like many baseball seasons in its era, this one was spiced with beanball wars, innovations, brawls, threatened lawsuits, implausible injuries, suspensions, tape-measure home runs, no-hitters, an assaulted umpire, plenty of public trash talk, players benched for weighing too much, a player sent to the disabled list for weighing too little, and critical fielding plays both outstanding and disappointing.

The fans' emotional swings could be extreme. Even in August a two-game losing streak seemed like it would take a team out of pennant race contention. Only a day or two might separate ecstasy and despair over a home team's prospects. The players were on the same roller coaster. Six weeks of a tight pennant race were grueling. After every loss, reporters crowded the clubhouse asking if the pressure was finally getting to them. In 1967, star players were expected to be heroes. In the crucible of the final weeks stars stepped forward, playing the best baseball of their successful careers. They really were heroes, carrying their teams of lesser players toward the finish line.

And then there were the contending teams' managers. One was replaced after only two months and he was the only one who had ever managed a team to a pennant. Two had never managed in the major leagues, but two others had started managing at least 12 years earlier. One was denigrated for trying too hard, while another claimed to embrace the opposite philosophy—under-managing. There was a teetotaler and one who resumed smoking under the stress of September. Some had reputations as bullies, while one spent much of the season as his team's verbal punching bag. And in the end, there was one reduced to wishing wistfully for team harmony.

One manager loomed over the entire season as a much-larger-than-life personality: Eddie Stanky. In his second year managing the White Sox, Stanky was widely disliked. His baseball knowledge, though, was not just appreciated, but also revered. In succeeding sentences he could provide unique baseball insight and then unexpectedly launch a venomous attack. Filled with contradictions, he was creative and authoritarian, outspoken and subtly manipulative, pious and profane, magnanimous and vengeful. His intimidation of opponents, writers and his own players was so thorough that each pronouncement was parsed for hidden psychological daggers. Stanky was effective. To a remarkable extent, he seemed to spend much of the season inside the heads of opposing managers, and their players.

In an era when there was little nationwide television sports programming outside of actual games, Stanky's opinions were published across the country almost daily. (Other managers might get a mention when their team was in town.) Stanky dominated the American League. It did not make him popular, but it gave the season a uniquely colorful commentary.

The stars of the 1967 pennant race are, to the greatest extent possible, the stars of this book. All four teams experienced a plethora of turning points: both euphoric exhilaration and stunned despondency. Retrospectively, it is easy to find those key moments for the ultimate victor. In the throes of the race, no one knew which team that would be.

As the final weeks unrolled, carefully crafted assumptions changed unpredictably. Pundits flagged, their energy sapped by repeated failure to judge players and teams. The drama increased. Some players and managers wilted or cracked under the pressure. Others were energized by it. In the midst of the final day of the season with three teams tied for the lead, two staff aces dueled in Boston, while the Tigers took the field for their fourth game of the exhausting weekend.

Well before August, managers began predicting a tight finish to the season. By mid–August, sports columnists were proclaiming it the best pennant race ever. Those seemingly overblown expectations came true.

Prologue

On a dusty summer afternoon in the 1945 season, the second baseman for the Brooklyn Dodgers scored from third base on a sacrifice fly. It was not surprising. It was not even noteworthy. Eddie Stanky was often on base and had a knack for scoring. He led the league in scoring runs that year, including at least 13 on sacrifice flies. He was not fast, but he was inordinately determined to win.

On a deep fly ball, any player could saunter home after tagging third base. On a short fly that an outfielder had to sprint in to catch, no player would be able to beat a competent throw. Between those extremes were fly balls on which a fast baserunner could score, but a slower one would be forced to remain on third. Stanky wanted to be able to score whenever the fastest player on his team could score.

He knew that a runner with a running start could cover the 90 feet to home faster than one with a standing start. He eased a step behind third base on one mid-summer fly. Timing the ball's flight, he started running just before the ball reached the fielder. Tagging third as the ball landed in the fielder's glove, Stanky beat the throw home. Eventually, he was taking a few sprinting strides while the ball finished its flight.[1] He was creating runs where no one else believed they existed.

Teammates loved playing with Stanky because he thought endlessly about how to win baseball games. Before Stanky, no one had taken a running start to tag up on a sacrifice fly. Once he did it, its effectiveness was obvious. The practice slowly spread to a few other players. The innovation was not welcomed. After the season the commissioner outlawed the tactic with what was initially referred to as the Stanky Rule. This decision was codified and remains part of baseball.

In admiration, Branch Rickey once described Stanky the player, "He can't hit. He can't run. He can't field. All he can do is win."[2] In an era of celebrated feisty middle infielders, Stanky was more intense than any of them. It seemed that he would actually do whatever it took to win. This intensity was no accident.

Stanky grew up in a large, insulated Polish neighborhood of Philadelphia. The first time he left this cocoon was as a young man to play Class C ball in Greenville, Mississippi. Not surprisingly he became homesick and wrote home saying he was returning. He soon received a reply.

> Edward,
>
> I have tears in my eyes while I'm telling you this, but if you do come home, please do not come to 951 East Russell St. We do not want quitters in this family.
>
> Your mother.[3]

Stanky stayed in Greenville.

Lacking physical talents that were the basis of most major league careers, Stanky spent eight years scratching his way out of the endless layers of minor leagues by developing and perfecting a myriad of small skills. Unlike many young players who could focus on their powerful swing or their throwing arm, Stanky eventually learned to pay attention and absorb nuances that typically came to the attention of only veterans or managers. None of that would have been enough to launch his major league career without his single-minded pursuit of winning.

Stanky's face was like a piece of quarried granite, flat and hard. What his opponents remembered, though, were his unflickering blue eyes. These were always described as cold: cold and mean, cold and nasty, cold and hard, cold. Every move he made on the field seemed to be calculated. Instead of a game, Stanky appeared locked in almost a life or death struggle. He had to win. He played on the edge of control, and the pursuit of victory harnessed his emotion.

Off the field, Stanky's intellect allowed him to warm those eyes. Teammates liked him. He successfully cultivated sportswriters. Baseball men at all levels, from superstars to scouts to executives, were impressed by his baseball insight and innovation. He developed a speaking style that imbued his opinions with a moral authority.

Increasingly through his playing career, Stanky was infamous for his ability to distract opponents and cause them to play below their usual capabilities. When he reached first base, Stanky would bend over and scrape dirt from the basepath into two small piles. He would scoop one pile into each hand. Base running with his hands clenched around dirt helped prevent him from injuring his fingers when sliding headfirst into a base. Stanky was notorious for another tactic with the dirt. Approaching second base when an infielder was trying to make a pivot on a double play, Stanky would not only slide into the fielder, but also throw the dirt into his eyes. After receiving a face full, or two, of dirt every shortstop and second baseman in the league was acutely aware every time Stanky stood on first base.[4] On a double play ball, the pivot man had to catch, tag the base and make a hard accurate throw to first, all while shielding his eyes from the hard-sliding Stanky. This not only increased the difficulty of the maneuver, but also forced the player to think instead of instinctively completing a well-practiced motion. After a while, Stanky rarely had to throw the dirt because his opponents knew that it might be thrown. Despite his slow speed, Stanky was a constant distraction anytime he was on first base.

He was often on first base. As a perennial on-base percentage leader, Stanky's skill at drawing walks was renowned. It was written, "He could wangle walks the way a con man bilks a rich widow."[5] He walked more times per plate appearance than almost any other player in baseball history, setting the National League record in 1945. This was in a decade when on-base percentage was a little-used stat and baseball opinion still disdained walks.

Stanky's success was much more than a disciplined adherence to the strike zone. He purposefully fouled off pitches to extend his at-bats, often frustrating pitchers in the process. His teammate Alvin Dark recalled that Stanky "would do anything to get on base. He'd step on a catcher's toe, or drop a bat on it, duck under a fourth ball, tap the bat on the plate and flip it so that it landed on the catcher's foot."[6]

On fly balls, second baseman Stanky would grab a runner's shirt as he tagged up, delaying him just enough to discourage him from taking third. Other times he sat on basestealers after an errant throw from the catcher went into center field. When baserunners were standing on or near second after a play, Stanky would step on their feet. Many of his opponents recalled the pain of Stanky's metal spikes sinking into their feet when he caught them in a moment of inattention. A player worried about his feet and trying to keep track of Stanky was not quite as aware and might miss something on the field. Stanky's carefully cultivated reputation as an intimidator could obscure his substantial skills. In 1947 he set a record for National League second basemen with a .9853 fielding percentage.

There were a number of critical influences in Stanky's baseball career, but none as important as Leo Durocher. Stanky played more than five and one-half seasons of his career for Durocher. Their attitudes toward baseball were so similar that Thomas Kiernan observed, "When they made Leo Durocher, it was as if they didn't throw away the mold until Stanky was born. Stanky could have been Durocher's son. Their behavioral responses to any given stimulus were almost identical."[7]

On a superficial level, both were notorious for verbally abusing opponents. When Stanky rode opponents from the field or the dugout, he wasn't kidding them or teasing them. He said whatever he could think of to rile them. The angrier they got, the more successful he had been. Stanky was often successful. More than once he was described as the most hated man in baseball during the 40s and 50s. Far more than dislike, this hatred was visceral. Decades later, the mention of his name could infuriate men he played against. Plenty of opponents could, in calm moments of reflection, praise his teammates and Durocher, but few contemporaries complimented Stanky.

While he undoubtedly learned many of the techniques for disrupting opponents from his mentor Durocher, the never-ending motivation was all Stanky's. Considered the best manager in baseball during the 1940s and 50s, Durocher was revered for his incisive understanding of baseball tactics and his decisive, often dramatically successful, in-game maneuvers. His players believed that Durocher was smarter than other managers and would always find an edge to help them win.

Durocher had an ego the size of a Macy's Parade float and a temper to match. He demanded full, constant effort from his players the entire time they were at the ballpark, often in clubhouse-shaking rants. Nicknamed "The Lip," Durocher was direct in his approach to players, umpires, writers, everyone. He criticized friend and foe alike. Despite his temper and egotistical personality, most of his players loved Durocher. As manager he was not merely an authority figure, but an extraordinary leader.

Stanky had played for Durocher on the Brooklyn Dodgers for two and a half years when he reported to spring training in 1947. During his playing career many teammates and writers referred to Stanky as a southerner, or a true southerner. This is an oddly frequent designation for someone born and entirely raised in Philadelphia to Polish immigrant parents and who played the first nine years of his major league career in the northern cities of Chicago, New York and Boston.

Dodgers owner Branch Rickey was planning to break baseball's color barrier by adding Jackie Robinson to the team's roster in 1947. Spring training would be the first hurdle to this plan and acceptance if not enthusiasm from his teammates might be critical. It was not long before Durocher realized that Stanky and his teammate Dixie Walker were circulating a petition among their teammates stating that they would never play with Robinson. Durocher immediately held a late night team meeting that fully resolved the situation. Durocher, who never cared what his players did outside of the ballpark, made it clear that he was no social crusader. He wanted to win. And he wanted the best players to help him win. Stanky's petition never saw the light of day.[8]

Durocher had no doubts about Stanky. His opinion was soon confirmed. Both Durocher and Robinson remembered one of Stanky's first interactions with Robinson that spring. He told Robinson, "I want you to know something. You're on this ballclub and as far as I'm concerned that makes you one of twenty-five players on my team. But before you play I want you to know how I feel about it. I want you to know I don't like it. I want you to know that I don't like you."[9] Like Durocher, though, on the field Stanky cared only about winning.

Once the season started, Stanky was a loyal teammate, fanatical about helping his team win. Robinson recounted how, in his first season playing an unfamiliar position at first base and against unfamiliar players, second baseman Stanky was constantly giving him tips about subtle advantages he could gain with small positioning changes. Near the beginning of the season when Robinson was enduring particularly vicious racial taunts from Dixie Walker's ex-roommate, Phillies manager Ben Chapman, Stanky yelled across the diamond, "Listen you yellow-bellied cowards. Why don't you yell at someone who can answer back?"[10] It did not end the taunts, but it made it clear to Robinson that even a true southerner like Stanky had his back on the field.

At the end of the year after the Dodgers lost the World Series in seven games, Stanky was traded to the Boston Braves to make room for the more talented Robinson to move to his familiar position at second base. Alvin Dark was a rookie shortstop for the Braves in 1948 and considered a defensive liability. Dark credited Stanky's constant advice with helping him improve rapidly in the field. Stanky batted a career high .320 and was selected as an All-Star for the second time that year. The Braves surprisingly won the pennant. After the 1949 season Stanky and Dark were traded to the New York Giants who were now managed by Durocher.

During a close game in the heat of August 1950, Stanky came up with a new idea for infuriating opponents. Braves third baseman Bob Elliott had already gone 2 for 3 with two doubles, an RBI and two runs scored. When he came up in the eighth, Stanky moved to stand near second base in Elliott's line of sight. As reliever Dave Koslo wound up, Stanky waved his arms to distract Elliott. Stanky picked on the right man. Elliott went down on strikes.

A couple of days later with Phillies catcher Andy Seminick at bat, Stanky began waving his arms and doing "hop straddles." Seminick had a hot temper. He already considered Stanky the dirtiest player in baseball, so he was in many ways a perfect target.[11] There was no rule covering these actions, so Stanky continued despite orders from the umpires to stop. After the game, Seminick's fury was not helped by both losing the game and getting hit painfully on his elbow by a Sal Maglie pitch in the eighth inning. He publicly vowed revenge. The Phillies protested the game, but National League President Ford Frick was too busy to make a ruling before the following game. Lacking the ruling, Durocher promised the umpires that Stanky would not continue his antics during a pitch.

The first time Seminick came to the plate in the second inning, Stanky started jumping around, stopping just before each pitch was delivered. Seminick did not hide his anger. Pitcher Sheldon Jones walked him. Seminick was fuming as he took first base. The next batter singled to left field where Whitey Lockman fumbled the ball before throwing to third. Seminick rounded second and kept sprinting. When third baseman Hank Thompson took the throw and bent to apply the tag, Seminick slid hard delivering a violent forearm shiver to Thompson's head. Thompson was knocked cold, losing some teeth and the ball in the collision. Seminick continued home to score.

In the fourth, Seminick came up to bat again and Stanky resumed windmilling his arms. After the second pitch, Seminick threw his bat across the diamond at Stanky. Realizing that the game was getting out of hand, the umpires ejected Stanky for conduct detrimental to the game. Seminick reached on an error. The next batter hit a groundball to shortstop. Needing just one out, Dark threw it to Stanky's replacement at second base, Bill Rigney. Seminick crushed him. Rigney came up fighting. There followed a lengthy, fist-swinging brawl—described as a riot. Eventually, the umpires had to call in policemen to restore order. Rigney was ejected with Seminick. When he reached the clubhouse with his face bleeding from the fight and body swelling from the collision, he found Stanky calmly sipping a cold Coke.[12]

Ford Frick found the time to ban the practice the next day, after calling Durocher and Stanky to his office to admonish them. This second Stanky rule also remains in place.

The following year the New York Giants came from 13 games back in August to tie Robinson's Dodgers at the end of the season. This incredible run indelibly validated Durocher's genius. The teams played a three-game tie-breaking playoff for the National League pennant.

The Giants won the first game, played at Ebbets Field, Brooklyn, 3–1. The second game was played at the Polo Grounds and the Dodgers won 10–0. The third game featured Brooklyn's 20-game winner Don Newcombe against the Giants' 23-game winner Sal Maglie. The teams had already played each other 24 times that season, so there were few surprises. The score was 1–1 when the tiring Maglie took the mound in the top of the eighth. The Dodgers scored three runs on four singles, a wild pitch and an intentional walk. Newcombe looked strong, retiring all three batters in the eighth. He started the bottom of the ninth with a seemingly secure 4–1 lead.

Newcombe gave up two singles before recording the first out on a foul pop. The fourth batter doubled, producing one run and a broken ankle. While the Giants' Don Mueller was being loaded on to a stretcher at third base, Ralph Branca replaced Newcombe on the mound. The first batter he faced, Bobby Thomson, hit the game-winning home run to left field—the Shot Heard 'Round the World. Twenty-six years later when the 1967 season got underway it was still the most famous baseball game ever played.

Six of the Giants players on that day became major league managers including three—Stanky, Dark and Rigney—who managed in the American League in 1967. Each consciously emulated Durocher. Two of the Dodgers—Gil Hodges and Dick Williams—also managed in the 1967 American League. They had less affinity for Durocher's managerial style.

With the possible exception of Hodges, all of them believed in what was known in the 1950s as National League–style baseball. This style was clearly delineated in the 1951 World Series when the Giants played the Yankees. On a failed hit and run, Yankees shortstop Phil Rizzuto waited confidently with the ball to tag out Stanky at second—a mere formality. Stanky kicked the ball out of the startled Rizzuto's glove and continued on to third base.

In this National League–centric differentiation of the two leagues, American Leaguers played with decorum, admiring strong pitching and waiting for big hits. Durocher's players fought for every small advantage they could identify. The Yankees' frequent World Series victories during the decade did little to dissuade Stanky and his contemporaries from their belief that their style of baseball was superior.

The 1950s were the training ground for the American League managers of 1967. All ten managers played regularly during the 1950s, except for Detroit's Mayo Smith. He was a National League manager from 1955 to 1959.

As a group, they were highly respected by baseball men. Four of them were major league managers either before or within a year of their retirement as players. Three more were major league managers only two years after retirement. These were not old men. Smith was the oldest at 52. Stanky was only a few months younger, although at the time his age was uncertain. He was believed to be as many as four years younger. Most were in their mid-40s. Cleveland's Joe Adcock and Boston's Dick Williams were still in their 30s.

Adcock, who had retired at the end of the 1966 season, and Williams were both new as major league managers. The others had at least four full seasons each managing in the major leagues. Together they had won over 3,300 games. Only three of the eight had losing records. Two of those losing records were compiled with expansion franchises.

These were the men who would evaluate and select players during spring training and then deploy them during the long season ahead.

Joe Adcock, Cleveland Indians
Hank Bauer, Baltimore Orioles

Alvin Dark, Kansas City Athletics
Gil Hodges, Washington Senators
Ralph Houk, New York Yankees
Sam Mele, Minnesota Twins
Bill Rigney, California Angels
Mayo Smith, Detroit Tigers
Eddie Stanky, Chicago White Sox
Dick Williams, Boston Red Sox

Chapter 1

"A bastard every day"

American League standings before play on April 14.

	W	L	GB
Baltimore Orioles	2	0	–
Kansas City Athletic	1	0	½
Boston Red Sox	1	1	1
California Angels	1	1	1
Chicago White Sox	1	1	1
Detroit Tigers	1	1	1
New York Yankees	1	1	1
Washington Senators	1	1	1
Cleveland Indians	0	1	1½
Minnesota Twins	0	2	2

The prospect of opening day for the Boston Red Sox brought more than the expected optimism from the large and opinionated corps of local sportswriters. The *Boston Globe* had each of its seven sportswriters pick the final standings of the American League. Four of them picked the Red Sox to finish fifth; two more predicted a sixth place finish and the pessimist in the bunch expected them to be eighth.

Outside of Boston this could be seen as the irrational hopefulness that prevails in each major league city just before the season starts. The authoritative *Baseball Digest* picked the Red Sox to finish ninth citing their poor morale and noting that they were "slack everywhere."[1] In their baseball preview issue, *Sports Illustrated* also picked them for ninth. They condemned the Red Sox because they "never have been able to execute the fundamental maneuvers that win ball games." Left fielder Carl Yastrzemski, one of the team's stars, was lambasted for his poor rapport with managers and his inability to throw a fielded ball to the correct base.[2] These same basic previews could have been written about the Red Sox in almost any year since the 1950s. It was widely accepted that the Red Sox possessed the worst team culture in baseball.

There was one potential bright spot. Both national and local writers hailed, or at least noted, the arrival of a new, young manager, Dick Williams. Williams' blond crew cut made him look younger than his 38 years. His no-nonsense, often abrasive approach left no doubt in his players that he was in charge.

Williams started in major league baseball with the Brooklyn Dodgers in 1951. He had a military exemption that year, which created an extra roster spot for him, but also prevented the Dodgers from sending him down to the minors where he belonged. He had no role on the team, which was loaded with talent and future hall of famers.

Charlie Dressen, the Dodgers manager, had little use for him. Dressen was in his first year with the Dodgers, taking over from the mild-mannered Burt Shotten. On a veteran team filled with high intensity individuals, there was almost no one to impress with his sharp baseball mind. He assigned Williams the job of yelling at opposing players from the dugout to distract them. Williams did this so well that later he boasted of being the third best in the major leagues, behind only Eddie Stanky and Leo Durocher.[3] It was a task that made almost every opposing player loathe him.

Red Sox rookie manager Dick Williams used spring training to eradicate the team's long-lived country club atmosphere. His no-nonsense emphasis was on fundamentals and conditioning. National Baseball Hall of Fame and Museum.

Williams was on the bench watching every futile move that the anxious Dressen made as his team collapsed during that September. Williams disdained Dressen. In 1952, Williams saw slightly more playing time. That August in St. Louis while diving for a fly ball in the outfield, he fell awkwardly on his shoulder enduring a "three-way separation." He threw the ball to the infield and then collapsed. Dressen's only response was to yell, "Get him out of there." It was left to the St. Louis player-manager Eddie Stanky, reputedly the meanest man in baseball, to help Williams to the Dodger dugout. Dressen would not even acknowledge his presence. Williams never forgot either gesture.[4]

With his throwing arm permanently injured, Williams eked out 11 more years in major league baseball as a utility player. Unable to rely on skill, Williams studied the game looking for advantages that would enable him to prolong his tenuous career. Williams played over 100 games during each of five seasons, so he was not merely a fixture on the bench.

His last two years as a player, Williams played for the woeful Boston Red Sox, a team whose culture of entitlement he despised. Still, Williams was known as a company man, one who would not rock the boat. After his last season in 1964, he was hired to manage in the Red Sox' minor leagues. A series of unlikely personnel changes left him managing their top farm club in Toronto. His teams won the International League championship the next two years. Almost immediately after the Red Sox completed their 72-win 1966 season, Williams was appointed manager of the major league team.

Williams was given a one-year contract. Even if he wanted to, there was no time to ease into the position of Red Sox manager. He had no reason to think that he would ever get a second chance to manage in the major leagues if he failed to greatly improve the Red Sox in 1967. Williams was determined to eradicate the country club atmosphere. He publicly announced that Carl Yastrzemski would no longer be captain. During spring training Williams repeatedly told his players that he was the leader and they were the followers.

Spring training for the Red Sox had long been a relaxed affair. Players slowly worked their bodies back into athletic shape. Even those reputed to be working hard had plenty of energy for late nights in a vacation atmosphere. Most spent more time concocting practical jokes than worrying about where to expect the cutoff man on a throw from the outfield. When Yastrzemski was a rookie, social status was important on the team. The wives of veteran players refused to acknowledge the presence of his wife Carol because he was a mere rookie. For years players had spent hours warming themselves in the morning sun or sitting in the cool afternoon shade while Ted Williams talked about hitting. No coach would interrupt the Red Sox' greatest hitting legend just to take a player to practice bunts.

Spring training was different under Williams. His first spring training experiences had been with Branch Rickey's Dodgers. Every player in their entire system worked on fundamentals the same way every spring. The 1967 Red Sox worked and worked on fundamentals. No one went at half speed. Williams appeared everywhere on the practice fields, yelling, coaching, and correcting with his sarcastic and abrasive tone. No player was safe.

First baseman George Scott was about to begin his second major league season. He had started almost every game in 1966 and might have enjoyed a comfortably secure spring training. Instead, Williams worked him hard to reduce his weight and then started him in the outfield during games. That experiment ended after Scott knocked himself out running into an outfield wall at full sprint. Remembering this spring, Scott would later say that Williams was "a bastard every day."[5]

Further ruining the traditionally casual attitude was another of Williams' idiosyncrasies. He demanded that players be ready on time. Two pitchers showed up 30 minutes late, once. Both were gone by June. Williams preached that players had to give 100 percent and avoid mental mistakes. In his mind being on time was part of achieving the correct mindset.

Williams was also an early believer that baseball players needed to be in good physical condition. At the beginning of spring training Williams noted that Tony Conigliaro was supposed to be the new Ted Williams, but had been a bust at the beginning of the 1966 season because he was in poor shape. Along with Yastrzemski, Conigliaro was the biggest star on the team and a local hero in Boston. If Conigliaro was not safe from criticism, no one was. As spring training progressed it was widely noted that Conigliaro was out on the practice field early every day.

Instead of sending pitchers out to leisurely shag fly balls during batting practice, Williams had them play volleyball to help their conditioning, footwork and competitiveness.

The Boston writers could not miss these changes. His players never found Williams lovable and he certainly was not during spring training. Still, this was a welcome change from the 1966 manager Billy Herman, whose only interest was golf. He had been negative from the first day of spring training, always in a hurry to get away from the fields and out on the golf course.[6] The newspapers told their readers that all recent Red Sox managers had talked tough in spring training. Williams was the only one to back it up.

Williams had spent the spring demanding accountability. In one of the last spring training games, Conigliaro dropped a fly ball for an error. In previous years he would have dismissed it, or given reporters excuses. In the clubhouse after the game, Conigliaro showed that he had gotten the manager's message and took responsibility for the error, vowing improvement.

For all of his gruffness, Williams was not insensible to the fact that players need to be motivated differently. In 1966 Billy Herman had made second-year shortstop Rico Petrocelli's life miserable. He seemed determined to destroy the young player's fragile confidence. One time he fined him over 11 percent of his total annual salary. After the team collected it, Herman loudly demanded that the team trade Petrocelli. Later in the season with Petrocelli sitting on the bench on a pillow because he was in such pain, Herman told the press that Petrocelli was a hypochondriac who lacked desire to play. To make his point Herman said, "When I played for the Cubs, my double play partner, Billy Jurges, was shot by a showgirl and was out of the lineup about a week. Petrocelli is out that long with a hangnail."[7] A week later, after he was admitted to a hospital, a large cyst was surgically removed from Petrocelli's abdomen. When Herman was fired in September he claimed that Petrocelli had cost him his job.[8] While many players would have ignored such a ridiculous statement, it deeply wounded Petrocelli.

Williams started spring training by telling Petrocelli that he would have to become the take-charge guy in the infield. Under Williams' tutelage, Petrocelli became convinced that the double play was the most important play in the game of baseball and that on the Red Sox he was responsible for it.[9] Within a week the timorous, insecure player of 1966 evolved into a leader. Petrocelli needed to take responsibility for the middle infield because he spent the spring with three different partners at second base—the two who stayed with the team were rookies and one those, Reggie Smith, was converting from center field. The first and third basemen, Scott and Joe Foy, were both entering only their second season in the major leagues, so at 23 and in his third season Petrocelli was the veteran.

Right before opening day the Boston papers reported Williams' prediction "We'll win more games than we'll lose this year."[10] This standard preseason bromide would be harmlessly reported in almost any city in the country. The hard-boiled Boston writers could not let it slide by. Williams was claiming that the Red Sox would finish in the top half of the American League. It was a belief that none of them shared.

The next day, the papers hoped for a crowd of 20,000 for opening day at Fenway Park against Eddie Stanky's White Sox. Instead, the game was called off in the face of temperatures in the mid–30s and 40 mph winds.

Stanky celebrated his 25th wedding anniversary far from his wife and holed up for a third day with a painful gout attack. The discomfort may have contributed to Stanky's irritability about Boston's Fenway Park where team officials denied the White Sox' request to practice the day before opening day. An odd winter combined with poor scheduling left the field in shambles in early April. Papers showed photos of road graders and earthmovers working on large piles of earth where the playing field should have been. Stanky told reporters, "It's the biggest disappointment of the spring. A million dollar organization and they can't get the field ready."[11] These were not the last harsh words he would have for the Red Sox.

The next day still in pain from the gout, Stanky held a team meeting before the game. On a blackboard in the clubhouse he had written, "From Opening Day until October you belong to me."[12]

In weather almost as cold, 8,000 spectators showed up to see Rico Petrocelli hit a home run and power the Red Sox to a 5–4 victory. Before the game,

Stanky told reporters, "I hear they are going to do some running, bunting, etc., too, aren't they? Well, that's good. That's the way to play the game."[13] After the Red Sox stole three bases during the game, the level of his admiration was not recorded. The Boston papers could write about nothing else. The previous season, the Red Sox stole only 35 bases. Three in one game was a complete change. After the game, Stanky demanded that his players behave less gentlemanly on the basepaths.

The Red Sox lost the season's second game in familiar fashion by giving up five runs in the ninth in a hail of five errors and blunders. On the field, the White Sox took Stanky's demand for more aggressive baserunning to heart. In the second inning, Tommy McCraw slid three feet wide of second to spike second baseman Reggie Smith, leaving his sock visibly in tatters. In the ninth, Tommie Agee smashed into Smith as he tried to start a double play, knocking him cold. It was a game that set the tone for the teams' season series.

Although not heralded in the Boston papers, these opening games of the 1967 season were the first time that the Red Sox had more than four black players on their major league roster. It was a subtle sign that times were changing. Not all of Boston's professional teams had an aversion to black players. Bill Russell was ending his first NBA season as the first black head coach of a major professional sports team, the Boston Celtics.

After the White Sox series, the Red Sox went to New York where Williams trotted out a novel lineup against the Yankees. Promising left-hander Billy Rohr, only 21 years old, would make his first start in the major leagues. He had never seen Yankee Stadium. His catcher Russ Gibson would also be playing in his first major league game. For the night before the game in New York, Rohr requested Jim Lonborg as his roommate. The 24-year-old Lonborg, a Stanford graduate, was a veteran of two major league seasons.

The two took a cab from their hotel to a restaurant for dinner. The gregarious New York cabbie held forth on baseball. "What's the matter with the Red Sox anyway," he asked rhetorically. "Throwing a kid like Rohr in there against the Yankees? That's not right making a kid pitch his first game in the Stadium."[14] Rohr and Lonborg replied noncommittally, maintaining their anonymity. After dinner, they spent hours that night discussing every hitter in the Yankees lineup. Eventually Lonborg had to give Rohr a sleeping pill to calm him down.

Before the game, the 6'3" Rohr—described as a French-Indian from San Diego—was so nervous even people in the stands thought he looked scared. He would be opposing the great Whitey Ford who had started over 400 major league games. It was the veteran who had trouble. Reggie Smith led off the game by hitting his first career home run.

Rohr quickly got past his nervousness and Gibson's inexperience. He took a no-hitter into the bottom of the eighth inning relying almost exclusively on his fastball. Yankees manager Ralph Houk inserted the aging Mickey Mantle as a pinch-hitter hoping to awe the young pitcher. When Mantle flied harmlessly to Conigliaro in right field, Yankee fans cheered. Even they were rooting for Rohr and his no-hitter.

Tom Tresh led off the ninth against Rohr. With a three-run lead, the outfielders all played shallow to prevent a bloop single that would ruin the no-hitter. Rohr was beginning to tire and the count went to 3–2 before Tresh lined a ball toward Yankee Stadium's enormous left field. Instantly it seemed that the no-hitter was over. On contact, left fielder Carl Yastrzemski turned and sprinted toward the long scoreboard on the left-field fence, dove and caught the ball over his shoulder as he crashed to the ground. Somersaulting, he came to his feet holding the ball in his bare hand. It was an incredible play requiring an instinctive break on the ball and great physical control. The fans did not hold back. It was a catch to remember. Decades later when his long career was over, seven-time Gold Glove winner Yastrzemski remembered that catch as the best defensive play he ever made.[15] The no-hitter was intact.

The next batter flied out and the whole stadium started cheering for Rohr as he faced the last batter, former MVP Elston Howard. The year before Williams had managed Rohr at Toronto. Rohr had taken a no-hitter into the ninth and lost it with two outs. Williams did not want to see that happen again. He went out to the mound to settle the pitcher, dispense managerial wisdom and remind Rohr that Howard loved to swing at the first pitch.

Rohr got Howard to swing at a low fastball and ran the count to 1–2. Gibson would always claim that the next pitch, a fastball, was a perfect strike, but it was called a ball.[16] After another ball, Gibson called for a curveball on the 3–2 count. With the crowd roaring in anticipation, Howard poked the pitch into right field for a dinky single. The emotion drained from the stadium and the players. The fans recovered first, loudly booing their hometown player as he stood at first base.

Despite losing the no-hitter in his first start, after the game Rohr basked in his celebrity that included a request for a signed baseball from the widowed Jacqueline Kennedy and her son John-John who had been at the game. Rohr moved on to enjoy his sudden fame. He was thrilled to be paid $500 to appear on the Ed Sullivan Show, but not without a reservation. "I hope it will be taped," he allowed. "I don't want to walk out on stage before all those people and also feel all those people watching me on television."[17]

If Rohr's psyche was largely unaffected, Howard's hit caused a deep and lasting change in the hardened and aloof Dick Williams. He publicly accepted blame for unnecessarily going out to mound and breaking Rohr's pitching rhythm. There was no good baseball reason for that. Later as he agonized over his action, he came to a critical realization. A manager cannot throw a no-hitter, but he can ruin one. By extension, only players can win a pennant. A good manager should stay out of the way, give credit to his players and remember how lucky he is to sit in their dugout.[18]

No matter how this effected his future decisions, it did nothing to mellow Williams' demeanor.

Chapter 2

"Hairy-chested home run hitters"

American League standings before play on April 30.

	W	L	GB
Boston Red Sox	8	5	–
New York Yankees	8	5	–
Baltimore Orioles	8	6	½
Chicago White Sox	8	6	½
Detroit Tigers	8	6	½
California Angels	7	8	2
Cleveland Indians	6	7	2
Minnesota Twins	5	8	3
Washington Senators	5	8	3
Kansas City Athletics	5	9	3½

About two weeks into the season, half the American League teams began Sunday, April 30, within half a game of the lead. The previous day the Red Sox beat the Athletics who let their star closer Jack Aker pitch for 8⅓ innings before he finally gave up the winning run in the 15th. Asked for his opinions on the young season, Eddie Stanky predicted, "The league is so well balanced that this could be one of the wildest, wide-open pennant races the American League has ever seen."[1]

The Tigers were wrapping up their four-game series in Baltimore with a doubleheader. The teams had split the first two games of the series. The Tigers' Denny McLain lost the first after serving up a grand slam in the first inning. Mickey Lolich won the second in a complete game.

To conclude the series, Earl Wilson started for Detroit in the first game of the Sunday doubleheader. With Bill Freehan catching, he tamed the mighty

Orioles bats for seven innings, allowing just two inconsequential hits. In the eighth, Wilson struggled with his control. After loading the bases by walking Orioles pitcher Steve Barber, Wilson yielded a run on a sacrifice fly.

Coming to bat in the top of the ninth the Tigers trailed 1–0. Barber, who had already thrown a one-hitter in the young season, was working on a no-hitter. Unlike Wilson, he had been wild throughout the game, walking seven, throwing a wild pitch and hitting two batters in eight innings. Finally having the lead did not help Barber's control. He walked Norm Cash and then walked the light-hitting Ray Oyler. Wilson laid down a sacrifice bunt and the Tigers had runners at second and third with one out. Slugger Willie Horton entered the game as a pinch-hitter. He had been sidelined since spring training with what was generally described as a calf injury. This was his first at-bat of the season. His foul pop was caught for the second out. Barber threw a wild pitch to the next batter allowing a run to score. After walking the batter, Barber was replaced by a reliever. His no-hitter remained intact. The Tigers scored the winning run on an infield error. Despite being no-hit, the Tigers won the game 2–1. While that outcome was a notable baseball oddity, it was most important for its benefit to the Tigers' psyche.

The Tigers also won the second game of the doubleheader later that day. They placed a lot of importance in taking three out of a four-game series against Baltimore on the road. Most baseball men picked the Orioles to win the pennant, or at least be in the race until the end. The Tigers saw a two-team race between themselves and the Orioles. One of the keys to their season was expected to be their head-to-head record against their rival. This series confirmed that they could play with the Orioles.

This upbeat mood was a big change from the year before when they had the same talent, but struggled with events beyond their control. At the start of 1966 their manager had been Charlie Dressen. He was starting his 16th year of a managerial career that began in 1934. Younger players like Willie Horton, who had recently lost both his parents in a car accident, and Denny McLain viewed him as a father figure.

Dressen suffered a heart attack in May and was hospitalized. He was replaced on an interim basis by coach Bob Swift. Dressen was still trying to rejoin the team when Swift entered the hospital with violent gastroenteritis. His temporary replacement was coach Frank Skaff who officially took over in the middle of July. In August while suffering in the hospital with kidney problems, Dressen had another heart attack and died. By that time, Swift had been diagnosed with terminal lung cancer and Skaff finished the season as manager. Swift died in October. It was a season of turmoil and emotional lows.

Immediately after the season, the Tigers hired Mayo Smith, a scout who had managed in the National League during the 1950s. The move was greeted with skepticism. Incapable of snappy one-liners, Smith seemed drab and a little dim. He did not compare well with the colorful Dressen who always had time to explain the genius behind his managerial moves. The Tigers had veteran, established position players and a talented group of young pitchers. Fans wanted a brilliant game manager who would skillfully use all the talent supplied to him. Smith's first move was acclaimed. He hired Johnny Sain, the highest profile pitching coach in baseball.

It was not enough to win over his critics. Entering spring training, Smith was clearly on trial in the eyes of Detroit sportswriters. One of his first moves was to place the team's biggest star Al Kaline in center field. Kaline complained loudly. Smith quickly backed down, returning Kaline to right field where he had played earlier in his career.

Kaline had entered the major leagues as a bonus baby right after high school graduation and won a batting title at age 20 in 1955. Now 32, he had already won nine Gold Gloves and twice been an MVP runner-up. He was a 12-time All-Star, perennially selected for the All-Star game even if injuries limited his playing time.

Protective of any perquisites that might accrue to him as the biggest star on the team, by the mid–1960s some in the Tigers clubhouse vaguely resented Kaline.[2] While almost all stars collected extra perks, Kaline's constant attention to his status wore thin with some of his teammates. A few years earlier his then-teammate Rocky Colavito, the possessor of a sizable ego himself, famously called Kaline "a little tin god."[3]

Kaline's public complaint about Smith's plan to play him in center field was typical. He knew he would win. By venting his displeasure through the newspapers he established that his opinion mattered more than the new manager's. Although Kaline had played many games in center field including much of the previous two seasons, he preferred right field because it was easier.[4] He looked better making throws from the shorter right field than from deep in center.

For all his clubhouse prickliness, Kaline was a dream on the field. He hit for some power as well as average. Considered the model of an ideal outfielder, he had one of the best outfield arms in the American League. The season was not even one month old and he had already thrown out three baserunners. No one accused Kaline of loafing on the basepaths, or failing to run out an infield pop fly.

There was one concern. As he aged, Kaline became increasingly injury-prone. He missed significant portions of four of the past five seasons with shoulder, knee and foot injuries.

Smith recognized as clearly as anyone that if the Tigers were going to overhaul the Orioles they would need Kaline secure in his status and performing like a star on the field. Kaline was desperate to play in a World Series and publicly commented that this team might be his best chance.

During spring training Smith also moved Dick McAuliffe to second base, replacing him at shortstop with Ray Oyler and Dick Tracewski. Both were exemplars of good field/no hit. McAuliffe was a fiery player in the 1950s mold who was determined not just to win, but to crush the opponent. Teammates assiduously avoided him during the hour before a game because he became aggressively mean.[5]

Smith emerged from spring training garnering public praise from his players for his game-managing acumen. Writers lauded his adept handling of the veterans' personalities. In this context columnist Pete Waldmeir found a reason to approve Smith's decision to return Kaline to right field.[6] In the optimism that surrounds the new season of a contender, Smith's quiet, almost lifeless, demeanor was determined to be the calming influence that a veteran team needed.

The Tigers liked veterans. The *Detroit News* estimated that backup catcher Jim Price and relief pitcher George Korince were the first rookies to start the season with Detroit since 1954.[7]

The veteran Tigers were a stoic group on the field and in the clubhouse, displaying little emotion. Their first baseman, Norm Cash, was an exception. He was famous throughout the league for arriving at the bar early and staying late. Despite almost nightly binges, he arrived each day eager to play and worked hard at drills before every game. Cash fielded his position aggressively and in 1964 had a league-leading .997 fielding percentage.

In 1961, his second full season in the major leagues, Cash batted .361 with 41 home runs and 132 RBIs. Bill James described it as the most famous fluke season in the history of baseball.[8] Cash never batted over .285 again, but he continued to hit with power. Detroit fans booed him frequently enough that Cash could claim, "When 50,000 people boo, you don't really hear it. But when one or two guys are on your back, they drive you nuts."[9]

Cash had a renowned sense of humor and would doff his cap in appreciation as boos rained down on him. In one game, Cash was caught leaning the wrong way and cleanly picked off first base. Instead of futilely diving back and into the tag, or sprinting for second and getting caught in a rundown, Cash stood where he was. And, signaled for a timeout.[10]

During a different game, Cash was on second base when rain stopped the game. After the delay, Cash took his position on third base. The umpire told him to move to second. Cash replied that he had stolen third. The umpire asked him when and Cash readily replied, "During the rain."[11] Cash was capable of attracting unusual statistics even without using his creativity. In 1963 he played an entire game at first base without a fielding chance: no putouts, no assists, no errors.

One advantage of a veteran team was that the players held few surprises. There was nearly universal feeling in Detroit that the Tigers would contend for the pennant. The vast majority of writers picked them to finish first or second. With Smith apparently a competent manager who had his players' respect, there were only a few questions lingering about the team. Poor batting at the shortstop position was a concern, although no one expected the Tigers to lack run production.

Many noted that the Tigers were relying on Johnny Sain to improve and get consistent production from the pitching staff. While talented, three of the starters Mickey Lolich, Denny McLain and Joe Sparma had well-established reputations as oddballs and inconsistent head cases. The other starter, Earl Wilson, was an established major league pitcher who had already fulfilled his potential. He was reliable rather than gifted. One of his most admired traits in Detroit was a superlative won-lost record against the Orioles.

The final place of uncertainty was the bat of catcher Bill Freehan.[12] In 1964, he had hit .300 with 18 home runs and 80 RBIs. He had followed that with two years of hitting .234 with decreased power. He was a Gold Glove catcher, so there was no question of replacing him. However, a batting order with a no-hit shortstop, a poor-hit catcher and a pitcher at the bottom had a huge void.

Before the draft was instituted in 1965, it was common for major league rosters to have local talent. Freehan was only one of a number of Tigers players who grew up in Michigan including Mickey Stanley, Jim Northrup and fellow Detroiter Willie Horton. Horton and Freehan met when Freehan was 13 and they were opponents in a sandlot league. Freehan remembered, "In one game he tried to run me over at the plate, and I tagged him out, and we began rolling over and grabbing at each other. A bunch of people poured on the field and pulled us apart, and I wasn't too unhappy about being pulled away from Willie. He's tough."[13] Later, they played together on successful all-star teams.

The 210-pound Freehan attended the University of Michigan where he played football and baseball. He batted a Big Ten record .585 as a sophomore and signed with the Tigers. Two years later in 1963 he was the Tigers' regular catcher.

After his breakout season in 1964, the Tigers hierarchy tried to maneuver him into a leadership role by appointing him captain. The Tigers had a leadership void. A few years earlier, Tigers manager Bob Scheffing suggested to ten-year starter Kaline that he be captain. Kaline was aghast.[14] Backing away from any responsibility, he pointed out that his play on the field should be all the leadership he needed to contribute. He was more comfortable in the background neither confronting teammates nor engaging with reporters.

Freehan, though, took the task seriously. For his efforts, he was derided by his more veteran teammates as "Big Ten Billy" for his overt enthusiasm and to mock his education.[15] The added responsibility and possibly the frustration at his teammates' dismissal of his efforts may have contributed to the decline in his hitting performance. Freehan was also building his skills handling pitchers. He admitted, "When I am alone I concentrate so hard on the game that my car is on automatic pilot."[16] Freehan lamented that the other fielders had only their hitting to think about, while he spent most of his energy recalling the at-bats of opposing hitters.

Freehan did not sacrifice his desire to his teammates' cynicism. Entering spring training in 1967, he and Mickey Stanley were the only Tigers who had worked out over the offseason. Freehan knew that he had to continually prepare his body to handle a season of catching. Even at 25, a season behind the plate took a physical toll.

When the season began, veteran Detroit reporter Watson Spoelstra noted, "Freehan hasn't been particularly sharp behind the plate this spring. Some feel he is too engrossed in his duties as the Detroit player representative."[17] Management of all baseball teams was resistant to the newly formed players' union, so readers in a union-heavy city would have no difficulty identifying this as the reporter's sop to management. Regardless of his union duties, Freehan was preoccupied with something else. Johnny Sain had many unique ways of handling pitchers and it took Freehan time to adjust. He had to spend more energy thinking about how he called each game, instead of relying on the instincts built by hard-won experience.[18]

By the beginning of May things had changed. Freehan's bat was on fire. Tied for the league lead in RBIs, he was third behind Kaline in hitting. "Freehan's throwing has never been better and the catcher is quite aware this is related to his batting success," wrote Spoelstra.[19] "When you're hitting, you catch better and you play sharper defense," said Freehan, who was batting sixth in the lineup.[20] He had thrown out four of the eight runners who tried to steal a base on him, and picked off another player.

After the Baltimore series, the Tigers had a day off and then were scheduled to play two games with the White Sox. It would be a series between the two early season league leaders. At stake was first place in the tightly packed American League. The first game was rained out.

The next game could not begin quickly enough for Freehan. He was eager to play the White Sox. During the last series with the White Sox the previous season, Freehan had been on the receiving end of a serious collision while blocking Don Buford from the plate. Although not big, Buford was aggressively competitive. He crashed hard into Freehan just after the ball arrived and both men sprawled to the ground. Buford was the third out. There was no dispute. Freehan not only held onto the ball, but so effectively blocked the plate that Buford never touched it. Freehan made the play look so effortless that it passed almost without comment.

After the play was over, Freehan had been slow to get up. White Sox third-base coach Don Gutteridge, on his way off the field, offered Freehan a hand. With Gutteridge's help, Freehan stood and tested his body to see if the sharp pain of a serious injury would pierce the dull ache from the collision. Through his numbed brain, Freehan's attention was forced toward the source of outraged yelling. It had nothing to do with the play at the plate. White Sox manager Eddie Stanky had left his dugout and come on the field to scream at Gutteridge for helping an opponent. After the season ended, Freehan noted that Stanky fired Gutteridge.[21] Stanky's attitude perplexed Freehan; the play and the inning, after all, were both over. It bothered him enough that he remembered this incident for years.

The game was expected to showcase the hitting and pitching of the Tigers against the White Sox' pitching. The Tigers collected eight hits and twice loaded the bases with no outs, but could manage only one run against White Sox starter Gary Peters and none against Bob Locker who pitched the final two innings of the 2–1 White Sox victory. Eddie Stanky crowed after the game, "Those hairy-chested home run hitters scare you, but we peck them to death."[22]

The White Sox scored both of their runs off Denny McLain in the first inning. With two outs, Tommie Agee lowered his shoulder into an inside fastball. Stanky was almost ecstatically proud: "That was a big play, taking a close pitch on the arm."[23]

Agee was the White Sox' biggest star. He had arrived unheralded at spring training in 1966 after an undistinguished and injury-ravaged minor league career. By the end of the season he had won the Gold Glove as a center fielder and rookie of the year honors. He also led the batting-challenged White Sox in home runs, RBIs, and batting average while contributing 44 stolen bases. After the season it was determined that he had been playing for weeks with a broken hand.

With the speedy Agee on first, Pete Ward checked his swing and left the bat extended high over the plate. It was enough to disrupt the hard-throwing Freehan as Agee stole second. Two singles sandwiched around a couple of errors gave the White Sox their winning two runs. This was exactly the type of game that Stanky had built his team to win.

On his way out of town with the win and tied for first, Stanky had one last gem for the Detroit writers: "Tigers are best at winning no-hitters. I knew when they got the first hit off Peters, we had them."[24]

Chapter 3

"A bucket of warm spit"

American League standings before play on May 25.

	W	L	GB
Chicago White Sox	22	11	–
Detroit Tigers	21	13	1½
Boston Red Sox	18	17	5
Baltimore Orioles	17	17	5½
Cleveland Indians	17	17	5½
Kansas City Athletics	17	18	6
Minnesota Twins	16	18	6½
New York Yankees	15	19	7½
California Angels	16	22	8½
Washington Senators	14	21	9

Entering May 25, the Minnesota Twins were seventh, two disappointing games under .500. Coming into the season, Minnesota fans considered their team the best equipped to challenge the Orioles. They had the core of their 1965 pennant-winning team largely intact and had added pitching ace Dean Chance to their roster in a trade with the Angels over the winter. That trade for first baseman Don Mincher and left fielder Jimmie Hall was designed to fix one of their biggest flaws, a lack of starting pitching. It was now their strength. *Sports Illustrated* gushed that their starting rotation of Dean Chance, Mudcat Grant, Jim Kaat (all three recent 20-game winners) and Dave Boswell was better than the White Sox starting pitchers.[1]

The trade for Chance had only upside for the Twins. Although Mincher hit for power and was a good fielding first baseman, trading him allowed the Twins to try to hide Harmon Killebrew's fielding woes at first. Killebrew's fielding was an important issue for the team. Longtime *St. Paul Pioneer Press* sports columnist Don Riley described Killebrew's fielding: "Big Harm was called Snowshoes at third, the Deer Slayer. He could butcher a bunt with either hand. His agility was comparable to the Himalayas. He carried anchors in his shoes and his idea of getting a jump on the ball was to shag it down in short left. He'll never move laterally better than a Mack truck."[2]

The loss of Hall was even less significant. He had never fully recovered from a terrible collision in the outfield with Bob Allison. His hitting and power diminished each year. Worse for an outfielder, he had become cautious, pulling up as soon as his feet hit the warning track.

If there was a perceived problem, it was the Twins' batting. It was accepted among the Minnesota writers that the Twins were transitioning from a slugging team to a running team. Hall and Mincher ranked third and fourth on the team in both home runs and RBIs. That left Harmon Killebrew as the only pure power threat from the 1966 team. Entering his fourth season, right fielder Tony Oliva was one of the league's best all-around hitters, a two-time batting champ who launched 25 home runs in 1966. No one else on the current team had hit more than 10 home runs or driven in more than 41 runs in 1966.

By contrast, the 1967 Twins were loaded with speed. In addition to shortstop Zoilo Versalles, both second-year player Cesar Tovar and rookie Rod Carew had dangerous speed on the basepaths. Oliva and outfielder Ted Uhlaender had shown that they were threats to steal bases in 1966.

Between the trade, slumps in 1966 and an influx of young players, the lineup had been in question when the Twins left spring training. Besides Killebrew who was moving from third to first base and Oliva, Versalles was the only player assured of starting. Every other position was available to whichever player started the season strongly. For a team slated to contend, this was a lot of uncertainty. There was more. Versalles had been the league's MVP in 1965. In 1966 his hitting fell off precipitously. His doubles, triples, home runs, stolen bases and RBIs were all less than half the 1965 totals. Any optimistic view of the Twins season included Versalles' return to form.

The other problem from 1966 was the marked decline in batting from slugger Bob Allison. More than almost any other player, except his road roommate Harmon Killebrew, Allison's career mirrored the fortunes of the Twins over the past eight years.

The Twins were born after the 1960 season when the Washington Senators moved west to Minnesota's twin cities for the 1961 season. (Confusingly, an expansion team called the Washington Senators began playing in 1961.) The team had played in Griffith Park in Washington, which was by far the worst slugger's stadium in the major leagues. It appears to be a misprint, but in 1945 only seven home runs were hit there during the entire season. As if by magic, the 1961 Twins became sluggers, a feature that characterized them through the 1966 season.

Twins veteran left fielder Bob Allison remained an athletic fielder even when his hitting slumped. Manager Sam Mele kept him in the lineup and this confidence was eventually repaid. As the season progressed, Allison's power returned. National Baseball Hall of Fame and Museum.

When the 1967 season began, Allison was an eight-year veteran who had already hit over 200 major league home runs. This was second behind Killebrew in the 66-year history of the franchise. He was hoping to rebound from a poor season in 1966 when he was platooned and saw his batting average fall to .220 while hitting only eight home runs. Allison's baseball career and his attitude toward it were largely shaped before his rookie season in 1959.

Allison always considered himself as an athlete rather than just a baseball player. He had earned 11 high school varsity letters. Three of those letters were earned as a sprinter. A successful football player in high school, Allison accepted a college scholarship to play football. No feature on him throughout his playing career failed to mention that he had been a star running back at the University of Kansas.

It did not matter that Allison played only one year of varsity football. That season he backed up one of the two halfback positions and ended the year as the fifth leading rusher on a poor Kansas team. Allison was a large man for a baseball player, 6'4" and weighing about 210 pounds when he began his first full major league season in 1959. On a baseball diamond Allison looked every bit the part of the intimidating, physical football player. The Senators trainer, George Lentz, also trained the Washington Redskins. He was quoted for years as having said that Allison was stronger than any of the Redskins players.[3] (Lentz said the same thing about Harmon Killebrew. The fact that two players on a bottom-dwelling baseball team were stronger than any of the Redskins players helps explain why the Redskins won only five games from 1959 through 1961.)

After a successful season playing college baseball at Kansas, Allison played four years of minor league baseball. He immediately established his fielding prowess. Playing center field he had excellent range, while his arm was reputedly the strongest in the Senators farm system. With thick, jet-black hair and his large powerful build, Allison basked in the nickname "Mr. America." Allison could hit the ball a long way, but he rarely did for three frustrating seasons.

His career finally began to take a positive turn during the 1958 season when he played for manager Cal Ermer at AA Chattanooga. That season Killebrew was his teammate and they began rooming together on the road. While Allison was both demonstrative and emotional on the field, Killebrew was the opposite—even-keeled. According to Allison, Killebrew "was not one to worry about his mistakes or to cry over spilled ballgames."[4] While Allison, like other players, might stay out and have a beer after eating at night, Killebrew watched television. After they both made the major leagues, Killebrew became famous for his television watching.[5] In an era with only three national networks, he would tell players on both teams exactly which shows would be on during each time slot every night.

Allison's performance at Chattanooga earned him a late season call-up to the Senators where he played in 11 games and batted an anemic .200.

The big change in his career came that winter when he played in Cuba. From the late 1940s through the mid–1960s, it was not unusual for some American ballplayers to head south during the winter to play in the Caribbean and Latin American winter leagues. Although the leagues were professional, the salaries were not sufficient to make them attractive to most major leaguers. Although few of the players in these leagues were Americans, a remarkable number of successful major leaguers made a significant breakthrough in performance after playing winter ball.

This may reflect the uneven quality or lack of focus of many coaches in American professional baseball. Some coaches were baseball lifers carefully guarding a small sinecure that allowed them to spend their days in the sun with no untoward effort. The recipe for success in this lifestyle emphasized babysitting players and flattering superiors. As if to highlight this, despite his speed and athleticism, in four years of minor league baseball no one had ever shown Allison how to run bases.

The Cuban coaches on Almendares taught him both the basics and many of the nuances.[6] The Cubans, both players and coaches, wanted to win and were not afraid to work to perfect fundamental skills. Their attitude was different. They practiced hard and played hard. While Allison liked baseball, his Cuban teammates and fans were passionate in their determination to win. Allison blossomed. A gregarious, open man, Allison thrived in cosmopolitan Havana.

It was an interesting season. When Allison arrived, armed rebellion with pitched battles involving thousands of soldiers engulfed much of the island. Cuba's revolution ended mid-season on January 3, 1959, with Fidel Castro's revolutionary army entering Havana where Almendares played. Baseball continued unabated, but political trials, killings and executions were daily news. At season's end, Allison's team went to Venezuela to contest the Caribbean World Series. Allison assumed this would bring some relief from the constant presence of armed soldiers in Cuba. He was wrong. The Venezuelans were passionate about their team beyond anything Allison had imagined.

In the minors, he had played in front of the polite fans of Chattanooga. During his brief call-up to the floundering Senators at the end of 1958, he had seen 4,200 fans thinly spread through cavernous Griffith Stadium in Washington. Venezuela was different. As far as Allison could tell there was no limit to the number of fans allowed in the Caracas stadium and they never stopped screaming. Twice during games the fans stormed the field in protest. Allison and his Cuban teammates dashed for their clubhouse in fear of bodily harm or even death both times. After beating the Venezuelan team in the series' last game, the limo carrying Allison and some of his teammates was stoned on the way to the airport.[7] It was an exclamation point to a fruitful winter.

Allison arrived at his first major league spring training camp in 1959 competing for the center field position occupied by Albie Pearson, the 1958 rookie of the year. Allison was proud of his arm and tried to showcase it by always throwing directly to a base, ignoring the cutoff man. Repeatedly making the same mistake to show off did not endear him to his teammates. He more than made up for it in the eyes of the coaches by hustling constantly. He ran hard in every drill and during every game. Although cynical veterans mocked his efforts, Allison opened the season as the starting center fielder. Unknown to Allison, manager Cookie Lavagetto had recommended to Senators owner Cal Griffith during spring training that he send both Allison and Killebrew back to the minor leagues because neither would ever be a major leaguer. Griffith refused. Frustrated by this meddling from the owner, Lavagetto confided, "The two of them together aren't worth a bucket of warm spit."[8]

Albie Pearson was traded in May. Allison hit 30 home runs, led the league in triples and was voted Rookie of the Year in 1959. Killebrew led the league with 42 home runs that year.

Griffith, who served as general manager, was unceasing in his attempts to upgrade his team. This meant a steady stream of changing players throughout Allison's career. Each player brought strengths and liabilities. The strengths were mostly hitting and the liabilities were often fielding. To fit the players together, Griffith's managers moved players from position to position. Even slugging superstar Harmon Killebrew regularly played three different positions during the next seven years.

As a rookie Allison was a center fielder. The next four years he played right field. In 1964 the Twins had a promising rookie outfielder named Tony Oliva and Allison was asked to convert to first base. He had his best season and was one of the best players in the league. In 1965 the Twins, tired of seeing other teams consistently run on the weak-armed Killebrew, moved Killebrew to the infield.[9] Allison was moved to his spot in left field. He did not hit as well, but the Twins won the pennant. In the second game of the World Series that year the Twins faced Sandy Koufax who was at the height of his pitching prowess. In the fifth inning with the game scoreless and the Dodgers threatening, Jim Lefebvre hit a curving line drive to left field off Twins pitcher Jim Kaat, who described the play. "Allison was playing Lefebvre quite a way off the line and he had a long run to even get near the ball. Nobody thought he had a chance to catch it but he made a tremendous effort, lunged for the ball, caught it and slid maybe 20 feet after hitting the ground. It was a great catch, one of the four or five best catches ever made in the World Series. That catch was definitely the turning point of the game."[10]

Allison entered spring training in 1967 under pressure. His performance had gone sharply down over two seasons. If it did not improve, his baseball career was finished. The Twins were flush with outfielders and talented young players. Despite the questions about Allison's diminishing capabilities with his bat, he never lost his innate hustle. Even after his poor 1966 season, Allison was widely regarded for his ability to turn a single into a double if an outfielder was lackadaisical.

Although a worrier by nature, Allison had a lot of self-confidence. He knew that he had major league skills and he was determined to show them. There was a promising rookie at spring training who was routinely described as having blazing speed. Allison, the possessor of three high school letters for his sprinting, repeatedly challenged this kid, a Panamanian who had grown up in New York named Rod Carew, to a footrace. It was a no-win situation for Carew and he refused every challenge. One of the few loquacious and quotable players on the Twins, Allison was a favorite of the Minnesota baseball writers who reported these exchanges. The result was the distinct impression among fans that Allison was indeed faster than this young speedster. Without ever running a race Allison had made his point that he still had well above average range in the outfield and was a threat on the basepaths.

Before opening day, Twins manager Sam Mele committed to using Allison as his every day left fielder. Even with that apparent vote of confidence, Allison had a lot to prove. Bill Veeck writing in the *Chicago Sun-Times* commented that expecting Allison to rebound was just the "wishful thinking department."[11] His performance backed up that sad assessment. After the first week of May, Allison was hitting a weak .203 while the team struggled around .500.

Allison's batting was almost the least of the Twins problems. Game after game the Twins struggled with fundamentals. Fly balls were misjudged, routine throws dropped, bases left uncovered and double play balls misplayed into runs scored. Carew was twice picked off first base. The lowlight came against the Tigers on April 21. With Cesar Tovar on first, Tony Oliva blasted a home run to right field. He rounded first base watching the ball disappear over the fence and passed Tovar who was mindlessly returning to the base to tag up. Oliva was credited with a single and then called out for passing a baserunner. To sportswriters, the coaching staff detailed ten baserunning blunders by Tovar alone during the young season.[12]

As May started, the Twins bats came to life. They scored 13 runs against the Yankees in the coldest major league baseball game ever played in Minnesota's Metropolitan Stadium. Just over 8,000 spectators braved the game-time temperature of 32 degrees with a 17 mph wind. When reliever Al Worthington retired the last batter two and a half hours later, the wind chill was estimated at 9 degrees. A week later they scored 11 runs against the Senators.

They followed those outbursts with a week of low scoring efforts. By the middle of May, Cal Griffith pronounced that he was disturbed by the Twins' slow start. He insisted that the record would have to improve before the beginning of June.[13] There was little doubt that this ultimatum was directed at phlegmatic manager Sam Mele.

A week later after the embarrassment of losing three in a row at home against the lowly Kansas City Athletics, Mele scheduled batting practice during a rare day off. *Minneapolis Star* columnist Bill Hengan reported that the main beneficiary was Allison who spent a long time practicing a more open stance. This was possibly in response to Griffith's earlier criticism of what he called Allison's "top-heavy, pigeon-toed, knee-crouching stance at the plate."[14]

The Twins improved after that and went 5–2 heading into a series-ending game against the White Sox on May 24. The Twins finished their home stand by taking a 14–1 beating from the light-hitting White Sox. Bob Allison collected his 1,000th career hit in the game and registered the Twins' only RBI. The Minneapolis papers paid scant attention to the rout, and failed to mention

Allison's milestone. Of much greater interest were a legion of disclaimers from every level of the Twins organization about a supposed feud between pitcher Mudcat Grant and shortstop Zoilo Versalles that originated from a botched double play a few games earlier. It was a sign of dissension that did not bode well for Sam Mele's professional future.

The next day with the Twins on the road at Kansas City, the *Star* headlined that Allison would be trade bait for the Athletics. Allison went 1 for 6 combined in the first two games. Neither performance was likely to boost his trade value. In the third game of the series, Allison shone. In the first inning he tripled with the bases loaded and ended the game with four RBIs on two hits in three at-bats.

The lengthy series ended May 28 with a doubleheader. Mele started his new acquisition Dean Chance. Chance had exceeded his reputation having already won seven games. He continued by blanking the Athletics on one hit through four innings. In the top of the fifth of the scoreless game, Allison drew a walk with two outs. He did not have a reputation as a basestealer, but in the past four seasons he had stolen 32 bases and been caught stealing only four times. He got the sign to steal and took off. Throughout the league, Allison was known for waiting until he was about two feet from the base before hitting the ground in his slide. He would slide through the base and usually the unfortunate infielder covering it.[15] Middle infielders did not relish making a play at second with Allison bearing down on them.

Young Athletics shortstop Bert Campaneris, weighing less than 150 pounds, covered the base waiting for the arrival of both the throw and the charging football player. Campaneris was well aware that only five days earlier Allison had crashed into the 200-pound White Sox catcher Duane Josephson while trying to score from second on a single. Allison was out on the play, but Josephson's damaged thumb would keep him out of the lineup for a month. It is not hard to imagine how relieved Campaneris was when the throw was late and offline, allowing him to hop out of the way of Allison's hard slide. Two pitches later Rich Rollins singled to left. Running hard on the hit, Allison scored easily.

In the second game, the Twins started Jim Kaat who was having a baffling season. The American League pitcher of the year in 1966 (the last year with only one Cy Young Award and it went to Sandy Koufax), Kaat entered the game with a 6.95 ERA. He lasted six innings giving up three runs, which was his best outing of the season. The Twins were held scoreless until the seventh when Allison hit his second double of the day and scored after advancing on a single and an error. In the ninth, Allison doubled again, scoring on Rollins' single. It was not enough as the Twins lost 7–2. With a stolen base, three doubles, two RBIs and four runs scored, 18,000 fans saw Allison have his best day of the young season.

There was no more trade talk. Instead, the next evening the *Star* wrote a glowing feature that attributed Allison's 6 for 12 series against the Athletics to his hard work. His average had climbed to .237. His 21 RBIs already surpassed his entire production in 1966. Ever-obliging to the popular player, the paper printed Allison's opinion that his success was "just a matter of playing often."[16]

When all of the games ended, the Twins were tied with the Red Sox for fifth place. After splitting a four-game series with the Angels, the league-leading White Sox were heading to Detroit for a two-game series with the Tigers.

Chapter 4

"Watch where you are going, Bush"

American League standings before play on June 3.

	W	L	GB
Detroit Tigers	27	16	–
Chicago White Sox	25	16	1
Boston Red Sox	23	21	4½
Baltimore Orioles	21	20	5
Cleveland Indians	22	21	5
Minnesota Twins	21	23	6½
Kansas City Athletics	20	24	7½
Washington Senators	20	24	7½
New York Yankees	18	23	8
California Angels	19	28	10

Nowhere in the American League did Sunday, June 3, dawn more brightly than in Boston. Less than a week before at the end of May, they had been one-half game out of seventh place. Now they were in sole possession of third place and gaining ground on the Tigers and White Sox ahead of them. The buzz in the Boston neighborhoods, though, was all about the return of their premier slugger, right fielder Tony Conigliaro, who had been missing from the lineup for two weeks.

Conigliaro had excelled at every level of organized or unorganized baseball growing up in in the rough, working class streets of East Boston and later the equally tough town of Revere.

Even at a young age he was a driven athlete. He decided that he wanted to play hockey in middle school, but had never learned to skate. Too proud to let his friends see him struggle to learn, he taught himself on the frozen puddles in the dirt parking lot of the local horse track. By eighth grade, he was a star. For high school, his father Sal picked a Catholic high school, St. Mary's, in the more upscale town of Lynn that had a highly respected baseball coach and a reputation for not letting studies get in the way of its star athletes. Conigliaro prepared to play football, hockey and baseball. His father, however, believed that hockey was too dangerous and forbade it. Conigliaro picked up a basketball for the first time, shot hoops endlessly in his driveway, and made the varsity team by his sophomore year.

As a baseball player, Conigliaro dominated throughout high school. A couple of Boston area players signed contracts for big bonuses during those years. It was obvious to Conigliaro and his father that a big payday waited after he graduated in 1962. To enhance that and possibly because his son was only 17, Sal had Tony play that summer in a high level American Legion league. The draft had not yet been initiated, so scouts were a common sight at the games.

In mid-summer the Red Sox invited Conigliaro down to Fenway Park for what they called a special workout. The team was on a road trip and the stadium was empty. Conigliaro arrived and dressed in the batboys' locker room. On the field he met Tony Horton, another prospect who had been flown in from California. The workout started with Horton pitching batting practice to Conigliaro who felt good hammering line drives throughout the park. Then the two prospects switched positions and Conigliaro started pitching to Horton. Horton deposited the first two pitches in the stands. Conigliaro had an abundance of pride and Horton's obvious superiority embarrassed him.

Conigliaro made one transformational observation. Both players were 6'3". Conigliaro was a tough but rail-thin 170 pounds. Horton bulged with muscles and weighed 210. A week later Horton signed with the Red Sox for a reported $125,000. Two months later, Sal Conigliaro arranged a single day bidding process for his son's services. Fourteen teams sent scouts with contracts. In the end the highest bidders were the Orioles and the Red Sox at $20,000.[1] This was not the Horton money that they had expected. They picked the Red Sox. (Susceptible to letting his pride get the better of the truth, two years later Conigliaro would tell a national baseball writer that his signing bonus had been "the equivalent" of $125,000.)[2]

That winter Conigliaro funneled his humiliation and desire into an intense workout regimen. He had seen what a $125,000 bonus player looked like. He bought some weights and a lead bat. Baseball players did not lift weights in the 1960s. Baseball coaches and managers accepted as fact that weightlifting left a player muscle-bound. Conigliaro had to create his own program. He spent hours and hours every day in his parents' basement swinging the bat and lifting weights.[3] To hone his swing and make sure that it exploded through the strike zone, Conigliaro devised a new drill. Heading to his parents' basement at night, he would light a candle. After setting the candle on a table, he would grab his lead bat and turn off all the lights. In the darkness with just the candle in front of him, Conigliaro would swing and swing and swing. His goal was to extinguish the candle by swinging hard and close to the flame, but never touch the candle with his bat.[4] It required nearly a perfect swing. When it was time to report to minor league training camp in Florida, Conigliaro had a huge right arm and was possibly the most physically fit player at camp.

The 1964 Red Sox featured entrenched veterans with apparently little motivation except to extend their major league careers with the least possible effort. They spent spring training doing their best to ignore younger players, hoping that they would duly disappear back to the minor leagues. One morning, Conigliaro started out of the dugout to stretch on the field when a ball whizzed by his head. Furious, he looked to see veteran backup Dick Williams who sneered, "Watch where you are going, bush."[5] Conigliaro retaliated with the same trick the following day. Only the sizable Dick Stuart kept the two from fighting.

Conigliaro, possibly the only Red Sox player to report to spring training in shape, started the season as the team's center fielder. To the joy of the local press and a large contingent of family and friends, Conigliaro hit a home run off Joe Horlen in his first at-bat at Fenway Park.

When teams traveled, players would sleep two to a room. Stars might pick their own roommates, but otherwise the manager decided. It was accepted practice that young rookies should room with older veterans who might instill good habits. The Red Sox roomed Conigliaro with Williams. The two men were equally fierce, but at opposite ends of the spectrum of baseball life and experience. Conigliaro claimed, "There was no way we could get together."[6] Williams fell back on what was then a hoary cliché, saying that he roomed with Conigliaro's suitcase because he never saw the rookie.[7] While Conigliaro was out at nightclubs, Williams' wild and hard partying days were behind him. He called his wife every night.

Conigliaro missed games with a hairline fracture of his left wrist and later with a broken right ulna as a rookie in 1964, but still hit 24 home runs. His injuries were the result of his batting stance. Conigliaro crowded the plate and then leaned over it. Pitchers hated it. In the 1960s pitchers were expected to throw at the heads of offending batters. Conigliaro actively practiced dodging beanballs in drills during spring training and during batting practice throughout the season.[8] His attitude eventually impressed even the sour Williams who allowed, "Say what you will, the guy is a fighter."[9] Conigliaro's more famous teammate Carl Yastrzemski told papers that summer, "[Conigliaro] has tremendous determination. He just keeps attacking,

attacking, attacking, attacking. He never backs off at the plate—*never* backs off at the plate."[10]

That offseason Conigliaro became a rock star. He formed a recording company, cut a record and sold it out. He performed at Boston venues and on a couple of national shows.[11] Conigliaro possessed what were admiringly described as matinee idol looks. Reporters wrote in amazement that most of his fan mail came from young ladies. It was the era of Beatlemania. Teenage girls viewed him as a heartthrob. Women of all ages came to Fenway Park to see him, not the Red Sox, play.

He continued his extensive basement workouts. At spring training, the press lionized him as the worthy successor to icon Ted Williams. The entire city referred to him as Tony C, as if he was just one of the many Tonys who lived down the street. Since youth, Conigliaro had talked big and then backed it up. Although he broke his right wrist on another hit-by-pitch, in 1965 he led the American League with 32 home runs as a 20-year-old.

The Red Sox in these first years of Conigliaro's career were famous throughout baseball for their undisciplined culture. On the road, curfews did not exist, or were unenforced. It was a poor atmosphere for a successful and highly social young player to develop life habits as he grew into manhood. In this environment where players had so few responsibilities, Conigliaro began to have problems with too much drinking, too many late nights and no respect for the club's few rules.[12]

Conigliaro's high times stopped abruptly on the day after the 1965 season. The change had little to do with Conigliaro or the Red Sox. In the beginning of 1965 President Lyndon Johnson decided that the military advisors in Vietnam needed to be reinforced by combat troops. The first of these arrived in Vietnam in March. On April 6, President Johnson formally changed the Army's role when he authorized troops to engage in direct combat. In July 1965 President Johnson announced plans to have 175,000 troops in Vietnam by the end of the year. By the end of the following year that number would more than double to 385,000.

These manpower demands strained the military, which was still occupying parts of Germany and had a large battle-ready force on the ground in South Korea. The president announced a greatly expanded draft to meet the Army's requirements. Conscription, or the draft, had been a part of the military's ability to fill its ranks since World War II. During both World War II and the Korean War, many young American men had volunteered for service in the armed forces. Many more were drafted into the Army. During the Vietnam War era over 2.2 million men were drafted into the army and it encouraged another 8.7 million to volunteer for military service.

Tony Conigliaro became one of those volunteers. On August 19, 1965, while he was still recovering from his broken wrist, Conigliaro avoided the draft by enlisting in the Army Reserve. His basic training at Fort Dix, New Jersey, started the day after the season ended and lasted through February, ending just before spring training.

Conigliaro was not alone. Major league baseball teams were eager to exploit the unique position of the National Guard and Army Reserve.

In 1960, the National Guard and the Army Reserve contained almost one million men. The purpose of both organizations was to have soldiers ready to serve on short notice. (Both the Guard and the Reserve were fully funded by the federal government and the Reserve was theoretically integrated into the Army command structure. Both the federal government and the state in which it was based commanded Guard units.) A brief call out during the Cuban Missile Crisis in 1961 had demonstrated that these troops were generally poorly trained, undisciplined and ill equipped. Secretary of Defense Robert McNamara estimated that it took longer to prepare a National Guard unit to serve in battle than it did raw recruits. His solution was to drastically reduce both the Guard and the Reserve. Through the early and mid–1960s he was able to make some small reductions, but real reform was effectively blocked by Congress. No congressman wanted to lose a Guard or Reserve unit from his district. They served as a consistent source of federal subsidy. It was estimated that over 100 congressmen during this period were active or retired Reserve officers. One had served as president of the Reserve Officers Association, the primary lobbying group for a large Army Reserve.

Once it became clear that service in Vietnam was hazardous, these same congressmen lobbied hard to protect the Reserve and Guard units from their districts. Under this "storm of protest" and the military reality that many of these units would be useless in combat, in his July 1965 announcement President Johnson explicitly refused to mobilize Reserve and Guard units for active combat service in Vietnam.[13]

Draft-eligible players and the teams that employed them had clear choices. Drafted men served in the Army and had a two-year commitment. It was widely accepted that the vast majority of draftees would become infantry soldiers in Vietnam. There were a large number of ways to postpone draft-eligibility or avoid the draft, but none were easily applied to physically active baseball players. One way to avoid the draft was to volunteer. The Air Force and Navy were exclusively manned by volunteers and the Marines almost entirely volunteer. All these services required a longer commitment of three or four years or longer depending on the extent of training. Either two years in a war zone or four years in another branch of the military would damage or end the career of a young baseball player. There was no public pressure for players to actively serve as there had been during the Korean War and World War II.

Teams steered their players to sign on with either the Guard or the Reserve. Sponsorship from powerfully connected team owners was critical. Reserve officers from this period remember long waiting lists of applicants eager to avoid the draft by enlisting in the Reserve.[14] The exact service requirements wavered both locally and over time. Typically, a Reservist served full-time for about four to seven months of basic training and then had a six-year commitment. During those years each Reservist had a required annual two-week training period and 48 meetings each year. The meeting could be a weekend or an evening, but they were essentially a weekly requirement.

Tony Conigliaro entered the 1966 season after his tedious winter of basic training underweight and understrength. He started in a prolonged slump, but for the first time in his professional career finished the season without breaking a bone. He hit 28 home runs and was named the Red Sox MVP, a small consolation on a terrible team.

After the season, Conigliaro received the kind of news that was becoming commonplace throughout the United States. His best and only close friend from St. Mary's High School, Freddie Atkinson, had been killed in Vietnam.[15] Although he had played three seasons of major league baseball, Conigliaro was only 21. Atkinson was one of many contemporaries who were serving in the war zone. Basic training had been a miserable waste of five months, but that had been washed away by seven months of easy and pleasurable living during the ensuing season. Freddie Atkinson was never returning to the easy life.

Possibly in response to this, Conigliaro went on an African safari during the offseason and spent many days alone, just thinking. It was not unusual for a wealthy ballplayer. The safari coincided with his two-week annual Reserve training, which he missed. Conigliaro later said that he assumed that his commitment would be taken care of, as had most of his Reserve requirements after the end of his basic training.[16]

During the spring of 1967, the draft system became the center of intense interest. Heavyweight boxing world champion Muhammad Ali announced that he would refuse to be inducted into the Army. Sports pages around the country carried updates on the story every day for weeks leading up to his induction date at the end of April. The topic was fraught with patriotic, racial and religious subtexts. Ali based his deferment request on the fact that he was a minister for the Black Muslims, a racially segregated group seemingly radical and at odds with the white, Christian status quo. Many papers referred to Ali almost exclusively as Cassius Clay, the name he was given at birth and used when he won a gold medal in boxing in 1960. Typically, but not universally, they rarely used his legal name and then only with the prefix "his Black Muslim name." Legal maneuvering for Ali's draft deferment twice reached the Supreme Court without success. When Ali attended his draft board on schedule and refused to step forward to be inducted, it was front-page news and fodder for impassioned editorials.

Attention to Ali's case focused scrutiny on what had been a chummy system. Suddenly, Reserve commanders began adhering to the letter of the law. Reservists who failed to fulfill their two-week annual commitment were automatically de-activated. At the beginning of May, Conigliaro was notified that his lapse made him newly eligible for the draft. To avoid that, his father arranged for him to sign on with the Army Reserve 412th Engineering Company based in nearby Lynn, Massachusetts.

The unit shipped out for two weeks of training on May 19. Conigliaro took his bats with him, so that he could fly directly to Cleveland to join the Red Sox after his Reserve commitment was over. He also took a weighted bat with him, but later reported that peeling potatoes and washing garbage cans tired him out so much that he never used it.[17] While Conigliaro was at Fort Drum, the Defense Department announced that total United States casualties in Vietnam had passed 10,000.

Throughout the 1967 season, major league players missed games or weeks to fulfill their military commitments. Some starting pitchers received a pass to pitch during their regular spot in the rotation. Others received no special treatment. In some cities, the papers assiduously chronicled the military absences of their team's players. Other papers left it unmentioned.

These commitments could be onerous. Conigliaro had to be in Lynn every Wednesday evening for drill. If the team was on the road, Conigliaro flew home to fulfill this requirement. Often this required at least one red-eye flight.

In his first game back Conigliaro went hitless, but was hit by a pitch and scored a run. The Red Sox won 6–2 behind two doubles and a George Scott home run. The Tigers and White Sox both lost, while the Orioles and Twins won. The top six teams were now within five and a half games of the lead.

Largely ignored in both Chicago and Boston was a trade of veteran players who were discontented with their authoritarian managers. The Red Sox who were desperate for pitching traded reliever Don McMahon who had shown an unfortunate tendency to walk batters with the bases loaded and serve up home runs. In return, the White Sox sent them starting second baseman Jerry Adair who despite strong fielding had been benched while batting an anemic .204.

Chapter 5

"What are you crying for?"

American League standings before play on June 6.

	W	L	GB
Detroit Tigers	29	18	–
Chicago White Sox	16	18	1½
Baltimore Orioles	23	21	4½
Boston Red Sox	24	22	4½
Minnesota Twins	24	23	5
Cleveland Indians	23	23	5½
New York Yankees	21	24	7
Kansas City Athletics	22	26	7½
Washington Senators	20	27	9
California Angels	20	30	10½

For weeks St. Paul and Minneapolis papers had speculated on the possible firing of Twins manager Sam Mele. According to one columnist, Sabath Anthony Mele (the initials led to Sam) possessed the best career record of any manager in the major leagues, except only Walter Alston.[1] This record was undermined by the team's careless play contributing to a surprisingly weak start.

Cal Griffith hired Mele as a coach in 1959, the year after he retired from an undistinguished playing career. Two years later, manager Cookie Lavagetto was encouraged by Griffith to take a vacation after 49 games. Mele filled in as manager for seven games. Speculation about Lavagetto's probable firing was intense, but Lavagetto returned. His relationship with the players only worsened. What appeared to be the longest firing in major league history ended ten games later, when Mele became manager.

Mele knew what it was like to play under a tyrannical manager. Playing for the Red Sox under Joe McCarthy in 1948 and part of 1949, Mele experienced the enervating effects of a manager who was capricious if not mean. While McCarthy ruled through fear, Mele wanted to be both fair and firm. He was largely successful. Mele's calm attitude allowed players to focus on playing.

Mele successfully guided the Twins to 91-win seasons in both 1962 and 1963. But after a seventh place finish in 1964, Griffith fired all of Mele's coaches and hired the replacements himself. These included pitching coach Johnny Sain, hitting coach Jim Lemon and third-base coach Billy Martin. Mele was given a last chance in 1965. The Twins responded with a franchise-record 102 wins and a World Series appearance.

According to Billy Martin, it was the World Series that created the beginning of Mele's downfall.[2] Before the third game, Sain convinced Mele to exclude Martin from the meeting to decide the starting pitcher. Camilo Pascual started and gave up three runs in five innings. Martin's preferred starter, Jim Merritt, relieved and gave up another run in two innings. The Twins were shut out. They eventually lost the Series in seven games. Never one to overlook the smallest slight, Martin spent the offseason and much of 1966 season making life miserable for Sain. Martin picked his fights and had Mele on his side in every disagreement. This was not difficult because Sain was a notoriously prickly character. Fiercely loyal and devoted to his pitchers, he was never capable of getting along with managers or management. Neither man was likely to let this spat be quickly forgotten. Many felt that Martin's and Sain's mutual dislike began when they were teammates on the Yankees in the early 1950s.

Sain turned to the bullpen coach Hal Naragon for support. Jim Lemon did his best to remain neutral and without an opinion. It was a toxic year. Sain moved out of the coaches' dressing room and into the clubhouse with the players. For most of the year Mele and Sain spoke only through Naragon who spent every game in the bullpen.

Griffith was frustrated at Mele's inability to manage his coaches. At Mele's request, Sain and Naragon were fired after the season. But even that did not end the dissension. Furious at losing his pitching coach, Jim Kaat who had won 25 games that year wrote an open letter to Twins fans. It included a staunch defense of Sain as an extraordinary pitching coach, who was far more valuable to the team than the manager. Kaat made it easy to see Mele's shortcomings in contrast, especially his poor communications with the Twins players. The letter and its contents continued to be a source of discussion during Kaat's poor start in 1967.

The sloppy play of the Twins in 1967 was easily viewed through the lens of Mele's apparently inadequate communication skills. These were again questioned when Zoilo Versalles and Mudcat Grant let slip a few intemperate remarks about each other to reporters after a botched double play in a loss.

It was a squabble worthy of no more than a day or two of attention. Instead, two weeks later the controversy was still in the papers. This fed the perception that Mele was incapable of dealing with even the slightest dissension on the team.

June 5 generated news more welcome in Minnesota than Mele's employment status. Fans read in their morning papers that Harmon Killebrew had hit the second home run in the history of Metropolitan Stadium to reach the facing of the second deck in the outfield. This was more impressive because he had hit the first home run to travel that far only two days earlier. That titanic 520-foot blast had landed in the second deck and was already marked by a seat painted red.

The magnitude of these home runs was not unusual for Killebrew. He had led the league in home runs in 1959, 1962, 1963, and 1964. In 1962 he hit the first home run to clear the left field roof in Tiger Stadium, which at the time had hosted major league baseball for 50 years. He held the stadium record for longest home run in other American League cities.[3] Killebrew's power was so intimidating that the Angels' George Brunet had already intentionally walked him, with the bases empty and two outs in the first inning of an early season game.

The newspapers bestowed on him possibly the least appropriate nickname ever—"Killer." Killebrew was almost universally proclaimed the nicest, most pleasant player in baseball during the 1960s. Even the umpires liked him.[4] A balding man who looked shorter than 5'11" and appeared to carry a few extra pounds, he looked like a salesman at the local hardware store. His interests were highly accessible: hunting and fishing locally, and watching television. Unfailingly courteous and polite, Killebrew had been a favorite of Twins fans from the day he arrived. Although ubiquitous in pre-game photographs for years, Killebrew claimed to be shy. Deferential local reporters almost never intruded by pestering him with questions in the clubhouse. Even after this historic performance, Killebrew basked unmolested at his locker.

While the home run was headline material, beat reporters filled space with Bob Allison's continued resurgence at the plate. The Twins won the game in the tenth inning on his squeeze bunt. Writers at the *Minneapolis Tribune* could not contain their enthusiasm, designating him "Twins best stand still bunter."[5] It was an odd category, but Allison's play demanded a superlative.

Most readers were stopped before they leafed to the sports section by a bulletin, shoe-horned into the top of the front page. The *Minneapolis Tribune*'s announced, "Arab-Israel Fight Starts."[6] Papers across the country struggled with presenting the news of this momentous war, which began not long before their papers had to physically go on the press. Reports were brief and often contradictory as the papers quoted government-sponsored radio broadcasts from the combatants. Official sources from both Egypt and Israel claimed that the other had attacked first. Many papers did not have time to pull lengthy stories inside about the planned—but now unnecessary—visit of the Egyptian vice president with President Johnson to discuss ways of avoiding war.

Americans had read for months as small border raids had increased in frequency and then with ferocity. Eventually in response to a successful Israeli air raid inside Syria, Egypt had sent troops as a threat onto the Sinai Peninsula. To further intimidate the Israelis, Egypt asked the UN peacekeeping forces under the command of Norwegian General Odd Bull to evacuate from the Israel-Egyptian border. (General Bull's grandfather was English. Odd was a Norwegian given name.) Egypt's President Gamal Nasser anticipated, and wanted, a long rhetorical contest over this request. Surprisingly, UN Secretary General U Thant complied almost immediately.

Now a war had started that no political leaders really wanted. The United States' and Soviet Union's leaders fell over themselves assuring the other side that they would not enter the battle. Despite more than a decade of bellicose rhetoric, neither wanted the Cold War to turn hot.

Even the next day, June 6, there was still little clarity about the war in the morning papers. The *Minneapolis Tribune* ran a typical headline: "Israel-Arab War Rages on Ground; in Skies; Both Sides Claim Victories."[7] If Mele's problems stemmed from his leadership style, or lack of leadership, the war in the Middle East presented an extreme contrast in approaches to leadership.

Almost since the conclusion of its war of independence in 1947, Israel's armed forces had been founded on five bedrock principles. The synthesis of these led to two strategies: Always attack first and attack relentlessly. Junior officers were given strategic goals, and expected to overcome all obstacles with their own initiative to reach them.[8]

By comparison, Egypt's armed forces featured an almost soviet command structure. At the highest levels were many political allies of Nasser and his chief of armed forces Abdel Hakim Amer who had little military training or duties. These political generals typically outranked professional officers who might actually run a military campaign. This dichotomy existed throughout the officer corp. Professional, effective officers commanded some units and political hacks were in charge of others.[9]

Editors throughout the United States had labored for months trying to explain the war in Vietnam with its transitory, almost ephemeral, military objectives and nonexistent front lines. They reveled at this war. Coverage with extensive maps and first-person accounts dominated entire sections of many papers.

The war continued to rage while Cal Griffith spent the afternoon of June 8 at Metropolitan Stadium watching his team erase a 3–1 deficit to the Indians in the eighth by scoring four runs with two outs. Sam Mele let reliever Al Worthington bat for himself and make the third out. A right-hander, Worthington began the ninth inning with a 2.76 ERA and retired the first batter. Griffith sat fuming as Mele left Worthington in the game to face seven batters. Worthington wild pitched in the tying run and then served up a two-run home run. The game ended with a 7–5 Indians victory.

Cal Griffith was born Calvin Robertson in Canada. His father's sister was the wife of Washington Senators owner and Hall of Fame player, Clark Griffith. The Griffiths were childless and Cal's father proved incapable of supporting his large family. After a visit when he was 10, Cal and his sister Thelma moved permanently to Washington with their aunt and uncle. Although he was never legally adopted, Cal became Cal Griffith and Clark treated him like a son. Every night when Clark came home from working, he spent part of his evening talking baseball with Cal, who was explicitly raised to run a professional baseball team. Cal recounted learning a certain fearless pragmatism from his uncle, "You must make a few mistakes in this world if you want to accomplish things."[10] He served as a bat boy, cleaned the stadium, sold tickets and concessions, played and managed in the minor leagues and later ran minor league teams in Chattanooga and Charlotte for his uncle.[11, 12]

One of Cal's earliest baseball memories was perhaps the highlight of Clark's long tenure as owner of the Washington team. Cal was a 12-year-old batboy when the Senators won the dramatic 1924 World Series after two errors in the bottom of the 12th inning of Game Seven. During the excited on-field celebration that followed, all the baseballs disappeared from a cage where they were held behind home plate. These were one of Cal's few responsibilities. While others reveled, Cal cried in fear at the thought of what retribution his uncle might take when he found out.[13]

For most of the 30s, 40s and 50s the Senators were consistently losers. From 1934 through 1960 the Senators finished over .500 only four times. When Clark Griffith died in 1955, Cal had already spent 13 years in the Senators small front office with his uncle evaluating players and running the business.

Cal and his sister Thelma inherited 52 percent of the franchise, which Cal used to fully control the team. Cal was famously single-minded. Everyone who knew him through the rest of his career confirmed his reputation: he had no hobbies or even interests to distract him from baseball.

Griffith had learned much during his long apprenticeship. He moved energetically to invigorate the moribund franchise. Griffith knew that talented

Cuban and other Latin players would sign with no bonus and for a low salary. The Senators became the first team with a full time scout in Cuba. This resulted in a long line of every day and All-Star players. Breaking with his uncle's frugality, Griffith extended substantial signing bonuses to unproven players of great potential.

Griffith struggled with a team drawing around half of a million fans per year, sometimes averaging fewer than 6,000 per home game. Only leasing his stadium out for wrestling matches and football games allowed him to break even.

Even though league president Joe Cronin was his brother in law, the other American League owners initially refused him permission to move his franchise. Griffith persisted with his usual tenacity. Five years after taking control, the Senators moved to Minnesota.

There were immediate dividends. The stadium was new. A single local beer sponsor paid five times the team's entire radio and television income in Washington. Attendance started at over 1.2 million. By 1963, they led the league in attendance drawing fans from seven states.

Griffith was a relentless scout and talent evaluator. He frequently overruled baseball men and insisted that his managers play young players that he favored. In addition to overruling Lavagetto in 1959 about Killebrew and Allison, Griffith later promoted Zoilo Versales over the objections of Sam Mele and minor league evaluators. During spring training in 1967 he presented the very raw Rod Carew who played Class A ball in 1966 to Mele: "This is your second baseman. End of discussion."[14] Those four players won two Rookie of the Year awards, 34 All-Star designations and three MVPs. Two were inducted into the Hall of Fame.

The Twins were run as a family business. Griffith's brother Sherry Robertson, an ex–major leaguer, oversaw the minor league teams and players. Billy Robertson was the Director of Stadium Operations. Billy's twin Jimmy Robertson oversaw concessions. His decision to include sauerkraut as a condiment at Metropolitan Stadium merited coverage in a full-length feature in one local paper. Thelma's husband, former major leaguer Joe Haynes, worked in the Twins front office until he died of a heart attack in January 1967.

The Twins may have been open to charges of nepotism, but the business was lean. During the 1967 season, visitors to Metropolitan Stadium could walk unannounced through Cal Griffith's open office door.[15] The Griffiths watched their marketing dollars. Near the end of Sam Mele's tenure, the Twins ran a rare ad encouraging fans to see a game at Metropolitan Stadium. The small design ran thriftily, deep in the sports section of the *Tribune* buried with the out of town box scores. It prominently listed convenient local outlets where fans could buy tickets. It was a diverse list that included: The Broiler Café in Mankato, Security Bank and Trust Company in Owatonna, Greyhound

Bus Terminal in Winona, Becker's Bar in New Ulm, and Newberg's Men's Wear in LaCrosse, Wisconsin.[16]

Despite its big-league team filled with international stars, Griffith's open door was not unique in providing a small-town atmosphere to the Twins' home cities. Later in the summer, the *Minneapolis Tribune* would announce with breathless excitement, "ABC sent a film crew in from New York to do some film on the Twins that will be seen on national television."[17]

When Griffith woke up on June 9, he had already decided to make a change. He called Cal Ermer, the manager at AAA Denver, to inform him that he was being promoted. To avoid news being leaked before Griffith was ready to make the formal announcement, Ermer flew to Minneapolis under the alias Griffith picked for him, Charles Cabin.[18]

Although Billy Martin was described as having watery eyes and some players were quoted lauding Mele, the firing was not controversial. However, Minnesotan politeness was offended by the timing. Columnists lamented that Mele was fired on the same day that his wife and large family were flying in to join him for the summer. Mele was famously quoted while greeting his wife at the airport, "What are you crying for? All these years you've been saying you'd like to have me home for the summer. Well, that's where I'll be now."[19]

Griffith claimed to have been grooming Ermer for years, but he was a complete unknown to the major league world. Most had assumed that Billy Martin was the manager in waiting. Ermer had a calm demeanor like Mele and he favored the same aggressive style of play. They even looked vaguely alike. Reporters had repeatedly confused the two during spring training earlier in 1967. Griffith had lost patience with Mele, but valued his basic managerial traits. He had built his team for that type of manager and was still convinced that the team would succeed.

Chapter 6

"A great manager from the ankles down"

American League standings before play on June 10.

	W	L	GB
Detroit Tigers	31	20	–
Chicago White Sox	28	20	1½
Baltimore Orioles	26	23	4
Boston Red Sox	26	24	4½
New York Yankees	25	25	5½
Cleveland Indians	25	26	6
Minnesota Twins	25	26	6
Kansas City Athletics	25	28	7
California Angels	23	32	10
Washington Senators	21	31	10½

On June 10 in his first start under Cal Ermer, Jim Kaat finally won his 100th career game on his 11th try, an 8–1 complete game victory over Baltimore. On the same day, Israel concluded two days of attacks on Syria by taking Mount Hermon and the Golan Heights in the hours surrounding the formal ceasefire deadline. The soon-to-be-named Six Day War was over.

Since the beginning of May the White Sox had battled the Tigers for the league lead. Frustratingly for Eddie Stanky, the Tigers had stayed on top for the past two weeks. After a 13-inning loss to the Athletics during which the White Sox went 11 consecutive innings with a total of only two hits, Stanky held a team meeting. In the most vehement terms he criticized his players for not putting forth enough effort to win. After blistering the team, he calmed his voice to a conversational level. June had barely begun. He told them that if they finished the season in second place by one game, they should remember that they lost the pennant here. They would have only themselves to blame. It was a theme for Stanky after close losses. He had browbeat his team with the same logic after leaving Gary Peters in to throw 158 pitches in a 4–3 loss at the end of April.[1]

Stanky had suffered through the 1966 season with a team that averaged barely three and a half runs per game. For 1967 he had replaced all of his coaches. One of these new coaches was Grover Resinger who would serve as the base-running and batting coach. Everything about Resinger was aggressive. Instead of a dog, Resinger had a pet wolf. As a minor league manager, Resinger's teams had consistently led their leagues in stolen bases. He ardently preached that an aggressive base-running team created far more runs than a team intent on playing it safe.[2]

Despite Resinger's coaching and great optimism during spring training, the White Sox had struggled to score during the season's first couple of months. Although overall their scoring per game had risen slightly, that was due primarily to two blowout wins. It was not so much that the batters were significantly underperforming but that none quite matched expectations. With the exception of Tommie Agee, the lineup consisted of players who had never been good hitters, were rookies, played irregularly or played injured. Prominent in this last category was Ron Hansen.

An above-average shortstop for most of his career, the 6'3" Hansen fell awkwardly after stepping on a stray ball during batting practice before a May 1966 game. He was lost for the year with a severe back injury, requiring surgery. Stanky believed that the veteran Hansen would be the key to the White Sox' season and had done all he could to build his physical condition during the spring and early season. Hansen's body was not ready. He noticeably wobbled in the field during games at the end of spring training.[3] His fielding range never quite recovered. Stanky told reporters that Hansen would play every game unless he specifically asked to be out of the lineup. Despite his weakened condition, Hansen started every game.

Throughout his career, Hansen had a nose for the ball. Since joining the White Sox with its plethora of groundball pitchers, Hansen led the league in assists each full year he played. In 1965, he set the record for the most chances handled in one day—28. Hansen still fielded a lot of balls and was on pace to lead the league again. This statistic was more the result of the pitching staff than Hansen's range. (The assist total of the four White Sox shortstops who split the 1966 season would have led the league by a substantial margin.)

Hansen's batting average was another victim of his injury and his weakened state at the beginning of the season. It had spent the entire season well below .200. Despite that, Stanky considered him one of his most important batters, believing Hansen had an uncanny knack of driving in winning runs.

Stanky claimed that the White Sox had statistics showing that Hansen had driven in more winning runs than any other player from 1963 to 1965. (Writers repeating these claims seemed to assume that no one else had access to these statistics or the interest in reviewing the hundreds of box scores necessary to duplicate them.) With only inexperienced catchers and a carousel of fielders at second base and third base, Stanky was willing to sacrifice some hitting and fielding range for Hansen's leadership.

Stanky's team was now entering a busy period of 11 games in nine days. To start this stretch, Stanky sent left-hander Gary Peters to the mound. Peters entered the game with a 2.13 ERA, and a chance to regain the league lead for strikeouts. This was Peters' fifth full season as a starter, making him the veteran of the four starting pitchers Stanky expected to use during the season.

There was little to predict Peters' success as a pitcher. He never played organized baseball until he joined a sandlot team in his teens as a first baseman. He had never pitched until injuries in Class D Holdrege (Nebraska) during his first minor league season made it a necessity. From Holdrege it took him six minor league seasons to make the White Sox' roster in the spring of 1962. For the last couple of years in the minors, Peters would get occasional coaching from Ray Berres, the White Sox' longtime pitching coach. Berres had a distinct pitching philosophy that promoted groundballs. Peters developed the standard Berres pitching repertoire: primarily sinking fastball and slider augmented by curveballs. Peters also had a straight changeup and a second fastball that ran inside to right-handed batters. Despite Berres' departure after Stanky forced him out before the 1967 season, Peters like the other White Sox starters maintained this ingrained style.

After pitching 14 innings combined over the course of three late-season call-ups, Peters started the season with the White Sox in 1962. After five relief outings he had compiled an unimpressive 5.68 ERA. The White Sox demoted him and he spent the rest of the year in the minors. He regressed to an 8–10 record. Disappointed and frustrated, Peters headed south to Puerto Rico to pitch winter ball. There he finally became a complete pitcher.

Peters again made the White Sox out of spring training in 1963. The White Sox had made it known that if he did not succeed in the major leagues that year, they would release him. His baseball career would be over. He began the season 0–2 as a reliever, but began starting in early May. By mid-season he was dominant. In one stretch he completed 10 of 11 starts, including complete games of 11 and 12 innings. He won 19 games and Rookie of the Year honors. Peters followed that with a 20-win season in 1964.

When Eddie Stanky became manager of the White Sox, he instituted an interesting incentive system for his pitchers. Every time a starter won a complete game with at least 21 groundballs (whether outs or not), he would buy them a new suit at Spencer's, a premier clothier in Chicago. Three of his best starters, Peters, Joe Horlen and Tommy John, won seven suits between them in the first half season according to Peters.[4] Stanky complained that he was going broke on the deal and was a little slow in buying one of Peters' suits. Peters told him to forget about it. A week or so later Stanky found Peters sitting in the locker room dressed in burlap sacking and surrounded by laughing teammates. Peters had told them that it was the only suit that Stanky could afford. He then headed out onto the field where he wore the burlap for batting practice.[5]

Peters' maturity and success made him one of the few players on the White Sox who had the confidence to rib Stanky. When longtime White Sox trainer Eddie Froelich retired during the 1967 season, he said, "Gary Peters is not only a physical gem but also a man of wonderful emotional balance."[6] Peters could view Stanky's violent outbursts impersonally. Peters' first manager on the White Sox had been Hall of Famer Al Lopez. Peters believed that while Lopez was aloof, he was a master psychologist, getting the most out of each player. Peters contrasted that to Stanky. "The problem with Ed was that he'd be friendly towards a guy and then a few minutes later he'd terrorize them. Some guys couldn't take that and had their careers ruined. I know from being around him that he'd say something and ten minutes later he'd regret it. But Eddie wasn't the type of man who was ever going to apologize for something he did."[7]

Gary Peters warms up before a game at White Sox Park. Even in this photograph the infield grass looks overgrown. The state of the grounds in Chicago was widely believed to help White Sox pitchers. Its effects on the confidence of Chicago's batters were corrosive. National Baseball Hall of Fame and Museum.

During Stanky's first year in 1966, Peters started 27 games and completed 11 of them, including four shutouts, with a league-leading 1.98 ERA. It was a phenomenal season. His disappointing 12–10 record was a reflection of poor run support. Stanky found little reason to terrorize Peters, who took the ball and pitched with no complaints.

Like many ballplayers, Peters loved practical jokes. He favored novelty and effect over ingenuity. Early in the 1967 season he walked onto a team bus and dropped a rubber snake on the seat next to first baseman Tommy McCraw who was the team's other notorious prankster. McCraw's immediate terrified reaction was gratifying. McCraw was so embarrassed at being fooled that he left the bus and took a cab alone to the ballpark. Later in the season, Peters went shark fishing. He arrived at the ballpark before his teammates that day. One of them found the shark's still-bloody head leering out of his locker. Peters later repeated the feat with a bobcat he killed. He had a never-ending supply of hobbies: serenading teammates with a concertina and a harmonica during a long bus ride. He also successfully fished using a bow and arrow.[8]

Peters was far from being frivolous. He had the foresight and drive to complete a college degree in mathematics during the off-seasons of his minor league career. Peters loved being a major leaguer. He knew that the long season wore on many of his teammates. The intensity that Stanky required was even more stressful, especially on the younger, struggling players. If he could have a little fun and relieve some of his teammates' tension at the same time, that was part of why the team viewed Peters as their leader.

Peters was one of the few pitchers to take great pride in his hitting. He took batting practice before most games that he did not start. Peters was convinced that being a solid batter gave managers incentive to leave him in close games when normally they would pinch-hit for the pitcher. During the first few months of 1967, the team's beat writers made the claim that he was one of the better hitters on the White Sox. By June 10, Peters had already pinch-hit three times and had a .265 average with a home run and six RBIs. Not large numbers, but baseball writers could extrapolate them as if he was an everyday player and see that he would be a team leader. A couple of weeks earlier Stanky had publicly mused about batting Peters sixth instead of the pitcher's traditional spot at ninth.[9]

When Peters took the mound against the Yankees, it had been seven days since Peters had won his previous game over the Athletics. In that game he had hit rookie Rick Monday in the face with a pitch breaking his jaw. Peters was unapologetic. He saw that as a necessity after an Athletics pitcher had hit Pete Ward with no consequences during the previous game. It did not bother Peters when he was plunked in retaliation. In between, Peters had matched up against Boston's emerging ace, Jim Lonborg, in a game that was called on account of rain before it was official. Peters typically pitched on three days' rest throughout the season, so a third start in seven days was almost normal.

Peters was masterful in his June 10 start, pitching a complete game shutout. He helped himself with his bat getting two hits including a home run and two more RBIs. The White Sox had one of their biggest days of the season winning 9–0 with 18 hits. Better yet, the victory brought them back to within a half-game of the Tigers, who lost to the Angels.

The series provided a glimpse of technology gaining a toehold on baseball. The *Chicago Tribune* beat writer gushed in disbelief, "The Yankees have three television monitors in the press box for play-backs of big moments on the diamond."[10] Early in July, the Orioles would unveil an even more incredible sight. For two games, their fans would be treated to "a computer operated sports information and message board." IBM designed the 30-foot-long portable novelty. The *Boston Traveler* noted it "displays messages in foot-high letters on a panel which makes use of more than 7,000 lights." "The board will be able to analyze a pitcher's performance at any point during the game, including total number of pitches, called strikes, swinging strikes, balls, fouls and other facts."[11]

The next day the White Sox won both games of a doubleheader from the Yankees and passed the Tigers to take first. It was Bat Day at Yankee Stadium drawing 65,582 fans, the largest crowd to see a baseball game in two years.[12] In White Sox fashion, i.e., low-scoring and close, they won 2–1 and 3–2. After the second game, Stanky compared his team to the 1951 Giants. This was both his goal for the team, and his highest standard of praise.

There followed an epic. Playing a night game in Washington, the White Sox and Senators were tied 4–4 after nine innings and 5–5 after ten. In the 16th, with the bases loaded and one out White Sox outfielder Ken Berry was caught trying to steal home. The Senators won 6–5 in the 22nd inning. At six hours and 38 minutes, it was reputedly the longest game ever played under lights. Eddie Stanky held a team meeting at 3:00 a.m. to express his displeasure with the loss.[13] Stanky would later bar from his clubhouse the Washington reporter who wrote about the meeting a couple of days later.

Hearing about the lengthy game, Detroit pitcher Denny McLain told Detroit sportswriters, "I just don't figure Chicago is going to last. They are playing their best ball right now. It's too tough on a pitching staff with all those low-scoring games. The strain of no hitting help will tell as the season wears on."[14]

McLain was not the only one to question whether Stanky's team could survive the season. Stanky's every-game intensity struck many as inappropriate. While those in baseball would not be quoted, columnists bemoaned his seemingly excessive managerial maneuvers. It was a long season and some felt he managed every game like it was the World Series. It was not unusual for Stanky to employ 15 or even up to 20 players in nine innings. Except for his fellow Durocher disciples Bill Rigney and Al Dark, this was far above the norm in the American League.

Apparently inspired by Stanky's early morning rant, the White Sox took the next game 6–0 from the Senators and then moved to Boston. Although most major league teams appeared penurious to their players, the White Sox were uniquely cheap when it came to lodging. They booked the team into particularly low-budget hotels. Players remember rooms having no bureau and no closet, just two beds and three hooks on the wall with a bathroom down the hall.[15] The night before the Boston series, Eddie Stanky did not need to worry that his players would be distracted by television. There were no TVs in the rooms, or even in the lobby of their hotel.

Peters started the first game of a doubleheader. He did not pitch well giving up two home runs in the second and leaving in the sixth with a 6–5 lead. Knuckleballer Wilbur Wood struck out George Scott in the bottom of the ninth to end the game with the bases loaded, preserving the 8–7 win for Peters. It was Peters' worst game of the season, but Stanky's team showed the resiliency to win when its best starter was not at his best.

This series had received a big buildup in Boston.

In the season's second week, the Red Sox had journeyed to Chicago. Weather played havoc with the series. In the same week, a tornado killed 47 in Chicago and a late-season storm coated the city with three inches of snow concluding the snowiest winter in Chicago history. Only one game was played. The *Chicago Sun-Times* estimated the meager crowd at 400.[16] In the fourth inning of that lone game, Tommy McCraw slid well wide of second base smashing into Reggie Smith and breaking up a double play. This play was credited for the subsequent poor Red Sox infield play that led to unearned White Sox runs and their eventual victory. While the White Sox gloated, the Red Sox stewed.

Feelings did not improve during the teams' series in Chicago at the beginning of June. In the first game of that series the White Sox led 5–3 in the top of the ninth with one runner on. In the middle of the inning, Stanky switched Ken Berry, his best fielding outfielder, from left field to right field. On the next pitch, Boston's Dalton Jones drove the ball deep to right. Berry made a sensational leaping catch while crashing into the wall.[17] While that savvy managerial move received considerable play in Chicago, Boston papers focused on Stanky's comment that Red Sox star Carl Yastrzemski was "an All-Star from the neck down."[18] The insult pierced Yastrzemski's ego. The next day's game was rained out and Yastrzemski brooded. In the makeup doubleheader, Yastrzemski collected six hits. As he rounded third base after hitting a home run, he tipped his cap to Stanky in the White Sox dugout.

Boston papers continued to mention Stanky's remark almost every day. Stoked by sports columnists, Boston fans fixed on Stanky as a villain. When the mid-June series opened in Boston one wag held up a sign next to the White Sox dugout that read, "Stanky: a great manager from the ankles down."[19] There was real anger behind the jest and it erupted during the second game on June 14. Stanky became embroiled with the umpires when they ruled that an apparent home run by J.C. Martin was a foul ball. Later in the game with Stanky on the mound ignoring the umpires and wasting time to give a reliever extra time to warm up in the bullpen, he was ejected from the game. This provoked a spectacular tantrum from Stanky. As he walked from the field to the White Sox dugout, Boston fans pelted him with garbage. The Red Sox won 6-1 on a Yastrzemski home run.

After the game, Stanky informed reporters that he had instructed his wife to file lawsuits of $1 million apiece against the American League, Red Sox owner Tom Yawkey, and players' union president Marvin Miller if any physical harm to him resulted from the lack of security in Fenway Park.[20]

The series finale the next day was a White Sox–type of game. The game was scoreless through nine innings. In the top of the tenth, the White Sox threatened to score. A pinch-runner was thrown out trying to steal third and then John Wyatt struck out two batters. Stanky was furious about the umpiring and after lengthy comments from the dugout he was ejected. In the top of the 11th, the White Sox finally scored on a Ken Berry single. That extended his hitting streak to 20 games, the longest streak in the major leagues since 1964.[21]

In the Red Sox half of the inning John Buzhardt retired the first two batters easily. When Buzhardt entered the game, Jerry Adair, who had been traded only the week before to the Red Sox from the White Sox, told Tony Conigliaro that Buzhardt had a tendency to hang his curve. As he headed to the on-deck circle to warm up while Joe Foy batted, Conigliaro told Adair, "If Joe Foy gets on I'm going to hit a curve out of here."[22] Foy singled and then on a 3-2 curve Conigliaro homered to win the game 2-1. For a Boston team that had years of almost uninterrupted experience at losing games like this, the win was revelatory. Conigliaro exulted, "There's never been anything to compare with this in my life."[23]

Except possibly winning the World Series (or Bobby Thomson after the Shot Heard 'Round the World), players did not leave the dugout to congratulate a teammate for a walk-off home run. The Red Sox were a young team. More than once they were derided as reacting like little leaguers—with exuberant displays of emotion. They charged the plate and mobbed Conigliaro. In this game, Yastrzemski was the first to greet Conigliaro. It was the first time that had ever happened.[24] The two men had never been friendly and had had an uneasy rivalry.[25] However subtle, this was a sign that the two hitting stars were now connected as teammates first.

The next day the *Boston Globe* used the term "Impossible Dream" in a headline to describe the Red Sox' unusual comeback victory.[26] It was taken from a popular song of the same name in the Broadway hit *Man of La Mancha* about Don Quixote.

After the game Stanky described Boston as "a bush town," although the main target of his displeasure was umpire Larry Napp.[27] The following day, Stanky refused a request to meet with American League president Joe Cronin to explain his behavior. Cronin had, apparently, no further recourse. Stanky was not the only manager to publicly vent his displeasure at the umpires. That same day after losing both games of a doubleheader to the Senators, Dick Williams called Red Flaherty a "mushmouth." In case this was too ambiguous, he clarified that Flaherty was "an incompetent umpire."[28] Williams also received no discipline for expressing this opinion.

The White Sox traveled back to Chicago to play the Yankees. It was raining when the first game was supposed to start. The usual crowd was augmented by an estimated 20,000 teenagers who were lured to White Sox Park by two hours of live music supplied by three bands before the game. An hour after game time with rain still coming down Gary Peters, displaying another of his hobbies, waddled out on the field fully clad in his scuba gear and entertained the soggy fans by pretending to swim around the diamond.[29, 30]

The next day—June 17—Joe Horlen won, pitching eight shutout innings. On Sunday the teams played a doubleheader with Peters starting the first game. Against the Yankees he was all business, pitching a complete game and giving up only one earned run. It was his seventh complete game of the season and brought his ERA down to 2.16. Tommy John followed with a complete game shutout in the second game. In the three games White Sox starters pitched 26 innings and gave up only one earned run. By the end of the day, the White Sox had opened up a three and a half game lead on the Tigers.

Chapter 7

"I can win in the big leagues"

American League standings before play on June 21.

	W	L	GB
Chicago White Sox	36	24	–
Detroit Tigers	35	28	2½
Cleveland Indians	33	31	5
Boston Red Sox	32	31	5½
Minnesota Twins	32	31	5½
Baltimore Orioles	30	32	7
California Angels	32	36	8
Kansas City Athletics	31	35	8
New York Yankees	28	34	9
Washington Senators	29	36	9½

Going into their first game at home against the Twins, the Tigers were reeling from a rough stretch in June where they had gone 4–10. They lost consecutive series to the Angels, Twins and Athletics before winning two out of three from the Angels at home. They were still solidly in second place, but their pitching, especially their starting pitching, was below average. Sportswriters and fans searched for answers to a season that seemed like it might not end well.

The atmosphere was totally different in Boston. The Red Sox were tied for fourth, five and a half games out, and one game over .500. The team had been pathetic and apathetic for so long that normally cynical Boston sportswriters sometimes sounded giddy with even this mediocre, but spirited, performance. On a team of pleasant surprises, the biggest and best was pitcher Jim Lonborg.

Lonborg signed with the Red Sox after his junior year as a pre-med student at Stanford. After a season moving from Class A ball to Class AAA,

Jim Lonborg winds up at Boston's Fenway Park. An improved slider and determination to throw to the inside of the plate led to his breakout performance in 1967. Lonborg led the league in hit batsmen, strikeouts and wins. He won the season's Cy Young Award. National Baseball Hall of Fame and Museum.

Lonborg served six months of active duty in the Army Reserves. One of the men serving with him was another Red Sox hopeful, shortstop Rico Petrocelli. Petrocelli was amazed that Lonborg would go through a series of flashcards every day. These had short messages on them: "I have a major league fastball." "I can strike out any batter I want to." "I can win in the big leagues."[1]

That spring when Lonborg finally reported to a major league training camp, he stood out. Three years of college gave him a level of maturity surpassing other hopefuls. He made the 1965 Red Sox roster as a starter. Having reached the major leagues, Lonborg labored for two years on terrible teams slowly improving his pitching. A common complaint whenever Lonborg had some rough outings was that he overthought on the mound or that he overintellectualized pitching. It was almost impossible to refute such a charge. Many coaches, managers, sportswriters, and even general managers had no more than a high school education. Lonborg not only had completed his Stanford degree in the offseason, but had an easy way of making intriguing references to Beethoven or the Brandenburg Concerto as if they were normal topics of conversation. Sportswriters ate it up and nicknamed him "Gentleman Jim" because of this education. Almost as a defensive reflex, baseball lifers preferred to see his brains as a handicap.

Lonborg was 6'5", sparely built on a medium frame with long arms. Handsome, his demeanor and looks were often described as Californian. It was a way to define his carefree charm and a compliment both nationwide and in parochial Boston.

Toward the end of the 1966 season, manager Billy Herman convinced Lonborg that if he wanted to develop into an elite pitcher he would have to be more aggressive. Lonborg had to start knocking down batters, planting doubt in every batter's mind that the next pitch might be aimed at him. This would give Lonborg an edge to make all his other pitches more effective.

Unlike many of his teammates, Lonborg respected Herman. In August that year, Lonborg lasted only one-third of an inning in the first game of a doubleheader against the Tigers. It was his first start in a month. Lonborg was shelled for four earned runs. Between games, Lonborg wondered if his big-league career was over. In the second game to Lonborg's amazement, Herman signaled for him in the bottom of the tenth to protect a one-run lead with runners on first and third, and two out. On the mound Herman handed Lonborg the ball and said, "Keep the ball low on this guy McAuliffe. Make him hit it on the ground so we can get the hell out of here and go home."[2]

It took Lonborg two pitches. That show of confidence from Herman transformed Lonborg. He reportedly wept at his locker after the game.[3] He earned nine more starts and dropped his ERA by a full run over the last month of the season.

That offseason the Red Sox replaced Herman and most of their front office. Management sent Lonborg down to the Venezuelan winter league to work on his curveball. Instead, he followed Herman's advice and spent the time gaining confidence throwing his fastball on the inside edge of the plate, or even closer to the batter.

After the Venezuelan season ended, Lonborg went back to his native California and skied. "I figured that there couldn't be anything better for your leg and shoulder strength and your overall conditioning," said Lonborg.[4] He was not slowly snowplowing down a beginner's trail. He skied with a confident young athlete's energy and daring on steep slopes high in the Sierra Nevada mountains. By his estimation, he arrived at Red Sox spring training in 1967 in the best shape of his life.

Lonborg was not only physically set, he was ready to take on a leadership role on a young team. He could see during the first weeks of spring training that his teammates were all willing to work hard under their new manager. They wanted to shed their losing habits. Lonborg was able to discuss this with many of them. Using his methodical, scientific mindset, he explained that a successful team was more than just mastering the individual fundamentals of catching fly balls and getting base hits. It required a team attitude. Everyone liked talking with Lonborg and his charisma allowed him to easily broach even awkward topics.

For example, in 1966 Carl Yastrzemski annoyed, and eventually infuriated, Red Sox pitchers. When they gave up a home run to left field, he would stand still, staring into the infield as the ball sailed over his head and into the stands. Lonborg was able to calmly explain to Yastrzemski that he was showing up his teammates. It was irrelevant that he knew that he would not catch the ball. As a good teammate, he had to turn around and move after the ball. There was no emotionally charged confrontation, just two guys sitting and talking baseball. They agreed on what was best for their team.[5]

Lonborg was not all business. He enjoyed his life as a baseball player emerging into a star. He assumed special service in local restaurants charming owners with his casual smile. On Boston's crowded streets, he showed off by leaving his car in no parking zones.[6] He fully enjoyed nightclubs, and repeatedly reported nights at the Boston Symphony Orchestra. But all of these behaviors were tempered by his ingrained sense of responsibility and his striving to learn. Lonborg believed that he owed the team two good nights of sleep before every start, so his nightclubbing had to wait on those evenings.

Once the season started, Lonborg's new aggressive pitch selection became obvious throughout the American League. In all of 1966 Lonborg hit seven batters. By mid–June he had already hit eight, leading the league. There was more to his success than just pitching inside. Lonborg's sinking fastball was now complemented by a sharper action on his slider.[7] He also developed a new fastball for 1967. Lonborg threw it off the cross seams with a new release. While his regular fastball sank, Lonborg said, "My new fastball hops, raises and tails up."[8]

Lonborg's dominance of the inside of the plate brought inevitable comparisons with Red Sox pitching coach Sal "The Barber" Maglie. When Maglie was a pitching star for the New York Giants in the early 1950s, he earned his nickname for his exquisite control. He located pitches so close to the edges of the strike zone that it was as if he was shaving it. Scowling from the mound with glowering sunken eyes, Maglie was more famous for his intimidating presence. His repertoire frequently featured a fastball that would arrive just under a batter's chin, sending him sprawling out of the way. That set up his wicked curveball, considered one of the most devastating of the 1950s. So, his nickname came to mean that he was throwing so close to batters' faces that he was shaving them. The name Sal the Barber became a byword for aggressive inside pitching.

Maglie had been a loner in his playing days, famously refusing to use his teams' scouting on opposing batters. During games when he was not pitching he sat silently in a dugout corner—his body language keeping teammates away. No one knew what he thought while he sat impassively. His initial success with the Giants in 1950 and then his reputation for independence allowed him to ignore the advice of managers.

Perhaps having refused coaching as a mature, successful player, Maglie assumed that other pitchers should learn the same way. Maglie's strengths as a pitcher—precise control, mound presence, increasingly thorough understanding of hitters—proved difficult for him to transfer. To many of his pitchers, he had little to offer and no interest in them. One described Maglie's approach: "Sal was just ... he was just there."[9]

Maglie spent three years as pitching coach of inept Red Sox teams. At the end of the third year, Boston's manager/general manager Pinky Higgins relinquished his managerial role. In the shakeup, Maglie lost his job. But, Red Sox owner Tom Yawkey liked Maglie, which in the early 1960s was the key element to employment with the team. Yawkey reached out to Maglie a year or so later when Maglie had other professional commitments. He finally convinced Maglie to return by offering a two-year contract that started with the 1966 season.

Dick Williams' hiring for 1967 was difficult for Maglie. Williams made no secret that he wanted to hire a different pitching coach. Maglie, for his part, looked down on Williams with disdain as merely a utility player, just "one of those holler guys in the dugout."[10] Tension between the two men seemed inevitable.

Maglie remained outspoken. Just as he had ignored managers' advice as a player, Maglie retained his disdain for management. After Gary Bell arrived on June 4 in a trade from the Indians, Maglie told Boston reporters that Bell would never last in the league because he threw across his body.[11] (Bell already had over 100 career wins and was in his tenth major league season.)

On the other hand, he could appear sycophantic. The day after Williams stated, "I don't want a pitcher to pace himself," Maglie was quoted as saying, "Pace yourself and you are out of this game."[12]

Although during the preseason Maglie had complained that strikeouts gave pitchers a swollen ego, he did not mind that Lonborg was leading the league with 98 strikeouts heading into the June 21 game with the Yankees.[13] The game at Yankee Stadium was the second in the series with Lonborg going against rookie Thad Tillotson. The day before, Joe Foy who grew up in New York had hit a grand slam in the Red Sox' 7–1 victory. After the game he found out that his parents' home had burned to the ground. Foy spent the night trying to salvage whatever remained and then resettling his parents.

The Red Sox started fast on June 21, scoring four runs in the first inning. They had a runner on base in the second when Tillotson beaned Foy. Foy staggered as he took first base. Whether Tillotson was retaliating for Foy's grand slam or not, none of baseball's unwritten rules justified it.

Tillotson batted in the bottom of the inning with two out and a runner on first. Lonborg left no doubt, drilling Tillotson on the shoulder with a fastball on the first pitch. The beefy Tillotson jawed at Lonborg on his way to first base. Joe Foy responded coming over from his position at third base until the first-base umpire gently restrained him. Both benches emptied in a baseball brawl of shoving and yelling.

It appeared that violence would be avoided until fellow Brooklyn natives Rico Petrocelli and Yankee Joe Pepitone began yelling at each other. Despite being restrained by teammates and at least one umpire, they rushed each other trying to throw punches. In the melee policemen came on to the field to help separate players and restore order. One of them was Petrocelli's brother who tackled Pepitone while Mickey Mantle jumped on Petrocelli. There was speculation in New York after the game that Petrocelli's brother was too concerned with the safety of the Red Sox' shortstop. Whatever his motivations, he was never again allowed to work on the field level at a Yankees game. Petrocelli emerged unscathed, but Pepitone hurt his wrist and left the game.

In the fourth inning, Tillotson knocked Lonborg down with a head-high fastball.[14] Not surprisingly in the next inning Lonborg hit pinch-hitter Dick Howser in the helmet with a fastball. Howser went down to first base and then collapsed. He had to be helped from the field, but apparently suffered no long-term consequences. There was no retribution against Lonborg in his last two at-bats.

After the game, Lonborg was clear about his intentions: "I meant to keep the ball up and in to Tillotson. I had to protect my teammates."[15] He was practicing the lessons on teamwork that he had preached. Lonborg set the tone and his teammates got the message. Teammates needed to stick up for each other. Lonborg had their back.

Dick Williams was secure enough with reporters to tell one after the game that when he walked into the middle of the brawl he looked both ways "to see if I was going to get it from my own players or the Yankees."[16]

Lonborg's next start would be in Minnesota on the June 26. The Red Sox arrived in Minneapolis in third place, a game ahead of the Twins and five games behind the White Sox. Rookie pitcher Gary Waslewski was scheduled to start the second game of the series. It would be his third career start after being called up from AAA Toronto. Waslewski did not know anything about the Twins hitters. He described the scene of approaching his pitching coach, Maglie, for information. "Jim Lonborg and I asked him about how to pitch to the Twins and he told us how to pitch to the Dodgers! 'Well you know, Campy was kinda like Killebrew, and I would do this with Campy...' and he was telling us about throwing a slow curveball."[17]

Neither Lonborg nor Waslewski threw a slow curveball. Waslewski gave up on Maglie after that, concluding, "Sal was useless."[18]

Lonborg lost his start 2–1 to the rejuvenated Jim Kaat, but the next day Waslewski earned his first major league win 3–1 over Dean Chance. The White Sox continued to open up their league lead with Joe Horlen winning his ninth game. Cleveland pounded Earl Wilson and the Tigers 8–1.

Chapter 8

"Hope like hell it goes somewhere"

American League standings before play on July 1.

	W	L	GB
Chicago White Sox	42	28	–
Detroit Tigers	38	33	4½
Boston Red Sox	37	34	5½
Minnesota Twins	36	34	6
Cleveland Indians	37	35	6
California Angels	38	38	7
Baltimore Orioles	33	38	9½
New York Yankees	33	38	9½
Kansas City Athletics	34	41	10½
Washington Senators	32	41	11½

On June 26, the visiting White Sox trailed the Orioles 4–3 in the top of the ninth inning. They loaded the bases with only one out. Recently acquired pinch-hitter Jim King hit a ground ball to first baseman Boog Powell. Powell threw the ball home for an easy force out. Hoping for an inning-ending double play, catcher Andy Etchebarren held the ball while the lumbering Powell tried to get back to first base. The *Chicago Tribune* admiringly wrote, "[Tommy McCraw] slid hard and hooked his legs out to the left neatly. It was as neat a clip as any football player could have pulled off."[1] Etchebarren went down hard. The next batter hit a two-run single, providing the White Sox with their winning runs.

While Eddie Stanky basked in his team's resilience, the Orioles felt that there was some unfinished business. During the next day's game in the fourth inning with Frank Robinson on first base, Brooks Robinson hit a groundball.

The third baseman fielded it cleanly and threw toward Al Weis covering second. Running at full speed, the much larger Robinson went headfirst into Weis. The force of the collision sent Weis' attempted relay bouncing wide of first base. Robinson was knocked cold.

Third-base coach Billy Hunter ran to Robinson and was kneeling down trying to get a response when right fielder Ken Berry ran in, demanded the ball and tagged the prone Robinson out. This alertness was one of the reasons that Berry appeared to be Stanky's favorite position player.[2]

Weis was removed on a stretcher having "shattered the front and back ligaments" of his left knee.[3] After surgery, it was expected that Weis would spend 12 weeks in a cast before starting to rehabilitate his knee. Even though they had traded their starting second baseman only three weeks earlier, the loss of a backup middle infielder caused little apparent concern to the first-place White Sox.

The collision was consistent with baseball's unwritten traditions. Stanky did not need to mention that he would have done the same thing. Unbidden, reporters dredged up Leo Durocher's almost-20-year-old opinion that Stanky would run over his own grandmother if she stood between him and home plate.

The Orioles loss was immediately and obviously much more important. Robinson led the league in hits, runs scored, batting average, and RBIs. He was second in home runs. It took over four minutes for Robinson to recover consciousness. Diagnosed with a mild concussion, he missed over a month of the season with double vision. The White Sox won 5–0 behind Joe Horlen's complete game.

It was on the back of this victory over the Orioles that the White Sox headed to Detroit with a 5½ game lead over the second-place Tigers. The Tigers limped in after a rough stretch playing 6–15 since the first week of June. They had lost five of their last six games.

On July 1, Joe Horlen started the second game of the series for the White Sox and took a 6–2 lead into the seventh inning. One run was in and two men on when Stanky replaced Horlen with Bob Locker, a sinkerball specialist. Locker gave up a single scoring another run. The next batter smashed a fastball back at the pitcher. The ball hit Locker so hard that it rebounded to catcher J.C. Martin in time for him to throw the batter out at first. Locker had to leave the game.

While Locker was being attended to, Hoyt Wilhelm made his way to the mound from the bullpen. He wandered in with a slow, almost meandering gait. His long neck hitched to the side as if afflicted by a permanent injury. This left his round face cocked, compensating for a so-called lazy right eye. The slightly mismatched eyes appeared to focus in different directions, heightening the discomfort of some batters.[4] Wilhelm was almost 45 years old, a knuckleballer with a slight frame, almost the opposite of the big, overpowering Locker. Locker possessed a dominant 2.08 ERA; Wilhelm's was a league-leading 0.74. He entered the game having thrown over 15 straight scoreless innings.

After giving up another run, hurt mostly by his own fielding error, Wilhelm settled down and closed the win out over the last 2⅓ innings. The error was much more of a surprise than the scoreless innings. It brought to an end Wilhelm's record streak of 319 consecutive errorless appearances that began in 1963. The *Detroit Free Press* the next day printed what almost everyone in the American League felt: "It's not fair using Hoyt Wilhelm."[5] An opposing manager would say later in the year after watching his batters' futility against Wilhelm, "Only God can make a pitcher, but the Devil makes knuckleballers."[6]

Wilhelm was the only World War II veteran playing in the major leagues in 1967, and had been for several years. He had been a sergeant during the Battle of the Bulge when exploding ordnance wounded him in the back and his pitching hand.[7] Because of this experience, sportswriters dubbed him "Old Sarge." It did not fit the man. Wilhelm was quiet, an unobtrusive presence on the White Sox.

Unlike many knuckleball pitchers, Wilhelm focused on the pitch in his teens and threw the knuckleball almost exclusively. He taught himself the pitch after seeing a magazine picture of major leaguer Dutch Leonard's knuckleball grip.[8] The essence of a knuckleball is that it does not spin between leaving the pitcher's hand and arriving at the strike zone. The lack of spin makes it susceptible to every slight variation in atmospheric conditions, causing the ball to move erratically.

The pitch is thrown with the same arm motion as a fastball, but comes out of the hand much slower. The pitcher grips the ball with his knuckles bent and nails digging into the ball. Extending his fingers as the ball leaves his hand provides the ball with little or no spin. The most critical physical part of a knuckleballer's anatomy is not his knuckles or even necessarily his arm but his fingernails. They must be strong so he can grip the ball properly pitch after pitch. Wilhelm's pitching coach in 1967 Marv Grissom claimed with a theatrical shake of his head, "Hoyt spends as much time preparing his fingernails as a manicurist in a beauty shop."[9]

Knuckleball pitchers have never been considered good prospects. Wilhelm spent 12 years in the minors and the military before making his major league debut in 1952 with the Giants. Not wanting to appear so old as to be near the end of his career, Wilhelm subtracted a year from his age. He was listed as a 29-year-old rookie. Giants manager Leo Durocher did not think that Wilhelm could last a full nine innings, so he was used strictly as a reliever.

He was an immediate success going 15–3 over 71 appearances with a league-leading 2.43 ERA.

Four years later he was considered too old to have a future. The Giants traded him to the Cardinals. The Cardinals released him that September because their catchers had so much difficulty catching his pitches. Wilhelm struggled to a 4.25 ERA that year which was not good enough for a pitcher apparently approaching the end of his career. The Indians picked him up off waivers at the end of the season.

This would become a recurring problem for Wilhelm. His knuckleball was in some ways too good. Hitters were befuddled, but so were his catchers. One of Wilhelm's catchers set the record for most passed balls in an inning—four. Another, Gus Triandos, set the season record of 28. In the minors he once struck out four batters in one inning but gave up two runs because of four passed balls.[10] By the beginning of the 1967 season Wilhelm had already led the league in causing passed balls 13 times including the past nine consecutive seasons.

In mid-summer of his season with the Indians, Wilhelm became a spot starter. He gave up nine earned runs in four starts including a complete game loss. After that experiment, the Indians released him. Their catchers led the league in passed balls. His 2.49 would prove to be the best ERA of any Indians pitcher who pitched at least 20 innings that year, but it was the old knuckleball pitcher who was cut midseason.

Reliever Hoyt Wilhelm's slight frame and slightly mismatched eyes belied the effectiveness of his knuckleball. By the beginning of July, he had spent most of the season with an ERA under 1.00. He finished the season with eight wins and 12 saves in 89 innings pitched. National Baseball Hall of Fame and Museum.

The message was clear to Wilhelm. He was too old and the movement of his knuckleball was too problematic. He had to prove himself every game.

The Orioles picked him up in late August 1958 and allowed him to start four games. In one of them he no-hit the Yankees, who were on their way to winning the pennant and leading both leagues in runs scored. The next year Wilhelm was a regular starter for the first time. He led the American League with a 2.19 ERA, although his record was only 15–11. Wilhelm was so dominant that Leo Durocher publicly second-guessed his decision to put Wilhelm in the bullpen at the beginning of his career. To help their catchers, the Orioles had an especially large catcher's mitt designed. Its extreme size was later outlawed.[11]

The next year the Orioles found themselves with four strong young pitchers, a veteran starter and Wilhelm in their starting rotation. To give the youngsters the innings they needed to develop and form a strong starting rotation for years to come, Wilhelm was sent to the bullpen. Two years later, despite a 1.94 ERA, he was too old for Baltimore and they traded him to the White Sox.

Wilhelm knew that his career was on thin ice. He would start the 1963 season listed as 39 years old, an almost unheard of age for a pitcher in the 1960s. He maintained a mild-mannered, low-key baseball personality. He insisted to reporters that his knuckleball would not cause catchers difficulties. As it turned out, the White Sox got a great deal. In his first four years with the White Sox, Wilhelm's ERA was 2.64, 1.99, 1.81, and 1.66.

When Wilhelm arrived, the White Sox already had a knuckleballing reliever: Eddie Fisher. Fisher and Wilhelm spent considerable time over three seasons discussing their experiences as they tried to improve their knuckleballs. But in June 1966 with Eddie Stanky managing, Fisher was traded to the Orioles for infielder Jerry Adair.

During the next winter the White Sox acquired a still-young left-handed pitcher named Wilbur Wood. A conventional fastball/curveball pitcher, Wood's stuff was just not quite good enough for the major leagues. Before abandoning his dream, Wood decided to pin all his hopes on developing a knuckleball. He spent a year throwing it in the Pirates minor league system. His success there intrigued the White Sox who acquired him.

Wood's development became Wilhelm's spring project in 1967. On the second day of spring training Wilhelm told Wood that he had to fully commit to the knuckleball. To Wilhelm this meant throwing it at least 90 percent of the time. Wood had to throw the pitch whether he had confidence in it or not.

Wilhelm had more experience with the knuckleball than anyone in the major leagues. His discussions over the past few years with Fisher allowed him to develop and formulate clear ideas about the pitch. Wood was the beneficiary. Wood credited Wilhelm with explaining more about the pitch in one day than he had learned by himself in a lifetime.[12] Although Stanky publicly praised his pitching coach for developing Wood, Wood gave Wilhelm all the credit.[13]

Wilhelm could articulate both the necessity and the mechanics of throwing the pitch with a stiff wrist. Wood had a tendency to throw his knuckler three-quarters or side-arm. Wilhelm knew that made the pitch hang. By the time spring training ended, Wood threw only overhand. The ball began to drop like a rock when it got to the plate, just like a superior knuckleball is supposed to.[14] At some point that spring Wood began to understand the most critical part of succeeding in the major leagues as a knuckleball pitcher. The release and the release point had to be exactly the same on every pitch.

One thing that Wilhelm could not teach Wood was the fatalistic disposition necessary for a player whose success is at the mercy of the apparently random nature of the knuckleball. Wood described his pitch: "I just aim it for the middle of the plate and hope like hell it goes somewhere before it gets there."[15]

Although Wood had spent short stints in the major leagues in five different seasons including most of 1963, at 25 his status was almost like a rookie. To the press he was deferential. There were certain things that he could not change. Wood's speaking voice was loud and brassy. He had an undiluted Boston accent with harsh A's and silent R's. It contrasted with Wilhelm's quiet North Carolina drawl. The amiable Wood had a round, ruddy face and an optimistic smile when he was not on the mound. Combined with his quick tongue, he could seem cheerful at the wrong moments. This apparently flip attitude had doomed him earlier in his career with a demanding manager in Pittsburgh. Now it made him a natural target for Stanky's biting displeasure.

Wood's season began better than anyone could have expected. He did not give up an earned run until his fifth appearance. By the time July started his ERA was 1.03 in 21 appearances. Still, the White Sox bullpen was so deep that he was typically the fourth option. The four of them—Bob Locker, Don McMahon, Wilhelm and Wood—had pitched a combined 126 ⅔ innings with a 1.21 ERA. They were a daunting group for any team to prepare to face.

After the White Sox and Tigers split the first two games, Gary Peters threw a three-hitter in the deciding game. The White Sox lost 3–0 because two of the hits were home runs by Bill Freehan and Mickey Stanley. To add injury to insult, Tigers shortstop Ray Oyler spiked Tommie Agee when Agee stole second in the second inning. The White Sox had runners on third base in four different innings, but could not score. This highlighted a worrying trend for the White Sox. Since mid–June they had scored only seven runs in their eight losses. There were games that they could not win no matter how effective their pitching was.

As the White Sox returned home for another series with Baltimore, the *Tribune* detailed the attendance competition between the White Sox and Cubs. The Cubs recently turned away 10,000 fans as they won a game to move into first place in the National League. The White Sox, who had led the American League for three weeks, had drawn 28,000 fewer fans than at the same point in 1966.[16] Only recently they had played a game with 20,000 teachers admitted for free.[17]

8. "Hope like hell it goes somewhere"

The pitchers were happy to be back in White Sox Park (known both formerly and again later as Comiskey Park) where they pitched better. The *Tribune* published a story that summarized a series of charges that helped to explain this success. Jerry Adair, who was traded from the White Sox to the Red Sox earlier in June, had told Boston reporters that the White Sox stored baseballs in a damp place to deaden them. It seemed self-explanatory that a heavy, soggy ball would not travel as far after being hit as one that was dry and lighter. White Sox general manager Ed Short retorted with a personal attack: "Mr. Adair seems to have problems wherever he goes." Having dispatched the accuser, Short continued, "We don't put our baseballs anywhere that is not inspected by the American League."[18]

White Sox catcher Jerry McNertney would later state that it was his job before home games in 1967 to clean the mildew off balls that had been stored in the dampest bowels of the stadium. The same few clean boxes were used game after game because the boxes containing the damp balls were decomposing.[19]

There were more difficulties than just heavy baseballs to playing at White Sox Park. Adair was not alone in accusing the White Sox of allowing the infield grass to grow high to slow groundballs. Others complained that the infield was over-watered, keeping the dirt exceptionally soft. With his teeth tightly clamped on his ever-present cigar, head groundskeeper Gene Bossard dismissed these accusations as "ridiculous."[20] There was good reason that he failed to elaborate. During most of the season, he would go to work with a pickaxe on the area in front of home plate before a home series. After digging down about six inches, Bossard would use a hose to turn loose dirt into the consistency of oatmeal. A half-inch of dry dirt concealed his handiwork.[21]

The *Tribune* article did not address the common perception around the American League that Eddie Stanky also froze baseballs, thawing them only enough before games so that they were not noticeably cold. Intrigued, Angels catcher Bob Rodgers compared a White Sox game ball and a ball he brought from Anaheim. He claimed the White Sox ball felt cold and bounced only half as high when dropped on a concrete floor.[22]

While Ed Short had to refute these accusations of cheating, Stanky reveled in them. Each rumor planted doubt in the minds of the opposing hitters. Batters overcompensating to adjust for the perceived difficulties in hitting at White Sox Park were less likely to succeed.

(It is likely that the White Sox were not the only team manipulating the dirt around home plate. Twins rookie Rod Carew, who had already reached safely after an estimated 16 bunts toward second base, confided that he could not use that strategy in Kansas City or Boston because those batter's boxes were too soft.)[23]

The White Sox batters might not have been immune to Stanky's maneuverings. On July 3, the White Sox lost 1-0 to the Orioles in the 14th inning. The White Sox managed only four hits during the game. After the game reporters saw Stanky in his dressing room, stomping around an overturned chair and screaming "a four-letter word beginning with 's' over and over."[24]

At the end of the day, the Tigers, Red Sox, and Twins were tied, 3½ games behind the White Sox.

Throughout the season writers conveyed a sense that almost all of the White Sox position players were young and inexperienced. This description might include outfielders Tommie Agee, aged 24, Ken Berry, 26, and Walt Williams, 23, as well as first baseman Tommy McCraw, 26. McCraw had been considered a backup although this was his fourth full major league season. Berry was in his third year and Agee in his second. All the other everyday players were older and had spent more time in the major leagues than Berry. (Excepting rookie catcher Duane Josephson who had been injured for most of the season.) They were considered young because of their perceived lack of major league experience. Only Williams was technically a rookie.

The 5'6" Williams had competed vigorously with Pete Ward and the recently traded rookie Ed Stroud for the left-field position during spring training. Reporters wrote that he had won the job, but then had been used largely as a replacement for Ward, starting only 18 games through June. Williams did not just hustle. He sprinted everywhere on the baseball field. It was possible that this could be just an affectation to appeal to Stanky. That perception changed on June 14. With a man on second in a tight game against the Red Sox, Williams fielded a single in deep right field and threw it toward home to the cut-off man. Conceding the run, the White Sox infielders caught the batter in a rundown between first and second. Shortstop Ron Hansen's return throw to first was wide and headed toward the Red Sox dugout. Seemingly from nowhere, Williams dove, corralled the ball and threw the runner out at second. He had sprinted in from right field to back up first base. For both his effort and execution, it was an amazing play.

Soon after, Stanky anointed Williams as the everyday left fielder and Williams' batting average rose past .300.

Even as they tried to maintain the pace of other top division teams, the Red Sox had to adjust their infield. Shortstop Rico Petrocelli had been batting over .300 when he was hit on the wrist by the White Sox' Don McMahon's pitch in the middle of June. It was a frustrating injury that doctors had a difficult time fully diagnosing. Petrocelli continued to try to play despite the pain. Some days he could not block it out and would ask out of the lineup. When Petrocelli was out, Jerry Adair filled his shortstop position more than adequately. After about ten days of this uncertainty, Petrocelli was hit again, this time by the Indians' George Culver. Petrocelli did not start again for almost two weeks. With Adair playing as the starting shortstop, Dalton Jones became the only backup infielder as well as the primary left-handed pinch-hitter.

While sportswriters in Boston tried to determine if Petrocelli was porcelain-fragile or just snake-bit, front-page news detailed another round of escalation in Vietnam. President Johnson authorized sending an additional 45,000 troops to Vietnam bringing the total to 525,000. The Defense Department released its weekly figures showing that total U.S. combat deaths in Vietnam now exceeded 12,000.

The war had an immediate impact on the Red Sox. Jones departed for two weeks of military duty on June 28. Management had to go all the way down to their Class A Winston-Salem team to find a left-handed batting infielder. Ken Poulsen received news of his unlikely promotion three days before his wedding. Both families and many guests had already journeyed across the country from California to attend. While he hurriedly traveled to join the Red Sox, Poulsen's fiancé Vicki Swaton gamely told a North Carolina reporter, "We can always get married. How often does a guy get sent up to the big leagues?"[25]

Eddie Stanky and his ex-teammate, Angels manager Bill Rigney, were named the two coaches for American League All-Star team manager Hank Bauer. The *Chicago Tribune* dusted off Stanky's assertion from the previous season that he and Alvin Dark were the game's only serious managers. Rigney, Stanky had proclaimed, was merely "a television manager."[26] In Stanky's opinion, Rigney's confrontations with umpires on the field were theatrical.

Chapter 9

"The dry side of a fastball"

American League standings before play on July 7.

	W	L	GB
Chicago White Sox	45	31	–
Minnesota Twins	43	34	2½
Detroit Tigers	42	34	3
Boston Red Sox	40	36	5
California Angels	41	40	6½
Cleveland Indians	38	40	8
Baltimore Orioles	37	41	9
New York Yankees	34	43	11½
Kansas City Athletics	35	45	12
Washington Senators	34	45	12½

The Twins arrived in Chicago on July 7 with an eight-game winning streak having clawed their way from the back of the pack into second place in the month since Cal Ermer took over from Sam Mele. Twins ace Dean Chance took the mound against White Sox ace Gary Peters. This was a big game for the Twins, a chance to measure themselves directly against the league leaders.

The Twins scored a run in the top of the first with two doubles. They did not get another hit off Peters who departed for a pinch-hitter after pitching the eighth inning. Dean Chance was cruising with a shutout when he took the mound in the eighth inning. According to the *Chicago Tribune*, White Sox coach Kerby Farrell, "a Tennessean who is an old hand at noticing pine tar," spotted a foreign substance on Chance's hand.[1] Umpire Al Salerno sent Chance to the clubhouse to wash the substance off with alcohol before allowing him to continue.

His focus broken, Chance gave up a single and a walk before escaping from the eighth inning. He was not so fortunate in the ninth. He loaded the bases before Al Worthington relieved him. Stanky replaced two of the baserunners with pinch-runners including speedy pitcher Joe Horlen at first. With two outs, Worthington faced shortstop Ron Hansen and his .206 average. On an 0–2 count Hansen hit a medium-speed groundball to the left of shortstop Zoilo Versalles. In his rush to get the force at second, Versalles booted the ball. Two runners scored on the error ending the game. The White Sox had another one-run win. Versalles was devastated. The Twins ascendancy was checked.

Chance's use of a foreign substance on the baseball was not an isolated incident, although the use of pine tar was unusual. The era was thick with suspicion. Hitters and managers were frustrated that umpires did not stop pitchers from loading up the ball. Umpires felt helpless because it was almost impossible to prove that a ball was a spitball. Rarely was anything done.

In July, *Sports Illustrated* published a long cover story on the spitball. It portrayed the pitch as ubiquitous.[2] A properly thrown spitball was like a knuckleball: it barely rotated. The lack of rotation helped it drop unpredictably as it approached the plate. Pitchers with a good sinking fastball were often accused of throwing a spitter. The pitch was thrown with the same motion and grip as a fastball. The saliva, or other substance, helped the ball slide out of the pitcher's hand so that his fingers did not impart spin to the ball. It was not an easy pitch to master. Getting the pitch over the plate consistently was part of the problem. Most pitchers, though, gave up on the spitter because if the pitch rotated just a bit, it became a slow, straight fastball. A poorly thrown spitball was a home run pitch.

There were other illegal pitches that were lumped in with the spitball. The most commonly confused was the mudball. Whitey Ford was its most famous practitioner. Ford mixed a little saliva with dirt from the mound, or that he had secreted in his glove, to create a small amount of mud. He worked the mud into a spot on the seam of the ball. This build-up of mud would make the ball less spherical. As it spun toward a batter this asymmetry increased its movement.

In 1964 when Tony Conigliaro faced Ford in his first major league game, Ford's third pitch got away from catcher Elston Howard. Already brash, Conigliaro pounced on the ball. He presented the clearly visible evidence to home plate umpire Eddie Hurley loudly demanding that Ford stop throwing the illegal pitch. Hurley, aware that no rookie should ever be allowed to show up a veteran as established as Ford, quickly wiped the ball off and threw it back to Ford without saying a word.[3] Like the spitball, it took practice and expertise for a pitcher to take advantage of even a perfectly prepared mudball.

Dean Chance was not the only pitcher suspected of throwing illegal pitches on July 7. The Tigers continued their resurgence having won six out of eight before playing the visiting Red Sox. Behind Joe Sparma the Tigers led for the entire game after scoring twice off Gary Waslewski in the first. Sparma took a 4–1 lead into the ninth, but gave up a home run to Tony Conigliaro. The next two batters singled and rookie Mike Marshall replaced Sparma. Manager Mayo Smith had a lot of confidence in Marshall, using him 12 times since mid-June as he dropped his ERA from 3.60 to 1.19 entering this game.

Marshall was a Ph.D. candidate in kinesiology at Michigan State who could have been making a far better living in a lab. Back in the spring Marshall was pitching in the Tigers' minor league camp. One day he had been brought over to pitch batting practice to the major league players. With Mayo Smith and Johnny Sain watching, Marshall blew the ball past batter after batter. Finally Al Kaline turned and yelled, "Mayo, will you go away so the kid will let us hit a few."[4]

Reggie Smith greeted Marshall with a single to right scoring George Scott from second. Pinch-hitter Jerry Adair then hit a double to tie the game before Marshall retired another pinch-hitter, rookie Russ Gibson.

The Red Sox' top reliever John Wyatt came on and closed down the Tigers bats in the ninth and tenth. That changed in the 11th. With one out and a runner on first, Bill Freehan came to the plate batting a productive .279 with 37 RBIs. Wyatt threw him a steady dose of his forkball, which sank nastily as it approached the plate. Eventually Freehan caught one that did not sink and pounded it to left field for a double. Jim Northrup scored from first on the hit to end the game.

In its last issue before taking over a rival and becoming the *Boston Herald Traveler*, the *Boston Herald* reported, possibly with tongue in cheek, that Wyatt's last pitch to Freehan had "slipped off his hand."[5] When asked to describe his game-winning hit, Freehan chortled, "I hit the dry side of a fastball." To clarify, the *Detroit News* added that Wyatt had a reputation for using Vaseline on his pitches.[6]

John Wyatt took a long, hard road to the major leagues. He played in the Negro leagues, the Mexican League and parts of five years in the minor leagues starting in Class D. Wyatt was 27 in his first full major league season with the Athletics in 1962. He had been a workhorse reliever, appearing in as many as 81 games one season. Wyatt's fastball collapsed downward when it worked effectively. Wyatt referred to the pitch as his forkball, and later—more exotically—as a Cuban forkball. On each of the first four fingers of his glove, Wyatt had written the word "think." On the fifth finger he wrote, "When in doubt, use forkball."[7] It was widely believed that Wyatt's forkball was aided by a liberal dab of Vaseline on his fingers. Earlier in the year Yankee Joe Pepitone claimed, "Wyatt has so much Vaseline on him that if he slid into second base he would keep right on going until he hit the outfield fence."[8]

Wyatt's manager Dick Williams remembered seeing Wyatt in a rundown between third base and home. It was an unfamiliar position for a relief pitcher who was only on base a few times in his entire major league career. Wyatt was wearing his warm-up jacket and every time he changed direction something would fall out of the pockets: cigarettes, matches, car keys and eventually a little tube of Vaseline. Players on the Red Sox bench laughed uncontrollably, but Wyatt picked up the tube before anyone else noticed.[9]

When Wyatt was starting out with Kansas City he reputedly had a Vaseline-filled syringe in the thumb of his glove. After that was discovered, he pitched with a tube of Vaseline in his mouth. By squeezing with his teeth, he could deliver exactly the amount he needed.[10] By 1967, Wyatt had a new strategy. He hid small dabs of Vaseline all over his uniform. That way he did not have to go back to the same place and establish a pattern. He hid the biggest cache of all under his belt. It was referred to admiringly by his teammates as The Blob.[11]

After losing one of the hard-fought mid–June games to the Red Sox, Eddie Stanky publicly accused Wyatt of throwing a Vaseline ball.[12] It did not attract much notice. Wyatt coyly denied the charge. He claimed to like the attention because the speculation kept batters guessing.

It was better than some of the other attention Wyatt received. In May, he became one of the few pitchers to be beaned by a thrown ball while on the mound. Wyatt turned his back to the plate after delivering a pitch to Willie Horton. His catcher Bob Tillman hit him on the head while trying to throw out the stealing Al Kaline at second. Kaline ended up at third. Wyatt was knocked to the ground, but recovered and finished the game. Tillman was charged with an error and went into Dick Williams' doghouse.[13] He never emerged before being sent to the Yankees later in the season.

The *Sports Illustrated* article was bold in naming a number of major league pitchers suspected of throwing a spitball. It focused on a relatively obscure starter for the California Angels—Jack Hamilton. Hamilton was an odd choice because there were many more successful and well-known suspects.

He entered the National League with the Phillies in 1962 when he made 26 starts and pitched over 180 innings. That year he was mostly noted for his lack of control, leading the league in walks and wild pitches. He shuttled between the minor leagues and the Phillies and then the Tigers for the next three years. In 1966 he pitched almost 150 innings as a reliever and occasional starter for the woeful Mets. Hamilton was not a bad pitcher, just below average.

Big for a six-footer, Hamilton had a wide, powerful frame, not a large gut, although he was called Fat Jack on his high school football team in Morning Sun, Iowa. He started 1967 with the Mets before being traded to the Angels in mid–June.

Hamilton found himself in an ideal situation. The Angels had endured a terrible start to their season, but a few days before trading for Hamilton they began a streak where they won 10 of 11 games. After the hopeless Mets, Hamilton had joined a team on the rise. Better for him, Angels manager Bill Rigney was a Durocher disciple who desperately wanted to win every game the Angels played. Despite his mediocre skill, Hamilton was a fierce competitor. A laconic Iowa farm boy off the field, Hamilton burned to win once the game started. Unlike many starting pitchers on their off days, Hamilton sat in the dugout immersed in the game. Probably to Rigney's delight, he became a bench jockey annoying opponents and umpires alike.[14]

It did not take long for Rigney to appreciate Hamilton's tenacity. Within a week, Hamilton was a starter. Rigney needed another starter. Long before June it was clear that the pitching staff assembled by general manager Fred Haney was inadequate. There were only two established starters on the spring training roster. Marcelino Lopez pitched only nine innings before going on the disabled list with tendonitis. George Brunet pitched a lot of innings, but could not consistently win. He was 3–9 when Hamilton arrived and then lost his next two appearances. He was an end-of-the-rotation talent asked to be an ace. Rigney had been well aware of this shortcoming in spring training. He confided, "If we can afford to carry all these pitchers on the roster, I have an inkle we can use 'em all." An "inkle," it was explained, is like an inkling, only smaller.[15]

Rigney was helped by the unexpected emergence of Jim McGlothlin who was 6–0 with a 1.40 ERA. The other pleasant surprise was rookie Rickey Clark. Not slated to make the team when spring training began, by the end of April he was a regular in the starting rotation. That left the fourth starting spot. With little success, Rigney tried the ragtag assortment of pitchers that Haney had assembled. None worked out. Lopez, Nick Wilhite, Jorge Rubio and Jack Sanford were all traded or demoted.

Newly acquired Hamilton was the next to be given an opportunity. He responded with one solid outing after another. He still walked batters and rarely made it deep into the game, but that did not matter. The team won when he pitched. He got his first win near the end of June against the Senators in an unremarkable five-inning outing. After the game, Senators manager Gil Hodges blasted Hamilton to a small group of sportswriters. Hamilton threw "the most flagrant spitter I ever saw," said Hodges. "He made a farce of the game."[16] It may have been this tirade that marked Hamilton as the face of spitball pitchers.

The Angels entered the All-Star break with six straight wins. After the break they faced 15 straight games against Chicago, Minnesota and Boston, all contenders at the top of the league. The team and their newly energized fans viewed this stretch as an opportunity to earn the respect of the league and cement a position as a pennant contender. They lost two of the first three games with the White Sox. In the fourth game, on July 15, Hamilton took his 3–1 record to the mound against the struggling 3–6 Bruce Howard. The Angels started the game in fourth place, only five games behind the White Sox. For the White Sox this was just another in a long series of games against various contenders. They had been in first place for over a month and had become accustomed to see one challenger after another fall back. The game was much more important for the Angels players and their manager.

Hamilton rose to the occasion, pitching 8⅔ innings and winning 4–1. He gave up five hits and five walks, but he also struck out seven. It was his best performance since becoming an Angel. The Angels headed to Minnesota only four games out of first and convinced they had a chance at the pennant.

Instead, their hopes crashed. The next day Rich Rollins, the first Twins batter in the bottom of the ninth inning, hit a walk-off home run to beat the Angels 7–6 and sweep a doubleheader. Bob Allison had a home run in each game. The Twins set an attendance record with 43,419 fans in the stands for the Angels doubleheader. The second win was the Twins' sixth in seven games. The Twins stood solidly in second place only a half-game behind the White Sox. Pennant fever gripped the upper Midwest. The Angels fell five games out of first.

The Tigers were headed in the opposite direction. They had lost five in a row since the All-Star break.

They were a mess. Near the end of June Al Kaline fractured a bone in his hand slamming his bat into the bat rack after striking out. A few days after that, the team's best pinch-hitter Gates Brown had dislocated his left wrist. In a happier moment earlier in the season, Brown entertained reporters with his self-description "I'm as square as an ice cube and twice as cool."[17] The *Detroit News* ran a photo of the two of them trying to stay in baseball shape by shagging batting practice fly balls, each with a large cast on one hand.[18]

Willie Horton's ongoing problems with his legs made him an infrequent performer. In this latest defeat, Dick McAuliffe sat with an inflamed pancreas and Bill Freehan did not start due to "an acceleration of the heartbeat."[19]

After the All-Star Game, *Detroit News* beat reporter Watson Spoelstra noted some bigger issues. He excoriated manager Mayo Smith for complacency: "Maybe somebody ought to raise a little hell about losing." Nor did he excuse the players: "Detroit's failure to execute the fundamentals is the reason for their inferior quality of play in the last six weeks." Spoelstra then detailed poor bunting, bad throws to the plate and failed rundowns.[20]

Rumors of dissension had floated around the team since their poor performance in June. As the team sunk into another perplexing stretch of lackadaisical effort, Smith fined quite a few of his players for checking into their hotel ten minutes late one night. Demonstrating the team's perceived lack of respect for the manager, one of them was reported to say, "You might as well fine me right now for tomorrow night, too."[21]

Smith may have felt a little desperate. Even though it was the middle of July, he started Joe Sparma, his winningest pitcher, on two days' rest. Smith was developing a reputation for overusing whichever pitcher seemed hot. The Red Sox won 9–5 in a sloppy slugfest. A recently called up 22-year-old rookie with the curious name of Sparky Lyle earned his first save in the game.

After the Tigers committed three errors in the losing effort, the *Detroit Free Press* headline read "Mayo Blisters His Tigers." After verbally lashing his players for 15 minutes behind closed doors, Smith told reporters that his team "played like a bunch of little leaguers."[22]

The following day the Tigers held a players-only meeting. In it, some veterans lambasted younger players for their poor attitude and late hours.[23] Al Kaline later described the meeting as a man-to-man talk. He said, "If you can't take criticism from one of your teammates, you don't belong on the team." To reporters he noted, "The starting pitchers have been inconsistent."[24] Viewed from the outside, it was less about uniting the players as a team with a common goal than an exercise in finger pointing and blame fixing.

In addition to being hampered by injuries and publicly disrespecting their manager, the Tigers had now developed an open rift between a clique of veterans and their young starting pitchers. None of these boded well for their pennant hopes.

After the meeting the Tigers lost 7–1 to the Red Sox, their seventh straight loss.

The surprising Red Sox were a young team, the opposite of the veteran-laden Tigers who had only one regular starter under 25. Carl Yastrzemski was the veteran of the Red Sox starters and he was only 27. Tony Conigliaro who was in his fourth major-league season was 22. The average age of the typical starting eight fielders was 23.

While the veterans on the Tigers imposed a tight-lipped, unemotional approach to the game, the young Red Sox played unfettered. Their surprising on-field success landed them on NBC's Game of the Week for the first time. Twenty-three-year-old first baseman George Scott gushed with sincere excitement at the announcement. His mother and extended family in Greenville, Mississippi, had never seen him play. Now they would have a chance.[25]

While both Conigliaro and Yastrzemski were having strong seasons, some in Boston felt that the only indispensable player on the team was the shortstop, Rico Petrocelli.[26] Not yet 24, Petrocelli had just returned from missing a couple of weeks with an injured wrist to play in a few games including his first All-Star Game. His wrist was not healed. Just as he had at the end of June, Petrocelli spent the middle of July trying to play until the pain caused him to swing tentatively. Eventually Dick Williams became so frustrated with his shortstop that he publicly declared him benched until he could guarantee that he was fully ready to play.[27] The team needed more than just Petrocelli's bat. He headed up the most consistent infield in the league. With little pitching, the Red Sox' surprising defense was keeping them in games. Petrocelli missed 12 starts before returning in the last week of July.

It was widely assumed that the Red Sox, who had finished 1966 in ninth place only a half-game ahead of the tenth-place Yankees, would falter and return to the bottom half of the league. Their inexperience had already cost them. In a game against the Tigers, Dalton Jones had hit a shallow fly to right with George Scott on first. The wily Al Kaline who knew he could not catch the ball, jogged in while looking up as if settling to catch the fly. The callow Scott held up part way between bases, prepared to return to first. The ball bounced to Kaline, who easily threw Scott out at second.[28]

With the White Sox scheduled to play five games in three days, Stanky promoted Wilbur Wood to start one of them. Wood won his first start as they split a doubleheader at Kansas City. Despite his inexperience with the knuckleball, Wood remained in the starting rotation for almost a month.

Chapter 10

"Getting an alligator to play the piano"

American League standings before play on July 22.

	W	L	GB
Chicago White Sox	51	39	–
Boston Red Sox	49	40	1½
Minnesota Twins	49	41	2
California Angels	51	44	2½
Detroit Tigers	48	42	3
Washington Senators	45	49	8
Cleveland Indians	44	48	8
Baltimore Orioles	42	50	10
New York Yankees	39	51	12
Kansas City Athletics	39	53	13

On July 22, White Sox pitcher Tommy John was rushed to the mound in Kansas City from his two-week stint with the Indiana Air National Guard. John had been bothered by a mysterious intestinal ailment during his last days with the Guard. Despite feeling weak, he took the ball to pitch. After four pitches to two batters in the first inning, John collapsed. He was able to walk off the field, but felt dizzy and could not continue.

Only later was it revealed that he had not been able to eat for days and had lost 20 pounds from his already skinny frame. Although the source and exact cause of his illness was never determined, John was so weakened that the White Sox placed him on the 21-day disabled list. John already had won eight games and sported a 2.23 ERA.

In Anaheim, the Angels were increasingly confident as they prepared to start the middle game of their series with the Twins. They had just swept a home series with the White Sox. Those victories continued an impressive run for the team. On June 6, they had been 12½ games out of first place. Six weeks later they were in the thick of the pennant race. After holding off the powerful Twins 2-1 in a Friday game, the Angels were now only 2½ games out of first and a half-game behind the Twins. Manager Bill Rigney felt his team was the hottest in baseball.

Anaheim Stadium was packed with over 38,000 energized fans for the Angels' Saturday afternoon game against the Twins. The Twins had been within a game of league-leading Chicago for almost a week until their loss. Even now, they were inclined to look past the surprising Angels to their series with the Red Sox to finish July.

The Angels started Jim McGlothlin who grew up in the Reseda section of Los Angeles. Combined with his freckled face, the Angels' cap, which still featured an oval white halo on top, made McGlothlin look younger than his 23 years. He had not pitched for a couple of weeks, since his outstanding six-out appearance in the All-Star Game. Warming up for a start immediately after the All-Star Game, he felt a strain in his right shoulder. Rigney held him out of the game, but expected him back in a couple of days. The *Los Angeles Herald Examiner* then reported that he was "suffering a virus attack."[1] A few days later McGlothlin explained his continued absence: "The problem is not the joint, which is good. It's a bone bruise."[2]

Now apparently recovered, McGlothlin brought a 1.80 ERA and an 8-2 record to the mound. In the first inning the Twins pounded him. Rookie Rod Carew led off with a double. Cesar Tovar was the next batter. He tapped a grounder back to McGlothlin. Usually after fielding a groundball like that, a pitcher has time to look the runner back to second before throwing to first. McGlothlin fielded the ball and turned toward third base. Carew did not go back to second. He was running all the way. McGlothlin threw him out easily at third.

Slugger Harmon Killebrew was up next and McGlothlin worked carefully. In only his second full season in the major leagues, Tovar had speed to burn. Perhaps lulled by McGlothlin's focus on Killebrew, Tovar was given the steal sign. He was cut down by catcher Bob Rodgers' throw. With the bases now empty and two outs, McGlothlin surrendered a walk to Killebrew.

The next batter was the rejuvenated Tony Oliva who had raised his batting average from .204 at the beginning of June to .252. He doubled to left. Killebrew did not have the speed to go home from first, so there were runners on second and third for Bob Allison. McGlothlin induced him to ground out to first and escaped the inning with no runs.

After McGlothlin's difficult first inning, the game settled into a pitchers' duel carrying over from the Friday game. In the seventh with the Twins ahead

1–0, the Angels bats finally came to life against Twins starter Jim Merritt. Woodie Held, starting at shortstop for Jim Fregosi who pulled a leg muscle the day before, led off with a grounder to the Twins shortstop Zoilo Versalles. It was a fairly routine play, but Versalles threw a little wide and immobile first baseman Harmon Killebrew could not reach it. Held was safe. The next batter blasted Merritt's first pitch seemingly through the infield when Versalles tracked it down. He flipped the ball to Rod Carew at second who relayed it on for a double play that cleared the bases.

Eventually, the Angels won their second 2–1 game in a row over the Twins.

The loss highlighted two of the weaknesses that remained for the Twins: sloppy baserunning and the continued inconsistent play from shortstop Zoilo Versalles. He could turn a routine play into an error, but then reach a ball that no other shortstop could.

Baserunning was a common topic of discussion throughout the season. Sportswriters and columnists praised the concept of aggressive baserunning, or disparaged perceived timidity on the bases. As long as runners were safe and runs scored, both players and managers received plaudits.

Whenever a baserunner was tagged out, the descriptions changed. Writers covering the Twins claimed that these runners were sloppy, or just plain stupid. The Twins, on the other hand, believed that even some of these outs helped produce extra runs.[3, 4] The concept of aggressive baserunning varied substantially. This difference of opinion was not merely between baseball men and writers, but from team to team.

The base-running gambles that failed in the first inning against the Angels were examples of the aggressive running that had propelled the Twins to the World Series two years earlier. Players on every team ran hard on the bases, but their coaches and managers forbid them from advancing unless they were almost certain to be safe at the next base. The Twins were considered aggressive because they often tried to advance when the chances of being safe were far from certain. Although speed made some runners more disconcerting to fielders than others, the key to this was not the speed or effort of the Twins runners. It was their mentality, an expectation of taking an extra base. The results, like they were this July day, could be disappointing.

There were other types of aggression. Eddie Stanky and Al Dark both promoted themselves as aggressive managers. By contrast Stanky disparaged others as safety-first managers. Of the two, Stanky's tactics were almost daily on display. Their overall approach to a baseball game was much more like a chess match where the two managers dictated the moves of their players. As an example, the White Sox stood apart for their emphasis on pinch-runners, sacrifices and base-stealing ploys in the late innings of games. Stanky orchestrated these tactics from the dugout; the players followed his orders. If a White Sox player attempted to steal home, it was only because Stanky had made the decision. The base-running elements he used were not unique. Other managers used them less frequently and not to the same extreme.

The Twins aggression was different. Their philosophy required a manager confident enough to cede part of his control. They consistently encouraged players to make aggressive decisions on the basepaths. The runners did not have complete freedom. Base coaches still waved them on, or signaled them to stop. Runners who ignored these signs or made other egregious errors were censured just like on any other team.[5]

The benefit was much greater than the occasional extra base that a fast runner might take. With the threat of runners taking an extra base, opposing teams had to hurry every part of the fielding process on balls hit to the outfield. The outfielder had to rush to the ball. A hard throw to the cut-off man was more likely to go astray than one lobbed in with no pressure. Similarly a throw to a fielder trying to tag a baserunner had a small margin of error. Opposing fielders spent the entire series with the Twins outside of their comfort zone.[6]

Fielders, even superior fielders, made errors against the Twins that they did not make against other teams. It gave the Twins extra baserunners, often in better scoring position. Extra baserunners made the opposing pitchers work longer and harder.

The aggressiveness fit manager Cal Ermer's baseball philosophy, as it had Sam Mele's. The man who coached the Twins baserunners and instilled this sense of reckless aggression on the basepaths was third-base coach Billy Martin. He had relied on, and succeeded with, aggression since his childhood. Martin grew up in the poorest section of Berkeley, California, with a strong sense of living on the margins.

Martin remembered, "From the time I was about twelve years old until I was maybe fifteen, I awoke every morning knowing that there was a good chance I was going to have to get into a fight with somebody."[7] Always undersized and slight, Martin could not rely on strength or power. His biographer Peter Golenbock wrote that Martin always punched first. Often the fight was over before the other guy even knew that the fight had begun. Martin hit first, hit hard and kept hitting until there was no more fight left in his opponent.[8]

Martin was almost impossibly blessed in his early baseball career. After two years in the farm system of the Pacific Coast League Oakland Oaks, Martin was promoted and spent a season on the Oaks playing for manager Casey Stengel.

Although the teenaged Martin had a reputation as "a vicious thug," he was gregarious with a knack for cultivating strong friendships.[9] Stengel recalled that the 20-year-old Martin had a never-ending appetite for baseball. Martin and Stengel spent long hours discussing all the possibilities in each baseball situation. And then they would begin on the nuances of each of those possibilities. Stengel was much more than Martin's manager. He became a mentor and a father figure.[10] After one year Stengel moved on to manage the Yankees. Martin stayed with the Oaks and was managed by Charlie Dressen, a sharp baseball man who would eventually win over 1,000 games as a major league manager.

Stengel taught Martin how to analyze each situation in the game. Dressen showed him how playing the game aggressively could disrupt careful analytics.[11] Martin was transformed, yoking his visceral aggressiveness and a love of baseball to drive a developing intellectual understanding of the game.

Although many of his years were curtailed by military duty and injury, Martin played for the Yankees for seven years. His statistics were never great, but he always played much better in the World Series. After winning the World Series in 1956, Stengel said, "[Billy Martin] thinks he knows more about baseball than anyone else, and it wouldn't surprise me if he was right."[12]

He finished his 12-year major league career as a utility infielder for the newly minted Minnesota Twins in 1961. For three years after that, Martin scouted for the Twins and supplemented his baseball income by travelling throughout Minnesota doing sales and promotions for a local beer distributor. That all changed after the 1964 season. Despite scoring more runs than any team in baseball, the team finished 20 games out of first place with a losing record. After owner Cal Griffith fired all of the coaches, Martin was one of his first hires. He had many duties but one of them was to coach baserunning.

Martin was clear about his approach, "I believe in being aggressive. I believe in forcing the opposition into making mistakes."[13] Martin worked to instill a mindset in the team. Years later he claimed that during that first spring training he purposefully sent runners home when he knew that they would be thrown out.[14] He wanted every player to always expect that they would need to take an extra base.

Martin was far more than just a cheerleader or martinet. He started by teaching his players the most basic fundamentals of baserunning. During spring training, he carefully marked the exact route they should take running from first to third on a single to right. Every player practiced tagging up at third on a sacrifice fly so that they always led with the proper foot.

Martin had another primary responsibility on the 1965 team. He needed to improve the team's leaky infield. He started with the team's best fielder, the enigmatic Cuban Zoilo Versalles. The two men had many similarities. Versalles dropped out of school at the beginning of second grade and spent his youth roaming the streets of the dangerous Havana slum, Marianao. Like Martin, Versalles was undersized and intensely aware that he could never show any sign of weakness.[15]

He played various versions of baseball barefooted and barehanded, learning to field with improvised balls among rocks, ruts and debris. Too poor to own equipment, as a young teenager he would always use the glove of the other team's shortstop. After an open tryout, he earned a place on one of Havana's upper echelon teams. They gave him equipment and more importantly one or two large meals every day he practiced.[16]

When he started, he was barely five feet tall and weighed less than 100 pounds. Three years later he stood 5'7" and proudly signed his first professional contract on the dirt floor of his mother's house with the Senators Cuba scout Papa Joe Cambria. In 1957 Versalles was one of the young Cuban players arriving by boat whom Cambria delivered directly to a ballpark in Key West by packing them into the back of a pickup truck. This field was the Senators staging area where they could immediately cull players they knew would not succeed. Versalles was assigned to Charlotte. He knew no English and no geography. By the time the bus arrived at its fifth stop in Fort Lauderdale, Versalles had worn out the driver with his enthusiastic question "Charlotte?" every time the bus slowed. After three days in Charlotte he was sent back to Cuba to grow. Cambria gave him a potato every day and told him to eat it with milk.[17]

Cambria would sign over 400 players for major league teams during the 1950s and early 1960s, primarily for the Senators/Twins. The Twins had so many Cubans on the roster during their first years in Minnesota that when asked what the unfamiliar "TC" emblem on their caps stood for, players would reply with a straight face, "Twenty Cubans."[18]

Returning to the United States for the 1958 season, Versalles played for Class D Elmira. On the field, Versalles excelled. His fielding was outstanding, although embellished with plenty of showmanship. His fielding antics led one teammate to call him the biggest hot dog that he had ever seen.[19] The Senators minor league fielding instructor Ellis Clary had a different take. Teaching Versalles to play defense "was like getting an alligator to play the piano."[20] Versalles had almost an excess of ability, but was unpredictable.

Despite his success on the field, that first summer was brutally difficult. Versalles was still growing, but none of the food was familiar. Versalles always had trouble putting on weight. He would not fill out to 5'10" and 155 pounds for three more years.[21] Versalles made little effort to acquire English, poor communication exacerbating every situation. Perhaps too proud to acknowledge his obvious shortcoming, he earned a lasting reputation with his coaches and teammates for his moodiness. He fought a perception that he was a hypochondriac, or used phantom injuries as excuses.[22]

The cultural difficulties went both ways. Versalles recalled that the minor league coaches all used the same technique to communicate with Latin players who understood little English. They yelled everything as if the louder volume would make it clearer. Mostly though, the coaches ignored the Latin ballplayers and focused on Americans. Rod Carew had the same perception until a minor-league teammate explained that the yelling was a positive sign, "If no one shows interest, you are in trouble."[23]

At Cal Griffith's insistence, in 1961 Versalles became the Twins starting shortstop replacing another Cuban, Jose Valdivielso. In July after Fidel Castro's new government refused to allow Versalles' new wife to leave Cuba, Versalles holed up in a Minneapolis hotel room refusing to play or travel with the team.[24] The team's other Cubans all played. After two weeks of intense effort, Griffith secured Versalles' wife's release. Only after she arrived in Minneapolis did Versalles emerge from his hotel and resume his place on the team. Versalles learned that if he demanded extra attention, he would receive it.

Griffith's efforts were handsomely repaid. On the field Versalles blossomed as a major leaguer over the next three years. He was an All-Star in 1963 when he also won a Gold Glove as the American League's best fielding shortstop. Always intense on the field, Versalles typically fielded and threw with his tongue sticking out of his mouth, firmly clamped between clenched teeth.

Living in Minnesota year round, Versalles' English improved considerably. In the winter before the 1965 season Versalles represented the Twins in many speaking engagements around Minnesota. One of his frequent companions on these trips was his 1961 teammate and new coach, Billy Martin. Driving for hours through the snow-blanketed landscape with the car's heater blasting, the two talked baseball.[25, 26] Still rail-thin, Versalles' gaunt face looked thinner behind his oversized glasses. Plagued by unresolved back problems, Versalles would sometimes walk gingerly with a hunch like an old man instead of an athlete

The 1965 MVP, Zoilo Versalles, struggled at the plate in 1967. While they had been praised two years earlier, in 1967 his aggressive base-running and fielding tactics appeared sloppy or reflecting a lack of baseball judgment. National Baseball Hall of Fame and Museum.

in the prime of his career. His earnestness charmed winter-bound Minnesotans who struggled to follow his heavily accented English.

Martin, who had grown up with Mexican friends, understood Spanish. He was a charmer by nature, someone who thrived on creating new friends. By the time spring training opened, Versalles developed an empathetic bond with him. Martin announced to the press that Versalles would be his special project. To Versalles he boasted that he would make him an MVP.

For the first time in his professional baseball career, Versalles had a coach who explained the intricacies of positioning in the field. Versalles' speed, quickness and glove skills had always been his strength. Now he could start in the correct place and use his skills to put pressure on the hitting team. Throughout his career, Versalles' flashy fielding had occasionally been negated by erratic throws. Martin convinced Versalles to completely change the way he threw the ball.[27] This was an enormous concession for Versalles, a Gold Glove winner, who had a reputation for resisting all coaching.

Throughout the 1965 season Martin and Versalles sat together on planes, buses, at meals and in hotel lobbies talking about baseball.[28] Martin preached an aggressive approach to fielding that should yield more double plays and more importantly convince opponents to play it safe on the basepaths. Versalles listened. Although he led the league with a career-high 39 errors, he also led in double plays turned and was second in assists. He earned a second Gold Glove. The team allowed 78 fewer runs than they had in 1964.

Versalles' hitting was even more impressive that year. He was the American League MVP—the best player in the league whether judged by traditional metrics, or modern ones. His speed suited Martin's aggressive base-running tactics. He led the league in runs, doubles and triples, adding 27 stolen bases and 19 home runs. The 1965 Twins won 102 games and the franchise's first pennant in 32 years.

Hindered by his balky back, Versalles' play faltered in 1966. That was also the first year that Harmon Killebrew played a majority of his games at third base, a change that required Versalles to cover a much larger part of the infield. He arrived at spring training for the 1967 season determined to return to his dominant play, but his speed was diminished and so was the power in his bat.

By July 19 he was batting .229 with only two stolen bases and two home runs. After the game, he confessed that he was waiting for new glasses because he had broken his others when he got mad at them for a batting slump a few weeks earlier.[29]

For the final game of the Twins-Angels series, the Twins counted on their ace Dean Chance to change their fortunes. He could not do it. Behind Jack Hamilton, the Angels triumphed 2–1 for the third consecutive day to sweep the series. Having swept both the White Sox and the Twins, the Angels confidently looked forward to their upcoming series in Boston with the second-place Red Sox.

Despite the victory, the Angels lost a half-game in the standings to the White Sox who swept a doubleheader with Gary Peters and Joe Horlen each winning their twelfth game.

The Red Sox plane landed at Boston's Logan Airport late at night on July 23 bringing the team home from a six-game road trip with a ten-game winning streak. They concluded the trip by sweeping a doubleheader from the Indians, pounding out four home runs. Two of the young Red Sox—Joe Foy and rookie Reggie Smith—were finally rewarding Dick Williams' patience and hitting like they had in the minors.[30] The Red Sox were running, too. Smith stole home against the Indians. Suddenly the entire Red Sox lineup was feared.

Unusually, the plane parked at the freight terminal where the players disembarked into a chartered bus for the short trip to the passenger terminal. The bus did not get far. An estimated 10,000 fans swarmed onto the runway, cheering and surrounding the bus. The bus stopped and the fans started to rock it. In the dark with the disorienting airport lights and the incoherent crowd yelling, the players were unnerved. Trying to assess the unprecedented situation, Carl Yastrzemski asked, "There are not mad at us, are they?"[31]

A large contingent of state police had to be brought in to control the masses of cheering people. The players sat in the bus trying to adjust to this new way of life while the police herded the delirious fans off the runway. Safely in the terminal and now exhilarated by the fans, Yastrzemski confided, "I've never seen anything like this."[32] Only a couple of weeks earlier at the All-Star break only third baseman Joe Foy would pick the Red Sox to win the pennant. Now, the whole team had pennant fever. The players were eagerly looking forward to a showdown with the Twins at the end of the month, convinced that the pennant was now within their grasp. Headlines the next morning would call them the "Miracle Sox."[33]

Chapter 11

"155,000 rounds of ammunition"

American League standings before play on July 24.

	W	L	GB
Chicago White Sox	53	40	–
Boston Red Sox	52	40	½
California Angels	53	44	2
Detroit Tigers	50	43	3
Minnesota Twins	49	43	3½
Washington Senators	46	50	8½
Cleveland Indians	44	51	10
Baltimore Orioles	43	51	10½
New York Yankees	40	53	13
Kansas City Athletics	40	55	14

Like other contenders for the American League lead, the Detroit Tigers had a Sunday doubleheader on July 23. In the opening game, the Yankees scored three runs off Mickey Lolich sending him to his tenth straight defeat.

In the second game, the Tigers triumphed behind rookie pitcher Mike Marshall's fourth save in four days. He pitched 9⅓ innings during those four appearances. The offense was powered by Willie Horton's twelfth home run. Horton had been plagued since spring training with an injury to his right leg. Reporters variously described the ill-defined problem as effecting his shin, calf, foot, ankle or leg. After missing almost all of April with the injury, Horton hit nine home runs in May. Then in six weeks of June and July he hit only one more. It was a terrible slump and the whole team slumped with him. Now finally he was over it. This was his second home run in two days and his third in a week.

As the second game progressed in the sunny afternoon, smoke increasingly covered the sky. Fans sitting in the first-base stands and bleachers could see the smoke cloud grow. When the game ended, the public address announcer held the crowd. Slowly he read off the numbers of bus lines that would not be running from the stadium after the game. Many fans were stranded. This cryptic and unwelcome message was the first news for most of the fans that extensive rioting had closed down a large swath of Detroit.

Since the late spring, violent rioting had plagued a series of American cities. In June, Tampa erupted in riots after an African American teenager was shot and killed by police during a robbery. Two nights of looting, extensive gunfire and arson destroyed local businesses and homes despite the eventual presence of bayonet-wielding National Guardsmen. The dead thief and a sheriff's deputy who died of a heart attack during the opening hours of the riots were the only fatalities, but hundreds suffered injuries.

At the end of June riots shut down Buffalo for three days. In the middle of July Newark endured the worst, six days of rioting, looting and destruction that left 26 dead. Many other cities and even towns the size of Cairo (approximate population of 8,000), Plainfield (45,000) and Erie (130,000) experienced disturbances, rioting or mob violence that required calling the National Guard or police with riot gear.

All of these riots were described in major newspapers as race riots. They took place in relatively segregated African American sections of cities and most of the rioters were African Americans. The triggering event in most cases involved white policemen and an African American suspect. Newspapers covered these extensively on their front pages. Other cities suffered smaller episodes of looting and violence.

Remarkably, there seemed to be nothing out of the ordinary in photographs and descriptions of armed U.S. soldiers patrolling American city streets in combat formation, fingers on the triggers of their rifles.

In the early morning hours of Sunday, July 23, Detroit police raided a blind pig located over a print shop on 12th Street in a predominantly African American section of the city. Readers of the Detroit newspapers did not need to be told that a blind pig was an unlicensed bar. The raid was not unusual, nor was the arrest of all the occupants. There was no violence and no injuries. It took a few hours to arrange for the transportation of all of the suspects. In that time trouble started.

By the time the last police cruisers were leaving with their prisoners, bottles and bricks were being thrown at the vehicles. The police kept going. The crowd, which had swollen to a few hundred as daylight broke, began surging down 12th Street destroying as they went. By noon, thousands crowded the streets. When the police returned, the situation was beyond control. The rioters' focus had little to do with outrage at the already forgotten arrests.

Police, reporters, even the mayor described the mood as "carnival-like."[1] On the warm Sunday morning, the streets were packed with people enjoying the spectacle.

To help keep the crowds from growing, radio and television stations were directed not to report on the riots.[2] This directive was so comprehensive that even Tigers radio broadcasters Ernie Harwell and Ray Lane were ordered not to mention the clearly visible smoke billowing into the sky.[3] These ill-conceived precautions had little effect. As the area consumed by rioting expanded, public bus service through those areas was suspended stranding thousands of fans.

Tigers players became aware of the rioting by the time their second game ended. Even this news was so scanty that most players could not understand what was happening. Willie Horton did. He went directly from the game to a car and drove into the most affected areas on 12th Street. He was still in uniform.[4]

Unlike the rural or suburban upbringing of many of the Tigers, Horton had an urban childhood. He spent his youth and teenage years living and going to school near the 12th Street and Grand Boulevard intersection where the rioting was heaviest. He was the 21st and youngest child of his parents.

As a teenager in Detroit, Horton found himself in minor trouble with the law. He did not excel in high school except on the baseball field. Only the Tigers were willing to take a chance on a troubled youth, despite his hitting prowess in high school and in national sandlot tournaments. Horton was not particularly tall, but he was strong. Even as a teenager he looked like a power hitter. Famously, he broke a bat just checking his swing.[5]

At 20 years old, Horton was called up to the Tigers for the end of the 1963 season. He started 1964 as the left fielder. It did not go well. He struggled at the plate and in May he was sent down to the minors batting .167 with no home runs.

Willie Horton's entire 1967 season was hampered by his painfully injured ankle, which required surgery immediately after the season. When he hit with power, the Tigers flourished. National Baseball Hall of Fame and Museum.

Before the 1965 season, Horton went to Puerto Rico to play winter ball. On New Year's Day he received a crushing message. Both of his parents had been killed in an automobile accident. He returned to Detroit for their funeral and then remained, unmotivated and directionless. Detroit's veteran manager Charlie Dressen reached out to him during the last few weeks before spring training. That was the beginning of a tight, almost father-son, bond between the two.

Initially platooned in 1965, Horton became a full-time starter and earned a place on the All-Star team. He finished that first full year with big power numbers. He was third in the American League with 29 home runs and second with 104 RBIs. After that first big-league season, Horton began an off-season regimen that included volunteering at Northwestern High School, his alma mater. He was a frequent, highly visible presence working with youth in the Detroit neighborhoods where he had grown up. Despite the illness and eventual death of his mentor Dressen in 1966, Horton avoided a sophomore slump hitting 27 home runs and collecting 100 RBIs.

Horton arrived on the scene before darkness descended. The worst initial rioting on 12th Street was only a few blocks from Northwestern High. More than just a star baseball player, Willie Horton was a local hero made good returning to his own neighborhood. Earlier in the day, African American religious and political leaders had made frequent forays into the riot area. Without exception they had been shouted down, pelted with garbage and even attacked.

Standing on a car wearing his Tigers uniform, Horton was unmistakable. He pleaded, shouted, almost begged people to stop destroying their own neighborhood. No one threw garbage at him, but he was ignored. Hoarse and exhausted, he finally left having achieved nothing.

The riot was far beyond the persuasive ability of any single person. It stretched for miles along 12th Street and actively involved 10,000 people according to police estimates. Under the comforting cover of darkness, looting, arson and gunfire all greatly increased.

By the end of Sunday 800 people had been injured, eight from gunshots. Five had been killed. At the mayor's request, Michigan Governor George Romney mobilized 7,000 National Guardsmen and sent them to the city. The Tigers' Mickey Lolich had lost the first game that day. Like his teammates he saw the smoke and flames from the larger fires as he drove home on his motorcycle. When he arrived at his suburban home, his wife informed him that his National Guard unit had been mobilized. That evening he was standing guard in Detroit with his helmet on his head and a rifle in his hand.

Like the other men in his platoon, Lolich had not eaten dinner. With permission, he headed away from the platoon's guard post. Through the fire-illuminated night alive with the sound of sirens, shouts and gunshots, Lolich went in search of food. Although almost the entire city was shut down, Lolich found a hamburger restaurant, open and serving. He ordered burgers, fries and shakes for the entire platoon. With his rifle at the ready, Lolich escorted a delivery boy carrying the food back to the guard post.[6]

Lolich spent much of his duty time over the next week driving his captain around. Lolich was the best marksman in his unit and the captain wanted him nearby in case snipers pinned them down—a constant worry over the next few days. Because of this fear, Lolich's captain would not allow him to stop at traffic lights because that would make them a much easier target for the snipers.[7]

Lolich's captain was not the only National Guardsman to feel overwhelmed. A Detroit police lieutenant confessed after that first night, "These state troopers and National Guardsmen frighten me. They're so trigger-happy."[8] This estimate was not a flight of fancy. By the end of Monday, the National Guard, state police and Detroit police had exhausted all supplies of .30-.30 ammunition. An emergency supply had to be trucked into the city in a guarded convoy from a nearby munitions manufacturer.[9]

On Monday President Johnson sent paratroopers to the city and the National Guard was placed under their command. Although the paratroopers were able to almost immediately calm the sections of the city where they were deployed, the ill-led and poorly trained National Guard units proved incapable of restoring order over the next few days.[10] Each night the looting, burning and shooting returned. City jails and processing centers were completely overwhelmed. Exhausted and overmatched city and state officials floundered from one ineffective measure to the next.

While the politicians and law enforcement officials were busy trying to understand the violence and end it, the Tigers had a pennant race. The Orioles were expected to fly into Detroit to start a series on Tuesday night. First, they had to play an exhibition game in Cooperstown on Monday afternoon. By the time that game was underway, it was clear that the Tuesday game could not be staged in Detroit. The city and its police department were imposing a curfew and trying to keep people at home. No one wanted fans or players in the city for a night game in the midst of the riots.

The series was moved to Baltimore and the Tigers flew out of town. Meanwhile, hard-pressed city officials came up with a solution to the horrific rioting. It was estimated that possibly thousands of television sets had been stolen from stores and warehouses. If all of those looters could be kept inside and off the streets, it was assumed that the bulk of the trouble might cease. Why not encourage them to plug in and watch their newly acquired television sets? The biggest draw on television for a young male population was obvious: a Tigers baseball game. The more this idea was discussed, the more cleverly brilliant it appeared.[11]

Only 37 Tigers games were scheduled to be televised in 1967. So while not a rarity, viewers would not expect a game to be broadcast. The television crew was dispatched to Baltimore and heavy promotion of the game began. Both Tigers management and Larry Osterman, the play-by-play announcer, were fully aware that the fate of their city now rested on this game and broadcast. The arrangements were so hastily made that George Kell, the color man, never made the game. Osterman and Kell's replacement were both instructed to announce the game as if it had always been scheduled for Baltimore. Under no circumstances were they to mention the riots.[12]

The Tuesday afternoon game started auspiciously, but was halted for a rain shower. Bill Freehan noted that the game could easily have been restarted except for the unconscionably shoddy work of the Baltimore grounds crew.[13] They did slowly deploy a tarp on the infield, but failed to cover the basepath to first base. Instead of being kept dry, the water from the tarp drained onto this area. Even though the skies cleared, the umpires had to call the game off. It is possible that this is the only major league game to have been postponed twice, in two different cities.

A rainout would have been unnoticed under normal circumstances. As it was, the television crew was keenly conscious that their broadcast was being counted on to save the city of Detroit. There were no national broadcasts, replays, or Detroit studio hosts to fill the airtime as the rain came down. It was entirely on the crew in Baltimore to produce interesting television for their baseball-watching audience. There is no evidence that the broadcast had much viewership. The following day there could be no game because Baltimore's Memorial Stadium was rented out for a soccer match. By Thursday, a television broadcast of a baseball game was no longer considered vital to Detroit's survival.

The rioting lasted for most of a week with steadily diminishing energy. By midweek, there were relatively small, copycat looting and arson incidents in Chicago, South Bend, Rochester, Waukegan, Minneapolis, Phoenix, Flint, Cleveland, Saginaw, Grand Rapids, and Cambridge, Maryland.

By some estimates, gunfire, vandalism, looting and arson damaged over 1,000 city blocks in Detroit. Hundreds of people were injured, many by gunshot. Of the 43 people killed during the week of rioting, police or military personnel killed 31.[14, 15] This number does not include people shot by unknown gunmen, or "stray bullets." The Michigan National Guard expended a staggering 155,000 rounds of ammunition in five days. That is a lot of stray bullets.

The Twins arrived in Boston on July 29 for a five-game series. They had endured a difficult week. A seven-game losing streak (not counting a nine-inning tie with the Yankees) left them in fifth place. In the first game on Friday, Dean Chance beat Jim Lonborg, 9–2.

The 35,469 who watched the next day's doubleheader were the largest crowd in Boston in 11 years. In the first game's fourth inning, left fielder Carl Yastrzemski threw out Jerry Zimmerman trying to advance to third base from first on Jim Kaat's single. More impressively, in the seventh with the Twins ahead 3–2 Yastrzemski caught Kaat's apparent sacrifice fly and threw out Ted Uhlaender at the plate. Uhlaender was believed to be one of the fastest players on the Twins. The Red Sox came back to win 6–3 with four runs in the bottom of the eighth.

This was another side of Yastrzemski's game that had become increasingly obvious during July. Opponents began to take notice of his fielding and fear the strength of his arm. In a soon-forgotten game against the Angels, Yastrzemski had played no role with his bat in a three-run rally to tie the game in the ninth, or in the game-winning sequence in the bottom of the tenth inning. However, in the top of the tenth, he robbed pinch-hitter Moose Skowron of a likely RBI double with what one veteran scout in attendance called the best catch he had ever seen.[16] Two batters later, Yastrzemski threw Don Mincher out at the plate to end the inning. As July turned into August he registered six assists in 11 days. His defense had become another weapon for the Red Sox.

After taking a doubleheader from the Indians, the White Sox hosted a four-game weekend series with the Tigers. In Detroit, this was expected to be the Tigers' best chance to cut into the White Sox lead. For a change, there was good news. Al Kaline would return to the field just four weeks after he broke his hand.

Kaline had spent his career proud of his dedicated selflessness while playing. Allowing a frustration tantrum to cost him weeks of playing time humiliated him. His self-image was so wounded that he could not face his teammates for a week after the injury. Eventually, he used the embarrassment as motivation. Kaline kept a telegram pinned to his locker in Tiger Stadium while his bones healed. It had arrived a day after the accident. "Nice going. Dummy. Signed Bob Allison and Harmon Killebrew."[17]

Despite the month-long layoff, he batted .294 in the four games. While Detroit fans knew Kaline was back in the lineup, thanks to Eddie Stanky few recognized that he was performing well.

The Tigers lost the second game 4–3 despite pounding 14 hits. Stanky did not waste the opportunity to dig at the Tigers insinuating that Kaline's timid baserunning in the top of the ninth had cost them the victory. He smugly asked reporters about the Tigers, "What's holding them back?"[18] On the play in question, Kaline had advanced from first to third on a single. The Detroit papers feasted eagerly on Stanky's portrayal. Readers were left with the impression that Kaline's, and the whole team's, lack of desire was to blame for the loss.[19]

With Mickey Lolich still on duty in the streets of Detroit, Mayo Smith started Denny McLain in the Sunday doubleheader only two days after he won a complete game effort. He lasted two innings and lost 4–1 to Joe Horlen. Despite the perception in both cities that the White Sox gained an advantage over the Tigers, the teams split the series. Unnoticed and unremarked, the Tigers scored 18 runs against the vaunted White Sox pitching staff.

Chapter 12

"The dumbest pitcher I ever caught"

American League standings before play on July 31.

	W	L	GB
Chicago White Sox	57	42	–
Boston Red Sox	55	44	2
Detroit Tigers	53	45	3½
Minnesota Twins	53	46	4
California Angels	55	49	4½
Washington Senators	51	53	8½
Cleveland Indians	46	55	12
Baltimore Orioles	45	54	12
New York Yankees	44	55	13
Kansas City Athletics	43	59	15½

Despite challenges by the Red Sox and then the Twins in the middle of July, the White Sox entered August in first place by two games over Boston. The Tigers, Angels and Twins all faded in the last ten days of the month.

Duane Josephson, the White Sox' rookie catcher, was ready to return to a substantial role on the team. In the first weeks of spring training, Eddie Stanky had announced that Josephson would be the team's everyday catcher. Two weeks later, the Senators' huge slugger Frank Howard followed through on one of his big swings. A raw rookie who expected to learn his trade from the team's veteran pitchers, Josephson was not acquainted with Howard's swing. The bat caught Josephson in the head with a widely audible crack. Howard momentarily thought he had killed Josephson, who eventually had to be carried from the field. Although he did not lose consciousness, it took eight stitches to close the wound. The team was relieved that x-rays showed no conclusive skull fracture.[1] A few days later, Stanky showed reporters one of his innovations. It was a modified batting helmet for catchers to wear with their mask, protecting their head from swings like the one that disabled Josephson.[2] Although catchers had been wearing masks since the 19th century, this was reportedly the first suggestion that they wear a helmet for additional protection.

Never diagnosed with a concussion, Josephson had returned to play in April. At the end of May he blocked the plate as a throw arrived from left fielder Pete Ward. The Twins Bob Allison, trying to score from second on a single, crashed through him. Josephson had held on to the ball for the out, but missed a month recovering from a thumb injury. Three games after he returned from that, a foul tip broke a finger on his throwing hand. As the season entered its final two months he was finally healed—a fresh player eager to make his mark.

That was not the only change on the White Sox.

Well aware of their inability to score runs, general manager Ed Short acquired veteran third baseman Ken Boyer and then slugger Rocky Colavito. Both players were past their prime, but were deemed adequate to improve the White Sox' weak attack. Boyer had been the National League MVP in 1964 and had won five Gold Gloves as a third baseman. He had struggled at the plate over the past year and a half. Still, his .266 average with 14 home runs in 1966 looked almost gargantuan compared with Pete Ward's .240 average, Dick Kenworthy's .244 or Don Buford's .220. Boyer swung an enormous 40-ounce bat, a "wagon tongue." Boyer had begun his long career as a rookie under Cardinals manager Eddie Stanky in 1955. Now Stanky hailed his arrival as providing a big psychological lift to the White Sox.

Colavito was a hero in Cleveland and led the league with 108 RBIs in 1965. He had struggled in 1966. During spring training in 1967, first year manager Joe Adcock had platooned him with Leon Wagner—a strategy that made both players eager to move to a different team. In May, Colavito wrote a letter to general manager Gabe Paul demanding to be traded. Receiving no response, he distributed copies to the local papers. In contrast to his warm welcome of Boyer, Stanky's first public comments about Colavito emphatically disapproved of Colavito's public demand to be played or traded.[3] Colavito's request was neither unusual nor unreasonable. After he lost his starting position in 1944 Stanky had publicly demanded that his Cubs manager Charlie Grimm either play him or trade him. Within a few weeks Stanky was a Dodger.

With his 363 career home runs, it was hoped that Colavito could supply some power to the White Sox lineup. Sports columnists across the country speculated that Colavito might be the player who would assure the White Sox of the pennant. The White Sox' ability to claim Boyer and Colavito off waivers was mostly dependent on their willingness to take on the two outsize contracts. They would finish the season with what was possibly the largest payroll in the American League by a substantial margin.

The White Sox' eagerness to upgrade their roster in the middle of the pennant race was particularly dismaying to Tigers fans who found a new goat in every loss. Fans saw a team that drifted along in third or fourth place incapable of closing the gap with the White Sox.

Within the organization, this was viewed as a success. The Tigers had maintained their position about three games behind the White Sox despite losing their best hitter for over a month and enduring the turmoil associated with the riots. Their general manager Jim Campbell claimed to have little interest in overpriced veterans like Boyer and Colavito because, except for their weak-hitting shortstops, all the Tigers' position players were deemed markedly superior to them.[4]

Perhaps it was the Twins slide into fifth place at the end of July, but Cal Ermer received a surprising lack of respect for a manager who had taken over a floundering team and propelled it almost to the top of the league. In city after city stories appeared stating that Ermer had not changed anything about the Twins. He had just been lucky to be the manager when players started improving.

It was a disservice to Ermer. Sam Mele had aggravated a number of players, who welcomed a fresh start under Ermer. Soon after Mele's firing, third baseman Rich Rollins said, "It was a strain to play for Sam Mele who kept saying that the Twins needed help at third base."[5] And Ermer was not without his strategic maneuvers. Unlike Mele, Ermer frequently used defensive replacements for his regulars in late innings. This noticeably improved the morale of bench players. It also signaled to all the players that he valued defense.[6] His right fielder, Tony Oliva, may have appreciated this the most.

Oliva was another one of the outstanding Cuban players signed by the Twins. When he first came to the United States, he had used his older brother's birth certificate to obtain a passport and in the process changed from Pedro Oliva to Antonio Oliva, or Tony. Initially the Washington Senators assigned him to a tryout camp with about 25 other Cubans. Oliva hit .700 in four games, but was given his unconditional release. Although he was fast and had an above average arm, he was a horrible fielder. By his own admission, he waited under one fly ball that landed 40 feet away. He closed his eyes and turned his head away when fielding groundballs.

His pride would not allow him to go back to Cuba so he took a job doing maintenance for the Senators AA Charlotte team. As part of the arrangement, he regularly took batting practice with the team. It did not take the general manager long to realize that Oliva was the best hitter there. Still a terrible fielder he finished the season on a Class D team where he led all professional batters with a .410 average. Because of the revolution he was unable to return to Cuba, so he spent the winter in the Florida instructional league working hard on his fielding.

After another successful minor league season, Oliva was called up to the Senators for the last few weeks of the season. For the first time he saw his hero, the Tigers' Al Kaline. Oliva marveled at his grace and perfection in the field. He tried to memorize every move. During the next two winters he returned to the instructional league and took as much fielding practice as he could. Every day during fielding practice, Oliva emulated Kaline's fielding technique. He did not hide his ambition to become "the black Al Kaline."[7]

In 1964, he made the Twins during spring training as a starting outfielder. Although no one in the Twins' organization knew why, Oliva wore Kaline's number six. He immediately excelled, winning Rookie of the Year honors. He took the batting crown in both of his first two years in the major leagues. He was not just a singles hitter. He averaged 25 home runs and over 90 RBIs in his first three years.

The Twins' Tony Oliva was a fierce competitor. Twice in 1967 he was hospitalized after full-speed collisions with outfield walls. After an injury-plagued start to the season, he returned to form becoming one of the league's best hitters. National Baseball Hall of Fame and Museum.

Initially, his fielding was still suspect, but he worked on it constantly both in season and during the winter. Eventually he became known as a fluid right fielder with a good arm. In 1966 Oliva won the Gold Glove for right fielders. He said it meant more to him than winning another batting title.[8]

Oliva was a star, if not a superstar like Killebrew. The left-handed hitting Oliva made a devastating combination with the right-handed Killebrew.

Against left-handed pitchers Oliva used a large 35-ounce bat. Against righties he used a 33-ounce bat. The strategy worked well. He entered the season as the second best all-around hitter in the major leagues behind only Frank Robinson. Oliva began the season in a long and nasty slump. His poor batting (along with Jim Kaat's poor pitching) was considered one of the reasons the Twins got off to a slow start.

As his managers knew, Oliva was beset by injuries during the first two months of the season. He had a cracked rib; both elbows were swollen after being hit-by-pitches; his right foot was bruised after he fouled a ball off of it; he jammed his left hand sliding headfirst into second base; he twisted his right knee; his right hand was spiked when he tried to break up a double play so his middle finger was crisscrossed with stitches. On top of all that, he was plagued with a head cold that lasted for weeks.[9] In addition to these woes, Twins management had moved the right-field fence back 16 feet during the offseason. Oliva had to hit the ball farther for a home run. He also had more territory to cover when he played in the field.

Mele had been batting Oliva sixth as his slump worsened. Ermer immediately returned him to fourth in the order behind Harmon Killebrew and kept him there for six weeks as his health and batting average steadily improved. By mid–July Oliva was healthy enough to attempt a straight steal of home. He might have made it except for a heady play by Athletics pitcher Jim Nash. Believing that Oliva would beat his catcher's tag, instead of pitching Nash threw at the batter, hitting him. Hit-by-pitch results in an automatic dead ball, so Oliva had to return to third base.[10]

Heading into a big five-game series in Boston at the end of July, Ermer switched Oliva and Killebrew in the lineup. Oliva moved up to third. Against Boston he collected nine hits including two home runs. The Twins won three of five.

As July turned into August, Ermer came forward with another innovation. Dean Chance had not pitched sharply since the beginning of July. Ermer announced that he was installing a five-man pitching rotation for the month of August. He felt that the heat of August took more out of a pitcher than competing in the cooler months.[11] The five-game series in Boston, which included a doubleheader, had lasted only four days. Jim Perry started one of the games, but this did not give any of the other pitchers an additional day off. With doubleheaders commonly scheduled for Sundays especially during the hot summer months, teams often used a fifth starter just to give their pitchers a normal rest.

Ermer planned something different. He would give an extra day off between starts to each of his starting pitchers. Perry would stay in the rotation. When a doubleheader was scheduled, Ermer employed a sixth starter, Mudcat Grant, to absorb the extra game. Although other teams had used a regular five-man rotation (including some National League teams in 1967), none of the other teams in the American League did. In that context, it flew in the face of baseball convention. Successful starting pitchers in the American League could expect 35 starts in a season. Already Detroit and California had used starting pitchers on only two days' rest in July.

Much less visible was Ermer's firm discipline with his players.[12, 13] Mele had been infamous for letting infractions slide. Ermer never did, but he kept the issues out of the public's attention. Baltimore's Hank Bauer was constantly posturing as a tough ex–Marine. Ermer, another ex–Marine, did not feel the need to pose. He was more likely to be seen chatting with his players than most managers. This friendliness did not extend to allowing his rules to be bent or broken. He was fearless. Most memorably to his players, Ermer once raced to the back of the team bus to physically separate his starting outfielders Ted Uhlaender and Tony Oliva who were engaged in a fist-swinging brawl.

Minnesota's home series against the Red Sox in the beginning of August received a big buildup in both cities. Sportswriters masterfully fueled already raging pennant fever. A series between two teams considered in their hometowns as the best of the tightly packed bunch was a sportswriter's dream.

An unusual day off while the team traveled home from the East Coast gave Ermer's pitchers an extra day of rest. Jim Merritt shut out the Red Sox in the first game and Dave Boswell won the second giving up only one run. The day off allowed Ermer to start Dean Chance in the third game. After the first game of the series, Ermer had to juggle his lineup. Rookie second baseman Rod Carew would leave for a two-week training commitment with the Marines Reserve in San Diego.[14] Carew was hitting a surprising .300 when he left the team.

Chance looked forward to pitching against the Red Sox ace Jim Lonborg who had already won a league-leading 15 games. During his entire pitching career, Chance had possessed an abundance of confidence, maybe an overabundance. There was good reason. In high school, he once struck out 21 batters in a seven-inning game. His high school record was reportedly 51–1 with 18 no-hitters. Chance told scouts, "I'd have had a better record if I'd have been with a better club." He modestly told some minor league teammates, "I was the greatest high school pitcher in the history of Ohio."[15]

Chance's arrogance may have been overlooked in high school, but it did not sit well after he made the major leagues with the Angels in 1962. At one point his teammates filled his locker with garbage and posted a sign over it that read, "I'm not naturally stupid. I'm just practicing."[16] He did not antagonize just players. Chance also had a running battle over money with Angels general manager Fred Haney.

After Chance led the team's starters with a 3.19 ERA, Haney refused to give him a raise. Chance conducted such an effective off-season publicity campaign that Haney finally conceded and gave him a $3,000 raise to $18,000. Chance claimed that he was promised an additional $7,000 if he pitched well and had a good attitude. By June Chance was telling everyone who would listen that Haney had gone back on his word. He demanded a trade. He showed up around Los Angeles doing odd jobs claiming that he needed more money for his family. Eventually he publicly refused to talk to Haney. The Angels owners met with him and gave him the extra money.[17]

Chance responded by winning 15 games over the rest of the season and the Cy Young Award. Playing for a mediocre Angels team, he won 20 games overall with a 1.65 ERA. Chance threw 11 shutouts, winning six of those 1–0. Since Hall of Famer Pete Alexander in 1916, Chance and Sandy Koufax were the only pitchers with that many shutouts in a season. He owned the Yankees team that won the pennant. In over 50 innings against them he gave up one run. In one of those games, he threw 161 pitches over 14 shutout innings. Chance was so effective that near the end of the year Mickey Mantle said, "Every time I see his name on the lineup card I feel like throwing up."[18]

The Angels rewarded Chance with a big contract for 1965. Chance slipped back to a 15–10 record with an ERA of 3.15. In 1966 he suffered with shoulder tendinitis. He had a losing record and a 3.08 ERA. Still, he was the ace of the staff leading the Angels starters with ERA and innings pitched. It was a difficult season. In a move that did not exactly boost his trade value, Fred Haney portrayed Chance as a washed up malcontent. After his trade to Minnesota, it was speculated that Chance manufactured rifts so that he would be traded.[19]

Some of his ex-teammates were eager to criticize Chance. His catcher Bob Rodgers conspicuously called Chance "the dumbest pitcher I ever caught."[20] This had been given a lot of play in the Minnesota papers before the teams' first meeting back in May. Rodgers was mostly miffed that Chance had the nerve to shake off his signs.

Chance may have been too competitive for some of the Angels players. He was not willing to overlook sloppy play or lackadaisical effort. Chance not only wanted to win, he sought to annihilate his opponents. He was fierce on the mound, demanding to the point of arrogance. At times, he openly complained to fielders who committed errors behind him, but never complimented them for making routine plays.

He compounded this lack of social grace with aloofness off the field, rarely staying in the team's hotel. In California he spent most of his time when not on the mound actively managing his social schedule. The papers were full of his escapades during the baseball season whether it was partying or chasing starlets.

Chance may have matured. In Minnesota he appeared to crave a team atmosphere. While still likely to stay in a separate hotel, at the ballpark he turned his natural gregariousness more toward practical jokes. The *Boston Globe*'s Will McDonough reported in July, "Dean Chance pulled this one on John Wyatt this past week. Chance informed Wyatt that he was wanted on a pre-game show that paid $50. Wyatt went over to the announcer to introduce himself only to find out that he had been Chance's sixth victim of the same stunt."[21]

There was another change. In Minnesota his teammates viewed his aggressive desire to win as an asset. Tony Oliva noted with admiration, "Some [opposing players] were afraid of him because he was mean—he would hit you."[22]

Despite this competitiveness, Chance was a notoriously inept batter. In 1966 his batting average had been .026 with 54 strikeouts in 76 at-bats. He did not get his first hit in 1967 until July 28. Cal Ermer joked, "We got the ball from the umpire on Dean's hit and enshrined it."[23]

The right-handed Chance's pitching motion was unorthodox. Once he received the catcher's sign, Chance never looked at the plate again. He further unnerved batters by turning his back completely toward the plate as he wound up. When he delivered the pitch, he threw across his body. It was hard for batters to pick up the ball. It was a slow windup and that made Chance relatively easy to steal on. In July the Angels scored a game-winning run when Jose Cardenal pulled off a straight steal of home while Chance slowly swung his left leg around as part of his normal delivery.[24]

Chance was a fastball pitcher. He kept the ball low and the pitch was often referred to as a sinkerball. Many sinking fastball pitchers were believed to throw a spitball. He was one of those commonly suspected. Throughout 1967, teams asked umpires to check Chance for illegal substances. That accusation was strangely incongruous with his reputation as a control pitcher. Since his days in high school, he could put the ball exactly where he wanted it on the edges of the strike zone. Although Chance developed a curve and a changeup, in 1967 his second pitch was a viciously low slider. He pounded the bottom of the strike zone. Batters rewarded him with plenty of groundouts.

Chance was primed for his showdown with Lonborg who was granted leave in the midst of two weeks of military service in Georgia. (The Red Sox had a minor league catcher drive 150 miles each way to work out Lonborg every other day during his stint.)[25] Neither pitcher disappointed. Through 3½ innings only one batter reached base. A summer thunderstorm crashed over the stadium resulting in a 24-minute rain delay. Despite this extra time to cool down, Lonborg took only eight warm-up pitches. The Twins' big bats broke through for three hits and two runs in the bottom of the inning.

In the top of the fifth inning, Chance retired the Red Sox in order. In the bottom of the inning Lonborg struck out Chance and then a huge thunderstorm hit. The wind-driven rain short-circuited the scoreboard and knocked out the stadium lights several times. By the time the storm moved on, the umpires estimated that water was ten inches deep in right field. The game was called.

Dean Chance had pitched a perfect game.

Although the game was official, Chance was not credited with a perfect game or even a no-hitter because the game did not last a full nine innings. In the locker room, Chance was willing to call his effort "a cheapie."[26] He claimed that any no-hitter required plenty of luck. This self-deprecating attitude showed a maturity that Chance lacked when he played for the Angels. He could sincerely claim that it was more important that the team had prevailed against the league's winningest pitcher. The Twins had swept the series and moved into a tie for second.

After months of relying on inexperienced catchers to provide guidance to their struggling pitching staff, the Red Sox acquired veteran Elston Howard from the New York Yankees. A 13-year Yankee, Howard announced that he would retire rather than play for another team. Faced with this frustration of his team's plans, Tom Yawkey telephoned Howard. It did not take long for Yawkey to charm him. This loss in Minnesota was Howard's second game with the Red Sox.

Despite losing both ends of a doubleheader at Baltimore, the White Sox remained 2½ games in the lead. The Tigers split a doubleheader in Cleveland to continue playing at about a .500 clip, but they were only a half-game behind Boston and Minnesota. The Angels continued to struggle against the Senators; they compiled a 2–5 record over two series to fall 4½ games back.

•

Chapter 13

"Sometimes you wonder what these kids are thinking"

American League standings before play on August 12.

	W	L	GB
Chicago White Sox	61	48	–
Minnesota Twins	60	50	1½
Boston Red Sox	60	51	2
Detroit Tigers	60	52	2½
California Angels	60	53	3
Washington Senators	56	58	7½
Cleveland Indians	53	61	10½
Baltimore Orioles	50	61	12
New York Yankees	49	61	12½
Kansas City Athletics	50	64	13½

Respected *Detroit Free Press* reporter George Cantor profiled White Sox manager Eddie Stanky. None of his observations necessarily broke new ground, but his frankness was a change. "While [Stanky] is easily the least liked man in the league, he has performed the most astounding juggling act in many years. He has taken this team of retreads, banjo hitters, kid pitchers and jackrabbits and looked back at the league for the best part of the summer." "In the course of his two years with the [White] Sox it seems as if Stanky has almost deliberately set about to antagonize everyone in sight."[1] The awkward juxtaposition of distaste with unexamined admiration would be repeated often, becoming a newspaper staple during the rest of the season.

The correlation between baseball stars and leadership can be a tricky thing. The reticent Harmon Killebrew was certainly a superstar and fan favorite, but barely interacted with many of his teammates. A genial man, he demonstrated little interest in baseball except when he stood on the diamond. Earlier in his career when he had been appointed captain, he had been not merely humble, but astounded. While Killebrew maintained that his batting performance would be the extent of his leadership, some teammates felt that the Twins might have benefited from "a little more of a firebrand type."[2]

Throughout his career Killebrew had been a streaky hitter. His home runs came in bunches. In 1967, the Twins had played poorly through the middle of June, but Killebrew had pounded 22 home runs by June 23. While Killebrew went 20 days without a home run, the Twins started a surge that took them to within a half-game of the lead in mid-July. When the Twins slumped eventually falling five games behind, Killebrew smashed ten home runs in the second half of July. Cause and effect cannot be determined, but Killebrew seemed to have an innate ability to perform when his team was struggling and needed a lift.

The Washington Senators signed Killebrew soon after his graduation from high school in 1954. Clark Griffith was alerted to Killebrew's existence and baseball prowess by an unusual scout: one of Idaho's United States senators. It was harder for the Senators to get a regular scout to Payette, Idaho, than it was for them to scout prospects in Cuba. That summer Killebrew was playing in the bush leagues of Idaho and western Oregon. Proceeding without haste, it took the Senators senior scout Ossie Bluege the better part of a week to arrive in Payette. He was greeted by days of rain. He used the time to negotiate with 17-year-old Killebrew's older brother and mother. Still, he needed to see Killebrew play.

Eventually Bluege announced that he would leave the following day even if he had not seen the prospect play. Soon after, the rain finally stopped leaving the field soaked. It was too wet to play. The entire town and surrounding region were aware of Bluege's presence. In an effort to ensure that their young star could perform in front of the Senators scout, locals reportedly burned gasoline to dry the field.[3] Both the process and the results conjure a variety of images. In the game that evening Killebrew responded with a massive 450-foot home run while going 3 for 4. (Bluege paced the distance to confirm its length the next morning.)[4] His two errors on the uneven field were irrelevant. Bluege signed him for the then astronomical sum of $30,000.[5]

The major leagues had a bonus rule at the time, which required any player who signed such a large bonus to spend two years on the team's major league roster. Killebrew joined the Senators in Chicago. Killebrew had been a shortstop and he fielded that position during practice before his first game. Manager Bucky Harris was unimpressed noting, "The kid throws like a girl."[6] There was no question of Killebrew playing except as a pinch-hitter.

The mild-mannered Harmon Killebrew was known for his powerful swing, which intimidated pitchers throughout the season. He tied for the league lead in 1967 with 44 home runs. National Baseball Hall of Fame and Museum.

In the Senators dugout during one of Killebrew's first games, veteran Johnny Pesky who had been assigned as the young rookie's roommate started to describe the team's positioning of the cutoff man on throws from the outfield. It was during this conversation that Pesky realized how raw Killebrew was. He had never heard of a cutoff man and did not know that such a concept existed in baseball.[7]

Killebrew's lack of fielding ability made it hard for him to play for the Senators. During spring training before the next season, his fielding was so bad that his manager openly complained to reporters, "How do they expect me to win games when I have to use players like Killebrew?"[8] To try to boost his baseball IQ, the Senators roomed him with coach Cookie Lavagetto during this second year. Lavagetto struggled to get Killebrew to focus on baseball.

When the two-year waiting period was over in June 1956, Killebrew was sent down to the minors where he finally got playing time. He played at Class A Charlotte where he hit .325 with 15 home runs. He was despondent at playing at such a low level, but came back in 1957 expecting to make the Senators. Instead, he spent the season at Class AA Chattanooga.

In 1958 the team believed he would become the Senators starting third baseman, but his fielding was so poor that he lost the job to Eddie Yost in spring training. Killebrew sat on the bench for about a month before the Senators shipped him down to Class AAA Indianapolis. Killebrew visibly sulked at the demotion. His hitting was poor and he committed 11 errors in only 38 games. The Senators decided to send him back down to Class AA Chattanooga. Killebrew refused the demotion. He called Bluege, who had served as a mentor throughout his time with the Senators, and told him that he was quitting baseball.[9] He had threatened this before each time his career had suffered a little adversity, but this time he was adamant. Bluege got him to agree to stay in Indianapolis and not head west immediately. The Senators had a lot of time, money and hope invested in Killebrew. Bluege and owner Cal Griffith realized that Killebrew's career was at a critical point. They believed that they could lose him.

Killebrew's wife Elaine had recently given birth to their second son. Nonetheless, she arrived in Indianapolis barely two days later.[10] That was about as fast as it was humanly possible to travel from the Killebrews' home in eastern Oregon to Indianapolis in 1958. Within a day, Killebrew reported to Chattanooga while Elaine packed up his apartment and prepared to follow. She stayed in Chattanooga for the entire season working on Killebrew's precarious confidence. For the first time in his professional career, he voluntarily took extra fielding practice.[11]

Griffith traded Yost before the 1959 season. Still, Killebrew's spring training performance was poor. He was lost at the plate. During his trying spring, Killebrew incorporated one big improvement to his hitting. Veteran Jim Lemon tried to discuss Killebrew's approach to a specific pitcher. Killebrew at first did not understand, but Lemon persisted over the course of a few days. Eventually, Killebrew realized that successful hitters study pitchers before they arrive at the plate to bat. It was a revelation.[12]

Despite Killebrew's disappointing hitting and his manager's disdain, Griffith insisted that Killebrew start the season at third base. Killebrew hit a home run in his first game. In May he hit 15. For the year, he tied for the league lead with 42. Playing third base, he led the league in errors. The errors did not matter. He was a major leaguer for good.

Frustrated by his team's inability to overtake the White Sox, Griffith mentioned his disappointment in the Twins bullpen to beat writers.[13] In the month after the All-Star break, the Twins registered only three saves. Statistics did not bother him as much as what he saw on the field.

His frustration boiled over after a particularly galling loss to the Senators.[14] Dave Boswell took a 7–0 lead into the seventh inning. He allowed two runs to score and was replaced with a runner on first and one out. Jim Grant and Ron Kline combined to allow another five runs to score that inning as the Senators tied the score. Kline quickly got in trouble in the eighth inning and had to be relieved by Al Worthington. Worthington pitched his best game of the season, holding the Senators scoreless for 8⅔ innings. Despite that, the Senators won 9–7 in the 20th.

It was not the first time that the bullpen had failed to hold a substantial lead. The Twins relieving corps was centered around two veterans, Ron Kline and Al Worthington. The other four bullpen regulars included Jim Perry and Jim "Mudcat" Grant who contended to be the fifth starter and were used primarily in long relief. Jim Roland rarely pitched unless both Worthington and Kline were unavailable. Jim Ollom pitched primarily in games that were out of reach. (The Twins had perhaps the most Jim-centric pitching staff in baseball history: Starters Kaat, Merritt, Grant and Perry along with relievers Roland and Ollom.)

While Griffith's comments were general—including the entire bullpen, manager Cal Ermer used them as cover to take action against 14-year veteran Ron Kline. Kline's ERA was above the league average at 3.64, but he had had some fine outings. The ERA did not show an unfortunate tendency to allow inherited runners to score. Ermer was frustrated by 6'3" Kline's visibly growing midsection. While there were other rotund pitchers in the majors, it struck Ermer as a sign that Kline lacked sufficient commitment. At the beginning of August, Ermer benched Kline until he lost 19 pounds.[15] Kline was far from this goal when Ermer sent him into the August 9 game against the Senators. Kline gave up a three-run home run and stayed off the field for another week.

Even before the benching, the relievers were not happy with Griffith's comments.[16] Their spokesman, who fired back through the press, was Al Worthington. The 38-year-old Worthington fit naturally into the role. He was glib, typically spending his innings in the bullpen ceaselessly chatting. It was not just a monologue. He casually engaged all his teammates with his southern drawl and open face.

Despite his easy-going demeanor, Worthington had a unique reputation for confronting management. A long-serving veteran, Worthington began his career when he was called up to the New York Giants in the middle of the 1953 season. Raised in Birmingham, Alabama, he was astounded by New York City. His first day in New York, he took a ride on the subway. He later proclaimed that as one of the biggest shocks of his life.[17] The next day he was to start against the Dodgers at Ebbets Field.

A teammate drove him to the game. Worthington could not believe that it was possible to drive through a tunnel under the East River and arrive in Brooklyn. These wonders may have taken off some of the shock of the Brooklyn fans who sat, seemingly on top of the field, hemming the players in. Most astounding to the young country boy: the fans booed during the introductions. This aggressive disrespect momentarily scared the solidly built 6'2" Worthington.[18] His pitching was unaffected. In this, his second appearance in the major leagues, he threw his second complete game shutout. It was the only game all season that the Dodgers were shut out. Worthington was the first National League pitcher since 1898 to throw complete game shutouts in his first two career starts.

Worthington was still with the now San Francisco Giants in 1958. A lifelong churchgoer, Worthington became a born-again Christian. He unabashedly proselytized his teammates, later admitting that he scared some of them and forced the rest to shun him. Late the next season with the team locked in a pennant race, Worthington went to manager Bill Rigney and insisted that he would go public with his accusations if the Giants continued to steal the opposing catcher's signs with a hidden telescope beyond the outfield. The Giants had done this since their days in New York—for Worthington's entire career. Only now did he feel strong enough to tell Rigney that it violated his Christian beliefs. Rigney gave in to the blackmail and allegedly stopped the practice.[19] The Giants finished four games out and Worthington was traded in the offseason.

The following year, after a disastrous start to the season playing for Boston, he was brought in to pitch for the White Sox who were making a run at the pennant in the first days of September. Within a few days he realized that they too were stealing signs. An inconspicuous light on the scoreboard was flashed to alert the batter about the coming pitch. He went to manager Al Lopez and threatened him with disclosure. Lopez cut him the same day.

Worthington spent the next two years in the minors.

By 1965, Worthington was the bullpen stalwart during the Twins run to the World Series. Still a fervent Christian, he no longer proselytized his teammates. He had a serviceable fastball delivered by his powerful frame. During his stay in the minors he learned a sidearm curve. This broke wickedly at an unusual angle, often leaving batters swinging at pitches that were far from the strike zone.

Worthington, who was proud of blackmailing two managers, was not going to be intimidated by Cal Griffith. The tempest in a teapot subsided after Griffith issued a placating statement through the press. Although they won the war of words, the relievers, especially Worthington, continued to feel underappreciated.

Ron Kline was not the only player who lost playing time while he tried to shed weight. While Kline was on the bench, the Red Sox headed west to Anaheim for the last stop in a long road trip. The Red Sox entered the series leading the league by a substantial margin in runs scored, but Dick Williams was not happy with all his players. Safely away from the maelstrom of criticism that his actions would create in Boston, Williams publicly benched young corner infielders Joe Foy and George Scott for being overweight just before the team landed in Anaheim.

While Boston pundits deplored the move, Red Sox players had a different reaction, one that did not find its way into the papers. If not immediately, eventually Williams gained respect. It is easy to proclaim rules, but much harder to uphold them especially during a slumping road trip. Williams made it clear that he was willing to take some heat if his rules were not followed. After this, his players knew that he would follow through.[20]

Despite his sincere interest in having his players in shape, Williams could be as hidebound as his older colleagues. During spring training, a reporter asked him about Mike Andrews who was not able to participate after injuring his back while weightlifting during the offseason. Williams replied, "That weightlifting business by Andrews really gets me though. No baseball players should be doing any weightlifting because all it does is buildup muscles that tighten them up. Sometimes you wonder what these kids are thinking of."[21]

Williams was typical of major league managers who disdained weightlifting. When faced with Joe Horlen's statement crediting offseason weightlifting and isometric exercises for his great start earlier in the season, Eddie Stanky told a reporter, "Isometrics have nothing to do with your brains. And that is where Joe is showing the most improvement."[22]

Many players had attitudes toward conditioning that were similar to Harmon Killebrew's. He believed that he kept in shape during the offseason by hunting for pheasant.[23] Killebrew may have had a more relaxed regimen than most. After all, when describing his devotion to hitting to a biographer after the 1965 World Series season, Killebrew noted that he *once* took extra batting practice, in 1963.[24] Killebrew was also famous for his devotion to the offseason banquet circuit, accommodating every request that he received. This may partially account for the extra pounds he carried around in 1967.

In this, Killebrew was not unusual. Nutrition was not a concern for major leaguers. It is doubtful that they would have seen the results of a new medical study that tied diet to Americans' increased rate of death from cardiovascular disease. The culprit was an unfamiliar chemical called cholesterol.[25]

This was not the first time Williams had benched Scott because of his weight. A big man, the 6'2" Scott was recognized as the best fielding first baseman in the league. He was quick, had soft hands and was exceptionally agile. Balls did not get by him. Red Sox infielders could heave off-balance throws in the direction of first base and be confident that Scott would bail them out. He was also fast—an asset rather than a liability on the basepaths. Only two weeks earlier, he had hit an inside-the-park home run to Fenway Park's short right field.[26]

Although eager to hit what he called "big taters" out of the stadium, Scott had disciplined his swing as a rookie so that he cut down on his strike-

13. "Sometimes you wonder what these kids are thinking" 119

outs and put the ball in play. He arrived in California batting .289, among the top ten in the league. In addition to his fielding and hitting, Scott was a tough player. Just a week after this road trip ended, he would be knocked cold in a collision while making a play at first base during the first game of a doubleheader. He was carted from the field, but returned to play the entire second game driving in the game-winning run.

None of this diminished Scott's unparalleled reputation for weight gain. It was claimed that he could add pounds just by walking past a restaurant, or looking at an ice cream sundae. No columnist was without a story of Scott's eating prowess. Legend had it that he once gained ten pounds in a single day.

Youthful looking, Scott's baby face was dominated by innocent eyes and a hopeful smile. Even when Williams was riding him for his excessive weight, Scott's wide frame looked almost slim in his uniform. Although he had powerful arms and legs, his chest was still waiting to develop muscles.

With baseball players' traditional knack for turning any quirk into a nickname, Scott's teammates began to call him "Twiggy."[27] His namesake was perhaps the first international supermodel. As the 1967 season progressed she had begun to morph from merely a model into an inescapable phenomenon. In contrast to Scott, Twiggy had an ultrathin, waif-like look.

Benching his overweight players did not bring Williams satisfying short-term results. The Angels swept the series winning each game by one run. Angels fans were ecstatic. Their team ended the series only 1½ games out of first. They were firmly ensconced in the pennant battle. All of southern California was excited; the floundering Dodgers were little distraction for most casual fans. Since the beginning of July the Angels had been competing for respect. Only a couple of weeks earlier a local headline boasted, "Stanky Studies Angels; Calls Them Contenders."[28] The actual quote was fairly innocuous, but finally the papers could run an outside assessment of the pennant race that did not exclude the Angels.

The Red Sox slumped home with a 2–7 record on a "near-disastrous road trip." The only good news that the *Boston Herald Traveler* could report the next day was that Scott's weight was down to 212 pounds from its high of 221.[29] Amid the gloom, Boston sportswriters failed to notice that the fifth-place Red Sox were only 2½ games out of first with 49 games left to play. Fans in Boston were either more observant, or just wildly optimistic. Calls to the Red Sox ticket office overwhelmed the local telephone system and led to a breakdown.[30]

A more notable sweep concluded the same day in Minnesota. Over the weekend, Twins starters Dean Chance, Jim Kaat, and then Jim Merritt each held the White Sox to two runs in winning efforts. In the first game, White

Sox third baseman Ken Boyer leaned down to field a routine grounder and pulled a hamstring. He had to be helped from the field.

An estimated 47,643, the largest crowd in the history of Metropolitan Stadium, saw the Twins take over first place in the last game of the series. A thrilled Cal Griffith declared, "We'll win the pennant."[31] It was the first time in two months the White Sox did not lead the league. In contrast to the Twins starters who were in the middle of a streak that would see them pitch 70⅓ of a possible 71 innings over eight complete games, none of the White Sox starters lasted more than six innings in this series. A Minnesota columnist proclaimed that pennant-race pressure was effecting the White Sox pitching. Their starters had completed only two of the 31 games since the All-Star break.[32]

The Tigers, who were back in Tiger Stadium, took three out of four from the Orioles and moved into third place only a game behind the Twins.

Pennant fever was hot. "The Great Race: 5 AL Teams" proclaimed one headline.[33] Columnists, with no sense of hyperbole, proclaimed this the best pennant race ever. It was still only the middle of August. The managers were not immune. Before Jim Lonborg took the mound against the Angels, Dick Williams tried to impress Lonborg's greatness upon the Los Angeles press. "I can envision Lonborg and Chance pitching for it all on the last day of the season at Fenway."[34]

In Los Angeles the papers broke down the remaining schedules of the five contenders by home and away because of the Angels perceived superiority in home games. In Chicago, a sportswriter completed the same exercise but based on games against other contenders. In all five cities, exhilaration and despondency on the sports pages could be separated by only a couple of days.

Chapter 14

"Die right here in the dirt"

American League standings before play on August 18.

	W	L	GB
Minnesota Twins	65	50	–
Chicago White Sox	63	51	1½
Detroit Tigers	63	54	3
Boston Red Sox	62	54	3½
California Angels	62	56	4½
Washington Senators	58	61	9
Cleveland Indians	57	62	10
Baltimore Orioles	53	64	13
New York Yankees	51	65	14½
Kansas City Athletics	51	68	16

At the baseball owners meeting, NBC announced a new $50 million TV contract for three years. NBC agreed to make 28 weekly broadcasts, in addition to televising the All-Star Game and the World Series.[1] Despite securing such a lucrative television deal, the meetings were not easy. Afterward, Cal Griffith noted that they were the most contentious since they voted not to rehire commissioner Happy Chandler in 1951.[2]

American League owners voted to have two divisions in 1968. The winner of each division would face off in a three out of five series to determine which team would go to the World Series. National League owners were furious because they had not been consulted on this change. National League President Warren Giles complained, "I don't think baseball should be put in a position where it is possible for a fourth place club to play a first place club in the World Series."[3]

Bill Freehan revealed that the players union had lobbied the owners at their meeting to raise the minimum major league salary from $7,000 to $10,000. He noted that reliever Mike Marshall was being paid only $5,800 because he had been brought up from the minor leagues during the season and did not have a major league contract. Freehan claimed that 10 of the 25 players on the Athletics roster were making $10,000 or less.[4]

Ed Penney was Tony Conigliaro's business manager and the "Penn" in Penn-Tone Records, the label that had released Conigliaro's records. He enjoyed living a fan's dream, frequently socializing with major league baseball players. In the summer of 1967 he sent his two young sons to Ted Williams' baseball camp in Lakeville, Massachusetts. On the last day of the camp, he arrived late to pick up his sons. Trading on his association with Conigliaro and undisturbed by other parents who had already left, he enjoyed a long chat with the Red Sox legend. In the course of the conversation, Williams asked Penney to pass along a piece of advice to Conigliaro.[5]

Unlike his teammate Carl Yastrzemski, Conigliaro had never displayed interest in Williams' intellectual, almost philosophical, approach to hitting. Williams intuitively understood this and this advice was purely physical. Williams thought Conigliaro was crowding the plate more than usual. He told Penney, "Tell him to back off. It's serious time now. The pitchers are going to get serious."[6]

Penney dutifully delivered the message when he met Conigliaro on the morning of August 18. Conigliaro, who spent most of the season believing that he was in a hitting slump, responded, "Who'd want to hit me, the way I'm hitting?"[7] His batting average had fallen 15 points in the past 10 days, but he was still hitting .287 with 20 home runs and 67 RBIs. He had recently been feted as the youngest player ever to hit his 100th career home run.

Conigliaro had always been an aggressive batter. Just as he had for his entire career, Conigliaro still practiced dodging beanballs during batting practices. Earlier in spring training, reliever John Wyatt had broken Conigliaro's left shoulder blade during such a drill. He missed only two weeks with the injury.

Conigliaro was convinced that the midst of a slump was the wrong time to adopt a timid approach at the plate. He told his brother, who had heard Penney's message, that he would do the opposite of what Williams recommended. He planned to crowd the plate more than ever.

Conigliaro and Carl Yastrzemski had always been rivals as well as teammates. Until 1967, Yastrzemski had hit primarily for average and Conigliaro was the team's slugger. Yastrzemski's newfound power changed that dynamic. As the summer had matured, both men pushed themselves to perform at a higher level. Similarly, they were aggressive in expecting high performance from their teammates. While Yastrzemski endured fame and its attendant responsibilities, Conigliaro basked in it. Conigliaro was slightly jealous of Yastrzemski's expanded success. He was not going to let up now.[8]

The Red Sox were hosting the Angels that afternoon. The Angels, who had been dominant in Anaheim, had arrived in Boston after losing all three games at home to the Twins. They felt the pressure to win the series in Boston and stay in the race. Jack Hamilton was starting for the Angels against Gary Bell who had pitched well, but lost to the Angels in Anaheim less than a week earlier.

Before the game Red Sox owner Tom Yawkey visited with Bill Rigney while the teams took batting practice. Both were gregarious, friendly with men throughout baseball. They basked in the excitement of the tightly packed teams at the top of the standings. Yawkey concluded, "What a great pennant race we'll continue to have as long as no one gets hurt."[9]

In the context of Rigney's gamesmanship during earlier series, Dick Williams repeatedly demanded that umpire Bill Valentine instruct Hamilton to wipe his fingers before pitching.[10] By the bottom of the fourth inning, the teams were engaged in a pitchers' duel. The only hit had been Conigliaro's single in the second. George Scott changed that, leading off with a smash to center field. For all the talk of his extra weight, Scott was deceptively fast for such a big player. He rounded first and dug hard for second. Jose Cardenal's throw just beat him and he was tagged out. The fans had been on their feet with the hit, but sank down dejectedly.

Fenway Park's left-field grandstand ran to within a few feet of the foul line and one fan tossed a smoke bomb out of those stands and into the outfield. It produced a substantial cloud of smoke that took more than 10 minutes for the grounds crew to douse with a fire extinguisher and then remove.

The smoke lingered. Irregular wisps clumped persistently in the outfield. Despite the wait, Hamilton did not look stiff when he retired Reggie Smith on a fly ball for the second out. Conigliaro was the next batter. After consulting with Scott, he was looking for a slider on the outside of the plate. Hamilton threw a fastball that tailed up and in. He felt it got away. Valentine thought that it followed Conigliaro's head as the batter tried to move back.

The ball hit Conigliaro flush on the cheekbone at his left eye. With a horrible squishing sound, his head jerked back toward third base. The impact was audible up in the open press box. All the pitch's energy dissipated into Conigliaro's head. The ball landed with a harmless thud on home plate. Conigliaro sprawled face down in the batter's box.

Along with the intense pain, Conigliaro's mind was filled with a loud screeching. He could not fill his lungs with air. Writhing in agony, he prayed, "Oh God, let me breathe. Don't let me die right here in the dirt at home plate at Fenway Park."[11]

The rest of Fenway Park was intensely silent with fans on their feet trying to see Conigliaro. The only sound was of people breathing.

Valentine immediately motioned for help. When Conigliaro rolled over onto his back in agony, catcher Bob Rodgers thought he was bleeding from his ear, mouth and nose. It was so disturbing that he ran out to turn Hamilton away so that he would not see.

Rushing over from the on-deck circle, Rico Petrocelli knelt by Conigliaro and tried to console and soothe him. Conigliaro never heard him. Almost unconscious but in excruciating pain, he was loaded onto a stretcher by teammates and the trainer from each team. Conigliaro's oldest friend in professional baseball, catcher Mike Ryan, Jim Lonborg and the two trainers hustled him through the dugout to the clubhouse. His head was filled with unending whistling. Both eyes were shut. His mouth was filling with a choking fluid.

In the stands, some fans sobbed quietly. His teammates were shaken in cold disbelief. As the scene slowly played out, that changed to anger. Yastrzemski in particular yelled threats at Hamilton from the dugout steps. He became incensed as the extent of the injury became clearer, certain that Hamilton had purposely thrown a beanball. By the time play resumed, most of the team was threatening Hamilton.

The next batter was Rico Petrocelli. He arrived at the plate full of hot emotion.[12] Hamilton was drained. Petrocelli hit a pitch hard, deep into Fenway's center-field corner—an oddity created by the right-field bullpens. He legged out a triple then continued home on adrenalin, scoring on Jim Fregosi's error. That was the winning run as the Red Sox took the game 3-2.

Despite the proximity of a number of nationally renowned hospitals including the Massachusetts Eye and Ear Infirmary, Tom Yawkey had Conigliaro transported across the Charles River to the obscure Sancta Maria Hospital in Cambridge. By the time Conigliaro arrived at the hospital and eye specialists were summoned, the swelling in his eye was too extensive for doctors to make an informed diagnosis. Swelling would not subside for three days.

A major, longtime benefactor of the hospital, Yawkey was able to order them to deny entrance to all visitors except Conigliaro's immediate family. Yawkey stayed by his hospital bed, for which Conigliaro was always grateful. Initial reports guessed that Conigliaro would miss about three weeks recuperating.

There was immediate speculation that Hamilton hit him with a spitball. Sal Maglie, who had a clear view from the Red Sox dugout, promoted this idea.[13] It was a poignant accusation because Conigliaro went down almost exactly 47 years after Roy Chapman was killed by a beanball, leading to baseball's outlawing of spitballs. Whether the pitch was a spitball or not, Conigliaro was the first and only batter Hamilton hit in 1967.

Others felt that it was a purposeful, tactical beanball. Hamilton had ridden the Red Sox hard from the dugout during the Angels' July visit to Fenway. Maybe he held a grudge. Or maybe he was encouraged by manager Bill Rigney to go after a Red Sox slugger as a way of energizing the slumping Angels. Eddie Stanky repeatedly stated through the rest of the season that the pitch was a direct retaliation for the many batters that Jim Lonborg hit.

Hamilton and Rodgers steadfastly denied all the speculation. Hamilton was sincerely remorseful.[14] He prominently tried to visit Conigliaro at Sancta Maria Hospital and was turned away.

Chapter 15

"A menace to baseball"

The American League standings before play on August 19.

	W	L	GB
Minnesota Twins	66	51	–
Chicago White Sox	64	52	1½
Detroit Tigers	64	54	2½
Boston Red Sox	63	54	3
California Angels	62	57	5
Washington Senators	59	61	8½
Cleveland Indians	57	63	10½
Baltimore Orioles	54	65	13
New York Yankees	52	66	14½
Kansas City Athletics	51	69	16½

Farther south on August 17, the Kansas City Athletics flew into Washington for a game the next day between two teams with no implications for the pennant race. Little had been expected of the Senators and Athletics before the season and both had performed to those expectations.

The Athletics were the only team in major league baseball that did not fly exclusively on chartered planes. As they boarded their commercial flight from Chicago that day, their manager Alvin Dark informed each of the players that there would be no drinking of alcohol on the flight.[1] Many commercial flights did not serve alcohol, so this was not a controversial request.

The Athletics were a team of below average veterans and not-quite-ready young players with well above average potential. Alvin Dark had been hired as the manager before the 1966 season. He had played and roomed with Eddie Stanky on the Boston Braves during their pennant-winning season in 1948, winning Rookie of the Year honors. The Braves Billy Southworth, a Hall of Fame manager, was soft-spoken and non-confrontational. His strength was positive reinforcement. It worked in 1948. But in 1949 the team dissolved in disharmony as players, most prominently led by Stanky, revolted against Southworth. Over the winter, Dark and Stanky were traded away to the Giants as troublemakers.

Dark was appointed the captain of the 1951 team that overtook the Dodgers from 13½ games behind to tie them at the season's end and set up the dramatic Shot Heard 'Round the World. During his six years with the Giants, Dark was an above average shortstop. He batted over .300 in three of those seasons and had enough power to collect almost 100 home runs as a Giant.

Dark and Stanky roomed together during road trips for Dark's first four years in the major leagues. Because they were both active Christians, neither participated in the stereotypical baseball activities of womanizing and drinking during the many idle evenings on the road. Most games were still played in the afternoon during the 1940s and 1950s. Instead, the two spent hours obsessively discussing baseball. They especially enjoyed dissecting the moves made by their manager Leo Durocher.

During a typical evening, the two would eat dinner at a restaurant, maybe see a movie and then retire to their hotel room. A medical theory of that time advised that a player's legs would be fresher if excess blood was allowed to drain back into the body. So, each would lie on his bed with legs propped high on the wall letting the blood drain. Then, they would begin to discuss the nuances of the game.[2]

Dark played for Durocher for five years and two World Series. Toward the end of that time, Dark consciously studied Durocher to prepare himself for a career as a manager. He distilled Durocher's instinctual methods to his own pithy philosophy: "A winning team is consistently aggressive. It makes things happen."[3]

Dark played for four other clubs before retiring at the end of 1960. In 1961 he became the manager of a strong Giants team. The following year his team won 103 games and the National League pennant, losing the World Series in seven games. He was fired after the 1964 season despite winning 90 games. In his four years with the Giants, Dark earned a reputation as a good game manager and handler of pitchers. Dark believed that there was no such thing as taking a pitcher out. There was only bringing another pitcher in.[4]

In imitation of Durocher, Dark employed fiery speeches in the Giants clubhouse. After one frustrating loss in 1962, he punctuated a comment by throwing a metal chair as hard as he could against the wall. As the chair left his hand, his index finger got caught in a sharp metal angle, bloodily ripping the end of the finger completely off.[5]

That helped him focus on his determination to model his managerial behavior on Durocher's. It did not take Dark long to realize that he was not a yeller and screamer by nature. He tempered his speeches after that. The result was clear. Young players blossomed under his tutelage. Dark came to believe that the most important part of a manager's job was in the way he interacted with and motivated his players. During spring training in 1967, he and Eddie Stanky engaged in a friendly debate through *The Sporting News*. In contrast to Dark, Stanky claimed that "handling men" was a vastly overrated quality and that the ability to instruct was the most critical part of a manager's duties.[6]

Dark was like Durocher in many of the ways he treated players. Off the field, he did not much care what the players did. Dark made a point of always sitting at the front of a team bus or on a plane ride. He did not want to see or hear what the players did. They were responsible for themselves.

After the Giants fired Dark, he was out of baseball for only one season before the Athletics hired him for the 1966 season. Athletics owner Charlie Finley wanted a manager who could get the most out of a group of young players coming up from the Athletics farm system.

Finley bought the Athletics in 1960 and had refused to follow commonly accepted baseball wisdom. A self-made man with an insurance empire in northern Indiana, Finley had learned the power of meticulous attention to detail. Despite having no baseball background, Finley oversaw everything to do with signing, developing and trading players. Unusually for a new owner with little baseball background, Finley had not acquired well-known veteran players. Instead, he invested heavily in building and stocking an extensive farm system. Despite year after year of lousy records and poor attendance in Kansas City, Finley stubbornly stuck to his plan of developing young talent.

Finley lived in Indiana. He talked regularly and at length to his manager and other administrative personnel by telephone. So great was his need to be on the telephone that he had one installed on a tree in his backyard, so that he could talk while he was outside with his kids. Because of this incessant communication, very little escaped his notice. Dark assumed that Finley knew every detail of the team's day-to-day existence.

Finley's focus on player development was invisible to the public, obscure and ignored by the baseball community in 1967. Like many successful people focused on details, Finley was publicly viewed as meddlesome. The baseball establishment through baseball writers accused Finley of getting in the way of seasoned baseball men. There was truth to this. In the first seven years of his ownership, Finley had seven managers.

The public did see his relentless marketing, which flew in the face of accepted baseball practice. He changed his team's colors to gold and Kelly green, which contrasted to every other team's variations on gray and white. For the first game of every series Finley insisted that his team don gold uniforms.

The players hated them. Sportswriters typically referred to them as hideous. In what might be seen as a confirming opinion, Italian fashion designer Emilio Pucci declared that these uniforms with their "wedding gown white" trim were the most beautiful athletic uniforms in the world.[7] A Minnesota columnist echoed the snobbish disdain of much of baseball referring to the Athletics as "the improbable creatures in Kansas City who wear gold and green uniforms and white shoes, giving them the appearance of large rabbits."[8]

Until 1967 every player in organized baseball wore solid black spikes. Finley changed that. The Athletics wore white spikes, which Finley claimed were made from the skin of albino kangaroos. These were so outrageous that Cleveland manager Joe Adcock planned to protest the first game of the 1967 season when his team played the Athletics.[9]

Perhaps more astonishingly, the Athletics had a live mascot. Charlie O was a mule visible on the field at home games and named after Finley. Any man capable of naming a mule after himself and promoting it has either a great sense of humor, or a secure sense of his self-worth, or both. Nonetheless, it helped establish that Finley was eccentric, egocentric and a little bit too odd to be taken seriously. In short, Finley was widely regarded as inept in his baseball decisions and buffoonish otherwise. The *Detroit News*' Pete Waldmeir called him "baseball's reigning kook."[10]

One of Finley's promising players was first baseman Ken Harrelson. Nicknamed for his prominent nose, "Hawk" Harrelson was a power hitter from South Carolina with a young family and a penchant for flashy clothes and fast cars who got himself deeply into debt on his $8,000 minor league salary. Promoted to the major league team, Harrelson wanted to buy a house in Kansas City. Finley lent him $6,000 with the agreement that he would withhold part of every paycheck Harrelson earned to pay the loan off. Before the 1966 season, Harrelson was given a raise to $12,000, but still felt impoverished because paying his debt significantly reduced every check.[11] Even after Harrelson was traded to the Senators that June, Finley continued to garnish each paycheck by arrangement with the Senators. For a big spender like Harrelson, this was a constant impediment to the lifestyle he wanted to lead. Before 1967, Harrelson convinced the Senators to stop cooperating with Finley. Harrelson felt as though he had received a large raise because he finally received his entire salary. Despite that increased financial security, Harrelson quarreled with manager Gil Hodges and started the 1967 season terribly. Finley wanted his money and Hodges was eager to be rid of an underperforming first baseman, so the Senators sold Harrelson's contract back to Finley.

For all of his oddities, Finley could be charming. Before a home game, Harrelson agreed to Finley's request to ride Charlie O around the field. Although Harrelson assumed that there would be a saddle, he gamely climbed on even after he found out that there was none. Between the mule's ungainly gait and a sudden increase in speed, Harrelson ended up almost upside down clinging to Charlie O's neck as the mule galloped toward fans offering popcorn. As soon as the mule stopped, Harrelson let go and fell to the ground. Ever the ham, he bowed extravagantly to the crowd. His teammates were in hysterics. Dark was furious that one of his young stars might have been seriously injured. Harrelson was mostly disappointed that instead of paying him, Finley gave him a $25 Stetson.[12] Pictures of Harrelson on Charlie O made all of the papers and Finley had Harrelson repeat the stunt, although he now paid Harrelson $100 for each ride. This arrangement gave Finley his publicity and Harrelson more spending money. It drove Alvin Dark crazy. Beyond the obvious chance of injury, it violated his firmly held belief that players needed to be totally focused on winning each day's game.

Although it did not end here, the Charlie O distractions for Dark's team peaked in the middle of the 1966 season. Finley announced that Charlie O would be appearing at other ballparks when the Athletics were visiting. Because of a long-standing personal feud, White Sox owner Arthur Allyn publicly forbid Finley from bringing Charlie O to White Sox Park.

During the late innings of one game in Chicago, Harrelson was in the clubhouse sneaking a cigarette when Finley arrived. He proudly showed Harrelson a mule that he had somehow smuggled into the stadium in a huge crate. Finley wanted the mule on the field, but the beast wisely refused to enter the dank, confined runway. Finley's persuasiveness, combined with Harrelson's willingness and sense of indebtedness, convinced Harrelson to help. While Finley tugged at the mule's halter, his emerging power hitter was pushing the recalcitrant half-ton mule through the dimly lit hall from behind with his metal spikes slipping and skating on the wet concrete. Harrelson knew he was on the wrong end of the mule, praying that he would not only survive but be able to sire more children. The ordeal was not over quickly and Harrelson had plenty of time to compare this reality with his naïve expectations of a major league baseball career.[13]

Finley and Harrelson did eventually prod the mule onto the field, just as reliever Jack Aker was beginning to wind up and deliver a crucial pitch. As the unrestrained mule dashed about the field, the umpires halted the game; the crowd cheered, booed and yelled in disbelief; Finley stood on the dugout steps taunting Arthur Allyn high up in his owner's box. His concentration shattered, Aker glowered from the mound. Although most of the Athletics bench joined Finley in his triumphant laughter, Dark did not.

Harrelson missed a week with a sore foot. The mule had stepped on him.[14]

It was this carnival-like atmosphere that made it hard for the baseball world to initially take the dispute on August 18 seriously. The day before the team had left for Washington, Finley called Dark and told him to fine pitcher Lew Krausse $500 for being drunk and disorderly on a team flight back on August 3. Dark replied that he would look into it. He had great rapport with Harrelson and respect for his relationships with his teammates. Harrelson had been sitting directly behind Krausse on the flight and told Dark that there had been no loud or unseemly behavior. When Dark refused to levy the fine, Finley assured him that the team's radio announcer, Monte Moore, had witnessed Krausse using deplorable language in front of a mother and her child. In an apparent compromise, Finley ordered Dark to prohibit drinking on all team flights. When the team reached the clubhouse in Washington on August 18, Finley (who was not in Washington) had the team's representative to the Players Association, Jack Aker, read a statement that defamed the players implying that they were irresponsible drunks. The players were furious and had Aker phone Finley asking for a retraction. Finley responded that he had already released the statement to the press.[15] The next morning, the players drew up a response and voted unanimously to endorse it. In it, they denied that there had been any incident on the plane and then condemned Finley for using "unauthorized personnel" for collecting information about the players.[16]

Harrelson remembers going to Dark's room with Aker before the game so that Dark could read it.[17] Aker gave the statement to the press after the game. Unknown to the players or Dark, Finley was flying to Washington and landed that night after the game ended. Arriving at the Shoreham Hotel he summoned Dark to his room. After Dark again refused to fine Krausse, Finley fired him.[18] This relieved the tension. The two then discussed the fine prospects that the team had going forward. Two and a half hours later in much better spirits, Finley rehired Dark and gave him a raise. To celebrate, Finley called in four of the club executives and Monte Moore. This celebration went on for about an hour until Paul O'Boynick, the *Kansas City Star*'s Athletics beat reporter, came to Finley's room to get his reaction to the statement released by the players.[19]

When O'Boynick read the sentence "We players feel if Mr. Finley would give his fine coaching staff and excellent manager the authority they deserve these problems would not exist," the mood changed in a hurry.[20] After getting the statement word for word, Finley called down to Aker's room. Aker had missed curfew and was not in yet, so the seven men jammed in Finley's room. While they waited, Finley grilled Dark about the team's attitude. Under this probing, Dark insisted that he had not known what was in the statement.

An hour later, around three in the morning, Jack Aker presented himself at Finley's door. He had already had a long night and was not looking forward to what promised to be an uncomfortable interview with his boss. A sidearm, sinkerball pitcher, Aker had been baseball's reliever of the year in 1966. He was arguably the best player on the team, so he was not afraid of the consequences to his baseball career.

The door opened and Aker was hit by a wall of stale air filled with the odor of seven men who had been sweating through the humid summer night. Finley wasted no time before trying to browbeat Aker into agreeing to retract the statement. Aker refused because his teammates had unanimously approved it. Defensive in the face of Finley's aggressive accusations, Aker tried to defuse the charges by pointing out that Finley's manager had seen the statement before it was released. This did not improve Finley's mood. Ratcheting up the acrimony did not change Aker's position.[21]

Unable to make headway, Finley ordered everyone to leave the room. An hour later he called Dark and fired him for a second time.[22] He needed a scapegoat. Dishonesty and disloyalty made Dark the only possible candidate.

The next day, the game against the Senators was called because of rain. Players were in the clubhouse packing their gear for the bus ride to Baltimore when Dark came in to say goodbye. He had developed a strong bond with many of the young men on the team. Dark choked up addressing the players. An emotional man, Harrelson was in tears.[23] After Dark left, a pack of baseball writers trolled the clubhouse looking for quotes. Still distraught, Harrelson remembered telling one of them that Finley's firing of his mentor and friend Alvin Dark was bad for baseball. That evening, Harrelson was watching the news on TV when the sports announcer claimed that Harrelson had called Finley a "menace to baseball."[24]

Harrelson knew he was in trouble. The next morning when Finley called, Harrelson agreed to retract the word "menace" but not the gist of his actual statement. Finley was furious. An hour later, Finley called and told Harrelson that he had been placed on the irrevocable waiver list. He'd been fired.[25]

Harrelson was in debt to his ex-boss and had just lost his job making $12,000. As a player, he was at best an average major league first baseman. In his favor, he could be described as a right-handed power hitter with an average glove at first base. He was still young enough to have potential. Best of all, his bat had been hot since he rejoined the Athletics.

Harrelson's teammates immediately recognized that he had hit an almost unprecedented jackpot. In 1967 there were no free agents. Major League Baseball was still the possessor of a unique right in America called the reserve clause. Once a player signed with a team, he could only play for that team, or its farm teams. The team could trade the player, or sell his contract. The player had no option to change teams.

Before each season, teams would offer each player a one-year contract. The player could negotiate, and many stars held out, but the only option to signing a contract was to retire. Salaries had escalated through the mid–1960s, but not far. As an example, in 1966 seven-time All-Star Frank Robinson won the Triple Crown, his second MVP award and led his team to the World Series championship. For 1967 he was reportedly rewarded with a $100,000 contract.

Harrelson found himself in a unique and potentially lucrative spot. He was a free agent in a world where there were no other free agents. All doubt was erased when White Sox general manager Ed Short called Harrelson within a few minutes of the firing. Everyone in baseball knew the White Sox were desperate for hitting. Short asked Harrelson how much money he wanted. This was such an astounding request that the usually glib Harrelson had no reply. They talked briefly but without any definite offer being made. Finally, Short asked Harrelson to think over playing for the White Sox.

In an industry where employees had almost no bargaining leverage, general managers had a natural arrogance in all player relations. That arrogance was on full display when Short concluded, "I'll tell you this, though. We're not going to get into a bidding contest. Bidding contests are bad for everyone—for you, for us, for baseball."[26]

Harrelson did not miss the real message. There would be a bidding war and it would greatly benefit him. Baseball's rules about an irrevocable waiver stated that the player would not be free to sign with other teams for four days. Stranded in Baltimore for a couple of those days, Harrelson was directly contacted by the Tigers, Twins, Angels, Red Sox and many other teams including the Athletics. Charlie Finley wanted him back. Many wanted his services, but none offered him a specific salary number. As he was going to the airport to fly home to Kansas City, the Red Sox called. Harrelson agreed to meet with their player personnel director Haywood Sullivan who had once been Harrelson's teammate.

They met at the airport and worked out a contract for $88,000. It was the first firm offer that Harrelson had received. Harrelson was not allowed to sign any contract before the four days had passed, but he took the offer back home to Kansas City. In Kansas City his wife presented him with a long list of baseball men who urgently needed to talk to him. It was overwhelming. Before talking to the Atlanta Braves, Harrelson realized that with such a huge raise, he really needed to decide what else was important to him. Atlanta was the closest city to his native South Carolina. It boasted year-round golf, with which Harrelson was obsessed. (Harrelson wore a golf glove when batting—possibly major league baseball's first batting glove.)[27]

When the Braves offered him $112,000, Harrelson committed. The decision was a relief. Throughout the process, he had waffled between feeling that he might destroy his reputation by being too greedy and fearing that he was squandering an opportunity by signing too cheaply.

He immediately had second thoughts. Nearly every team had asked him to call before he made his final decision. He spent an exhausting day honoring that commitment, letting each team know that he was going to Atlanta.

Tony Conigliaro lying in a hospital bed in Boston was far from Harrelson's thoughts. No one in Boston could think of anything else. Although initially uncertain, a few days after the beaning the doctors made it clear that Conigliaro would probably play baseball again, but not in 1967. The Red Sox had lost a critical part of their big hitting lineup. There were a couple of journeymen outfielders available, (the Red Sox signed one of them—Jim Landis—who had recently been waived by the Tigers) but none approached Hawk Harrelson's potential as a right-handed power hitter. Tom Yawkey had not had a team near the top of the league since 1950. Pennant fever gripped him as hard as anyone in Boston. He made it clear to his general manager that the Red Sox needed the best available bat to replace Conigliaro in the lineup.

That night as Harrelson was at the door to head out with his wife to celebrate their good fortune, the phone rang. It was Red Sox general manager Dick O'Connell. He cut right to the point: "Kenny, we have got to have you here in Boston." He refused to be put off and immediately demanded, "Exactly how much will it take for us to get you up here?"

Harrelson tried to avoid giving an answer. He did not want more negotiations. O'Connell persisted. Under this duress, Harrelson blurted out a ridiculously high figure, "A hundred fifty."

"You've got it," replied O'Connell so quickly that Harrelson was left wondering if he could have gotten $200,000 or even a quarter of a million.[28]

Harrelson called his golfing friend Paul Richards, the general manager in Atlanta, who released him from his verbal commitment. The next day Harrelson, a .238 hitter with only 57 career home runs, flew to Boston to sign his contract. All of baseball, but especially players, noted the size of this contract for a barely average player. It was obvious what free agency would mean. Once the Harrelson contract was signed, there was no stopping free agency. It could only be delayed.

Harrelson joined the Red Sox in New York where they were playing the Yankees. It was an odd night. A Yankees spokesman claimed it was the first time that they had held an awards ceremony to honor a visiting player.[29] August 28 was Carl Yastrzemski Night to celebrate the star on the visiting Red Sox. Harrelson sat on the bench watching his new teammates and trying to become acclimated to playing meaningful games in front of big crowds. A crowd of 27,000 many of whom bussed in from Yastrzemski's home area of eastern Long Island watched with him as the Red Sox won 3-0 behind Reggie Smith's seventh home run of the month. Yastrzemski did not hit safely, but collected an RBI on a first-inning sacrifice fly.

Harrelson had admired Yastrzemski as an opponent, but he was astounded after watching him up close as a teammate. Even before it was his time to go to the on-deck circle, Yastrzemski focused on the pitcher. Once he got to the plate, his eyes never left the pitcher for a moment. He seemed to know more about what the pitcher was doing than the pitcher did. Harrelson had never seen anything like it. Yastrzemski was locked in all the time. It was obvious to Harrelson: "The difference between real greatness and just average success is [Yastrzemski's] power of concentration."[30]

The next day the teams played a Tuesday evening doubleheader. Harrelson hit a home run in his first Red Sox at-bat. New England residents apparently dominated the unusually large crowd of over 40,000 as the unfamiliar chant of "Go, Red Sox, go" echoed frequently through Yankee Stadium.[31]

Chapter 16

"That runt"

American League standings before play on Thursday, August 24.

	W	L	GB
Chicago White Sox	69	53	–
Boston Red Sox	69	55	1
Minnesota Twins	68	55	1½
Detroit Tigers	69	56	1½
California Angels	64	61	6½
Washington Senators	60	65	10½
Cleveland Indians	59	67	12
Baltimore Orioles	57	68	13½
New York Yankees	54	70	16
Kansas City Athletics	53	72	17½

The Angels, who had been only 1½ games out of first on August 13, were swept by the Red Sox after the Tony Conigliaro beaning, capping a seven-game losing streak. This sweep concluded with a soul-destroying 9–8 loss after they led 8–0 with ace Jim McGlothlin on the mound. The Angels never recovered. By the end of August, they were eight games out. While they played the contenders even through the last month of the season, their run as a challenger for the pennant was over.

Back in first place after more than a week in second place, the White Sox' Eddie Stanky proclaimed, "Dropping out [of first place] and then coming back is another thing. It's the mark of a champion."[1] In his telling, at least, the White Sox were ideally positioned for a triumphant run to the pennant.

Starting in the last week of August, each of the remaining contending teams faced an exhausting schedule of at least 20 games in 15 days. Just as the Angels disappeared from the race with just one bad stretch, it was widely assumed that these two weeks would be decisive in determining the pennant winner.

The leading teams continued their aggressive search to upgrade their rosters. On August 17 the same day that starting third baseman Don Wert pulled his hamstring trying to run out his double play grounder, the Tigers acquired Eddie Mathews from Houston for a player to be named later. Mathews had played his entire career until 1967 with the Braves. He was the only Braves player to play in all three of their hometowns: Boston, Milwaukee, and Atlanta. Paired with Henry Aaron in the middle of the Braves batting order, he was part of the most prolific home run hitting duo in history. A third baseman, Mathews arrived in Detroit with 503 career home runs, the seventh player to reach the 500 home run plateau.

The Twins visited Detroit for a three-day, five-game series including consecutive doubleheaders that began August 22. In the first game of the first doubleheader, the Tigers roughed up Dean Chance early and knocked him out of the game in the third inning. Earl Wilson cruised to his 17th win despite giving up three solo home runs. Mathews, playing only his third game for the Tigers, hit a home run for the last run in the 7–3 win.

In the nightcap, the Tigers went down 1–0 when Bob Allison scored on an inning-ending double play in the second inning. Starting pitchers Mickey Lolich and Jim Kaat dominated. The game was still 1–0 when the Tigers came to bat in the bottom of the ninth inning. Kaat, who had given up only three hits in the first eight innings, surrendered a single to Dick McAuliffe. Then Al Kaline doubled, scoring McAuliffe. Al Worthington relieved Kaat and retired Horton, Freehan, and Northrup without allowing Kaline to advance. Recently promoted Tigers reliever Fred Lasher and Worthington continued to close down batters until McAuliffe led off the bottom of the 11th inning with a triple. Kaline fouled out to Twins catcher Hank Izquierdo. Izquierdo was a 36-year-old rookie from Cuba who had been called up at the beginning of August. This was his fourth major league game. It was speculated that he and the 38-year-old Worthington might be the oldest battery in major league history.

Before this inning Worthington, and his odd sidearm curveball, had faced only one batter with Izquierdo behind the plate. Worthington threw his first pitch to Willie Horton past Izquierdo. McAuliffe scored on the wild pitch to end the game. The Tigers were easily the least emotional team in the American League, but even they expressed satisfaction at taking a doubleheader from the league leaders. They were now tied with Minnesota only a game behind the White Sox and Red Sox.

Despite throwing eight shutout innings against the league's second highest scoring team, Kaat received a no decision in the loss. His record remained

9–12. The *Detroit News* ran an interview with Twins coach Billy Martin. Noting that Kaat had only one win during the tense month of August, Martin blamed Kaat's disappointing season on the letter he wrote and had published on the day after Johnny Sain was fired in October 1966.[2] This was a public example that Martin was incapable of releasing his grudge with Sain and now Kaat.

The Tigers won the opening game of the next day's doubleheader 10–0 behind Joe Sparma's four-hitter. Twins pitcher Jim Merritt gave up five runs before being taken out in the third inning. Playing at home against the Twins who were arguably the most complete team in the league, the Tigers had taken the first three games of the series. They were beginning to make their pennant run and now led the Twins in the standings.

Merritt, who in mid-summer had led the league's qualifying pitchers in ERA, would come back to pitch to Eddie Mathews with the bases loaded in the day's second game. Mathews singled, scoring two runs. That was the last hit in the game. The Twins held on to win 4–3. During the game, both managers began running out of players. The pressure remained. They were keenly aware that they needed to win every game if their team was going to keep pace. After the gimpy Willie Horton doubled, Mayo Smith brought in the not-so-athletic Mickey Lolich as a pinch-runner. Later in the game, he sent up Earl Wilson as a pinch-hitter for Pat Dobson. In all, Smith used 18 players in the game.

In the last game of the series, Harmon Killebrew hit a home run for the winning run in the eighth inning and the Twins piled on 14 hits as they beat Denny McLain 4–2.

The Tigers won three of the five games, but felt as if they had lost the series by losing the last two games. They were back in fourth place.

Two days after the Tigers added Mathews, the White Sox activated Tommy John from the disabled list. To make room for him on the roster, they demoted Bruce Howard to Indianapolis. Only three days earlier, Stanky had pledged to keep the struggling Howard in the starting rotation.

Howard's season had been a baffling disappointment. A prodigy, Howard threw his first major league pitch when he was barely 20. Two years later, he was the fifth starter in the White Sox rotation with 22 starts. He had a breakout year in 1966. His record was only 9–5 but he dropped his ERA to 2.30. During spring training in 1967 he appeared to have matured. A tall 6'2", he no longer looked like an overgrown boy. His round face had lost the look of baby fat. For the first time since childhood he had allowed his blond hair to grow out from a crew cut.[3]

This would be Howard's fifth year in the major leagues, although he was still only 24. He was bound for a long career. His only physical problem had been recurring finger blisters. Howard had spent the winter trying to toughen the skin on his fingers. His solution was to handle a baseball whenever he had leisure time. Every time he watched television in the evening, he would take a baseball and keep flipping it in the air.[4]

Despite his success the year before, Howard was not a Stanky favorite. In 1966 despite Stanky's order for a beanball, Howard had refused to hit Detroit pitcher Joe Sparma in retaliation. Instead, he just brushed him back. Stanky's tirade in the clubhouse was leaked, revealing that Stanky ordered his pitchers to hit batters. Months later, what could have been a minor incident was still in the Chicago papers because it had led to the benching and eventual trade of catcher John Romano, arguably the best hitter on the team. Stanky made it clear that he blamed Romano for divulging his orders to the press.[5]

Perhaps because of his success at a young age, Stanky believed that Howard lacked necessary discipline and toughness. During spring training, Stanky had been pleased with his improvement touting him as a candidate to pitch opening day. "What has helped Bruce in my estimation is the conditioning that Marv Grissom [the White Sox new pitching coach] stressed. He's a kid that had the soft body of an old man or a bank clerk. He needed hardening up."[6]

In addition to conditioning, Grissom changed Howard's delivery so that it was more to Stanky's liking. Just before the season started Stanky assessed Howard as a 20-win pitcher.[7] Stanky was not the only one to value Howard highly. *Chicago Daily News* beat writer Dave Nightingale pronounced that he would be the number one starter on five of the ten American League teams.[8]

Howard started the season well, but then missed the first three weeks of May. When he returned, he was in the bullpen. As the schedule became more crowded with games, Howard earned 13 starts in the next 11 weeks. He still pitched in relief between starts and his outings became noticeably shorter. If the White Sox were behind by even one run as early as the fourth inning, Howard was convinced that Stanky would lift him for a pinch-hitter. Every time he allowed a run, Howard could not keep himself from glancing impulsively into the dugout to see if Stanky was about to emerge. He felt the burden of having to be perfect.

Howard had been called the Nibbler for his penchant of pitching to the corners of the plate. Under Ray Berres this had not been a concern. In 1966 he issued only 44 walks in almost 150 innings. With his new motion, Howard had a little less control and his walk frequency went up.[9]

By August, Howard had been in a slump for over a month. He desperately tried to follow the advice coming at him from all directions. It did not help. Each suggestion just reinforced that he was pitching poorly. His confidence was gone. In an interview, Howard described his season as an "utter disaster."[10] His control became so bad that he walked Dean Chance.

When Howard was finally sent down, a local columnist bid him goodbye, describing his stint with the White Sox as two seasons of mediocrity.[11] The bar was pretty high for White Sox pitchers. In those supposedly mediocre seasons of 1966 and 1967, Howard made 38 starts with an overall ERA of 2.79.

It was about this time that a *Sports Illustrated* article under Eddie Stanky's byline hit newsstands.[12] It hit publishing gold by immediately becoming fodder for sports columnists nationwide. Its myriad of themes would play out over the remainder of the season.

Of immediate interest was the mainstream acknowledgment that Stanky had barred Vice President Hubert Humphrey from the White Sox clubhouse after the August 13 loss that saw the White Sox fall from first place. Humphrey was a vocal and unabashed Twins fan, but mindful of his status as a national figure garnered publicity by visiting the clubhouses of the opposing teams when he attended a game. By the time the *Sports Illustrated* piece was released, Stanky was able to brandish a framed letter from Humphrey on the wall of his clubhouse office absolving Stanky and praising his sportsmanship.

Typically capable of projecting a high moral tone, the strain of close games seemed to be taking a toll on Stanky. That same week a reporter asked a question about Humphrey. Stanky replied, "What do I care about Humphrey? He can't hit."[13] Of course, it was reported nationally.

Even as Stanky's press conferences became more volatile, many assumed in print that he was lashing out to foster an "us vs. them" mentality on his team. After being shut out by the Yankees dropping the White Sox into a tie for first on August 24, Stanky exploded in such a "stormy tirade" to reporters that his press conference drew far more attention nationwide than any of the day's games.[14]

For weeks his most consistent point repeated, or at least recycled by writers, almost daily was that the White Sox were unfairly denigrated as dull. He presented himself as sticking up for his apparently talentless players who won on guts and determination. It did not go over well with the young position players. Their confidence had become increasingly battered by the handicap of trying to hit in White Sox Park with its swamp-like infield. This was almost certainly maintained to Stanky's desired standards. As a team, they were hitting close to .200 at home—about .050 lower than their road average. The team's road batting average was better than that of every team in the league except the Red Sox and Tigers. Not surprisingly, the White Sox scored far more often on the road than at home.

Psychologically, the White Sox batters were beaten down. Stanky ruled his clubhouse with intimidation and fear.[15] The easiest targets were the young, underperforming players. Many of these lost significant playing time after the trades for Colavito and Boyer at the end of July. The favored status of these two high-priced veterans undermined the younger players' confidence. Team chemistry among position players evaporated.[16] Like Howard, some had lost their resilience. Rather than help his players navigate the pressure of the increasingly tight pennant race, Stanky amplified every stress. He often lost his temper and screamed at the team after a loss. His anger was so violent that he scared some players. Scared players often do not play well.[17]

In the dugout, Stanky would often bark questions at players to make sure that their attention was on the field. To a few veterans, this confirmed Stanky's passion and his devotion to constantly teaching his players.

Master strategist Eddie Stanky enjoys a light moment, or does he? As the season wore on, Stanky psychologically intimidated his opponents. Increasingly his on-field tactics and off-field comments dictated the actions of opposing managers. © Ron Vesely/Chicago White Sox.

To many White Sox, it was constantly wearing, an additional source of stress that they did not need. Pitcher Joe Horlen spent games that he did not start standing on the top step of the dugout because Stanky would only question players when he could look into their eyes. Horlen successfully avoided the grilling, but it made him conspicuous when Stanky was looking for pinch-runners.[18] Horlen pinch ran 26 times in 1966 and an additional 12 times so far in 1967.

It is likely that the real issue was that the Cubs were outdrawing the White Sox in Chicago. Comparing the two clubs' attendance was a staple of the city's papers. Stanky blamed the Chicago sportswriters for the attendance disparity. Certainly some local columnists regularly criticized him and even mocked him as "Little Caesar."[19] But to others, he could do little wrong. It is hard to find any reference to the White Sox as dull, except Stanky's repeated assertion. They remained one of the biggest road draws in the league.

At the end of August, a historic vote took place in the United States Senate. President Lyndon Johnson's solicitor general, Thurgood Marshall, was confirmed to serve as a justice on the Supreme Court. Marshall had been the first African American Solicitor General and became the first African American Supreme Court justice.

As the Senate vote took place, the Red Sox arrived in Chicago with a contingent of 12 sportswriters for a five-game series with the White Sox. It was a big series, receiving more coverage in both cities than the vote. Carl Yastrzemski, who by this point in the season was the face of the Red Sox, admitted that he had never been so nervous for a series.

The two managers provided a notable contrast. While Stanky managed as if he alone could propel the White Sox to victory, Dick Williams had begun mentioning that he was trying to under-manage his team.

The first game matched up the staffs' two aces. Gary Peters was shelled for four earned runs and was pulled in the second inning. According to the box score, he had pitched poorly giving up eight singles in less than two innings pitched. Peters knew that he had pitched well. The singles had almost all been groundballs that found their way through his slow-moving infielders. Although upset that he had not led his team to victory in the first game of this big series, mentally Peters was already preparing for his next start.

Jim Lonborg pitched a complete game for the 7–1 win. Even in such a lopsided game there was controversy. With two out in the sixth and the score 6–0, Wilbur Wood knocked down Yastrzemski with each of his first three pitches. The fourth pitch was thrown behind Yastrzemski's head to the backstop. Message sent. Yastrzemski would say after the game, "[Stanky] wants to win at any cost. He'll do anything to win. And so will I."[20] After the walk Yastrzemski proved his point by coming around to score the Red Sox' final run.

Dick Williams pointedly stated that he knew Wood was not a pitcher who threw at batters on his own. Angered by the thinly veiled charge Stanky replied, "I'm not a knockdown manager."[21] This was reported in the Chicago papers with no indication of the obvious irony.

Stanky would continue to complain indignantly for the rest of the season about other pitchers—especially Lonborg who led the league—who hit batters. While fans could frequently read these assertions, they would have no idea that the White Sox as a team were well on their way to leading the league in hitting batters by an overwhelming margin.

The second game was the major league debut of White Sox starting pitcher Cisco Carlos. Carlos had spent six years in the minor leagues before his promotion to Class AAA in 1967. He had endured playing three years in Evanston. It took that team 14 hours by bus to play in Mobile; 13½ hours to reach Charlotte. Their closest competitor was a mere six-hour ride away in

Knoxville. Twice Carlos had told his wife that if he did not make the major leagues, he would retire at the end of the year. This was the second of those years. For most of his minor league career, Carlos had excellent control. In 1967 he changed his approach. Instead of aiming the ball, he just threw as hard as he could.[22]

With five games against the Red Sox in three days, the White Sox needed an extra starter and Carlos was brought up. For 6 ⅓ innings he mystified the Red Sox batters who had just pounded Peters. Stanky lifted him after a single and a sacrifice put a runner on second with one out in the seventh and the White Sox clinging to a 1–0 lead. The Red Sox would tie the game, but the White Sox won in the bottom of the ninth on a Ken Berry single off John Wyatt. As usual, Stanky was relentless looking for an edge that might lead to a run. He used 16 players, which was not unusual for the White Sox, and in this game had Berry play all three outfield positions. In the decisive ninth inning, he used a pinch-hitter, two pinch-runners (including Gary Peters), and a sacrifice bunt to set up the winning hit.

After the game, the managers sparred again. Stanky crowed that he knew the White Sox would win the second game when the Red Sox sacrificed their runner to second in the seventh inning. Ripping Williams for playing for a tie, Stanky claimed that because the Red Sox were briefly in first place Williams lost his nerve and was playing it safe. Stanky's opinion was echoed in headlines and columns across the country.[23] "Safety-first" was a pejorative used by Stanky and Al Dark throughout the season to describe other managers. In this case, it was an empty insult because Stanky had spent the season winning games by sacrificing runners. The purpose here may have been to goad Williams into having his hitters swing away. Or Stanky could have decided to create the perception that Williams was wilting under the race's pressure. Stanky's opinion was so highly regarded that his assertion about Williams was accepted as fact.

Following Lonborg's lead, the Red Sox had become known as a team that protected their hitters. They were aggressive about it. Boston writers grilled Williams about the lack of response to the White Sox pitchers throwing at his batters. Williams explained that he ordered his pitchers not to throw at the White Sox batters under any circumstances. He would not allow Eddie Stanky to fool him into allowing extra baserunners because the White Sox were so talented at turning every one of their baserunners into a run. As an experienced holler man himself, Williams felt he knew better than to allow the White Sox manager to draw him into a series of escalating reprisals that played to the White Sox strengths.[24]

Boston won the Saturday game 6–2 behind 3-for-5-with-1-RBI performances by their fourth and fifth hitters, George Scott and Reggie Smith. A switch-hitter, after a mid-season slump Smith had adopted an hourglass stance while batting left-handed. He claimed that it was based on a karate position, the Sanchin stance. This exotic configuration allowed Smith to pop his hips, a key component of Ted Williams' hitting philosophy. The effect was noticeable. Smith had 19 RBIs since the beginning of the month. Just a week earlier he had hit a home run from each side of the plate in a single game.

Smith's August had not been all triumph. At the beginning of the month with a man on second and the weak-hitting Mike Ryan on deck, Athletics manager Al Dark seemed to signal for an intentional walk. On a 2–2 count, the pitcher threw a soft pitch well outside. With Athletics catcher Phil Roof standing and signaling for another wide pitch, Smith relaxed. Pitcher Bill Stafford struck him out with a fastball down the center of the plate.[25] Williams benched Smith for the following game. Smith was perhaps the most intensely competitive player on the Red Sox. A week later playing the final game of the year in Kansas City, Smith stood at first base with the bases loaded. Jerry Adair singled to left scoring the two runners ahead of Smith. Running too aggressively, Smith sprinted around third. As he approached home, catcher Phil Roof waited, ball in hand and body blocking the plate. Smith lowered his shoulder as he continued at top speed. When Roof braced for impact, Smith jumped over him kicking the ball from his hand. Smith was safe. Roof's hand was spiked so badly during the play that he had to leave the game.[26] Dark and Roof had made Smith look silly and now he had returned the favor.

There was another, unseen, drama that played out after Saturday's game in Chicago. Carl Yastrzemski was relentless in his approach to hitting. He sent the clubhouse man to ask the White Sox if he could use the field to take some extra batting practice. He had been 1 for 4 and scored a run in the day's game but wanted to work on his swing. The clubhouse man eventually returned saying that Eddie Stanky would be using the field for infield practice, but Yastrzemski could use it when they were done. Yastrzemski sat in the dugout and watched sluggish backups purposelessly fielding grounders for about an hour before leaving. Yastrzemski went back to the clubhouse to get his pitcher. They were set up to begin when Stanky popped out of the dugout with his dog, a toy poodle named Go-Go. Stanky said that he needed to walk the dog in the outfield and only then could Yastrzemski use the field. Yastrzemski stood in the dugout fuming and glaring, while Stanky pretended to ignore him. Twenty minutes later Stanky left, graciously granting Yastrzemski the field as if bequeathing a huge favor. He hit for about 15 minutes before it became too dark to see the ball properly. While even that short amount of batting practice helped, the greatest benefit became apparent only after Yastrzemski had time to reflect on the incident. He realized that he had demonstrated that his determination was stronger than that of the hardest, most ruthless man in baseball. He entered September confident that he could impose his will on the pennant race.[27]

Stanky continued his season-long efforts to intimidate and unsettle the other American League managers. Although he did not use this tactic on Williams, Stanky often needled other managers with disparaging notes on the lineup cards. Stanky also sometimes employed a more damaging tactic. Before the first game of the series-ending doubleheader, Dick Williams walked to home plate with two lineup cards. Stanky had a reputation of changing his lineup at the last moment, forcing his opponent to continue with an unfavorable set of matchups. Young right-hander Fred Klages had been expected to start the first game of the doubleheader, with left-handed Gary Peters starting the second game. Williams felt he had to be ready in case Stanky switched them.[28]

In the fourth inning of Sunday's first game, Red Sox first baseman George Scott heard Stanky yell to Klages while pointing at Scott. Klages hit Scott on the elbow with his next pitch. Scott was furious and so was the Red Sox dugout. Even the usually levelheaded veteran Elston Howard was incensed. After the games with his emotions still strong, he told reporters, "I've never hated many people in this game, but I don't want any part of that runt and you can quote me on that, too."[29] To newspaper reporters, Stanky confirmed his complicity by irrelevantly blaming the incident on Boston's Jim Lonborg because he led the league in hit batsmen.[30]

In the fifth inning and again in the seventh, Yastrzemski hit solo home runs to make the score 4–1. The White Sox narrowed the score to 4–3. After a double and a sacrifice bunt, the White Sox were threatening with one out and the fleet Ken Berry on third in the bottom of the ninth. Stanky brought in Duane Josephson to pinch-hit for Hoyt Wilhelm. Williams countered by replacing Gary Bell with John Wyatt. The Red Sox were all well aware that this was the White Sox' strength: a late inning rally where one runner is sacrificed around the bases to score a tying or winning run. Josephson and Wyatt dueled before Josephson lofted a fly to right. Right fielder Jose Tartabull was an excellent fielder with a reputation for a below-average arm. He backed up before coming in to catch the ball. With that momentum, he let the ball fly directly to home. His throw was on line, but very high. Catcher Elston Howard leapt straight up, fully extended, and caught the ball high over his head. In a single sweeping motion he brought the ball down, directly on to the sliding Berry for the third out.

It was a beautiful and athletic play, unusual in a catcher. It appeared impossible because Berry was sliding before Howard even caught the ball. The well-positioned umpire saw Howard's left foot land directly in front of Berry's left foot as it stretched for the plate. Berry's momentum carried his slide past Howard, but his left leg bent completely under him. His foot never reached the plate.[31]

The aggressive Berry was stunned; the Red Sox ecstatic. Stanky refused to believe what had just occurred. He stormed the field and repeatedly bumped umpire Marty Springstead during his ensuing protest. Springstead later explained that he could not eject Stanky because the game was over.[32]

The next day, even with 33 games still left on the schedule, the *Boston Globe*'s Harold Kaese wrote, "At the end of the season, Howard's left foot may go down as the first left foot ever to have won a pennant for the Red Sox."[33]

During the eighth inning of the second game a Chicago fan, dressed neatly in a suit and tightly knotted tie, exacted revenge for this call. He made his way on to the field and threw a full cup of beer in Springstead's face.[34]

In that second game, Stanky started Gary Peters on only one day of rest. Incredibly, Peters entered the game confidently. He had recently told a reporter that this was the first time since the beginning of 1965 that he had not had pain in his left arm.[35] The White Sox started the game two games behind the Red Sox. Peters was determined that he would perform his best in what could be a dire situation. He threw 11 innings of shutout baseball to win 1–0.

After this heroic performance, Stanky was asked to appraise Peters' pitching. There was nothing special, Stanky insisted. Peters pitched merely as Stanky expected, nothing more. At the other end of the clubhouse, Peters said it was the most important victory of his career.[36]

Peters was not the only ace to come up big. Pitching near his hometown and in front of his parents, Dean Chance threw a no-hitter in Cleveland. Counting his rain-shortened perfect game against the Red Sox, this was his second no-hitter of the month. The victory propelled the Twins back into first place, for one day.

The standings were chaotic. In the previous week, the White Sox spent four days in first, two days in second and a day in third. The Red Sox had been in first place three separate times for a total of four days. The Twins were even more volatile: starting the week in first before falling into a tie for third. They regained sole possession of first, before losing it the next day. They ended tied for the lead with Boston.

Chapter 17

Four-Way Tie

American League standings before play on Tuesday, August 30.

	W	L	GB
Boston Red Sox	75	58	–
Minnesota Twins	73	57	½
Detroit Tigers	74	58	½
Chicago White Sox	71	59	2½
California Angels	65	65	8½
Washington Senators	63	69	11½
Cleveland Indians	63	70	12
Baltimore Orioles	58	70	14½
New York Yankees	59	73	15½
Kansas City Athletics	54	76	19½

As August turned to September, both the Tigers–Twins and the White Sox–Red Sox played a second series. For both sets of contenders, this would be the last time they would face each other during the season.

Players had already endured weeks of questions about the pressure. Boston's young first baseman George Scott described the situation best. He noted that there is pressure to succeed during every major league at-bat, regardless of the team's place in the standings. That had not changed. What was different was life away from the ballpark. For the first time, he was having trouble sleeping. Except when his adrenaline was pumping during the game, he felt constantly exhausted. He could not escape that feeling.[1]

The players were not the only ones feeling drained. The day after the Red Sox lost in 20 innings to the Yankees in the televised second game of a doubleheader, Boston Edison reported a 6 percent increase over the normal electric power usage during the last two hours of the game that ended around 2:00 a.m. The only explanation was that televisions throughout Boston had remained tuned to the game. Fans in their living rooms were not the only ones wrapped up in the game. When policemen asked the only witness to a parking-lot shooting in Boston about the time of the incident, the witness replied, "The best I can say is that there was one out in the last of the 19th inning."[2]

After finishing that seemingly endless, 29-inning doubleheader, Dick Williams told reporters he thought Yastrzemski might be tired and that he would rest him. When reporters relayed this, Yastrzemski told them that he would not let his teammates down by missing a single game during the pennant race. Reporters returned to the manager. The tough chief was surprised and invited Yastrzemski into his office. Reporters stood by in the hallway wondering how the meeting would go between the strong-willed star and the fiery manager. The two soon emerged and it was clear that there was no discord. Williams was thrilled to have the best player on his team so determined to play.[3]

Yastrzemski hit a game-winning home run in the 11th inning the next day.

Yastrzemski was much better suited to thrive under pressure than most players. He normally thought deeply about his hitting and constantly analyzed his approach to every hitting situation. The pennant race focused him with increasing intensity. He responded with the best month of his career. Players who had a more unconscious approach to the game could tighten up as the pressure caused them to begin thinking through each at-bat and fielding play.

The Red Sox arrived home after that game in New York having played 40 innings in two days. Boston was in first place, 2½ games ahead of the fourth-place White Sox. Stanky's maneuverings in the previous series had set his team up for success. He had shown the Red Sox batters that his pitchers could throw at them with no fear of reprisal. Stanky's yearlong pattern of aggressive managing had prodded Dick Williams into publicly stating that he had ordered his pitchers to avoid hitting the White Sox batters. So now heading into this critical series, his pitchers could fearlessly intimidate the Red Sox batters and his batters could crowd the plate on the Red Sox pitchers.

Even with that edge, the players had to win the game. Cisco Carlos started the series' first game and again shut down the Red Sox big bats. Stanky pulled him out of the game with a 1–0 lead in the seventh even though he had allowed just one hit. After the game Stanky defended his actions saying that he would pull his own son if he thought it would help his team win.[4] This was headline material in Boston and reported, like many of his quotable opinions, throughout the country. Many columnists shook their heads figuratively at Stanky's unorthodox tactics, which unnecessarily deprived this deserving rookie of his first major league win for the second time.

Stanky was way ahead of the pundits. For him, Carlos was a relatively fresh arm at a point in the season when all the players were exhausted. Alone of all the contenders, the White Sox had a deep bullpen—one of the major leagues' first modern bullpens. Stanky had plenty of reliable, highly effective pitchers to finish games. And he knew how to use them. Most managers expected their starters to pitch nine innings, and became disgruntled when they pitched fewer. Stanky planned to use relief pitchers.

Despite their season-long lack of power, the White Sox homered twice in the eighth inning of the first game, coming from behind to win 4–2. Pete Ward delivered the game-winning two-run home run. It was his eighth during August.

This month was a big change from his 1966 season, which had been a disaster. Early on in 1966 after a rainout, he had been driving to see the Black Hawks[5] in a Stanley Cup playoff game when his car was rear-ended. He suffered a whiplash injury, but played though the pain and immobility.[6] His poor play was frustrating, but Stanky's insistence at using him at four field positions angered him. The son of an NHL player, at one point Ward was ready to fight Stanky.[7]

Those differences had been patched up. During spring training, Ward had wielded a hot bat. He started the season as the team's cleanup hitter. Error-prone as a rookie, Ward's fielding remained a perceived liability. He played mostly in left field, often leaving for defensive replacements. His batting had floundered in May and June before he found his power stroke in mid–July. With the newcomers, Ken Boyer and Rocky Colavito, Ward now provided a solid middle to the White Sox batting order. When the three of them played, the White Sox finally had an intimidating part of their lineup.

Power hitting could not help the White Sox in the second game. The Red Sox knocked Gary Peters out by scoring seven runs in the first two innings. For the second time in three critical starts against the Red Sox, Peters felt that he had pitched well despite taking a lopsided loss. He accepted accountability. In his mind, that was part of being a leader on a major league team.

Others could describe a more complete and accurate picture. Headlines in Chicago labeled the team, "Losers."[8] They followed up on a familiar theme noting that, although there were no errors, horrible infield play led to the four first-inning runs. This included the embarrassing failure to cover second base on a successful double steal. The *Chicago Daily News* concluded that the White Sox' infield defense was "a myth."[9] Even Stanky lamented his infield's lack of range.[10]

Commentators were quick to disparage the play of shortstop Ron Hansen. On a team with a different lineup in nearly every game Hansen had been Stanky's constant. Despite his balky back and initially poor hitting, Hansen started nearly every game. Hansen had not been helped by the fact that the left side of the White Sox infield saw more groundballs than any other in the league. He had been hobbling with leg issues since the middle of August. Hansen's diminishing range was only highlighted by the arrival of the relatively immobile Ken Boyer at the end of July. Now with Boyer playing first while he tried to return from his own leg injury, Stanky tried Ward at third. While Ward may have been better than his poor fielding reputation suggested, his adventures increased the ground that Hansen was trying to cover.

Hansen was the opposite of a prima donna. He accepted that Stanky's constant scheming created an ephemeral constellation of infielders around him. Like Peters, Hansen was an even-keeled veteran capable of turning down the volume of his manager's personality and providing an anchor to younger and more effected teammates. Stanky was well aware of his value. With only a month left in the season, he singled Hansen out as the most valuable position player on the White Sox. Hansen was more than just steady. He had a fearless toughness. After Willie Horton bloodily spiked him during a game at the end of May, Hansen went after the Tigers' burly slugger.[11]

Dick Williams sent Jim Lonborg out to start the series' third game. Lonborg had thrown complete-game victories in his last two starts. Playing at home and fresh off a decisive victory, the Red Sox were confident. Joe Horlen started for the White Sox. He admitted that he had been tired and had not thrown well for five games.[12] Despite that, Horlen was the one who pitched a complete-game 4–1 victory.

For all of their perceived difficulties at the plate, the young White Sox continued to play hard, maybe too hard. On consecutive pitches yielding fly balls, rookie Walt Williams and Tommie Agee collided in the outfield as they aggressively chased down the ball. Each of them got one ball and held on for the out.

The final game that the two teams would play during the season contained many archetypal elements of White Sox games. The infield committed an error and misplayed another groundball into a single, but it did not matter. Ward continued his power surge with a 410-foot home run. Most importantly, Tommy John threw a complete game five-hitter winning 4–0. John induced 21 groundballs.

After the game, John explained to the Boston media that his manager bought a starting pitcher a new suit if he won a complete game with at least 21 groundballs regardless of whether they were outs, errors, or hits. Stanky confirmed this practice adding, "I pay the bill when he gives it to me."[13]

Neither the Red Sox fans nor Dick Williams knew what hit them. The White Sox won three of four games, knocking the Red Sox out of first place.

In their three losses, the Red Sox scored a total of only three runs. They had been averaging almost four and one half per game.

After the series' final, disappointing game Yastrzemski returned to the field for extended batting practice. Pete Ward sat in the White Sox dugout and watched.[14]

After a months-long scandal involving the frequent jamming of the Army's new M-16 rifle in the rigors of combat, the House Armed Services Committee issued the official report of its probe. It found that the Army used the wrong type of lubricating oil and gave the wrong instructions for using the oil. Compounding that, the Army had switched to a new powder that was too hot for the gun. There was improper and insufficient training on cleaning the rifle. And after this was determined, no one informed the Chief of Training that there was a problem. The Marines, in an attempt to solve the oil problem, had begun using an oil that proved corrosive.

The Tigers arrived in Minnesota having won 10 of 14. They were a game out of first and only one half-game behind the Twins. They were ready to move back into first. The whole team was peaking. Their pitchers had a 1.57 ERA in the last 14 games with five shutouts. Their sluggers were not quiet either. In almost 13 years as the home to a major league team, only nine home runs had been hit out of Kansas City's Municipal Stadium onto the adjacent Brooklyn Avenue. The Tigers hit three there during their late August visit.[15]

Perhaps emboldened by the activity in other contenders' front offices, Tigers general manager Jim Campbell purchased outfielder Don Demeter from the Indians. The Tigers would be Demeter's third team of the season. Mayo Smith claimed that Demeter would give him a good option at first base against left-handed pitchers. Both Norm Cash and Eddie Mathews batted left. It seemed a stretch. Demeter was barely batting .200. As it turned out, Demeter never played for the Tigers. After delaying his arrival because of a newly discovered pulled muscle in his chest, Demeter turned up in his hometown Oklahoma City. Contacted by Tigers pitcher Dave Wickersham by phone, Demeter promised to fly to Detroit that afternoon.[16] Three days later he sent the Tigers a report claiming that a doctor found "indications of a disturbance in his coronary artery circulation."[17] While many players dreamed of being sent from a bottom-division club to one on the brink of winning a pennant, Don Demeter had effectively retired.

Despite Detroit's optimism, Minnesota won the first two games 5–4 and 5–0. The Twins suffered a scare in the seventh inning of the second game when second baseman Rod Carew sprinted after a popped bunt attempt. He ran into the concrete edge of the dugout roof at speed and was knocked unconscious.[18] Although he was dizzy after the game, it was expected that he would play the following day.

Playing center field for the Tigers during that second game, Mickey Stanley noticed holes in the field where he wanted to take his position. They were dangerous. The last thing he wanted was to trip in one while he was chasing a fly ball. Before the next inning he scooped up some of Metropolitan Stadium's uniquely black infield dirt and filled them flush. But the next inning, the dirt was gone and the holes were back. Corralling some blowing trash, he filled them again. In the next inning, the trash was gone. Watching closely, Stanley realized that Twins center fielder Ted Uhlaender was using the holes like starting blocks to get a quick jump on fly balls.[19]

Although the outfield holes did not effect Stanley's fielding, the Tigers committed so many errors that Mayo Smith had to assure reporters that the team was not cracking under the pressure. That second loss dropped the Tigers 2 ½ games back. Suddenly there was real concern that the Tigers might be on the edge of dropping out of the race.

For the third game of the series, Smith sent his newly designated stopper Earl Wilson to the mound. In his previous start, he had taken a three-hitter into the ninth inning, but lost the game 3–2. There was no doubt about this game. He shut out the Twins 5–0 beating Dean Chance who gave up four runs in seven innings. Side-arming Fred Lasher, who was Smith's current favorite in the bullpen, had let the winning run score in Wilson's previous start. He closed this game out. The Tigers were still in fourth place, but now they were only 1 ½ games back. In contrast to the White Sox–Red Sox series, the closest managers Mayo Smith and Cal Ermer got to trading jibes was when Smith said he thought Boston was now the team to beat instead of Minnesota.[20]

The Tigers headed home to Detroit for a five-game series against the Athletics. While the Tigers players could not escape the pressure of the pennant race, many of their fans were suddenly distracted. After weeks of fruitless negotiations, the giant United Auto Workers union selected Ford as its target manufacturer. Approximately 160,000 workers stuck at 93 Ford plants in 25 states.[21] The strike with all of its attendant rituals dominated Detroit news.

Despite losing three home games to the White Sox, the Red Sox trailed the league-leading Twins by only a half-game. The White Sox stood one game behind with the Tigers in fourth, 1½ games out. The standings remained unprecedentedly stable for the next two days as first each of the contending teams split a doubleheader and then each won.

On September 6, the Twins lost and the idle Red Sox made up their half-game deficit. In a game that saw the managers deploy a total of 39 players and pitchers throw 433 pitches, the White Sox beat the Angels 3–2 in the 13th inning to gain a game. The Tigers swept a doubleheader from the Athletics, gaining 1½ games on the Twins. Earl Wilson, pitching on two days' rest, threw a complete game becoming the first pitcher to win 20 games. In the past eight days, he had started three games, pitching 22⅔ innings.

With three weeks left in the season, all four teams were tied for first place.

It was by far the latest date that four teams had been tied for the lead of the American League. The pennant race was now as tight as it could possibly get. Scrutiny of the teams and their managers would only increase, as would the perceived importance of every game.

Chapter 18

"That friggin' skinny, shallow body"

American League standings before play on Thursday, September 7.

	W	L	GB
Chicago White Sox	78	61	–
Minnesota Twins	78	61	–
Boston Red Sox	79	62	–
Detroit Tigers	79	62	–
California Angels	72	67	6
Washington Senators	66	74	12½
Cleveland Indians	65	76	14
Baltimore Orioles	62	75	15
New York Yankees	62	78	16½
Kansas City Athletics	57	82	21

The Tigers were primed for the last three weeks of the season. Al Kaline was fully healed and had regained his hitting stroke. Gates Brown a backup outfielder and feared pinch-hitter had returned from his injury. Eddie Mathews' bat was providing just the pop that the Tigers needed. Even better, starter Mickey Lolich had won four straight after losing 10 in a row.

The Detroit papers had taken many opportunities over the past couple of weeks to point out whenever the Tigers failed. In particular they referenced Eddie Stanky's quote in his *Sports Illustrated* article that the Tigers should be leading the league by 10 games.[1] It fit nicely with the frustration that Tigers fans felt at their team, which repeatedly failed to win a critical game that would send them into first place. Radio and television reporters who covered the team disparaged them as underachievers. The resulting apathy of the fans completed the circle of negative reinforcement. Players were openly disappointed with the relatively small home crowds, which did not compare well with the citywide euphoria engulfing Boston and Minnesota's twin cities.

The form and utility of veteran leadership on a baseball team is typically speculative even in hindsight. The Tigers had a veteran core that neither led nor would accept leadership. No one either on the team or reporting on it had dared to publicly address this. As the summer progressed, more and more observers agreed that Bill Freehan was becoming the most important Tigers player. Freehan was in the midst of an incredible season that had seen veterans Kaline, Norm Cash, Willie Horton, Jim Northrup, Don Wert, and even Dick McAuliffe stumble in one way or another.

Eddie Stanky repeatedly pronounced Freehan the most valuable player in the league. Like many of his opinions, this was cynically examined for a hidden agenda. Whatever Stanky's intentions, Freehan believed that his assessment was genuine. It meant a lot to Freehan that baseball's preeminent genius would give him such an accolade. No one in Detroit was prepared to dispute it, but many of the players resisted the possibility that this should translate into leadership. It was fine for the college-educated Freehan to take on the burdens of player representative to the Major League Baseball Players Association, but that position did not give him any influence in the clubhouse. While Freehan's more veteran teammates increasingly accepted that their success was now dependent on his performance on the field, it was a slowly evolving attitude with no clear-cut turning points. If there was resentment, it remained deeply buried.

Ultimately, leadership descended on the clubhouse from an outside source. Away from ballparks, the fun-loving Eddie Mathews was known for his warm personality. On the field, his fierce black eyes drilled through opponents. A burly 6'1", he had spent most of his career feared as the toughest man in the National League—a designation he earned with his fists. Dedicated to his craft, Mathews broke his nose three times just practicing his fielding. There was no ambiguity for Mathews on the baseball field. He practiced hard and played hard. Others might praise his hustle, but he believed that he just played the game.

Mathews was the only everyday player on the team who knew what it was like to win at the major league level. He had won two pennants and a World Series as one of the best players on the Braves. (Jerry Lumpe and Dick Tracewski had both won pennants and World Series as bench players, a status they still occupied.) He had initially been mystified by the Tigers' team dynamics. Within the confines of the clubhouse, the veteran players had mocked manager Mayo Smith since spring training. In late May Smith pulled a leg muscle while sprinting toward Willie Horton's crumpled figure after the slugger crashed into the outfield fence trying to make a catch. Smith hobbled around the clubhouse for weeks while his players mockingly called him Chester, after a TV character with a pronounced limp.² The continuing sniping, both within his hearing and behind his back, led some players to disregard Smith's authority. As the pennant race headed into its last month, one Tiger wrote on the clubhouse blackboard, "Let's win this in spite of Mayo."³

After less than a month with the team, Mathews had seen enough. He called a players-only team meeting. He demanded that his new teammates give Smith the respect due a major league manager.⁴ There was no open disagreement. Mathews was, in every way, too formidable. For the first time the Tigers acknowledged that there was more to this pennant race than showing up on the field at game time. Critically, Al Kaline followed Mathews' lead. Although his overt influence had been inconspicuous, after this meeting Kaline engaged with reporters as the team's star. He finally accepted that his role demanded that he do more than just play right field.

During a rare day with no game, Eddie Stanky insisted that his players report to White Sox Park. Like all players they were physically exhausted by the schedule that had them playing six doubleheaders in the past two weeks. Unlike the other contenders, the White Sox players were enduring increasingly harsh diatribes from their manager. The stress may have been getting to Stanky. Even in his press conferences, he was beginning to lose the veneer of civility.

In an attempt to lighten the mood, Gary Peters along with his road roommate Joe Horlen and Tommy John gave Stanky a bicycle for his recent birthday after a New York paper ran a story about his impoverished youth. The presentation was choreographed for the Chicago press. There was plenty of staged banter. The team went out of its way to appear loose. Peters teased groundskeeper Gene Bossard, "When are you going to start cultivating that rice paddy out there?" referring to the notoriously overwatered and overgrown infield.⁵ The *Chicago Tribune* gamely wrote, "The White Sox have had a lot of laughs this year, most of them supplied by the irrepressible trio of Peters, Horlen and John." The grim faces in the background of the story's photos belied the paper's words.⁶

In July, Stanky had had a record player installed in the White Sox clubhouse. He proclaimed it a sign that he understood modern ballplayers. While the White Sox remained in first place, its jubilant notes proclaimed their upbeat attitude. It was self-evident that a team with music in its clubhouse was loose. Now the players lacked the energy to turn it on. When it did play, its noise could not mask the players' silence.⁷ It was another sign that the players' chemistry was broken.

The two veterans acquired to propel the White Sox to the pennant had proven largely ineffective. Both were liabilities in the field and on the basepaths. Ken Boyer hit for average but was hampered by injury. Rocky Colavito was in a lengthy batting slump. He admitted as if hoping to believe his conclusion, "Pressure, yes there's pressure, but I don't let it build up past a certain point."[8]

The only position player who retained the desire to optimistically engage reporters was Tommy McCraw. He assured them, "Everybody's got more spark. More life."[9] Heading into the series with the Tigers, Stanky announced that he would bench Colavito in favor of McCraw to make his team more aggressive. As it turned out, they both started.

Stanky had enjoyed gloating at the Tigers' expense for much of the summer. Before this series he disparaged Mayo Smith's physique, "He's got a pretty big tummy for a baseball uniform."[10] Stanky reveled in stirring people up. No matter how outrageous his statements, Stanky always claimed the high moral ground. After noting that a 14-year-old had yelled, "You stink!" at him from the stands, Stanky wrote, "I told him that I had an 11-year-old son who, if he had heard him saying those things, would beat his head in.... [T]hese things disgust me mostly because it *is* a reflection on the parents. One of my greatest faults may be that I put baseball on too high a pedestal." In the next sentence, he went out of his way to lie about his age.[11]

The Tigers arrived in Chicago tied with the White Sox for third place, but only a half-game behind the leaders. Demonstrating before the game that Stanky was not the only one capable of gamesmanship, the Tigers convinced a league representative to require the White Sox grounds crew to repeatedly roll the area around home plate because of "loose sod." Stanky was furious, yelling, "This is like Russia. They come in here and dictate to you about the condition of your field."[12] With unabashed relish at the delicious irony, the *Chicago Sun-Times* added one of Stanky's gripes: "I don't like dictatorship."[13] Perhaps Stanky failed to remember the June evening in Kansas City earlier in the season. As part of his on-going rivalry with Al Dark, Stanky complained to the umpires that the baselines were too sandy. The game was delayed while the umpires required the grounds crew to remove the sand in front of home plate.[14]

In the first game, Mickey Lolich won his fifth in a row 4-1. The Tigers got only four hits, but two were solo home runs. Their other runs were unearned, the result of White Sox infield errors. The third run scored when Lolich pulled off a suicide squeeze with two strikes. Smith called for the unorthodox attempt because he considered Lolich such a good bunter.[15] Even when plays were not scored as errors, there was a constant tension that the White Sox could turn almost any groundball into a hit. After this game, *Detroit News* columnist Pete Waldmeir wrote, "Sometimes [the White Sox] infield looks like four guys playing Twister."[16]

In the second game of the series Gary Peters dominated, taking a three-hit shutout and 3-0 lead into the ninth. Veteran White Sox radio announcer

Bob Elson was already wrapping up the victory for his listeners in anticipation that Peters would quickly finish the Tigers in the top of the ninth. The Tigers, who had entered the game tied for first, seemed destined to squander their chance to stay there. Then Al Kaline singled to open the top of the ninth. Still hobbling on his bad leg, Willie Horton flied out into a strong wind. As he limped back to the Tigers dugout, Ken Berry taunted him repeatedly from the safety of the White Sox dugout.[17] Horton was seething by the time he got in the dugout. One of the few emotional players on the Tigers, Horton's anger lit a fire under his phlegmatic teammates. The next batter, Bill Freehan, hit a blistering grounder to Ron Hansen at short. Hansen misplayed it into a single with both runners safe. The tiring Peters walked Eddie Mathews, the tying run. Stanky removed Peters. Four pitchers and 40 minutes later, the Tigers walked off the field with a 7–3 win. Elson was reduced to repeating inanely, "This is unbelievable."[18]

The Tigers staged a loud, wild celebration in their clubhouse. It was almost as if they had clinched the pennant. Mayo Smith proclaimed that he had never won a bigger game in his life. Norm Cash saw the game as a turning point.[19] He had broken out of an 0 for 11 slump to knock in the winning run. The dramatic win gave Detroit confidence and momentum. Although he cautioned after the game, "We have not won the pennant with this game," Smith was convinced in his heart that this victory would lead his team to the pennant.[20] The Tigers were finally over the hump. An admiring Chicago reporter wrote, the Tigers "certainly have the unmistakable look of champions."[21]

The White Sox room was like a morgue.

If the White Sox players and their manager were feeling stress before the series, this unexpected loss made it far worse. For the entire season, Stanky had relied on his superior bullpen. The White Sox did not lose a lead in the ninth, certainly not a three-run lead. This game violated a fundamental belief. Pete Ward felt that the team was on the brink of destruction. "Things are falling apart," he muttered.[22] The next day the lead in the *Tribune* read, "The bottom fell out of the White Sox pennant drive yesterday with a sickening thud in the ninth inning."[23] It reflected the team's belief.

The series would end with a Sunday doubleheader. The Tigers were eager for the games. Finally, they had won a big game and proven to themselves that they were winners. Now they hoped to put the hated Eddie Stanky and his team out of the pennant race.

Joe Horlen would be starting the first game for the White Sox. After a successful college career at Oklahoma State and a late-season call-up, Horlen had started the 1962 season with Chicago. It did not go well. He was sent down in June with an ERA over 5.00. The next year in spring training it seemed as though his career might be over. Then in a casual bullpen session the recently retired Warren Hacker showed him how to throw a cut fastball. Almost immediately Horlen lit up the Grapefruit League. The cut fastball tailed away from right-handed batters. Horlen's sinking fastball moved in on them. It was a brutal combination. Horlen was in the majors to stay.

Late that season he was throwing between starts in the bullpen. Hoyt Wilhelm asked why he did not throw that way in a game. Horlen was at first confused because he was throwing his usual pitches. Then Wilhelm pointed out how smooth and effortless his delivery was. In games, Horlen's delivery was tight, almost cramped, as he tried to perfectly spot every pitch. In the bullpen session, he just threw the ball.[24]

The discussion was revelatory. He followed Wilhelm's advice, relinquishing the desire for great control. The following year he made 28 starts and had a 1.88 ERA. His record for the light-hitting White Sox was only 13–9. His name was rarely considered in the Cy Young race between Dean Chance and Sandy Koufax.

Even as an established major league pitcher, Horlen remained receptive. His teammate Tommy John had a reputation for fearlessly asking any pitcher about his secrets. The two of them marveled at Whitey Ford's control of his curve. So before the next game with the Yankees, John and Horlen went right up to Ford and asked him about it. Ford taught them his unorthodox grip for a smaller curve that was easily controlled. It became Horlen's secret pitch. He could throw it for a strike even when he was behind in the count.[25] Horlen also had a slider, but he abandoned that pitch early in the 1967 season. That reduced the stress on his arm and Horlen felt that his fastballs had more life as a result.[26]

Despite having an ERA of 2.44 over the three years as a starter leading up to 1967, Horlen was considered a relatively anonymous journeyman pitcher. His record in those three years was 36–35, which accounts for

Joe Horlen pitched his best during the toughest part of the pennant race. After the end of August, he started eight games and completed five, compiling an ERA of just 0.84. National Baseball Hall of Fame and Museum.

his reputation. His supporters described him as a hard-luck pitcher who might give up one home run, but end up losing 1–0.

His detractors in the Chicago papers stated that he was a loser who would pitch not quite well enough to win.[27] It was a tough argument. In 1966, Horlen had a 10–13 record with a 2.43 ERA. He did not win a single game in which he gave up more than two earned runs. He lost seven games that year when he yielded only one or two earned runs in a start. Horlen had another five starts where he completed seven or more innings, giving up two or fewer earned runs without getting a decision. (By comparison the American League pitcher of the year Jim Kaat had a 25–13 record and a 2.75 ERA. In ten of those wins he gave up more than two earned runs.)

Horlen was 30 entering the 1967 season, but still delightfully eager. This perception was reinforced by his pronounced overbite, which could make him look like an awestruck teenager in relaxed settings. When asked about his unimpressive career record of only 55–51, he replied, "I admit it's probably cost me some money in the past because they are looking for victories. But I haven't worried too much about money. I have a comfortable life. I've got a real nice home in Texas. The big thing is that I'm playing here in the major leagues."[28] It was the sentiment of a wide-eyed rookie, not a five-year veteran.

Most fans outside of Chicago knew Horlen only because of his most famous quirk. Many pitchers chewed tobacco to keep generating saliva so they could dampen their fingers for a better grip on the ball. Chewing tobacco made Horlen vomit, even the smell of it made him nauseous. Gum, the most common substitute, upset his stomach.[29] Before each game, Horlen stuck a wad of tissue inside his bottom lip. It was widely reported that, for promotional reasons, a season's supply was delivered to him each year.

Spring training in 1967 had been difficult for Horlen. New pitching coach Marv Grissom instructed Horlen to change his delivery. Grissom had him move his foot position on the rubber and modify the way that he pushed off. Additionally, Horlen was told to drop seven pounds from his 1966 playing weight.[30] As a result of the weight loss, Horlen was tired and felt lethargic. He was terrible in his early spring training starts. Everyone hit him. Then Horlen crashed on his pitching shoulder while successfully avoiding a rundown at third base during one of these essentially meaningless games.

As if these physical difficulties were not problem enough, Horlen's name was linked almost daily to trade rumors. Throughout spring training and into the season, it was obvious that the White Sox needed to trade for hitters. In contrast, they had a surplus of superior pitchers. Horlen was to be the most likely pitcher to be traded—neither as young and promising as Bruce Howard and Tommy John, nor as successful as Gary Peters. Unfortunately for White Sox management, his trade value was low and diminishing. The Orioles, who wanted Horlen, refused to trade prospect Mike Epstein for him. Epstein would not make the Orioles major league roster and was traded early in the season as part of a package deal for a pitcher with a 4.64 ERA, Pete Richert. Horlen stayed with the White Sox only because no other team valued him.

As Horlen's spring training woes continued, Stanky stopped including him on his list of probable starting pitchers. Frustrated, Horlen abandoned Grissom's coaching and returned to his own delivery. The improvement was almost immediate. In July when Stanky credited Grissom for Horlen's improved performance, Horlen contradicted him in *The Sporting News*.[31]

Horlen started the regular season on fire. By the end of June he was 9-1 with a 1.96 ERA and made the All-Star team for the first time. Before that game, Horlen was sitting at his locker in shorts and shower shoes reading the paper. A movement made him look down. Below the edge of the paper he saw a pair of shower shoes that had "Yaz" written on them. Putting down the paper, he was confronted by Carl Yastrzemski. Shaking his head for effect and with a rare toothy grin, Yastrzemski said, "You mean that friggin' skinny, shallow body has been getting me out all season?" They both laughed. It dawned on Horlen that Yastrzemski respected him as an equal. He belonged, not just with stars, but with superstars. He was not the little kid playing with big boys any longer. He replied, "Yea, and it's going to keep getting you out."[32]

Even with the added confidence, Horlen began to sag under the pressure. Stanky kept reminding his starters that they could not allow runs. No pitchers in all of baseball were pulled more quickly than the White Sox starters. The ingrained mindset for starting pitchers throughout the major leagues was that they would complete nine innings unless they pitched poorly. At some level, these early exits sent a psychological message. Horlen became so anxious that he could not sleep without taking sleeping pills at night before his starts.

If Horlen felt insecure and anxious, few noticed. Chicago columnist Bill Gleason writing after an early September game commented, "[He's] a tough-minded individual—hard-bitten describes him." He went on, "A perceptive fan once said, 'Horlen seems like a nice guy and I've heard he has a good sense of humor, but he looks like he'd kill you for a nickel.'"[33]

In the most critical game of the season for the White Sox, Horlen would be starting against Detroit's Joe Sparma. This was Sparma's first appearance against the White Sox since Stanky wrote in *Sports Illustrated*, "Sparma is one of those pitchers with a reputation: 'Stay close to him and you'll beat him.' He tends to weaken when games get tough. He did it once against us already this year. Detroit can have all the super pitching coaches in the world like Johnny Sain to help the staff, but I don't know how much Sain can help a guy like Joe Sparma."[34] At the time it appeared to be an odd attack because the day it was published Sparma shut out the powerful Twins with a four-hit complete game.

Already a 14-game winner, Sparma was primed to succeed. After a career hampered by wildness and inconsistency, pitching winter ball in Puerto Rico before the 1967 season helped him fulfill his potential. Sparma was athletic, having played quarterback for Woody Hayes at Ohio State, so his inconsistencies were believed to stem from an inability to focus or maintain his confidence.[35] Sain was the ideal coach for a physically gifted pitcher held back by the mental part of pitching.

Sparma headed into this game surrounded by a team buoyed by optimism. He had extra motivation, having spent two weeks hearing about Stanky's opinion. He came out throwing too hard—overthrowing. He started the game by yielding a hit to Tommie Agee. Two batters and a stolen base later, Sparma dropped the ball trying to make a routine out at first base. Sparma's error allowed Agee to score. Shaken, he gave up three straight hits. Mayo Smith removed him from the game. Sparma was charged with five runs in one-third of an inning.

Horlen, on the other hand, started strong. He did not allow a baserunner until he hit Bill Freehan with a pitch in the third. Uncharacteristically, Freehan swore at him all the way down the first baseline. The Tigers in the dugout were in an uproar. Stanky had publicly stated that Freehan was the one player that the Tigers could not afford to lose. The Tigers assumed that would make Freehan a target for Stanky and his pitchers. Freehan had already missed games in the season after being hit by pitches. The White Sox had hit him the day before apparently in revenge after the Tigers completed their comeback in the ninth inning. Earlier in the season the Tigers might have emotionlessly accepted this as part of the game. Now, they were furious.

Horlen was not surprised when in his next at-bat Dave Wickersham threw the first pitch at his chin. The second pitch was thrown at his chest. Horlen sprawled in the dirt to avoid it and assumed that things were now even. The third pitch came in on his legs and hit him on the inside of his right knee. For the rest of the game when he was not on the mound, Horlen paced in the dugout or runway. He was afraid that if he sat the knee would stiffen.[36]

The only other Tiger to reach base was Eddie Mathews on a Ken Boyer error. He was erased in a double play. Horlen finished his no-hitter by inducing three groundball outs in the ninth. Every no-hitter is exciting. Horlen threw this one under the immense pressure of a tight pennant race against another contender. Most importantly, he had saved the White Sox season.

In the second game of the doubleheader rookie Cisco Carlos finally got his first major league win, a shutout with help from Hoyt Wilhelm and Bob Locker. The White Sox knocked Denny McLain out of the game after one inning. Increasingly desperate to regain his team's momentum, Mayo Smith used 19 players. After being hit by Horlen's pitch, Freehan spent this game in the dugout with his arm in a sling. The Tigers who had been on top of the world the day before were now faced with the same doubts that they could not win a critical game to solidify their hold on first place.

After the games, Stanky told reporters, "The zombie is still walking."[37] Presumably because zombie was such an unfamiliar word, many papers awkwardly translated that for their readers as "The walking dead are walking again."

In anguish Smith told reporters, "September in the American League is no place for people with faint hearts."[38] That night Smith, who had quit smoking years earlier, started smoking again.[39]

The next day, White Sox general manager Ed Short gave Horlen a new contract for the 1967 season. It was $1,000 larger than his existing contract. Major league baseball strongly discouraged giving players bonuses, so this was the way to reward Horlen for his no-hitter. Horlen's catcher had been J.C. Martin, who got nothing. Horlen wrote him a check the same day he got his new contract.[40]

In the weeks surrounding this series, columnists in the Chicago papers felt it necessary to rebuke fans for their low level of support for the White Sox. Even writers reliably antagonistic to Stanky and Short proclaimed their embarrassment at the low attendance figures in the middle of the most exciting pennant race in memory.[41] Bill Gleason wrote more succinctly than most, "The fans don't deserve this gutsiest [White] Sox team." "The only word is disgraceful." "[The fans] stink."[42]

Chapter 19

"A well-mannered colored boy"

American League standings before play on Monday, September 11.

	W	L	GB
Minnesota Twins	82	62	–
Boston Red Sox	82	63	½
Chicago White Sox	80	63	1½
Detroit Tigers	81	64	1½
California Angels	73	69	8
Washington Senators	68	75	13½
Cleveland Indians	67	78	15½
Baltimore Orioles	63	79	18
New York Yankees	63	81	19
Kansas City Athletics	59	84	22½

Coming off their decisive doubleheader win over the Tigers, the White Sox lost a home game to the Orioles in front of only 4,048 fans. Pete Ward spoke for many of his teammates when he complained, "For a while I thought we were playing an intrasquad game before a roaring throng like that."[1]

On Tuesday they opened a home series with Cleveland in a lightly attended doubleheader. They lost both games.

Just that quickly they were three full games out of first place and had fallen out of the pennant race. With only 16 games left, it seemed impossible that they could catch and pass the other three teams. Wednesday papers throughout the country began carrying the White Sox' obituary. They sounded a similar theme.

When the White Sox stumbled at the end of August, Eddie Stanky held his most explosive press conference. Amidst score settling with a long list of enemies both real and perceived, Stanky indulged in the theatrics that made him the most quotable man in baseball. He announced, "We are last in homers.

We're last in hitting and we're last in war and peace. But, we're first in guts and determination."² Two weeks later, after the losses to the Indians, Stanky became the one with the determination for taking a team of such underperforming players so far.³ Mixed with evident relief at his imminent departure from the pennant race, some touted him for manager of the year.

As if Detroit fans needed any extra bad news after the Sunday doubleheader loss to the White Sox, they were greeted by headlines on Tuesday proclaiming, "Mathews Falls.... Will Miss Orioles."⁴ On the night after the losses to the White Sox and with a day off on Monday, Mathews had traveled to his home in Milwaukee. In the sort of freakish accident that targets baseball players, he tripped and fell down a set of 12 stairs. It was variously reported that he suffered from a bruised hip, or forehead, or possibly damaged ligaments in his right thumb. He flew to Detroit early Monday morning and went to see a doctor at the Detroit Osteopathic Hospital. He was still in the hospital on Thursday, reportedly with a bruised thumb.⁵

There was no speculation in Detroit that it was odd for an athlete to spend four days in a hospital bed because of a bruised thumb.

Although missing from newspaper descriptions of the accident and its aftermath, Mathews had a long-established reputation as a heavy drinker. In the face of skepticism about his story, Mathews declared authoritatively and presumably from personal experience, "If I'd been drinking, I'd have been loose and wouldn't have gotten hurt."⁶ Mathews would pinch-hit and pop out in Friday's ninth-inning win over the Senators.

The Twins started the week having been in first place for 10 days and facing the second-division Senators. They were in the middle of a fortuitous, two-week road trip. In their absence from the daily Minnesota papers, the team's latest controversy had finally wound down. It started when unnamed players complained to reporters that Griffith was not committed to winning. They pointed out that other contenders had added stars to their rosters: Elston Howard, Rocky Colavito, Ken Boyer, Eddie Mathews, and Ken Harrelson. Griffith had done nothing.

When Griffith responded that he felt he had a team that did not need to be upgraded, players groused that the salaries of all the players on the Twins bench combined were less than Colavito's.⁷ The tit for tat continued even after Griffith insisted that the Twins had the largest payroll in the American League. It was an unlikely claim that no one, including the parsimonious Griffith, could confirm or disprove.

The Twins' weaknesses and strengths were on display in the opening game against the Senators. Three infield errors in the first inning led to five unearned runs and a 5–2 deficit. Dean Chance was lifted for a pinch-hitter after pitching just three innings. Behind seven doubles, the Twins went on to win 13–5. After the game, Ermer announced that Chance would be available for long relief in the next couple of games because of his short outing.[8]

The result confirmed the widely held belief that the Twins had powerful hitting and dominant pitching (Chance and Jim Perry had yielded no earned runs in the 13–5 victory), but their infield fielding was suspect. Their four starting pitchers were arguably the best staff in the league. As a team they had given up fewer runs than any other, except the White Sox. Offensively, they were the most balanced of the contenders. The heart of the batting order—Killebrew, Oliva, and Allison—was loaded with power. All three players were in the top ten in slugging percentage. While the power scared opposing pitchers, fielders were kept off-balance by the Twins' baserunning. The aggressive tactics leveraged each individual's speed. Entering the season's last two weeks, the Twins were the only contender that could take the field every day expecting to win with both their pitching and their hitting.

Before the game the next day, Cal Ermer finally lost his patience with the continual controversies plaguing his team. His declared target was the Washington writer who had claimed in the morning paper that there was dissension in the Twins clubhouse. Having vented his displeasure on an outsider, Ermer tried to sound reasonable by simply desiring 100 percent effort from his players. Jarringly, this implied that some of his players might be giving less than 100 percent in the midst of this pennant race. As he continued, Ermer seemed to be pleading when he added that harmony and unity in his clubhouse were all he wanted.[9]

Jim Merritt started for the Twins in the second game of the series. In his third major league season, and first season as a full-time starter, Merritt had been a pleasant surprise. The lefthander entered the game with an ERA of only 2.37. He had completed three of his previous four starts.

But even with the Twins expanded pitching rotation during August, he was beginning to feel worn down. At 6'3", he had a thin frame that had carried 200 pounds when the team left spring training. He had lost 20 pounds since then. His increasingly gaunt face made him look almost emaciated. Even his thin black mustache looked exhausted. Merritt was convinced that his fastball had lost some of its zip during the past couple of starts and he blamed the weight loss.[10]

Merritt's pitching success was based on his control and he had not lost that. He compensated for diminished speed by keeping all of his pitches at the bottom of, or below, the strike zone.

Like Joe Horlen, Merritt was quiet with the press and had an unassuming demeanor. Despite superior statistics, he was never considered as the equal of the Twins' two big starters, Chance and Jim Kaat. Even the more flamboyant fourth starter, Dave "Bullet" Boswell, whose ERA spent most of the season a full run higher than Merritt's inspired more confidence from the Twins fans.

Merritt's game against the Senators was a disappointment. Ermer lifted him for a pinch-hitter after six innings with the Twins trailing 4–1. The Twins eventually lost the game 5–4, after Frank Howard blasted an Al Worthington pitch for his 34th home run. Beat writers and columnists in the twin cities blamed the loss on over-aggressive baserunning by Zoilo Versalles that turned a seventh-inning double into an easy out at third.[11] Versalles had become their favorite scapegoat.

The following day, Billy Martin took the blame for Versalles' baserunning gaffe, explaining that he had been exhorting Versalles to take more chances on the bases.[12] During the same press session the club announced that Martin would be in St. Louis scouting the Cardinals during the Twins' critical upcoming series in Chicago.

This was not a surprise to the team's fans. Martin did not go to any of the Twins' games in Chicago during the 1967 season. What the newspapers referred to as his "legal problems," were really his ongoing attempts to avoid paying damages stemming from a baseball brawl in Chicago in 1960 when he stormed the mound and sucker punched rookie pitcher Jim Brewer breaking his jaw.[13] The initial award by a judge of $100,000 had been reduced to $35,000.[14] Now Martin hoped for a retrial. Martin was not the only one in the American League whose travel schedule was modified to avoid certain legal jurisdictions. Athletics shortstop Bert Campaneris never traveled to California to play the Angels in 1967. He was avoiding an attempt to serve him with papers in a patrimony suit.[15]

It was another week of unceasing pressure on the teams and their players. Players and fans of all four teams read the experts describing the demise of the White Sox, which resulted from no more than losing a doubleheader. Throughout the middle of the week, the Twins and Red Sox remained tied for the lead with the Tigers one game behind.

In Chicago on Wednesday, Stanky started Gary Peters in a must-win game against the Indians. Peters threw 180 pitches over 11 innings of a one-hit shutout. The White Sox finally won 1–0 in the 17th inning on Rocky Colavito's RBI single. It was the longest 1–0 game in American League history.

With that game, the three frontline White Sox starters possessed the three best ERAs in the league: Horlen at 2.20, John at 2.33, and Peters at 2.36. The White Sox got another extra-inning shutout from their pitchers the following day and prepared to welcome the Twins for a critical series having thrown 27 consecutive shutout innings.

With the pennant race remaining persistently tight, virtually everyone in baseball was asked for his prediction of a winner. American League players on teams not directly in the race were more eager to describe the team they wanted to win. Not surprisingly, the White Sox were the least liked team. A large number of players picked the Red Sox.[16] Many cited their hope that popular owner Tom Yawkey would finally win a World Series.

Tigers TV announcer George Kell noted, "It seems that the Boston Red Sox have been adopted across the country as the sentimental favorite. As one man put it, they seem to want it the most."[17] Yankee Joe Pepitone, who had no reason to like the Red Sox after he was injured in a June brawl, had a different perspective. He told reporters that he felt that the Red Sox had a perfect attitude. In what may have been a jab at the White Sox, he claimed that they constantly hustled, but from a desire to win rather than from fear. A six-year veteran, Pepitone had never played against a better all-around player than Carl Yastrzemski. In Pepitone's opinion, the Red Sox deserved to win.[18]

Not everyone in New York felt the same way. Baseball great Jackie Robinson had recently taken a job as New York governor Nelson Rockefeller's special assistant for community affairs. That took him around the state for frequent speeches. On more than one occasion he was asked for his preferences in the tight pennant race. He stated that he did not like the Red Sox. "I'd like to see them lose because [owner Tom Yawkey] is probably one of the most bigoted guys in baseball." He preferred the Twins and believed that they would win because of their talent. His comments were widely and frequently reported. There was no controversy associated with his remarks, even in Boston.[19]

The Red Sox had been the last team in the major leagues to integrate. In 1959 Pumpsie Green, an African American prospect who hit .400 in spring training, was selected for the team by general manager Bucky Harris. Manager Pinky Higgins went to Yawkey and had the decision overturned. Higgins was widely quoted, "There'll be no niggers on this ball club as long as I have anything to say about it."[20] To fans in Boston, he was doing little more than expressing Yawkey's and the team's long-standing attitude. This was, after all, the team that had refused to extend contract offers to Robinson, Willie Mays and Sam Jethroe, a future American League rookie of the year.[21]

After Pinky Higgins was fired part way into the season and Green was named to his second Class AAA All-Star team, he was finally promoted. More than 12 years after Robinson's debut with the Dodgers, there was still some unspoken tension on the Red Sox. This was smoothed over in the clubhouse at least because the team's star, Ted Williams, specifically warmed up with Green before every game.[22]

A week later black pitcher Earl Wilson was also promoted. While Green never projected as much more than a utility infielder who made sense for a

Red Sox team with a liability at shortstop, Wilson had star potential. He had been converted from catcher in the minor leagues and had that rare commodity—a fastball with lots of natural movement. He was 6'3" and powerful. More importantly he was driven by an unrelenting work ethic. The only thing holding his career back was wildness. His pitches had too much movement and Wilson too little control. His solution was to throw every pitch at the middle of the plate.[23]

His career with the Red Sox did not start well. The organization leaked a humiliating portion of their scouting report on Wilson. It stated in part, "He is a well-mannered colored boy, not too black."[24] To some this seemed to confirm that the Red Sox had a racist mindset. Reinforcing this perception, Yawkey brought back

Earl Wilson became the Tigers' staff ace in 1967, pitching injured and sick during the final two weeks. He tied for the league lead with 22 wins and led the Tigers in innings pitched and strikeouts. National Baseball Hall of Fame and Museum.

the openly racist, alcoholic and relatively unsuccessful Pinky Higgins as manager part way through the 1960 season. Higgins was then promoted by Yawkey and served as general manager of the Red Sox from 1960 until he was fired in September 1965 with the Red Sox suffering their first 100-loss season since 1932, the season before Yawkey bought the team. It is probably not a coincidence that these years were the team's nadir during Yawkey's long ownership.

After a year back in the minors in 1961, Wilson returned to the Red Sox as a full-time starter on their awful teams of the mid–1960s. He threw a no-hitter in 1962. Yawkey publicly rewarded him with a $1,000 bonus.

Through the 1960s the Red Sox had a variety of unwritten quotas for black players. There were always an even number of blacks on the team for road trips, so no white player would have to room with a black. The roster never had more than four blacks, so that a manager would not have the opportunity of putting a team on the field where blacks outnumbered whites.[25]

Wilson was the Red Sox' MVP in 1965 and arrived at spring training convinced that 1966 would be his breakout season. During spring training he went out to a local Florida bar called Cloud Nine with two white teammates, pitchers Dave Morehead and Dennis Bennett. (Bennett was a wild character, well known for carrying multiple handguns with him on road trips. One evening he argued with his roommate about who would get out of bed to turn off the hotel room light. The argument escalated until Bennett pulled out one of his guns. It was a tense moment. He pulled the trigger and shot out the light bulb ending the need for further discussion.[26]) The bartender took Bennett's and Morehead's orders, but refused Wilson saying, "We don't serve niggers here." The three players left.[27]

Wilson had a starting pitcher's mentality; he was aggressive to the point of fierceness on the mound. Wilson could let his temper go, too. Once he attempted to rip the Red Sox' clubhouse door off its hinges and destroy it with his bare hands. In Wilson's early years Dick Stuart, a veteran slugger, played first base. Nicknamed "Dr. Strangeglove" for his epic ineptitude in the field, in one game Stuart's misplays cost Wilson a late-inning lead. From the mound, Wilson let Stuart have it with what was termed "very blue language." Well aware that he deserved the rebukes, Stuart took it and the two remained friendly.[28]

Off the mound, Wilson handled himself at all times with dignity. After the Cloud Nine episode, he went to the Red Sox asking them to support him. Manager Billy Herman told him any acknowledgment would embarrass the organization. Herman claimed that Wilson was a troublemaker for putting himself in a situation of being denied service. He was forbidden to mention the incident to the press. After this response, Wilson knew his days on the Red Sox were limited.

In June 1966, the Red Sox traded for black players John Wyatt and Jose Tartabull. With that addition, there were six blacks on the roster. Two days later, Wilson and African American outfielder Joe Christopher were traded to the Tigers for the well-traveled, and white, Don Demeter. It was immediately recognized as a lopsided trade.[29] Even though the Tigers outfield was decimated by injuries to Al Kaline and Mickey Stanley, Demeter was batting around .200 and could not stay in the starting lineup. Despite hitting as a pitcher, Wilson would go on to collect almost as many home runs and RBIs as Demeter.

Immediately after the trade, Sal Maglie denigrated Wilson as merely a .500 pitcher. Wilson replied that he had always played on a sub-.500 team.[30] Proving Maglie wrong, over the last two and a half months of the Tigers' turbulent 1966 season Wilson went 13-6. Along with his success came the worsening of chronic back pain. Doctors in Detroit examined Wilson and discovered that his left leg was two inches shorter than his right leg. Wilson finished the season with a two-inch lift in his left shoe when he played. For 1967, he reduced the lift's thickness to only one inch.[31]

Spring training in 1967 was not quite as smooth for Wilson. The Tigers' new pitching coach, Johnny Sain, was entirely different from the coaches Wilson had experienced with the Red Sox.

Sain pitched in the late 1940s and 1950s. In 1947 he won 21 games and batted .346, possibly the highest batting average of any 20-game winner. In four different seasons he won 20 or more games, relying on an outstanding curve. He had a reputation as a workhorse, one year starting 39 games and pitching over 300 innings. After concluding his career, Sain spent one year as pitching coach for the woeful Kansas City Athletics in 1959. Two years later, Ralph Houk hired him before his first full year as manager of the Yankees. Legendary Yankees pitching coach Jim Turner had left only a year earlier. Turner was in one way the most successful pitching coach ever. In 11 years his pitchers led the Yankees to an unprecedented run of nine pennants and seven World Series titles. Turner's primary function had been to monitor pitchers while they warmed up and alert manager Casey Stengel if they were not at their best.

Sain's approach could not have been more different. He was the first person to chart every pitch.[32] Unlike everyone else in baseball who acted on accepted wisdom, Sain conducted ballistics tests to understand exactly what effected baseballs.[33] Already in the early 1960s Sain believed that the orthodox nine-inning start was doomed. He expected a team would typically deploy three pitchers each game. This would help save the pitchers' arms and prevent batters from becoming acclimated to one pitcher.

Sain was also brilliant at explaining technique to pitchers. Pitchers on most teams would just throw to warm up or between starts. Sain made them consistently practice perfect body control. Every throw had to be the same. It was an unusual mental strain that pitchers initially resisted.[34]

Most pitching coaches including Turner adopted the practice of having pitchers jog in the outfield. Sain famously disdained running for his pitchers. He claimed, "The reason pitching coaches run their pitchers is that they don't have a lot to tell them about pitching."[35]

Instead, Sain spent his time working on his pitchers' mental attitude and approach to each game. According to Bill Freehan, Sain insisted that his pitchers organize their minds to have their skills and strategies clearly in focus.[36] Sain adamantly believed that his main job was to keep each pitcher's confidence at its peak. While he demanded more than other pitching coaches, Sain also created more. He was loyal to his pitchers and had a knack for making the game fun even while he extracted maximum performance. Before he arrived in Detroit, his pitching staffs had formed an unusually tight clique within the team. Unlike many coaches who only associated with success, Sain had the self-restraint to leave his pitchers alone when they were doing well. But when they hit a rough spot, they knew that he would give them the support that they needed.[37]

Sain's approach was radical and therefore, not surprisingly, suspect. As the pennant race heated up in August, Billy Martin went out of his way to decry Sain's methods. After noting that Sain would be sympathetic with his pitchers after a loss, Martin proclaimed, "You're not supposed to feel good after a loss. You're supposed to think about a loss."[38] By contrast to Sain's practices, in 1967 Twins coaches did not give players alibis.

With Sain as his pitching coach, Houk's Yankees won three pennants and two World Series in three years. Hall of Famer Whitey Ford had his only 20-win seasons, as did Ralph Terry and Jim Bouton.

This success did not come without problems.

Sain was incapable of hiding the fact that he knew much more about pitchers and pitching than his managers. In short, he was difficult for managers and general managers to work with. After three years, the Yankees decided not to rehire him. In 1965, the cycle started all over again in Minnesota. His pitchers had career years, the team won a pennant and he was fired after two seasons.

In 1967 Sain brought his expertise to the Tigers. With the exception of Wilson, the staff was stocked with young, talented starting pitchers incapable of consistently harnessing their abilities. Spring training had required adjustment for all the pitchers. Wilson was the only reliably good pitcher during spring training, but manager Mayo Smith publicly considered only three white pitchers as the Opening Day pitcher. Neither Wilson nor Sain were wallflowers and Wilson mentioned Smith's oversight to the press.[39] Part of Smith's genius as a manager was his ability to appear oblivious to tension and controversy. Denny McLain started, and lost, on Opening Day.

Wilson started and won the home opener seven days later. After the game Wilson was asked about the pitch Jimmie Hall drove to Tiger Stadium's third deck. "That was a rising fastball. It kept rising 60 feet above the field out there." A reporter replied, "It's 90 feet to the third deck." Wilson did not miss a beat: "It was rising better than I thought."[40] Wilson was no grim warrior. He had a personality that teammates could gravitate toward.

The Tigers season had not been smooth for Sain's pitching staff. The starters continued their uneven performance. By mid–August, there was speculation that Sain would be fired after the season. One of his starting pitchers led the league in giving up home runs and another was mired in a 10-game losing streak. None of the four primary starters had an ERA under 3.00. That speculation died as the Tigers continued to win close games in September.

Mayo Smith, though, followed the lead of other managers who were insecure enough to feel threatened by Sain. When Sain was not at the ballpark, he secretly countermanded Sain's practices and workout schedules for the pitchers.[41]

The Tigers started their weekend series with the faltering Senators on

Friday, September 15. Joe Sparma started and lasted only a little longer than he had against the White Sox. He departed in the second inning having already yielded three runs. It took six Tigers pitchers to hold off the Senators.

Becoming the first Tigers catcher ever to hit 20 home runs in a season, Freehan tied the game with a three-run home run in the eighth. Willie Horton singled in the winning run in the bottom of the ninth for a 5–4 win. It vaulted the Tigers into a first place tie with the Red Sox, who lost to the Orioles, and the Twins who were whipped 7–3 by Joe Horlen and the White Sox.

With only two weeks left in the season, three teams were tied for first. The White Sox who were counted out of the race earlier in the week lurked only 1½ games back. Although it was still a four-team pennant race, the teams' uneven performance did not impress everyone. Bill Veeck wrote disparagingly, "It's impossible to figure whether there are four 4th place clubs struggling for a pennant or four pennant contenders struggling to finish 4th."[42]

The Twins visit to Chicago for a weekend series was the first time the teams had met since the beginning of August. The Twins, who always had small dissensions bubbling to the surface, had not been spared in Eddie Stanky's August *Sports Illustrated* offering. Somewhat innocuously, Stanky had claimed that utility player Cesar Tovar was the most valuable player on the Twins, specifically better than Harmon Killebrew, Bob Allison, Zoilo Versalles, and third baseman Rich Rollins.[43] Team MVP was an award of little interest to veterans Killebrew and Allison. (Although, later in the tension-packed month during a road trip to Kansas City Allison would travel to Raytown, Missouri, his hometown, to accept a key to the city. He also had time to receive an award as one of the ten best-groomed men in Minnesota from the Association of Master Barbers and Beauticians of Minnesota.[44])

Rollins' addition to the list could only be described as odd because he was below average as a third baseman whose hitting was in decline. Conveniently for Cal Ermer, Rollins had gone into a severe batting slump soon after the piece appeared. Tovar was now the regular third baseman. That source of friction was gone. Unlike Versalles, there was nothing in Rollins' reputation that made him likely to fuel a controversy.

Versalles was the tender spot for the Twins. He was struggling with a .210 batting average, but acting like he was still the league's MVP. A prickly teammate even in the best of times, Versalles was already a divisive character in the Twins organization. In 1965 he had been the team's spark. Now he was isolated, frequently portrayed as underperforming if not selfish.

Ermer had benched Versalles a number of times after poor decisions in the field or on the basepaths. After the last benching, Versalles went to Cal Griffith and complained that his production was hurt because he was a humiliating eighth in the batting order. Griffith reportedly clashed with Ermer, requiring him to reinstate Versalles and use him as the leadoff batter.[45]

When asked about his return to the top of the batting order, Versalles explained the situation: "It's like Hubert Humphrey and Lyndon Johnson. What LBJ tells Humphrey to do, he does."[46] Like other interventions by Griffith, this undermined Ermer's authority and promoted the feeling among other players that Versalles received special treatment.

Ermer benched Versalles for motivation, not as a long-term solution. He agreed with Griffith that Versalles' fielding was essential to the Twins success. Although Tovar was more popular with his teammates, he had demonstrated that he could barely field the shortstop position.[47] His poor base-running judgment and lack of focus in the field drove Billy Martin and Cal Ermer crazy. Versalles made mistakes on the basepaths, too and was leading the league in errors. Compared to Tovar, his failures were more spectacular and always figured prominently in newspaper accounts. While an official error looked bad to the fans, Griffith, Ermer and his coaches realized that many balls went past Tovar for hits that Versalles would have fielded for outs.

Stanky's elevation of Tovar to team MVP had some interesting consequences. Not surprisingly, it became immediate fodder for echoing columns in the metropolitan Minnesota papers. Within a couple of weeks though, columnists around the country were proclaiming that Tovar was the only indispensable player on the Twins. By the time the Twins arrived in Chicago, the rhetoric had ratcheted up to a much higher level. A Minnesota columnist declared that the *league* MVP should be either Tovar or Killebrew.[48] While this might have been a lot of empty speculation outside of the clubhouse, a week later his teammates would vote Tovar as the team's MVP.

In the second game of the Minnesota–Chicago series, Dean Chance started for the Twins against Tommy John. Chance was masterful and entered the ninth leading 4–1. He gave up consecutive singles, with a runner advancing to third on Tony Oliva's error.

Oliva was still feeling the effects of a horrific collision with the outfield fence in Washington only three days earlier. He had severely cut his face and hurt both knees so badly that he had been carted from the field. He still bore the stitches under his eye and walked like a man trying to simultaneously limp on both legs. Oliva was tough. There was little or no thought of waiting to heal from these injuries. He was in the starting lineup the day after the collision, arriving at the ballpark directly from the hospital. That was the Oliva's second full-speed collision with an outfield wall in 1967. He had missed one game in June after catching a Max Alvis fly in Cleveland while piling into the wall.

After the error, with runners on first and third and no outs Chance faced

Rocky Colavito. He was mired in a hitting slump, but still had three RBIs in his last four games. Chance threw him his sinking fastball. Colavito hit what appeared to be a double play groundball to Tovar at third. Tovar missed it completely, allowing a run to score and Colavito to reach first safely. Instead of two outs, the score was now 4–2 with two baserunners and still no outs.

The next batter attempted a sacrifice bunt. Chance threw the ball away to load the bases. A few days earlier, Ermer had successfully used Chance to relieve Jim Kaat in the ninth inning. Now he reversed the roles and brought Kaat in from the bullpen. Although he had already started 38 games in 1967, this would be his fourth relief appearance. Kaat threw a wild pitch to allow a run to score and the runners to advance. On the next pitch, Wayne Causey hit a sacrifice fly to tie the game. The Kaat-as-reliever experiment having failed, Ermer replaced him with Al Worthington. He intentionally walked the bases full and then pitched to Pete Ward who was in an 0 for 22 slump. Ward won the game for the White Sox with a hit that bounced off Harmon Killebrew's glove and into right field.

In Boston, the Orioles took a second consecutive game from the Red Sox defeating Jim Lonborg 4–1. Lonborg hit the first batter that he faced in the seventh inning with the score tied 1–1. He was furious that Dick Williams came to the mound and replaced him with John Wyatt. Wyatt allowed the winning runs to score on Boog Powell's three-run home run. Lonborg had thrown 163 pitches when he left the game. Like many players, Lonborg could not get over a tired feeling except when he was playing; he had lost more than 20 pounds since the beginning of the season.

That same day Earl Wilson took the mound in Tiger Stadium. On his second pitch of the game, Ed Stroud lined the ball off his pitching shoulder. It bounced in the air to Dick McAuliffe who caught it for the out. In the fourth inning, Wilson knocked in a run with a single. McAuliffe was the next batter and hit a groundball to the second baseman. Sliding hard into second to break up the double play, Wilson ended up with a bloody right knee and a spiked left ankle where the shortstop landed on him. He continued pitching into the eighth inning and departed with the Tigers ahead 5–2. When it came to pitching in pressure situations, Wilson was both mentally and physically tough. With the win, Wilson became the first major league pitcher in 1967 to win 21 games.

The Tigers stood alone in first place for the first time since early June. In the strange context of this pennant race, the full game lead was suddenly dominating.

Chapter 20

"Too big for us"

American League standings before play on Monday, September 18.

	W	L	GB
Detroit Tigers	85	65	–
Chicago White Sox	85	66	½
Boston Red Sox	84	66	1
Minnesota Twins	84	66	1
California Angels	77	71	7
Washington Senators	70	79	14½
Cleveland Indians	71	81	15
Baltimore Orioles	67	81	17
New York Yankees	66	84	19
Kansas City Athletics	59	89	25

Having watched his team fall apart behind their ace the day before, Cal Ermer tried a new tactic with the Twins. Before the final game of their series in Chicago he gave the team a pre-game fight talk, just like a football coach.[1] It did not work. The White Sox beat them 4–0 behind Gary Peters. The Twins managed only four hits, two each by Tony Oliva and Rod Carew. Almost as disappointing, another two unearned runs scored on errors by Rich Rollins and Carew.

The weekend sweep of the Twins allowed the White Sox to creep within a half-game of the league-leading Tigers who lost the last game of their series with the Senators 5–0. The Red Sox were swept at home by the Orioles who won all three games convincingly. Even after their disastrous weekends, the Twins and Red Sox were tied only one game behind the Tigers.

Each team was scrutinized for tiny differences that might lead to success or failure in this crucible of pressure. Dick Williams was believed to be the most relaxed of the managers. After a game where Ken Harrelson's early error led to a critical run in a loss, Harrelson sat head down in the despondent locker room. The other players sat somberly at their lockers. Williams' cleats clattered slowly across the concrete floor as he walked toward Harrelson. Harrelson braced for the well-deserved tongue-lashing. Williams stopped short, reached into the cooler and extracted a beer. He took a long, long drink. The beer glugged loudly as it poured out of the can and down his thirsty throat. There was not another sound in the room. Williams yelled, "Fuck it!" More quietly he added, "It's just another game. We'll get them tomorrow." Harrelson would have followed Williams through fire after that.[2]

The Twins left Chicago for two games in Kansas City, the last stop on their long road trip. Jim Kaat threw a 10-inning shutout to win the first game. Dave Boswell followed with a complete-game 8–2 win. Just that quickly, the Twins were back in first place and headed for an eight-game home stand.

Twins management ordered new uniforms to be worn if they made the World Series. Because the noticeable effects of weight gain, and more commonly excessive weight loss, were so widespread, tailors were brought in to re-measure every player.[3]

The White Sox flew to Anaheim. The first game of the series followed a familiar script. The Angels scored first after an error led to an unearned run. They took a 2–0 lead on Cisco Carlos before the White Sox came back to score two unearned runs in the eighth with Eddie Stanky employing a flood of substitutions: two pinch-runners and three pinch-hitters. The Angels spoiled the script, winning 3–2 on Rick Reichardt's RBI single in the bottom of the ninth inning.

Fans in all of the contending cities were concerned with the game's outcome. There was virtually no way for fans who did not have access to radio broadcasts of a specific game to find out results in real time. With a little luck and some patience, fans in Minnesota and Detroit might be able to find the 50,000-watt AM signal of Chicago's WMAQ. Fans in Boston could not count on that. Some called their local newspaper. The *Boston Globe* received over 40 calls between 1:00 and 3:00 a.m. early Tuesday morning asking for the status or result of this White Sox game on the West Coast.[4]

The rest of the series went the White Sox' way. Joe Horlen threw a complete game shutout to win 3–0. In the last game, Tommy John and Bob Locker held on to win 6–4. First baseman Tommy McCraw told reporters that the victories showed that the White Sox could "smell the money now."[5] World Series money, an obsession over these last few weeks, could more than double many players' regular season salary.

The inhabitants of Boston had lost almost all sense of perspective when it came to baseball. Even though Fenway Park was not filled for every game, the Red Sox dominated all facets of life. Nothing captured this better than a possibly apocryphal account that was often repeated during the season's final weeks. The city was built on a peninsula jutting into its harbor. While centuries of landfill obscured the original landform, egress to the northern suburbs was still blocked by harbor waters. A highway bridge and a long, two-lane tunnel were the only ways for thousands of commuters to pour out of the city after each workday. While traffic was typically awful, it was made much worse one day by a fan listening to the end of a game on his car radio. With Carl Yastrzemski at-bat in the bottom of the ninth, the man refused to enter the tunnel where he would lose radio reception for long minutes in the slow-moving traffic. He stopped his car. Other cars were blocked creating cascading gridlock back into the city center while he raptly listened to the broadcast.[6]

This attentive devotion led to intense scrutiny in the city's sports pages; 23 media members accompanied the team to Detroit. On his way out of town, Red Sox manager Dick Williams told reporters that his team might benefit from playing away from the pressures of Fenway Park.[7] This would provide grist for the mill of speculation that the Red Sox were choking. Williams clarified that his players were just pressing, but not afraid. There was little doubt that the Red Sox hitters would have to get hot. The Sox lack of pitching depth was obvious when they started late-season call-up Jerry Stephenson against the Tigers' Denny McLain in what was clearly a critical game.

Stephenson had not pitched for two weeks. Before he entered the game, the Red Sox had already pounded McLain for three runs in the top of the first. After the Tigers rallied in the bottom of the second inning to tie the game, McLain walked the first batter in the top of the third. Yastrzemski singled to right, his second hit of the game. Mayo Smith, nervous that McLain would again let the game slip away, went straight to the mound. He pulled McLain who furiously stomped through the dugout and into the locker room. The sound of him venting his frustration by kicking lockers echoed back to the dugout.

The Tigers came back to tie the Red Sox 4-4 in the sixth and then took the lead in the bottom of the eighth. Tigers reliever Fred Lasher had already pitched the eighth and he struck out Mike Andrews to start the top of the ninth inning. Lasher was a sidearm pitcher who threw almost underhanded. He entered the game with a 2.08 ERA.

The next batter was Yastrzemski. He came to the plate determined to wait for a fastball and then swing for the fences. Lasher threw what he later disgustedly called "a lollipop pitch" and it landed in the second deck of Tiger Stadium.[8] It was the first major league home run hit off Lasher. The game was tied. Backup third baseman Dalton Jones capped a 4 for 5 day by winning the game for the Red Sox with a solo home run in the tenth. After the game, Norm Cash who had hit two home runs in the losing effort confided, "That game was a crusher. We came back, went ahead, and lost it."[9] A despondent Kaline added admiringly, "Yaz is too big for us."[10]

Newspapers in Boston had been calling their team the "Comeback Kids" or more recently the "Cardiac Kids" after every late inning win for over a month. By now music stations in Boston were playing recordings of the show tune "The Impossible Dream" in a regular rotation, almost regardless of their format. While it had originally applied to a surprisingly successful game, now the dream it described was loftier: the American League pennant.

Carl Yastrzemski seemed like he could make the dream come true. Just 28, Yastrzemski was the rare player in any sport who took over from a superstar and held his own. In 1958, Yastrzemski had been the prize in a multi-team high stakes bidding war that saw a Yankees scout thrown out of the Yastrzemskis' Long Island home after flipping a pencil at the ceiling. The Red Sox eventually signed the teenager.

Carl Yastrzemski's hitting powered the Red Sox through the pennant race. In the season's final month he batted .417 with nine home runs, 26 RBIs and 22 runs scored. National Baseball Hall of Fame and Museum.

After a season in the low minors batting close to .400, Yastrzemski was called to Boston. He expected to finish the season with the Red Sox. Instead they sent him to their Class AAA club in Minneapolis where the team was just beginning the playoffs. Despite not being eligible, Yastrzemski was allowed to play. The Millers won and were rewarded with a trip to the Junior World Series against the Havana Sugar Kings in Fidel Castro's Cuba. The first game was delayed for a full two hours awaiting Castro's arrival. Armed guards took the Millers bats and balls when they tried to warm up. During the seven-game series, automatic weapons were regularly fired in celebration from within the stadium during games. This was Yastrzemski's introduction to playing professional baseball under pressure. After losing the final game, the veteran-dominated team drank heavily, committed a few indiscretions, and some were thrown in jail. Manager Gene Mauch had to contact Castro directly to have his players released so that they could fly out of the country.[11]

During the offseason the Red Sox announced that Ted Williams would retire after the 1960 season. Yastrzemski would replace the hitting icon. He spent 1960 back with the Millers learning to play left field. As planned, Williams retired and Yastrzemski entered spring training with the weight of expectations. Williams had ignored him the year before, but this spring he made Yastrzemski his project. The two men had similarities beyond batting left-handed. Both had an intellectual approach—spending hours thinking and dissecting everything about hitting. Williams gave Yastrzemski four tenets of hitting:

1. Close stance and move to the back of the batter's box.
2. Watch the ball. Don't take eyes from the ball. Ever.
3. Hit the ball through the middle.
4. Be quick with your hands. Know your pitch.[12]

Superficially, each was simple and straightforward. The more Yastrzemski thought about them, the more nuanced they became.

For his first few years in the league, Yastrzemski would go to Williams whenever he was in a slump. One time he casually asked Tom Yawkey if he knew if Williams was available. That night Yawkey finally reached Williams via high seas radio on a sport-fishing boat bouncing through big waves in the Gulf Stream off the Florida coast. Williams was at Fenway Park the next morning to take batting practice with Yastrzemski. All the attention paid off. In Yastrzemski's third year he was an All-Star, American League batting champion and won a Gold Glove. He was only 24.

The next few years he earned a reputation as a player who did not always hustle and who clashed with managers. The teams he played on were poor and received the minimal fan support that they deserved. At least twice Yastrzemski played games at Fenway Park with an announced attendance of fewer than 500. Following the 1965 season when Yastrzemski batted .312 and led the league in doubles and slugging, Ted Williams pressured him to become more of a pull hitter and begin hitting for power. Yastrzemski refused. He wanted to continue with the same things that made him successful.

Instead, 1966 was the worst year since his rookie season. Yastrzemski had little respect for manager Billy Herman whose only interest and topic of conversation was golf. Before the season started, Herman rigged a vote for team captain so that Yastrzemski would win. Then Herman declared that all communications from players to Herman would have to go through the captain. Similarly, he met with Yastrzemski every day and made Yastrzemski responsible for delivering his orders. Herman did not speak with his other players. He made all of the manager's headaches, Yastrzemski's.[13] The duties were a nightmare for Yastrzemski—a passive-aggressive punishment from Herman. Yastrzemski was a self-described loner who just wanted to be left alone to think about his own hitting. An introvert, he would much rather brood about the motion on an opposing pitcher's curveball than advocate for a second baseman in some never-ending petty squabble. Rather than becoming resentful when Dick Williams stripped him of the captaincy before the 1967 season, Yastrzemski was relieved.

After the 1966 season, Yastrzemski determined that he had to contribute more to the team. As with most important things, he thought about it for a long time. He set himself two goals for the offseason: He would arrive at spring training in the best shape of his life and he would follow Ted Williams' advice to become a pull hitter.[14]

Soon after setting those goals, while eating lunch with friends at a local hotel complex he announced that he would be training all winter. The complex's owner told Yastrzemski that they had a health club run by a Hungarian defector who had been the trainer of Olympic teams. After lunch, they went down to see the 60-something Gene Berde (pronounced birdie). On the spot Berde put Yastrzemski through a series of exercises, which Berde did with him. Gasping and exhausted, Yastrzemski could not complete any of them. Berde was not even breathing deeply. Apparently not one to consider his potential customer's feelings, Berde mocked and then taunted the much younger Yastrzemski in heavily accented English. It worked. Yastrzemski trained with Berde for six days each week all winter long.[15]

Yastrzemski spent the winter and much of his attention during spring training adapting his swing to create more power. Yastrzemski described his new approach as wristing the ball, claiming that it had taken him six years to learn the technique.[16] The first time that he understood power hitting was during a long batting practice tutorial from Ted Williams during an off day in his second year in the majors. After a couple of hours, Williams and Yastrzemski agreed that Yastrzemski had done enough. Dressed in slacks, loafers and a sport shirt, Williams grabbed one of Yastrzemski's bats and asked the pitcher for a couple more pitches. To Yastrzemski's amazement, Williams merely flicked his wrists and hit every ball into the stands. Williams appeared to be an old man to Yastrzemski, yet he possessed this effortless power. Yastrzemski needed to really step into a pitch with a big swing to hit a ball as far as Williams.[17]

During spring training in 1967, Williams devoted most of his time to Yastrzemski. He insisted that Yastrzemski focus on his hands and his hips. They worked together every day for three weeks.

Yastrzemski's 1967 season had started well and gotten better. He had set a goal of 20 home runs. He had 19 by the All-Star break. Yastrzemski had been an All-Star in three of the previous four years, but he had only played in the 1963 game. This year he was voted on the team as a starter. In the 15-inning game, he had gone 3 for 4 with two walks. The National League won 2–1, but the game provided an epiphany for Yastrzemski. Among the very best players in the game, he was a dominant hitter. Yastrzemski had read glowing press clippings for years, but at a deep level he had never believed them. This one game began to recast his self-image.

After the Detroit game, Yastrzemski led the league in every Triple Crown category for the first time all season. Of more interest around the country, there were again three teams tied for the lead in the American League with identical records. The fourth-place White Sox were only a half-game back. It had long been assumed that one team would put together a string of victories and pull away. Now the common wisdom had flipped. To commentators, a playoff seemed inevitable. No less of an authority than Eddie Stanky proclaimed, "There is no way to avoid a playoff."[18] One question echoed through the American League and its cities: Would the playoff involve two, three, or all four teams?

American League president Joe Cronin summoned representatives from all four contending teams to his offices in Boston. There, they would use a series of coin flips to determine the schedules for all possible playoff scenarios. Cronin had decided that each playoff would be best of three games. The loser of a flip would host the first game and then travel for the second and, if necessary, third games. Before he left Detroit, general manager Jim Campbell told Mayo Smith, "I'm a heads man. I always call heads." Smith was adamantly opposed. In this matter of critical baseball strategy at the highest level, he convinced Campbell to call tails. Campbell called tails every time and won every time.[19] The Red Sox lost every flip. In every playoff scenario involving them, they would host the opening game.

A complex playoff schedule was not the only issue that Cronin faced as a result of the tight race. It took time and money for teams to print and distribute World Series tickets. With only two weeks left in the season Cronin gave his permission for all four teams to print tickets. The actual printing would take more than a week. Each team would have to distribute the tickets by mail. To print a set of World Series tickets cost each team about $20,000. Three sets would never be used. The magnitude of this waste of money was hard to comprehend. It was so remarkable that papers repeated it almost daily for the remainder of the season while covering the printing of tickets, fans' ticket applications, the teams' lotteries and finally ticket distribution. The league would compensate the three teams that were not going to the World Series. That total bill was too exorbitant to print. In 1967, $20,000 was a lot of money in the world of baseball. It was the salary level for an average starting pitcher or an established, average starting infielder.

The Tigers and Red Sox had one more game to play. It was their last scheduled meeting of the season. Detroit fans were finally excited about their team. More than 42,000 showed up for each of the two weekday games against the Red Sox. They were not the only ones. The press box was overcrowded with 63 writers trying to work out of it. Not a day went by without papers commenting on the perceived effects of the pressure on players. Few game summaries of the contenders were written without mentioning that the team (or some players) had succumbed to pressure (if the team lost), or were energized by it (in victory). It was becoming a commonly held belief that one person was seemingly above the pressure: the Red Sox' rookie manager. During batting practice and fielding warm-ups, the media corps entertained themselves by trying to confirm a recent rumor that Dick Williams never blinked. He reportedly did not.[20] After the end of the series the sports editor of the *Detroit Free Press* concluded that Williams was the most relaxed of the four contending managers.[21]

In this last game, Williams started Lee Stange who had been a regular starter since the beginning of June. His ERA was half a run lower than ace Jim Lonborg's, but he received little run support. The Tigers started Mickey Lolich who had lost ten straight decisions in the middle of the season, but now was riding a six-game winning streak.

Stange took a 1–0 lead into the sixth. Al Kaline led off with a double. After a groundout, Jim Northrup homered and Stange was pitching from behind.

Lolich started the top of the ninth having faced only 19 batters since the second inning. He gave up two singles sandwiched around a walk to Yastrzemski, and a run. George Scott got the second single, but admitted after the game that he felt Lolich was throwing harder in the ninth inning than he had during the rest of the game. Mayo Smith had a different perception. He came out to the mound and replaced Lolich. Based on the results the day before, Smith was convinced that his bullpen was worn out. The score was tied 2–2 and he could not allow this game to slip away. He brought in his best pitcher.

This was Earl Wilson's first relief appearance of the season and only his fourth since 1963. Williams immediately pinch-hit the left-handed Dalton Jones for Ken Harrelson. Jones was intentionally walked. Williams pulled his All-Star shortstop Rico Petrocelli and sent up another left-handed batter, Norm Siebern. Wilson's first pitch bounced off Bill Freehan's glove and went to the backstop. Yastrzemski scored and George Scott sprinted into third. After Siebern was walked intentionally, Russ Gibson hit a sacrifice fly to score Scott.

The Tigers came up in the bottom of the ninth behind 4–2, but with the Red Sox infield in disarray. First baseman George Scott was playing third.

Second baseman Mike Andrews was playing shortstop. Dalton Jones, typically a third baseman in 1967, stayed in the game to play second. Norm Siebern was at first. Reliever Jose Santiago walked two of the first three batters. Slugger Eddie Mathews was introduced to bat for the light-hitting Ray Oyler. Williams replaced Santiago with rookie Bill Landis.

Landis had been with the Red Sox for the entire season. He had spent most of it deep in Williams' doghouse. Back in April, his first outing was not going well when Williams strode to the mound. In no uncertain terms he told Landis not to walk the next batter. Landis walked him and did not pitch again for three weeks. He pitched exactly once in June. He had thrown only 24 innings all season. Entering the game, he had not pitched in three weeks.

As Landis left the bullpen, he asked veteran Gary Bell who was also warming up if low fastballs would get Mathews out. Bell had no idea. He'd never faced Mathews. Trying to reassure the rookie who was entering a pressure-packed game in the bottom of the ninth with two on, one out and a suspect infield behind him, Bell agreed that it would be the best pitch. When Landis arrived at the mound, Williams did not immediately give him the ball. Instead he pointed and asked, "Do you know what that oblong thing is there?"

"Yeah, it's the rubber." No need to discuss tactics; Williams decided Landis would be fine. He handed Landis the ball and walked to the dugout.[22] This may have been the ultimate example of Williams' conscious decision to under-manage his team. Instead of ratcheting the pressure up on Landis and Gibson by dictating the pitching tactics, Williams distracted them with his ridiculous question.

Landis threw two low pitches to Mathews to get the count to 1-1. Neither Landis nor apparently his rookie catcher Gibson knew that Mathews had hit over 500 home runs by feasting on high fastballs. Landis' next pitch was a high fastball. Mathews had a famously beautiful swing. He unleashed it with all of his power, and missed. Buoyed by that success, Landis threw another high fastball. Mathews swung, and missed again. That was it for Mathews, and for Landis. Williams brought in Bell who claimed that he had thrown 200 pitches warming up in this two-game series.[23] Bell's appearance as a reliever struck many as incomprehensible because he was widely assumed to be the team's second-best starter. Al Kaline lined his first pitch to center where Reggie Smith made a difficult running catch to end the game.

With that one loss the Tigers, who had started the day in a three-way tie for first, fell to fourth.

In one way, Tigers owner John Fetzer was the polar opposite of Tom Yawkey. While Yawkey maintained a locker in his team's Fenway Park clubhouse and dressed in a uniform to play pepper on the field with the team's ball boys before batting practice, Fetzer had owned his team for 11 years but never once visited the Tigers clubhouse. He made an exception after this loss. "I don't feel this is a lost cause," he explained. "I want the players to know we are all with them."[24]

Chapter 21

"Short-winded"

American League standings before play on Wednesday, September 20.

	W	L	GB
Boston Red Sox	86	66	–
Minnesota Twins	86	66	–
Chicago White Sox	86	67	½
Detroit Tigers	85	67	1
California Angels	78	72	7
Cleveland Indians	72	81	14½
Washington Senators	70	80	15
Baltimore Orioles	69	81	16
New York Yankees	66	86	20
Kansas City Athletics	59	91	26

On September 20 all the contenders won. Jim Lonborg started for the Red Sox, but gave up four runs on three home runs before being replaced by a pinch-hitter in the eighth inning with the score tied 4–4. In the top of the ninth, Carl Yastrzemski, who had already hit his 41st home run, singled and advanced to second on a wild pitch. He scored the winning run on Reggie Smith's single.

Beyond his hitting, Yastrzemski seemed to have infected the Red Sox with his winning attitude. Nothing demonstrated this better than his approach to the pennant race. Since July, he had been asked almost daily about the pressure. Real pressure, he told reporters, was batting in the late innings of a lost game at the end of a hopeless season. This type of pressure was fun. He could not wait to get to the ballpark every single day. And he had proven that.

Joe Sparma bounced back with a complete game in Detroit's 10–1 win at home over the Yankees. Dean Chance collected his 19th win by beating the

Athletics in a complete game. Playing the last game of the day in Anaheim, the White Sox jumped to a 5–0 lead. Still-weakened starter Tommy John allowed a Rick Reichert solo home run and then single runs in the fourth and fifth innings. Bob Locker replaced him. He held off the Angels for the final four innings to earn his 19th save of the season.

The four contenders remained locked within a game of each other.

A different type of story was developing in Detroit. Mayo Smith had told reporters on Tuesday that pitcher Denny McLain was at home with a foot injury. It did not sound serious. McLain told Smith that he awoke Tuesday after falling asleep on the couch while watching television. According to McLain, his foot was also asleep and when he went to stand, his ankle gave way and he rolled it. The foot was now badly swollen. Smith told McLain to stay off the foot and rest it at home.[1]

By Thursday a doctor had examined the foot. There was no injury to the ankle, but two of McLain's toes were dislocated. McLain adjusted his story. He claimed that he had injured the toes Monday night rushing out to investigate a rattling noise coming from the trash cans in his garage. In good news for the Tigers, the team doctor felt that McLain might be capable of pitching over the weekend and certainly within a week.[2]

The Tigers had Thursday off while travelling to Washington for a Friday doubleheader. The story was little more than an afterthought to reporters covering the team. McLain's status became even less relevant after Smith announced that he expected Earl Wilson and Mickey Lolich to make most of the starts for the rest of the season.

To many, McLain's mishap was just another in a series of untimely and odd injuries that plagued the Tigers all season. Slugger Willie Horton had been hobbled since spring training by what was now believed to be an Achilles injury. Jim Northrup missed ten days in June after catching the mumps from his son. Al Kaline fractured his hand slamming a bat into the bat rack in a frustration tantrum. Two days later his likely replacement Gates Brown dislocated his wrist. Now in the final month of the pennant race both Eddie Mathews and McLain suffered improbable at-home accidents.

McLain's teammates, who had said nothing publicly about Mathews' injury, were not pleased. Anonymously they became openly impatient when McLain did not travel with the team to Washington. Many Tigers resented McLain who acted abnormally selfishly.

From the start of his baseball career, McLain had attracted an outsized amount of attention. He had plenty of talent and an outstanding arm. The White Sox signed him out of high school for the 1962 season. After his first year at the lowest levels of the minors, the White Sox decided to protect a different minor league prospect, Bruce Howard. The Tigers picked up McLain on waivers.[3] This remote decision involving minor leaguers was still remarkably alive for both teams. After a White Sox victory over the Tigers in a spring training game earlier in the year, Eddie Stanky had crowed that Howard's win over McLain entirely validated the White Sox decision. McLain gained motivation by never forgetting any slight.

His apparent rejection by the White Sox provided plenty of fuel. In 1963, the 19-year-old was promoted from Class AA to make a few late season appearances with the Tigers. The next year he made eight starts at Class AAA before becoming a starter with the Tigers. In 1965 he had a 16–6 record with a 2.61 ERA. He was a young star with what was considered a Hall of Fame future. In 1966, McLain's ERA slipped, rising to 2.92, but he won 20 games. At 22, he was the youngest 20-game winner since Bob Feller in 1939.

McLain was an aggressive strike-throwing pitcher and had set a Tigers team record in 1966 by yielding 42 home runs. Johnny Sain encouraged McLain's approach. He had again led the league in that category for most of the season.

Unlike most young pitchers who toiled in relative anonymity, McLain had a loud, brash personality. After a *Detroit Free Press* article mentioned that he drank 18 bottles of Pepsi every day, he became a spokesman for the local Pepsi bottler. They delivered free cases of Pepsi to him every week in addition to paying for his endorsement. McLain played the organ in lounges during the offseason and increasingly during the season.[4] He endorsed Hammond organs. By 1966, he was one of the few baseball players who made more from endorsements than from baseball. McLain had an active mind that was not particularly engaged by baseball. He once claimed, "My concentration span is about eight seconds."[5] It made him seem unreliable and uncommitted. Jim Northrup said at the beginning of the season that McLain was the only player on the Tigers that he did not trust.[6] McLain contributed to this perception. He could never understand why he needed to spend hours sitting in the dugout at a game that he would not pitch in. He freely expressed the frustration at wasting these precious hours of his life.

His biggest fan on the team may have been his catcher Bill Freehan. He could see and understand McLain's talent. Even when he did not have his best stuff, McLain would make outstanding pitches to escape from jams. Freehan's challenge was to get and then keep McLain focused. Even Freehan had to admit, "You just couldn't ever be sure of what McLain might do."[7]

McLain worked overtime creating distractions. He flew his own plane. He also invested in a variety of businesses. To some teammates, McLain treated the Tigers like one of his lesser priorities. Especially if things went poorly, McLain could make pitching seem like his hobby.

In addition to his business interests, McLain had begun to play the horses under the tutelage of former manager Charlie Dressen, sometimes taking Dressen's wagers down to the track on days he was not pitching.[8] Gambling was a common pastime in baseball and McLain wagered on a lot of things. He was not a successful gambler. The Tigers, like most teams, played a lot of cards typically for small stakes. A player who could be reliably counted on to lose was known as a fish. McLain was a big fish. Because of his lack of skill, McLain's nickname with his teammates was "Dolphin."[9] McLain reveled in the nickname and freely explained its origin. He continued to play cards, and lose.

McLain lost plenty of money gambling and realized that his bookie must be making substantial profits. Before the 1967 season McLain and his friend who ran the local Pepsi bottling company decided to set up a local bookmaking operation in Flint. They hired a local hoodlum to take the bets and kicked in some money to finance the operation. As the summer progressed, their employee came to them a number of times to make good on large losing bets. Only later did McLain realize that the bookie pocketed the winnings and had the partners make good any time there was a substantial loss.[10] Although this apparently absorbed a lot of McLain's attention, no one on the Tigers knew about it in 1967.

By Friday when the Tigers played a doubleheader in Washington with McLain still in Detroit, McLain modified his story to claim that he stubbed his toes chasing raccoons that had raided his garbage cans. It would later be charged that as a result of unpaid losses in his bookmaking operation, a local mafia enforcer summoned McLain during the evening of the 18th. In this version, he helped McLain understand his displeasure by stomping on McLain's toes.[11]

In Washington his ever-changing foot injury became just another reason to doubt McLain's commitment. Some speculated that the injury was self-inflicted. He had been seen kicking in lockers, and the clubhouse water cooler, after being removed from the Red Sox game. If a doctor said that he might be able to pitch over the weekend, many of his teammates felt that he should be with the team.

As the first hints of these dissatisfactions arrived in Detroit, McLain told reporters over the weekend that his story was too implausible to be made up.[12] He did not indicate which story. (Later in one of his autobiographies, McLain would claim that any of his or his teammates' stories could probably have been true.)[13]

As frustrating as it was for his teammates, McLain's absence was not a disaster for the Tigers. As the pressure of the pennant race had increased, McLain's pitching had gotten worse. He had not won since August. In his four September starts, he had given up 12 earned runs in only 13⅔ innings.

While McLain's story slowly unrolled, Thursday's American League schedule was light. In addition to the Tigers, the White Sox had the day off. The Twins beat the Athletics behind Harmon Killebrew's 40th home run and Tony Oliva's 17th. The Red Sox squeezed out a 6–5 victory over the Indians to remain tied with the Twins in first place. In the seventh inning of the game with the Indians threatening, pinch-hitter Lee Maye hit a hard shot deep to left. With his eyes glued to the ball, Carl Yastrzemski sprinted toward the outfield wall. Suddenly he pulled up, the ball bounced a few feet in front of him and jumped the wall into the stands for a ground-rule double. Dick Williams sat down in the Red Sox dugout while the prickly sweat of a sudden, panicked adrenalin rush subsided. He had momentarily seen his star about to crash into the unprotected wall at full speed. Cleveland's Municipal Stadium was the only one in the major leagues without a warning track. Earlier in the year it had claimed the Twins' Tony Oliva as a victim, sending him to the hospital. Fortunately, relievers in the nearby Red Sox bullpen had screamed at Yastrzemski to stop and he had listened.[14]

Entering the season's penultimate weekend, the standings remained as tight as ever. *Detroit Free Press* writer George Cantor, who like many other writers in different cities had trumpeted the success and then written off his home team many times already, finally gave up. "This is a pennant race without a turning point. It just goes on and on, with teams suddenly springing to life or collapsing without a hint of a reason behind it."[15]

As much as players and managers wanted to deny it, the weeks of a close pennant race had begun to stress almost everyone. Umpire Hank Soar, who was in his 18th major league season, confided, "I have never seen such tension as there is in the American League right now. The pressure is on the umpires because you don't want to make a mistake that could be costly. Our crew just came from the Detroit-Boston series and I've never seen so much tension."[16]

American League standings before play on Friday, September 22.

	W	L	GB
Boston Red Sox	88	66	–
Minnesota Twins	88	66	–
Chicago White Sox	87	67	1
Detroit Tigers	86	67	1½
California Angels	78	73	8½
Cleveland Indians	72	83	16½
Baltimore Orioles	71	82	16½
Washington Senators	71	82	16½
New York Yankees	66	87	21½
Kansas City Athletics	59	93	28

Friday seemed like it might be a big day, and not just because the Defense Department proudly announced that B-52s and other warplanes dropped over half a million pounds of explosives on North Vietnam in one day. All the contenders played second division teams. Both the Tigers and the Red Sox would play doubleheaders. The Twins hosted the Yankees.

The White Sox started Gary Peters against Luis Tiant in Cleveland. Peters gave up a run in the second on a walk and a double. The White Sox batters could not solve the 11-9 Tiant. In the top of the ninth, still trailing 1–0 with one out and Wayne Causey on second. Eddie Stanky sent pinch-hitter Smoky Burgess to the plate.

Burgess debuted in 1949 as a catcher with the Cubs. Now 40, he was used almost exclusively as a pinch-hitter. First Chicago papers and then others around the country referred to Burgess as the league's best pinch-hitter. While this could be legitimately attributed to Burgess' career numbers, Stanky had found a unique way to promote the legend of Burgess' prowess.

At the beginning of spring training, Stanky proposed that the American League adopt a new position—the designated pinch-hitter. This would allow the same player to pinch-hit more than once in the same game as long as he did not play in the field. No manager used more pinch-hitters than Stanky. Within a week of Stanky's proposal, American League president Joe Cronin gave him permission to use the proposed rule during "home" spring training games.[17] In the end, Cronin declared that the innovation would not be incorporated into the league's play, but all of the American League managers understood Stanky's interest in having Burgess bat more frequently.[18]

Burgess' performance in 1967 did not fully match this reputation. He strode to the plate batting .123. His actual ability did not matter. Almost every time he was announced as a pinch-hitter, opposing managers became defensive. It was not unusual for him to face a fresh reliever, pitching with extra care. Despite his pitiful batting average, Burgess had been walked 19 of the 78 times he came to the plate. Six of those walks were intentional. He was not a slugger; Burgess had hit only two home runs in the past two years. The league-wide fear of Burgess may have been one of Stanky's most successful con jobs.

Burgess' bat was not entirely punchless. He had nine RBIs.

Burgess hit Tiant's first pitch to right for a run-scoring single, his 10th RBI. Stanky had somehow put his team in a position to win another game. (The week before the White Sox had won two extra-inning games with the Indians that were tied 0–0 in the 17th and 10th innings respectively.) The Indians threatened with two on in the bottom of the ninth inning, but Wilbur Wood came on to strike out Richie Scheinblum to end the inning. Hoyt Wilhelm then shut down the Indians for three innings before being replaced by Roger Nelson for the bottom of the 13th. The first Indians batter, Tony Horton, homered to end the game. It was another surprising loss for the White Sox who had already won an American League–record 38 one-run games. Stanky used 23 players in the game. Afterward, Tommy McCraw remained optimistic, "I think we can do it. We'll have to. I believe it."[19] Taken without context, this appeared to be mindless cheerleading. McCraw was genuine, repeating the sentiment throughout the remaining few days of the season. It may have been his sense of humor that kept him loose. McCraw was one of the few White Sox position players whose play improved under the strain of September. He had entered the game batting .295 for the month.

In contrast to the White Sox' tight game, the Twins cruised to an 8–2 win over the hapless Yankees giving Jim Kaat his 15th win.

Neither of the Red Sox games was close. The Orioles lit up Red Sox starter Jerry Stephenson for six runs and coasted to a 10–0 victory in the first game. In the second game, Dick Williams started Jose Santiago who had been a reliever for most of the season. Backed by 14 hits he pitched a complete game winning 10–3.

In Washington, Earl Wilson started the first game for Detroit. Although he gave up two home runs, Detroit led the whole game and won 8–3. Wilson became the first pitcher to win 22 games.

Lefthander Mickey Lolich started the second game for the Tigers.

In 1964, Lolich's first full year in the majors, he went 18–9 for the Tigers becoming a young star. Reporters liked him because he was usually funny and often self-deprecating. Asked after one game what he thought of the gusty wind he replied, "When the wind was blowing to right, I was thinking to my left. When it was blowing to left, I was thinking to my right." Reporters entertained themselves and their readers by trying to determine if this was an exceptionally deep thought or mere frivolity.[20]

The youthful Lolich had a well-established reputation as a flake based on seemingly innocuous decisions like riding a fire engine red Kawasaki 350 motorcycle to the ballpark on days that he pitched.[21] Lolich defended himself by claiming exemption from baseball's rule of thumb that left-handed pitchers were nutty. He was not a true lefty because he did everything right-handed, except pitch. To many his logic only further reinforced the stereotype. Lolich pitched left-handed because of a motorcycle accident when he was three years old. It is a description that allows for a wide range of possibilities and a decade of media coverage gave free rein to many of those.

Despite more exotic interpretations, it is clear that Lolich pedaled his tricycle into a parked motorcycle, which fell on him breaking his collarbone, or arm, or shoulder. While the collarbone healed, Lolich began throwing things with his left hand. He never stopped. Which collarbone was broken, or why a six-week recovery period at age three would permanently set his pitching hand were explained in contradictory ways at different times by reporters, Lolich, and even his mother who could actually remember the recovery period. The extensive variation in the accounts only heightened the mythical quality of the tale.

There is an additional legend in Detroit that Lolich played his first baseball game as a 12-year-old. His father, a park employee, volunteered him to fill in as a left fielder on a short-handed team of older players. The team soon fell badly behind and the coach did not want to wear out his pitchers for games later that weekend. Although he had never thrown a baseball before, Lolich was summoned from left field to pitch. He effortlessly mowed down the opposing batters. This account only further reinforced the view that Lolich was blessed with an inexplicable, God-given talent.

Tigers starter Mickey Lolich had an odd season. After starting 5–2, he endured a ten-game losing streak. He missed almost two weeks of the season when his National Guard unit was mobilized, then returned to win nine of his last ten decisions. Lolich ended the season throwing 28⅔ straight shutout innings. National Baseball Hall of Fame and Museum.

Lolich supplemented these origin stories with verifiable, strange habits. During his first major league spring training, a team trainer approached Lolich and praised his throwing. This trainer told him that one of the best pitchers he had ever seen never allowed ice to touch his arm. Instead, after pitching he would take a long, very hot shower with the water pounding on his arm for 15 minutes. Lolich was naturally curious and asked who the pitcher was. The trainer told him, "Satchel Paige." Paige was not only one of the best pitchers of mid-century, but famous for pitching in the major leagues in his late 40s. Lolich's minor league career was undistinguished to say the least, so it is not clear if this was a practical joke gone awry. Regardless, Lolich followed this practice for his entire career. Like many of Lolich's idiosyncrasies, he did not take half-measures. He used water so hot that teammates would not shower next to him because the splashing water burned them.[22]

Of all Tigers pitchers, Lolich seemed most likely to welcome Johnny Sain. Even as a young player, Lolich had a noticeable potbelly. He did all he could to avoid prescribed running, claiming that he was short-winded. Despite his aversion to running, Lolich was not lazy. He believed almost fanatically in throwing every day during the season. He said, "The only way to build up your arm is to throw. The only way to improve your control is to throw. So, I throw every day."[23] When the team was at home, he would go out early on days that he was not scheduled to pitch. There was a chunk missing from the wall in Tiger Stadium's left-center field. Lolich would stand in the outfield and throw at that spot. He was serious about this regimen. He believed, "You've got to get tired to get strong."[24]

Despite his success in 1964, Lolich increasingly struggled in his next two seasons. His ERA ballooned to 4.77. His catcher Bill Freehan was convinced that Lolich's biggest problem was his confidence. If his curveball got hit in one game, Lolich would be ready to junk it and try to develop a new one.[25] He spent much of his early career as a fastball pitcher in search of an effective curve. When he had both pitches, he thrived. His fastball was not overpoweringly fast, but it was unusual. He threw a four-seamer with a tremendous amount of backspin, so it appeared to batters that it rose when it neared the plate.[26]

The 1967 season started well for Lolich. He developed a new curveball in spring training and repeatedly won games right after a Tigers loss. In the middle of May, he was 5–2. Then the bottom fell out of his season. His ERA climbed over 4.50 and he could not win a game. By the time he was deployed for the riots in Detroit, he had lost 10 straight games in 11 starts. Normally cheerful and a great locker room interview, he sat gloomily in front of his locker day after day. In 1966 he had won 14 games (only five pitchers won more), but the Tigers cut his salary by the maximum allowed. Now he was worried that they would cut it again by the maximum for 1968.[27]

Johnny Sain spent much of the summer working on Lolich's confidence on the mound using his recipe of positive reinforcement. There was another encouraging exception to the dejection that surrounded him: Tigers fans, who were tough on so many of their players, sincerely cheered Lolich through June and July as the losses piled up. While he had a few terrible games, in most he pitched well enough to win. He missed almost three weeks of the season because of his National Guard deployment. After he returned, Lolich started to get run support and to pile up the innings. His sunny attitude reappeared and so did his confidence on the mound. In eight outings he was 6–1 while his ERA dropped almost a full run.

When Lolich took the mound for the second game of the doubleheader, he was pitching with only two days' rest. The expectations were high; the pressure was on. The Tigers would go as far as Wilson and Lolich could carry them. Lolich started strong, throwing almost exclusively fastballs, but the

Tigers had trouble scoring. The game was close until Norm Cash hit his 22nd home run of the season in the eighth. Lolich pitched a complete game shutout to win 4–0. After the game Tigers TV color analyst George Kell wrote, "Lolich has developed into the Tigers' finest pitcher."[28]

Winning the doubleheader helped the Tigers vault past the White Sox into third place, a game behind the Twins. Better, the whole team was playing well. The bats had come alive and Mayo Smith had two strong pitchers ready for the final week.

Chapter 22

"$10,000"

American League standings before play on Saturday, September 23.

	W	L	GB
Minnesota Twins	89	66	–
Boston Red Sox	89	67	½
Detroit Tigers	88	67	1
Chicago White Sox	87	68	2
California Angels	78	74	9½
Cleveland Indians	73	83	16½
Baltimore Orioles	72	83	17
Washington Senators	71	84	18
New York Yankees	66	88	22½
Kansas City Athletics	60	93	28

In Minnesota, the Twins entered their Saturday game with an 11–5 season record against the Yankees. The game was played in the morning because the University of Minnesota would open their football season in Metropolitan Stadium against Utah that afternoon.[1] Dave Boswell started for the Twins. He had little command of his pitches, giving up six walks and a home run to a late-season call-up before being removed in the third inning. The Twins were never in the game, losing 6–2. After the game, Ermer announced that he expected Dean Chance to pitch three of the team's last six games including once on only two days' rest. Boswell, he believed, had lost his ability to control his pitches.[2]

The next day the Twins started strong against the Yankees, scoring seven runs in the first two innings. Dean Chance threw 139 pitches to win his 20th game. He gave up four runs in the complete-game effort, but was in command the whole way. Six Twins had RBIs in the 9–4 win. Bob Allison continued his outstanding year with his 23rd home run. Tony Oliva raised his batting average to .291 and scored a run. Harmon Killebrew pounded his 41st home run.

Chance admitted that he hoped to be relieved earlier in the game. With the big lead his mind wandered to the game on Wednesday. He wanted to save his arm.[3] Ermer did not trust his bullpen. That was the reason he had used both Chance and Kaat in relief in the past week. Ermer was convinced that he needed not just the maximum number of starts from his two best pitchers, but the maximum number of innings.

Despite Ermer's inner turmoil, the Twins emulated Harmon Killebrew's ever-placid exterior. Al Worthington described the calm confidence of the players: "I guess it's the experience of 1965 that has helped keep us from feeling the pressure. You realize when you've been through it that one game isn't necessarily the pennant. I honestly don't think this team is feeling the pressure like you'd imagine."[4] There had been no pennant race when the Twins won in 1965, but the scrutiny of the World Series had been surprisingly amplified. Worthington knew what that jolt of extra adrenalin could do. He had been a model of calm during the regular season in 1965, but in his first World Series appearance he gave up a two-run single to the first batter he faced. He fumbled a sacrifice bunt by the next batter into another run. By the time he left the game, the Dodgers had stretched their tight 3–2 lead to a decisive 6–2. He was confident that players on the other teams would feel the surprise of the extra adrenalin in 1967.

One person who definitely felt the pressure was Cal Griffith. Even though the Twins were in command for the entire game and it lasted just over two hours, he smoked a whole pack of cigarettes.[5] He confessed, "I don't know how much more of this I can take."[6]

At the end of the weekend, the Twins still led the league. Crucially, they were the only team with just 67 losses. The others all had 68.

The Red Sox had struggled with the Orioles, losing five of six games since the middle of the month. Dick Williams knew that the Red Sox had to win both of the weekend games between the two teams.

A week earlier he had announced that Lee Stange would be dropped from the starting rotation. Williams needed wins and Stange had won only two of his last ten starts. On the other hand, Stange's ERA had dropped from 3.02 to 2.61 over those starts. It did not take a baseball genius to identify the problem—a lack of run support. Williams thought he had identified the reason that the high-scoring Red Sox wilted at the plate when Stange pitched. He felt that Stange worked too slowly on the mound. As a result, players spent so much time in the field that they could not find their rhythm at the plate.[7]

Unfortunately, Williams had few other choices for starting pitchers. His only other option was Bucky Brandon whose ERA was over 4.00. There were good reasons he had not started since the beginning of August. Williams went with the better pitcher, Stange.

He would be pitching on only three days' rest, but that had become so common in this race that it passed without comment. Lacking the height desired in a major league pitcher, Stange compensated with toughness. Like many professional baseball players in 1967, the 5'9" Stange had starred at high school football. In high school he played the same position as his classmate Ray Nitschke, a future Pro Football Hall of Fame linebacker measuring 6'3" and weighing 235 pounds. Nitschke backed up Stange.[8]

Stange did not find redemption in this game. Curt Blefary, the second batter he faced, belted a home run. In the Red Sox' second, Orioles backup catcher Larry Haney threw out George Scott trying to steal second. After Ken Harrelson singled, Haney threw him out trying to steal, too.

Harrelson was a mess. Under the pennant race pressure, he had broken out in hives. His batting average was just .216 since he joined the Red Sox, although he had collected 13 RBIs in less than a month. He had long been a player who thrived on emotion, but now it was getting to him. In an attempt to calm himself, Harrelson had been getting a daily allocation of tranquilizers from Red Sox trainers.[9]

This was not Harrelson's day. In the third inning, he misplayed Blefary's fly ball into a double. It would have been the third out. The Orioles scored three runs that inning on another home run. Williams benched Harrelson. Stange was also taken out at the start of the fourth inning.

Despite this bad start, the Red Sox came back. Yastrzemski homered to give the Red Sox a 5-4 lead.

In the eighth, Williams brought in his best reliever, John Wyatt. Wyatt had been used in 27 games since the beginning of August. The pitching did not wear him out. It was the warming up.[10] Williams had him throwing during every close game. In some games he might warm four times and still not get in the game. All of those pitches took their toll. His arm had felt dead for a month.

Wyatt knew he was in trouble. His pitches had no movement. He did not have the power to throw a ball past the hard-hitting heart of the Orioles order. Frank Robinson singled. Brooks Robinson hit the game-winning home run. The Orioles won 7-5.

Players on both teams noted the number of bad bounces that infield grounders had taken. The previous weekend the Baltimore Colts had opened their season defeating the Atlanta Falcons at Memorial Stadium. (At 11-1-2, the 1967 Baltimore Colts would go on to have the best record of any team not to make the postseason since the NFL instituted playoffs.) Many baseball stadiums were also used for professional football games. Even in the best weather and with a competent grounds crew, a single football game could leave the infield turf in shreds. The Baltimore grounds crew had spent the season garnering a reputation for incompetence from visiting teams.

The Red Sox entered Sunday's game tied for second place only a half-game behind the Twins. Williams announced that Jim Lonborg would start three of the team's last six games. It was assumed that veteran Gary Bell would start the other three games.

Before the game, Lonborg took his customary nap. Unusually curious and open to new ideas, Lonborg learned what he called a "Yoga trick" from Reggie Smith earlier in the season. This allowed him to relax almost instantly to fall asleep.[11]

Just before taking the field to start the game, Lonborg showed teammates his glove. He used a marker to write "$10,000" on its thumb. That was expected to be the share for each player on the team that won the World Series. Lonborg wanted to remind himself how much might be at stake with every pitch.[12]

During the past weeks, barely a day had passed without some player discussing their motivation to increase their World Series share. It could be big money. These were calculated based solely on the first four World Series games. Fifteen percent of the gate went directly to the commissioner's office. The two owners received 25 percent. The remaining 60 percent went to the players' pool. From those funds, 70 percent went to the two competing teams in a 60–40 split. Fifteen percent was divided between the two second-place teams; 10 percent to the third-place teams; and, the last 5 percent to the fourth-place teams. The owners retained all revenue from any additional World Series games.

Lonborg easily wore the mantle of a natural leader. His charm motivated people. Teammates wanted to follow him. Strangers wanted to help him. Earlier in the season he flew from his Army Reserve unit to pitch on a one-day pass. His plane aborted one landing after a truck pulled onto the landing strip right in front of it. The pilots had to pull up on the next approach, too. The control tower had failed to clear the runway of a plane waiting to take off. Lonborg was unshaken. He thought he had plenty of time until his cabbie informed him that the game would begin in less than half an hour. Lonborg convinced the cabbie to run multiple red lights and then make an illegal turn to speed the wrong way down a one-way street. Lonborg made it in time to start the game, and collect the win.[13]

Now, he was using those same persuasive powers to help boost the confidence of his exhausted teammates.

Lonborg did not disappoint, pitching six innings of two-hit ball. The Red Sox' bats finally came to life against the Orioles and they scored in each of the first five innings. Lonborg departed before the seventh inning with the Red Sox comfortably ahead 7–0. Williams limited Lonborg's outing so that he would be fresh to pitch three days later. In this abbreviated start strategically calculated to save his arm, Lonborg threw 124 pitches.[14]

Bucky Brandon choked up six runs and blew out his arm before Williams finally pulled him in the ninth inning. The Red Sox won 11–7, but the victory only confirmed the opinion that their pitching after Lonborg was nonexistent. Even Williams seemed to despair of his bullpen.[15] The Red Sox would go only as far as their hitting would take them.

The Tigers had Saturday off before finishing their series with the Senators on Sunday. Joe Sparma started and gave up only three hits and one run in the first six innings. In the top of the seventh with the score tied 1–1, the Tigers scored three runs. Before Sparma took the mound in the bottom of the seventh Mayo Smith made a couple of defensive substitutions. Pitching with a 4–1 lead Sparma walked the first two batters. Smith signaled for Fred Lasher who immediately induced a double-play grounder to Dick McAuliffe at second. McAuliffe fumbled it and the bases were loaded with no outs. The next batter also hit a grounder and this time the Tigers turned the double play, but a run scored.

After a 1–2–3 eighth inning, the game came apart for Lasher in the ninth. The first batter singled and was replaced by Ed Stroud, a speedster who had been traded by the White Sox in June. Lasher got the second batter to hit a grounder to McAuliffe at second. McAuliffe decided to tag Stroud as he ran by on his way to second. McAuliffe lost his footing as he tried to lunge, and completely missed Stroud. His throw to first was too late. Instead of a double play and empty bases, there were two on and no outs.

After Lasher gave up a single and a run, Smith brought in another young pitcher, John Hiller. The first batter he faced flied out. If it had not been for McAuliffe's error, the inning and game would be over. The next batter was pinch-hitter Doug Camilli, a backup catcher. Hiller and Camilli battled through six fouled pitches before Camilli finally singled to right to tie the game. Hiller gave up the game-losing hit to the next batter on an 0-2 count.

After the game, McAuliffe was distraught about his fielding blunders and was widely blamed by the press for the loss. A haggard Smith could not contain himself, "You cannot lose games like this one."[16]

Sports pages nationwide had carried almost daily updates on Charlie Finley's various disputes since mid–August. These conflicts wove together in a confusing and complex way. When Finley fired Alvin Dark and Ken Harrelson, he also suspended without pay and fined pitcher Lew Krausse. Because of his subsequent intimidation tactics, that suspension led the nascent Players Association to file a grievance with the National Labor Relations Board.

Although this sounds straightforward, charges leveled on Finley's behalf by *The Sporting News* and nationally syndicated columnist Red Smith led to a myriad of rebuttals and counter-charges. Some continued almost daily for weeks. Much of it read like the cover of a supermarket tabloid.

In the middle of September, baseball's commissioner brokered a lengthy two-day meeting in New York that resulted in a compromise with the players agreeing not to pursue their grievance and Finley merely agreeing to obey the law in the future.

While many commentators echoed the belief that Finley had completely outmaneuvered the Players Association, ex-owner-turned-columnist Bill Veeck disagreed. He noted that for the first time owners were constrained to neither coerce players nor retaliate against them. These had long been standard aspects of the business relationship between owners and players. Veeck also pointed out to a national audience that Finley's assertions against Krausse were not just unproven. They were completely unknown.[17]

Simultaneously, Finley was travelling between Milwaukee, Seattle, and Oakland to secure the best deal if he moved his team. This earned him the enmity of the soon-to-be-spurned fans and newspapers in Kansas City. As the last week of September began, Finley exercised his option to not renew the Athletics' lease in Kansas City.

These were not separate issues. Finley needed the approval of the other owners to move his franchise. For all his quirks, Finley was a canny businessman. The other owners greatly appreciated his attacks on the Players Association, a new and possibly dangerous foe. Cal Griffith freely admitted that Finley's aggressive approach helped convince him to back the rumored move.[18]

Finley's strategy worked. As the end of the season approached, American League president Joe Cronin announced that the American League owners would meet immediately after the World Series, for an unspecified reason. It was widely assumed that the owners would approve the Athletics move during this meeting.[19]

The White Sox entered the weekend with the easiest remaining schedule of the contenders. They would finish their weekend series with two games against the Indians. Then, finish the season with two games against the hapless Athletics and a three-game series at home against the sliding Senators. Eddie Stanky was not shy about proclaiming the importance of pitching. He claimed to welcome a playoff because the White Sox' pitching was so superior. An oft-quoted aphorism stated that good pitching beats good hitting. The White Sox' starting pitchers were the league's best. While the other three contending managers were apprehensive about using their relief pitchers, Stanky had the only reliable bullpen in the league.

This pitching superiority was confirmed on Saturday. Joe Horlen threw another complete game shutout, this time using only 96 pitches. More encouraging, the White Sox pounded the Indians for eight runs.

In a standard post-game question, Stanky was asked if the pennant race had been an emotional drain. "I was accused in May of managing every game like the World Series. So, I must have been under the same tensions then that I am now."[20]

Inside the clubhouse the atmosphere was less optimistic. Despite the rare, easy victory, players dressed in silence. Even the usually ebullient Gary Peters just peeled off his uniform without the energy to engage teammates or reporters in conversation. During the past week, the players took little joy from their wins. They were drained both mentally and physically.[21]

The next day before the game coach Grover Resinger went to talk to Stanky in the manager's private office. "Eddie, I think the boys are a little tight," Resinger said.

Stanky stared at him.

"You know," Resinger said. "The guys aren't relaxed."

Still Stanky stared.

"They're afraid to make mistakes," Resinger said.

"What did you do?" Stanky asked. "Read a book on psychology?"

"No," Resinger said.

"Then get the hell out of here."[22]

Resinger was not the only one to sense the team's fragile psyche. The Indians starter, fireballer Sam McDowell, proclaimed before the game that the White Sox would not be in contention at the end of the week.[23] He may have overestimated his own abilities because he gave up three runs and was lifted in the third inning with an arm injury.

Stanky started rookie Cisco Carlos who entered the game well rested and with a 0.93 ERA. He retired the first six batters he faced. After Ken Boyer homered to give the White Sox a 3-0 lead, Carlos gave up a single in the bottom of the third and then walked a batter. Stanky immediately replaced him with veteran reliever Don McMahon.

McMahon pitched five scoreless innings. In the top of the eighth, he gave up back-to-back doubles. A run scored cutting the White Sox lead to 3-1. That was it for McMahon. Stanky brought in Gary Peters who had started and pitched six innings on Friday. He retired the only batter he faced. Bob Locker finished the game for the save. This was Locker's league-leading 74th appearance, but his sinking fastball was still brutally effective. Locker attributed his energy to his habit of eating a large spoonful of honey before every appearance.[24]

Stanky's quick removal of his pitchers, seemingly now just for allowing a runner to arrive at second base, was so unusual that even wire service reports denigrated his handling of the pitching staff. Throughout the past couple of months Stanky's quick hook had ratcheted up the pressure on his starters.

Stanky had set up his pitching staff in a revolutionary way. He expected to use multiple relievers in every game. Consequently, his bullpen was filled with high-quality pitchers—Wilhelm, Locker, McMahon, and Wood—who had spent the season pitching frequently in close games. Although he did not have a designated closer, his use of the bullpen pitchers was otherwise well ahead of its time.

By contrast, the Angels' Bill Rigney seemed to use Minnie Rojas in every close game all season. Rojas had already made 69 appearances. Detroit's Mayo Smith was a firm believer in using a hot reliever. In April and May, Fred Gladding had ten saves including twice when he had three saves in three games. In June Dave Wickersham had three of the team's four saves. Rookie Mike Marshall had the other one. He became Smith's favorite reliever in July. He had ten saves by the end of the month and a 0.87 ERA. In early August, Marshall lost a close game. Three days later a recently called up minor leaguer named Fred Lasher recorded his first save. Lasher would have nine of the team's next 10 saves. Heading into the season's last week, Lasher had made 11 appearances in 27 days. Marshall had only six appearances in September. There was little concern for protecting a reliever from overuse to promote his effectiveness during the rest of the season, or extend his career. Relievers had value for most teams only if they could currently pitch well.

There was no criticism of Stanky's pitching moves after Sunday's win over the Indians. The next morning the *Chicago Daily News* proclaimed, "It looks as though the [White] Sox are in the driver's seat."[25] They were not the only ones. The White Sox had won nine of their last 11 games. In those games they had scored 44 runs, far above their season average. They were still one game behind the Twins, but the Twins had to end the season with two games in Boston against the Red Sox. The White Sox had the advantages of momentum, the easiest schedule, and the league's best pitching entering the last week.

The Cardinals had clinched the National League pennant back on September 18. Their manager Red Schoendienst was asked over the weekend to predict the American League winner. He confidently picked the White Sox.[26]

Over the weekend, United States Secretary of State Dean Rusk celebrated the marriage of his daughter. In front page news on Monday, he offered his resignation to President Lyndon Johnson. Rusk felt his daughter's marriage to an African American would be so controversial that he was duty-bound to offer his resignation. A spokesman for President Johnson said that the president "gave the resignation no serious consideration."[27] Newspaper editorials found the wedding offensive and criticized Rusk.

Chapter 23

"We are now out of tomorrows"

American League standings before play on Monday, September 25.

	W	L	GB
Minnesota Twins	90	67	–
Boston Red Sox	90	68	½
Chicago White Sox	89	68	1
Detroit Tigers	88	68	1½
California Angels	80	74	8½
Baltimore Orioles	73	84	17
Cleveland Indians	73	85	17½
Washington Senators	72	84	17½
New York Yankees	67	89	22½
Kansas City Athletics	60	95	29

Minnesota and Detroit were the only contenders playing on Monday. Detroit traveled up to New York from Washington for a two-game series with the Yankees.

Before the game the *Detroit News* wrote, "It is hard to see how [Earl Wilson] can miss on the Cy Young Award in the American League."[1] He was the only pitcher in the league with 22 wins and had been the rock of the Tigers staff.

Mayo Smith was convinced that his team would have to win out their last six games to even make it into a playoff. He sent Wilson to face the Yankees on two days' rest. Wilson had been ill all night, not able to get to sleep until about 5:30 in the morning. He felt so terrible that he did not believe that he would make it through his warm-up pitches.

Despite his exhaustion and the pressure of a must-win start Wilson pitched strongly, going seven innings and giving up two runs. That should have been enough to win. It was not. The Yankees Al Downing shut out the Tigers with a four-hitter. No runner got past first base. It was a dismal effort.

After the loss, the usually stoic Smith staggered around the clubhouse. His answers to reporters' questions were barely coherent. One reporter described him as "dazed like a losing boxer."[2] Al Kaline, who had two of the Tigers hits, was asked the inevitable question about the players folding under pressure. He brushed the suggestion aside: "This is the most fun I have ever had in September."[3] Columnist Red Smith saw it differently. "The Tigers," he wrote to a nationwide audience, "lost like losers."[4]

During these last couple of weeks, managers of non-contending teams repeatedly confirmed that their teams would play hard against all the contenders. Before the Twins opened their home series with the Angels, Bill Rigney headed off accusations of playing soft. He claimed that he had saved his best pitchers for the last seven games, all of which would be against contenders. "This is our World Series," he proclaimed.[5]

This was not just talk for the press. Rigney had four pitchers leading the team with 11 wins each. He gathered his entire pitching staff before the series. Rigney laid out the situation. Each one of them would be negotiating a contract in the offseason. Those with 12 wins would make more money than those with 11 wins. Over the next few games, they would each have a chance to pitch their best and put themselves in a stronger bargaining position.

Cal Ermer sent Jim Merritt to the mound. Merritt was now so skinny that Ermer had nicknamed him "Bones." Along with the weight, Merritt had dispatched his mustache. He had another new look for the Angels. About a month earlier, Merritt had changed his uniform number from 26 to 17 in the hopes that it would lead to more run support. Like many superstitions, it worked for a while. But by now, the magic had worn off.

Merritt had not changed his habits on the mound. He still worked quickly with small, efficient movements. This was expected to be Merritt's last start in the regular season. Ermer had announced that Jim Kaat and Dean Chance would start Tuesday and Wednesday. The Twins had Thursday and Friday off before the final weekend series in Boston. Kaat and Chance would start those two games on regular rest, which was now only three days.

Although the Twins were in first place, their lead was tenuous. Ermer felt that the pennant winner would need 94 wins. That meant his team could not lose more than one of their remaining five games. Merritt certainly felt the pressure. He gave up four runs and did not make it out of the second inning. That was only the beginning of the nightmare for the Twins. Jim Perry finished the second and third innings, but was lifted for a pinch-hitter. Ermer brought Dave Boswell in to start the fourth inning. He was no better than he had been on Saturday, giving up three runs and getting only one out. He had to be replaced by Mudcat Grant who got the last two outs of the inning.

The Twins scored two runs in the bottom of the inning, but were never in the game eventually losing 9–2. Cal Ermer used 22 players desperately trying to manufacture runs. His batters did not fail him. They managed 11 hits, but could not turn them into enough runs.

In a sign that stress was getting to almost all the players, Zoilo Versalles criticized Rigney for playing "hot dog baseball" by sacrificing baserunners along with a 7–2 lead. Versalles claimed that "[Rigney] made every chicken move" in an attempt to help the White Sox win the pennant.[6] Rigney, like every manager, had been repeatedly asked for his pick to win the pennant. He had recently selected the White Sox because they were scheduled to play the bottom-dwelling Athletics and the staggering Senators, who had won only three of their last 11 games. Versalles' teammates pointedly refused comment on his claims.

Once it was printed, Versalles could see how embarrassing that statement was and futilely retracted it. Rigney who desperately wished the Angels were still in the pennant race fired back, "The Twins would be ahead by ten games if Versalles batted .270 instead of .202."[7] The Twins were now tied with Boston for the lead. It was time for their stars to step up.

With no Red Sox game to occupy them, Boston fans had nothing to distract their curiosity from their rivals' games. Over 200 calls per hour were logged at the *Boston Herald Traveler* switchboard from fans desperate to hear the latest score of the Twins-Angels game.[8] The *Boston Record American* had by now set up a special phone line just to handle inquiries about baseball scores. It was touted daily in the sports pages, which carried the plea not to call the paper's main number if the line was busy.[9]

American League standings before play on Tuesday, September 26.

	W	L	GB
Boston Red Sox	90	68	–
Minnesota Twins	90	68	–
Chicago White Sox	89	68	½
Detroit Tigers	88	69	1½
California Angels	81	74	7½
Baltimore Orioles	74	84	16
Cleveland Indians	73	85	17
Washington Senators	72	85	17½
New York Yankees	68	89	21½
Kansas City Athletics	60	95	28½

Tuesday dawned with observers sprinkling disdain on the American League pennant race. A National League scout anonymously opined, "No one is good enough to win the pennant in the American League this year, but several clubs are going to lose it."[10] A columnist observed that the teams looked like they were headed for a four-way tie for fourth.[11]

Each of the contenders had a scheduled Tuesday game.

It was 40 degrees with a snow flurry when the game started at Minnesota's Metropolitan Stadium. Many of the 8,012 fans were huddled under blankets or wore heavy parkas and ski hats. September 5 had been the last night game in Minnesota. Cal Griffith felt that September evenings in Minnesota were too cold for good baseball. This day game was cold enough. Angels players in the dugout donned long, football-type warm-up capes that the team had borrowed.[12]

The Twins started Jim Kaat who had regained his ability to challenge batters by throwing strikes. He explained, "I don't like to pitch around anybody. I'd rather try to get them out."[13] So far in September he had yielded only three walks and 12 hits in 54⅓ innings for a WHIP (Walks and Hits per Innings Pitched) of just 0.276.

Minnesota's Cal Ermer was desperate for a win. Another loss might drop his team to third with only three games left on their schedule. Kaat came through for him. He started strong but gave up three runs in the third inning, hurt by Tovar's error and Killebrew misplaying a grounder into a single. With three runs in and the bases loaded, Kaat ended the inning by striking out two batters. The Angels had only three baserunners the rest of the game. Kaat finished with 13 strikeouts in the game and 207 for the season. Joining Dean Chance and Dave Boswell, he was the third Twins pitcher with over 200 strikeouts.

It was not an easy win. The Twins were still behind when they came to bat in the sixth. After Tovar led off with a single, Killebrew smashed a Jim McGlothlin pitch 435 feet to the bleachers in center field. Killebrew had a league-wide reputation as a classy player, but he indulged in his one temptation: He stood at the plate admiring the ball as it soared into the stands before dropping his bat and trotting around the bases. That blow unnerved the Angels. Killebrew had done exactly what a superstar needs to do. He had made a big play at a critical moment to change the course of the game.

After Bob Allison walked, Rigney brought in rookie pitcher Jim Weaver. He allowed a single to Carew. On the next play, shortstop Jim Fregosi threw away a double play relay as Carew crashed into him, allowing Allison to score from second. Carew hit Fregosi so hard that he was still furious after the game. Fregosi vowed, "I'm going to break both his legs."[14]

After a walk, Kaat reached on an error by second baseman Bobby Knoop. On the error, Ted Uhlaender aggressively tried to make it all the way home from second. The throw beat him easily, but he kicked the ball from Bob Rodgers' glove for the Angels third error of the inning.[15] Desperate for a win, the Twins increased their typical aggressiveness.

Killebrew iced the win with another long home run in the seventh. It was his 43rd home run of the season. Allison collected three hits including a triple and scored three runs. So far in the month of September he had 17 RBIs and seven extra base hits. The Twins' two sluggers were swinging hot bats.

The Twins ended the game with one area of concern. With one out in the top of the ninth, Angels catcher Bob Rodgers hit a hard line drive that Kaat knocked down with his left hand. He picked the ball up and tossed it to first for the out. It was obvious that Kaat was hurt and the game stopped while Ermer and the team's trainer came out to examine Kaat's pitching hand. Kaat stayed in the game and struck out the last batter.

After the game, reporters saw the swollen and discoloring thumb. There was immediate anxiety about Kaat's effectiveness in his next start against the Red Sox. There was almost no speculation about whether Kaat would start. He had a long-established reputation as the toughest player on the Twins.

The 1962 Twins, in just their second season in Minnesota, were loaded with young players bonding into what would become a World Series team. In a close game that July, Detroit's Bubba Morton connected with one of Kaat's fastballs and lined it back into his face for a single to load the bases. Kaat was taken from the game missing two teeth and part of a third. After surgery, Kaat made his next start on only three days' rest. He threw over 40 innings in his next four starts. That set the standard for fortitude in what would become one of the Twins' foundational narratives. Like many inspirational acts, it quickly acquired mythical elements becoming one of Killebrew's favorite stories. As he told it, "With two outs in the inning, somebody hit a one-hop line drive back toward the mound and hit Jim in the mouth. The ball ricocheted to Rich Rollins at third and Rich picked it up and threw it to me for the final out of the inning. Like I always did after the third out, I looked at the ball to see if it was scuffed and I saw Jim's teeth stuck in the ball. He was such a tough competitor. He had oral surgery and didn't miss his turn in the rotation."[16]

After the Angels game, Kaat faced the inevitable questions comparing the pressure in this pennant race to the 1965 World Series. He replied, "There's more pressure in this race. In the Series you know that if you don't win you're still going to get a pretty good payday."[17]

The *Chicago Daily News* polled all major league players and published the results of their All-Star picks. Carl Yastrzemski received more votes than any other player in both leagues; Jim Lonborg led all pitchers.[18] Having the two players most highly acclaimed by their peers did not help the Red Sox on this day.

The visiting Indians scored three runs off Red Sox starter Gary Bell in the first three innings. His replacement, Jose Santiago, did little better giving up three runs in just two innings.

Indians manager Joe Adcock certainly did not ease up on the Red Sox. He had Luis Tiant issue an intentional walk to Yastrzemski with one on and one out in the first inning. With nothing to lose, Tiant had plenty of confidence during the game. He taunted Red Sox batters approaching the plate yelling, "Tight asses!" at them. Then giggled with his high-pitched laugh.[19] The laugh was so annoying, it made the batters press harder. The frustration of not hitting made the Red Sox even madder.

In the third inning, Tiant singled. The next batter singled to center. Always a competitor, Tiant challenged Reggie Smith's arm by continuing past second base for third. Smith's throw arrived well before Tiant. Maybe because he was angry at Tiant, Smith's throw to third was well over Dalton Jones' extended glove. It flew directly into the Indians dugout, smashing to pieces the phone to the right-field bullpen.

Later in the game Tiant would make his only serious mistake, leaving a pitch to Yastrzemski over the plate. Yastrzemski's 43rd home run was wasted as the Red Sox lost another home game 6–3. After the game, Dick Williams pointed out the obvious: "We are now out of tomorrows."[20] Others were even less optimistic, concluding that the Red Sox were already out of the pennant race. After the game, Adcock told reporters that he could see that the Red Sox played tight. It was an accurate observation of a team that had lost three of its last five games.

While many players were trying to raise their play to a higher level during this last frantic week, that was not the case with the Red Sox' hitters. Carl Yastrzemski had taken extra batting practice all season long. On a team that regularly started three rookies and two second-year players, Yastrzemski was the veteran. He did not need to say anything. Young teammates saw his success and scrutinized his work habits. They were eager to emulate him.

Yastrzemski did not take batting practice after this loss, but shortstop Rico Petrocelli did. Petrocelli had two hits in the game, so he was not struggling. He felt that he needed the confidence boost of seeing the ball pop off his bat. He had lost 25 pounds during the season, mostly in the last month. An athletic six-footer who weighs only 150 pounds is lean. Petrocelli was joined by rookie center fielder Reggie Smith. Smith had played great in the field and surprised many by collecting 15 home runs and 60 RBIs. Dick Williams would insert him as the cleanup batter in the next day's lineup. Mentally tough and willing to show it, Smith was the only player on the Red

Sox to bat without a batting helmet. He continued this even after Conigliaro's beaning.

The two of them hit for almost 45 minutes.[21]

In New York, the Tigers bats were again held almost entirely in check. They managed only three hits against the Yankees Mel Stottlemyre. Fortunately two of those came in the sixth inning. Then with the bases loaded, Eddie Mathews knocked in the game's only run with a long sacrifice fly.

In the ninth, with a runner on first, Mickey Mantle hit a double play ball right at Dick McAuliffe. Just as he had on Sunday, McAuliffe lunged for the runner and missed. This time he was able to get the slow-running Mantle with a toss from his knees to first. After the game, reporters urged Mayo Smith to criticize McAuliffe who had now made the same mistake twice. He refused, "I've learned you can't prevent a fielder from making an error."[22]

The Tigers' star was Mickey Lolich who pitched his second consecutive complete game shutout for the 1–0 win. While not flawless, it was an impressive performance with little support.

It was the league's 33rd 1–0 game. The 146th shutout tied an American League record set in 1909.[23] The record would soon be obliterated.

Despite the win the Tigers clubhouse was quiet, the players grim. Smith pointed out to reporters that the Tigers would probably need to win all four of their remaining games against the Angels. Perhaps tired of reporters asking if his players were feeling the pressure, the usually taciturn Smith unexpectedly answered, "My players are no tighter than the writers."[24] In that atmosphere, it passed for levity.

The mood in losing clubhouses during these last weeks was a constant part of game reports. Morgue and mortuary were commonly repeated metaphors; funereal and somber served as adjectives. Writers and presumably their readers expected players to show their disappointment. It was a sign that players cared and were accountable for their insufficient performance. Some writers even took teams to task for not being more distraught in defeat.[25]

The White Sox were in Kansas City to start their two-game series with the Athletics. A cold drizzle was falling at daybreak. The field, which was not in great shape, was soaked. The umpires called the game early in the day. The teams would make up the game with a doubleheader on Wednesday. Stanky told reporters, "I hate doubleheaders at this stage of the season. It's the worst thing that could have happened to us."[26]

The players did not feel much better about it. Monday had been a day off. Their manager had repeatedly berated them for having a terrible record after off-days.[27] At least some of the players were convinced that their record was as bad as 1–10. (It was actually 19–18 including both games of doubleheaders.) Players did not talk of being tired or needing a rest this late in the season. They wanted to reverse this record of poor performance.

Determined to do all they could to win, they voted to work out on Monday. There was nothing half-hearted about their workout. The team played a full intra-squad game to keep their momentum going. Now, Tuesday would be a second day off. With rain coming down and the field covered, there was no chance of another workout. For some, the delay had a corrosive effect on their confidence. Players had plenty of time during that inactive day to wonder if the team could win after a layoff.

Their manager projected a calm and poised demeanor, telling reporters that he would take advantage of the free day by attending to some fall shopping.

The day was not a waste for the White Sox. They moved into a tie for second with the Red Sox, but they led the Red Sox by one game in the loss column. Minnesota regained its sole possession of first place, a full game ahead of the second-place teams.

Chapter 24

"Black Wednesday"

American League standings before play on Wednesday, September 27.

	W	L	GB
Minnesota Twins	91	68	–
Chicago White Sox	89	68	1
Boston Red Sox	90	69	1
Detroit Tigers	89	69	1½
California Angels	81	75	8½
Baltimore Orioles	74	85	17
Cleveland Indians	74	85	17
Washington Senators	73	85	17½
New York Yankees	68	90	22½
Kansas City Athletics	60	95	29

Jim Lonborg started the Red Sox home game against the Indians on two days' rest. The Red Sox had only three games left in their season and would almost certainly need to win all three of them to qualify for a playoff.

After an easy first inning Lonborg suddenly lost the fastball that made him a 21-game winner. The Indians pounded him for three singles and two doubles while scoring four runs. Lonborg finished the inning, but was pulled for a pinch-hitter after he completed the third inning. Dick Williams needed extra batters more than he did a tired ace on the mound.

The Red Sox never recovered. Although they loaded the bases twice, they could not collect the key hit. In the sixth they loaded the bases with none out, but the Indians struck out Dalton Jones, George Scott and Rico Petrocelli in order. Indians catcher Joe Azcue started taunting each Red Sox batter as he approached the plate by chanting, "Tight. Tight. Tight."[1] It worked. The Red Sox struck out nine times. The Indians tacked on a two more runs for an easy 6–0 victory. After limply going out in order in the bottom of the ninth, their 18,415 Wednesday afternoon fans booed the Red Sox off the field.[2]

The players did not take their performance lightly. They knew that they had blown their opportunity to win the pennant. The locker room was uncomfortable. The gloom made the naked light bulbs seem dimmer. It felt like a wake with an open casket that no one dared to look in.

Jerry Adair sat despondently in front of his locker. A beer bottle hung loosely from his right hand. An unpuffed cigarette dangled from his lips trailing a wisp of smoke into his eyes. Throughout his season in Boston he rarely spoke to reporters, his dour demeanor keeping them at a distance. Maybe from exhaustion he allowed a sentence to escape, "A good year and it turned to nothing in the last two days."[3]

Most of the players just sat, too tired to take a shower. Their faces were drained, exhausted not from the day's game but from months of trying to live up to their billing as heroic over-achievers. Now their dream, which had appeared so close only two days before, had slipped out of their hands.

Exhausted and more than a little despondent, Lonborg told reporters that he felt center fielder Reggie Smith should have caught one of the Indians hits in the disastrous second inning.[4] Whether warranted or not, it was a needless criticism. Lonborg had broken with his team-first attitude that had carried the Red Sox so far.

The Indians exalted at sweeping the series. Manager Joe Adcock claimed, "I could see the pressure get to them."[5] After the daily focus on how players handled tension, Adcock knew that this was the toughest shot that he could take at the Red Sox players. He seemed to enjoy it, repeating the comment as different reporters entered his office.

While players on the contending teams had spent the past months struggling for a chance to win the pennant and increase their share of post-season winnings, players on the other teams were competing for little more than their next contracts. During the last couple of weeks, that had evolved. Increasingly they played for pride. Most of them were eager to avoid any sense that they allowed a contending team to take a poorly contested win. After this game, Azcue proudly proclaimed, "We put the nails in their coffin."[6]

The Twins also played a home game, although it started later than the one in Boston. Before the game Dean Chance confided his surprise to reporters. He had never been on a team near a pennant race, but had assumed that a team's spirit would transform. "I expected more rah-rahing during a pennant race."[7] He sounded disappointed.

He started strong, giving up just one hit over the first three innings. Like Lonborg, he was pitching on two days' rest.

It came apart for him in the fourth when Don Mincher led off with a home run. Chance was frustrated. His specialty was a sinking fastball, but he could not keep his pitches down. They just hung fat in the middle of the strike zone. Four of the next five batters singled. Chance intentionally walked the fifth batter.

Ron Kline relieved with the bases loaded and none out. After striking out pitcher Rickey Clark, Kline yielded a single to late-season call-up Aurelio Rodriguez. One run scored, but Rod Carew's relay caught Bob Rodgers lumbering home. After the tag, catcher Jerry Zimmerman threw down to Versalles covering second. He tagged out Rodriguez to end the inning.

The Twins fought. They collected hits in seven innings, finally scoring one run in the seventh. Bill Rigney tried hard to neutralize their power. His pitchers walked Harmon Killebrew three times. The Angels won 5–1, scoring their last run after Jim Merritt gave up a triple to Jimmie Hall and then wild pitched him home.

The Twins had started the day in first place and knew that the Red Sox had lost. While disappointing, their situation was not dire. If, as expected, the White Sox won both of their games that evening, the Twins would be only one half-game out of first.

Chance took responsibility, "I blew it—nobody but me. There's no excuse. I just made bad pitches."[8] After the game, he sounded almost desperate: "I'm ready to do anything they want me to do. I'll start or relieve. I never wanted to win a game more, but that's history now. We've got to win the next two."[9]

On the field before this last home game of the season, the Twins held a ceremony. They presented Dean Chance with an award as the team's winningest pitcher. The players had voted on the next two awards. Rod Carew was honored as the team's rookie of the year. A large trophy was presented to Cesar Tovar as the team's MVP. After the game ex–Twin Jimmie Hall who was part of the Dean Chance trade said, "If this team thinks Tovar, and not Killebrew, is its most valuable player, it's simply too dumb to win the pennant."[10]

Twins management announced that by special permission their Saturday game in Boston would be broadcast on local television.[11] The game was originally an exclusive part of the contract with their radio network. Earlier in the week radio executives had publicly refused to relinquish that exclusivity.[12]

Although Chicago fans had not turned out in large numbers at White Sox Park during the season, they were intensely interested in the pennant race. The operators at the *Chicago Tribune* logged 1,000 calls per hour throughout Wednesday afternoon requesting baseball scores.[13]

The Athletics' team that took the field to play the White Sox was greatly changed since Al Dark and Ken Harrelson were fired. Their owner had spent most of the past month threatening to disclose embarrassing details of the players' lives. Repeatedly they had voted on pursuing a labor action against Finley, each divisive vote further fracturing team unity. A steady stream of columns depicting them as thugs or gorillas for some still undisclosed action on the August 3 flight greeted them in every city they visited.

Luke Appling was not an inspiring manager. The team was 8–26 since his arrival, 1–11 in the last 12 games. Finley had publicly committed to moving the team to a different city for 1968, so fans had little to cheer for. These would be the last two home games that the Athletics would ever play in Kansas City. It is hard to imagine a more dispirited team with less to play for. The crowd for the evening doubleheader was expected to be small. The cool weather would likely keep all but the most fervent baseball fans away. It was so gloomy that the stadium's lights were on for the 5:00 o'clock start. Fans in Chicago would be able to see the games broadcast live on WGN. Its coverage was not scheduled to begin until 6:30, 90 minutes after the first game began.[14]

It was more difficult for Dick Williams to follow the games. Leaving his home and his family, he drove his car to the top of an obscure hill where his car radio could pull the static-filled AM signal from Chicago's WMAQ. He sat there in the deepening dark while players a thousand miles away decided the fate of his team.[15]

Before they took the field the White Sox knew that the Twins and Red Sox had both lost. This was exactly the opening that they needed. The White Sox now had fewer losses than any of the other contenders.

Eddie Stanky put his big hitting lineup out on the field. The still-gimpy Ken Boyer was at third base. Pete Ward started in left field with Rocky Colavito in right. Athletics starter Chuck Dobson was completing his first full major league season. He had won nine games with an ERA of 3.76, more than half a run worse than average in 1967. Players find unusual ways of motivating themselves. After the games, Dobson would confide, "One time in Chicago early in June, I had to cover first and Stanky called me a donkey. I've never forgotten it."[16]

Gary Peters would be the White Sox' starter. It was not easy to be a leader as a player under Stanky. Peters worked well with Stanky and he commanded respect in the clubhouse. He was not interested in maintaining perquisites like an Al Kaline. Peters fought for every win and constantly motivated his teammates to fight with him. Young players looked up to him not just because he was older, but because he cared about and connected with each of them.[17] There must be many ways to put a bloody bobcat head in a teammate's locker and later enjoy a laugh at his shocked expression. Peters was innately capable of pulling it off in a way that made the victim feel fully integrated in and appreciated by the team. Even though Joe Horlen had pitched better in September, Peters' leadership had earned him the start in the first game. He wanted and expected to lead by example.

Peters had not limped through the last month. Twice he had taken the ball in must-win games and pitched 11 shutout innings. Since the disastrous start at Boston on September 1, he had pitched over 40 innings with an ERA well under 1.00. It would be hard to imagine a more clutch month from a staff ace.

With Peters on the mound, Stanky hoped to get an early lead and then bring in defensive replacements. Peters was well rested. His last start was five days earlier giving him four days off, not including his relief appearance on Sunday against Cleveland.

The first Athletics batter in the second inning was Mike Hershberger. He hit a fly to left field. Pete Ward chased the ball to the wall before he collected it and threw it in to second. Hershberger had a leadoff double. Ward had injured his ribs diving for a ball in the Cleveland series. He re-injured them on this play and had to leave the game, replaced by Ken Berry.

With shortstop Ron Hansen playing deep in the hole to prevent any groundball from making it into the outfield, Hershberger took a sizable lead off second. Peters was a lefty, so he could not see Hershberger as he stood on the mound just prior to delivering each pitch. Hershberger had not attempted to steal a base since early in September, but he easily stole third. Two batters later Jim Gosger singled him home with the game's first run.

At the end of 5½ innings, the Athletics still led 1–0. The White Sox had had only two baserunners. Peters singled in the third and then he walked in the sixth.

The first batter Peters faced in the sixth was second baseman John Donaldson. He hit a grounder to third. It was Boyer's first chance of the game. He stopped the ball but fumbled it before he could get a throw off. Donaldson was safe at first. Late-season callup Joe Rudi laid down a sacrifice bunt with a little too much force. Peters came off the mound, fielded the ball and threw to Hansen covering second. Hansen dropped the ball. Umpire Bill Valentine initially ruled Donaldson safe, then changed his call. He decided that Hansen controlled the ball before he dropped it. Donaldson was out.[18]

Peters worked to Hershberger and set him up for a curveball. Peters' pitch was good for a strike but bounced off J.C. Martin's mitt for a passed ball allowing Rudi to advance to second. Peters eventually struck out Hershberger. The next batter was Rick Monday who was completing his first season. Back in June, Peters had unapologetically broken Monday's jaw with a pitch. This time Monday singled and Rudi came home with an unearned run.

That was the second run to score off Peters. Stanky removed him and brought in Don McMahon who entered the game with a 1.75 ERA. He had thrown five strong innings on Sunday giving up one run, but that was his only run allowed in his last six appearances. Five innings were the most he had pitched in one game during 1967.

Although this was his 11th major league season, McMahon was not impervious to the pressure. He started with a wild pitch allowing Monday to advance all the way to third. That further unnerved McMahon, who walked the light-hitting Sal Bando. Stanky replaced McMahon with Wilbur Wood to face the left-hander Jim Gosger, a utility outfielder who had started about half of the Athletics' games. While not a great batter, his batting average was better than that of most of Wood's teammates.

Wood was not at his most confident. While not exceptionally fast, Monday was a daring runner. Wood could see that Martin was not having his best game behind the plate. There was perhaps no worse combination with an aggressive runner on third than a left-handed knuckleball pitcher and a catcher he did not trust. Wood focused on coming off the mound toward home after every pitch—ready to get to the plate in case the ball got away from Martin.

With two outs, the White Sox expected Gosger to swing away. He fooled them and pushed a bunt up the third baseline. With his momentum carrying him toward the plate, Wood had to pivot toward the rolling ball.

Stanky had pounded his biting criticisms of each misstep into Wood and his teammates for the whole season. More than anything else in this high-pressure situation, Wood wanted to avoid making a mistake. While he chased the ball, he watched Monday sprint for home. Wood was neither fast nor a great fielder. He decided that he could not get the ball to Martin in time to be certain that Martin would tag Monday out. In addition to the tight timing, it would be an awkward throw for a left-hander running to his right. As he reached for the ball, Wood made a decision. Needing just one out to end the inning, he whirled and threw hard to first. It was a wild throw. Monday scored and the runners ended up on second and third. Wood pulled himself together and struck out the next batter to end the inning, but now the White Sox trailed 3–0.

The pressure was on the White Sox to generate baserunners. In the seventh, Berry singled and went to second on a wild pitch. Colavito ended the inning by grounding out to the pitcher. They had no baserunners in the eighth.

Hoyt Wilhelm came on to pitch in the eighth. He was as veteran as any player in the game. It may have been his nerves, or the misty drizzle. Something affected his knuckleball. He gave up two runs on three hits and two walks before being replaced by Roger Nelson. Nelson was Stanky's white flag. His entry with the game 5–0 meant that Stanky was saving his pitchers for the next game.

With the game seemingly lost, Tommie Agee tripled to open the top of the ninth. He had hit safely in five of the last six games. The next batter, Tommy McCraw, walked.

Luke Appling was not going to allow the White Sox to snatch this rare victory from his team. He replaced the tiring Dobson with Lew Krausse. With all the accusations and recriminations, Krausse's season was already a disaster. His pitching had not been good. This would be another poor outing.

He walked Boyer and then pinch-hitter Smoky Burgess, driving home Agee with the White Sox' first run. Colavito collected the White Sox' fourth hit of the game, a single, driving in McCraw and leaving the bases loaded with Boyer on third. Krausse left having allowed all three batters he faced to reach base. Stanky had young, fast players running for both Burgess and Colavito. A single would probably bring home at least two runs.

This was a position that the White Sox had been in all year. After eight innings of futility, they had scratched their way back into the game. The winning run was at the plate with only one out. The White Sox had life. Stanky sent Wayne Causey to bat for the pitcher. The left-handed-batting Causey had started 75 games at second base before the acquisition of Ken Boyer and a batting slump in August relegated him to a role as a late-inning replacement for Don Buford. He had only three hits in September and the last had been more than two weeks earlier.

Appling brought in the left-handed Paul Lindblad to face Causey. Although he had started 10 games, Lindblad had spent most of the season as an inconsistent reliever. Causey hit Lindblad's pitch awkwardly and poked it out toward center field. Rick Monday came in to make the catch in short center field and unleashed a strong throw to the plate. Ken Boyer did not even attempt to challenge Monday's arm. He stayed on third.

The next man to step to the plate was Ron Hansen. He was batting eighth for a reason. Unlike many of the White Sox, though, his .238 average was a sign that his batting had improved through the latter part of the season. He had demonstrated throughout the season an ability to provide a hit at critical moments in tight games. He was ready to feast on the inexperienced Lindblad who had lost his last five decisions.

Instead, Hansen bounced a grounder to Sal Bando at third base. Bando had plenty of time to set his feet and fire the ball across the diamond to first baseman Joe Rudi for the final out. The score was 5–2. The White Sox had lost.

With the temperatures dropping in the damp night, the 5,325 fans allegedly in attendance for the doubleheader were visibly reduced for the final game.

Joe Horlen started the game for the White Sox with a league-leading 2.04 ERA. He had been almost perfect for the entire month of September.

He had complete-game wins in five of his six starts. In the other game, he was lifted after eight innings for a pinch-hitter with the game tied 0–0. Over those six starts he had allowed a total of three earned runs. He was so dominant that columnist Jerry Nason of the *Boston Globe* rhetorically asked in the morning's paper, "Hasn't Joe Horlen just about put a lock on the Cy Young Award?"[19] He was not alone in that opinion. Dean Chance considered Horlen the obvious selection.[20]

Appling started 21-year-old Jim Hunter who was finishing his third major league season. Hunter had lost 16 games, but his ERA was only 2.81.

As so often happened in White Sox games, it started as a pitchers' duel. Through five innings each team had one hit. In the top of the sixth, Don Buford singled for the White Sox but was stranded.

In the bottom of the sixth Horlen knocked down Hunter with a high, inside pitch to start the inning. Hunter responded with a bloop single, his second of the game. Athletics rookie shortstop Ted Kubiak came to bat with a .144 average. Expecting a sacrifice bunt, White Sox third baseman Ken Boyer cheated, standing on the infield grass. His on-going leg issues left him with little speed or agility.

Kubiak sliced the ball past Boyer and into left for a single. Donaldson, the next batter, singled to left. Hunter raced around third and headed for home. Duane Josephson tried to block the plate as he received the throw from Colavito. Hunter hit him at full speed, knocking the ball loose. In the collision Hunter's knee hit Josephson in the right temple knocking him out. Donaldson and Kubiak stopped at second and third. The Athletics had a 1–0 lead.

Although he regained consciousness, Josephson had to be carried from the field. J.C. Martin replaced him. Hershberger grounded out with the runners holding. Ramon Webster the rookie who had replaced Harrelson at first base was the next batter. He collected another single. Both Kubiak and Donaldson scored to make it 3–0.

Stanky brought in Wood to replace Horlen. Rick Monday hit a grounder to Buford at second base—a double play ball. Buford dropped the ball taking it out of his glove, and both runners were safe. Gosger singled to Ken Berry in right. Webster tried to score from second, but Berry's throw home nailed him. Monday advanced to third and Gosger to second on the throw.

Stanky had already seen Wood pitching with Monday dancing off third base in the first game. He decided to replace Wood with Bob Locker, the only one of his star relievers who had not yet pitched. Martin missed one of Locker's pitches for another passed ball allowing Monday to score. Locker closed out the inning, but the score was 4–0.

Although McCraw doubled in the seventh and Buford walked in the ninth, no one could advance them. Hunter shut the White Sox out on only three hits.

In Chicago the debacle was immediately dubbed "Black Wednesday." The two starting pitchers took the losses the hardest. They knew that the team, and especially its manager, expected each to throw a shutout. Both felt that they had failed. The expectations had been so high and there was so much emotion invested in the games that the losses were devastating. Peters cried at his locker.

Stanky had no clever comments for reporters after the games. Rather forlornly he told them, "I guess I'll remember Kansas City for a long time to come."[21]

Trying to make sense of the losses, injured shortstop Al Weis hypothesized, "The Sox could have been very tight playing for Stanky."[22] Others guessed that facing such a poor team might have lulled some players.

Stanky acted more optimistic when he faced reporters after the team's plane landed in Chicago: "All we can do is win three straight and pray."[23] Given the way that the other teams were playing, winning 92 games could very easily put them in a playoff. In the immediate aftermath of such a feeble performance it was hard to be that hopeful.

Detroit was the only team that did not play on Wednesday. They gained a half-game on the lead going from fourth to second. After Wednesday, the winner of the American League pennant was assured of having lost more games than any pennant winner in history.

The day's losses were the most frustrating possible outcome for sports columnists across the country. One of these teams should have taken advantage of this opportunity. The narrative was well established: one team would embark on a winning streak and heroically win the pennant. Having all the contenders lose was crushing. In self-defense, pundits labeled the pennant race neurotic, unbelievable and daffy.[24]

There was now no possibility of a four-way tie. The Twins and Red Sox could not both be in a playoff.

The names of the four losing pitchers: Jim Lonborg, Dean Chance, Gary Peters, and Joe Horlen. They were four of the best five pitchers in the league. The pitchers who beat them—Sonny Siebert, Rickey Clark, Chuck Dobson, and Jim Hunter—had a combined record of 45–49.

The Coca-Cola Company heavily advertised its slogan, "Things go better with Coke." Leaving the White Sox dressing room in Kansas City after Black Wednesday Gary Peters slammed an empty soda bottle on the table and started toward the door. "No, dammit, it isn't true ... it isn't true. Things don't go better with Coke."[25]

American League standings before play on Thursday, September 28.

	W	L	GB
Minnesota Twins	91	69	–
Detroit Tigers	89	69	1
Boston Red Sox	90	70	1
Chicago White Sox	89	70	1½
California Angels	82	75	7½
Cleveland Indians	75	85	16
Baltimore Orioles	74	85	16½
Washington Senators	73	85	17
New York Yankees	68	90	22
Kansas City Athletics	62	95	27½

The only game scheduled for Thursday featured the Angels playing in Detroit. After scoring only one run in two games, Mayo Smith made some changes. He benched Willie Horton for Lenny Green. Eddie Mathews would start at first base for Norm Cash. Oddly Jerry Lumpe who had not played an inning at shortstop was expected to start there for Ray Oyler.

By midmorning with driving drizzle and the temperature not likely to exceed 48 degrees, the umpires called the game. With that decision, the whole league had the day off. It was a welcome breather.

The Tigers and Angels would play a doubleheader on Friday. Just as Eddie Stanky had on Tuesday, Smith bemoaned the necessity of playing a doubleheader. "We are just not a doubleheader club. They take a lot out of a player, especially the older ones."[26] He was especially worried about Al Kaline who had chronic foot problems. It is not clear if Smith knew or cared that the Tigers were 23–13 in 1967 doubleheader games—a far better winning percentage than their other games.

Back in Chicago preparing for a three-game series with the Senators, Stanky regained his swagger. When pressed he exclaimed, "Would I like to have Wednesday back? No.... I never look back.... I never look back."[27]

The Twins who had faced the possibility of no television coverage for their final game on Sunday announced that the game would now be on two local channels: Channel 5 KSTP and Channel 11 WTCN. The stations took out ads in the local papers stressing that their broadcasts would be in color, not the typical black and white.[28]

The weather in Detroit on Friday had not improved. It had only become colder and windier. Despite only a small chance that the weather would improve, the umpires waited until about 90 minutes before the first pitch before they called the games off. The Tigers and Angels would finish their seasons with a pair of doubleheaders on the weekend. Mayo Smith's plan of pitching Wilson or Lolich on two days' rest on Sunday was long gone. Now he would need four starters. He announced that Lolich and Wilson would start on Saturday and then Sparma and John Hiller would start on Sunday. In the event that the Sunday games were postponed, which seemed possible, the league announced single games would be played on Monday and Tuesday. Smith might be able to bring back one of his aces for that last game with the pennant on the line.

Denny McLain had reportedly received a cortisone injection for his toes. His doctor believed that he could pitch in this final series.[29] Before the game was called off, he had pitched a warm-up session in the bullpen under the eyes of Johnny Sain and Smith. His pitches looked good. McLain pronounced himself ready.[30] It was now up to Smith to decide how to use him.

The White Sox were the only contenders to play on Friday. Tommy John started against the Senators. He had not pitched for over a week. Stanky had been concerned with his continuing inability to regain weight and strength. Although John's pitches looked good in practice sessions, Stanky had been saving him for a big game. This was the game. If they won, Stanky could bring back Peters and Horlen to start over the weekend.

Despite the gloom that still covered the team after Black Wednesday and the obvious pressure of the pennant race, John was unfazed. He had faith in himself and his pitches.

John started with his best stuff. The first batter hit a sinking fastball on the ground to Ken Boyer at third. Boyer came up with the ball and threw to Tommy McCraw at first. McCraw dropped it. It was only his 11th error in over 1,200 chances. He had a better fielding percentage than George Scott, the best first baseman in the league. John remained calm, as if that first batter had been out.

The next batter was Hank Allen who hit a nice double play grounder to Hansen who relayed it to Don Buford covering second. Buford tagged the base and then threw the ball over McCraw's head and into the dugout. Allen stopped on second base.

Two batters, two grounders, two errors. The White Sox were as tight as a team could be. The Senators' big slugger Frank Howard was up next. With first base open, John pitched carefully to him and Howard walked. Right fielder Fred Valentine followed. Even with runners on first and second and just one out, John was still in a strong position. A groundball could easily turn into a double play and end the inning.

Like all of the contenders, the White Sox had begun preparing for the World Series, which would begin in the American League champion's park only two days after the season ended. They had greatly expanded the facilities for the press, building seats for an additional 100 reporters. NBC would be televising the games nationally. They wanted field level cameras in addition to ones looking down from the stands. At NBC's request, the White Sox had constructed a camera pit just in front of the stands next to the first-base dugout. To protect fielders who might be looking up for a foul pop, a stout, short chain link fence enclosed the small area.[31]

Valentine popped one of John's pitches into foul territory next to the first baseline. McCraw drifted over. He was well aware of having already made an error and was determined to rectify that. He had tracked countless pops into foul territory at White Sox Park and moved confidently after the ball. He was about two steps away from catching the ball and making the second out when he hit the new fence and fell over it.

McCraw was not hurt, but Valentine was not out. Valentine lined the next pitch into right field for a single. Allen scored from second, an unearned run.

The next batter grounded into a double play and the embarrassing half-inning was over with the White Sox behind 1–0.

The Senators started Phil Ortega who had had a good season, although his won-loss record had suffered as the Senators slumped in the latter half of the season. Before the game started he had guessed that the White Sox would be feeling tight after their losses to the Athletics. Their woeful fielding in the top of the inning confirmed it. Ortega decided to keep throwing strikes and see if the White Sox could hit them.[32] He struck out the first two White Sox batters, and kept going. No White Sox runner reached third base during the entire game.

The White Sox lost 1–0 on an unearned run. They were officially eliminated from the pennant race. They had two more losses than the Twins who could lose two to the Red Sox. But if the Red Sox beat the Twins twice then they would still have one fewer losses than the White Sox. The Tigers also were two games ahead of the White Sox in the loss column.

While Eddie Stanky could look ahead with a thread of hope after the Black Wednesday losses, this was final. He closed the clubhouse to reporters for eight minutes after the game. After the clubhouse was opened, he told reporters that he took responsibility for the losses.[33]

Stanky began, "I wish we had not lost tonight's game this way. I hate errors. I'd rather that we'd have been beaten by a home run or a good clean base hit."[34] Pressed to pick an eventual pennant winner, Stanky testily replied, "I don't give a damn who wins. I'm going down to Florida to watch our boys in the instructional league."[35] As he continued, Stanky became increasingly emotional as if his steely tough-guy demeanor was no longer necessary. The press conference ended when Stanky walked away with tears streaming down his face.[36]

Anonymous position players were free in blaming the team's awful hitting on the swampy basepaths and long grass in the infield at White Sox Park. Almost every player had a much higher average on the road than at home. But, as the *Chicago Daily News* gloomily concluded, Stanky had little choice because his infielders were "not blessed with great speed and range."[37]

The White Sox would go on to lose their last two games with the Senators. On Saturday Stanky sent Gary Peters out to pitch on two days' rest in this largely meaningless game. The Senators again shut out the White Sox sending Peters to his 11th defeat. No longer sentimental, Stanky delivered a long, profane soliloquy to reporters after the game. Jerry Green, a *Detroit News* beat reporter, noted the book on the desk in Stanky's office: *The Last Battle* by Cornelius Ryan.[38] An odd bestseller, it was an immense historical tome detailing Hitler's final, delusional days.

On Sunday, Joe Horlen went for his 20th win, an important milestone for him and the team. The Senators scored four unearned runs to win 4–3. Tommy John pitched to two batters and took the loss. The White Sox' two runs in the second stopped a scoreless streak of 28 consecutive innings

In the last five critical games, White Sox pitchers allowed 18 runs, but only ten were earned. The team committed nine errors and two passed balls. On the offensive side, they scored only five runs against the worst and the second worst pitching staffs in the league.

The famous 1906 White Sox team nicknamed "The Hitless Wonders" had provided a model for this team's success. They won a World Series while batting only .230 on the season. The 1967 White Sox batted .225.

Despite their poor batting, it is likely that the White Sox were undone by their fielding. Although one columnist covering the team claimed that they lost more than 20 one-run games due to unearned runs, it just seemed that way. The team did give up a lot of unearned runs—more than 17 percent of their total. By contrast, the slick-fielding Red Sox gave up 11 percent and the Tigers only 9 percent. *Chicago Sun-Times* columnist Bill Gleason concluded, "This was more than a poor defensive team. It was a pratfall act."[39]

No team in modern times had a pitching staff like the 1967 White Sox, boasting a staff ERA of 2.45. Eight pitchers threw 89 or more innings. Bruce Howard was the only one of that group with an ERA over 2.47. Two relievers in that group had ERAs under 1.70. The staff threw 22 shutouts—six each by Joe Horlen and Tommy John.

Chapter 25

"I'll make sure I hit one for you"

American League standings before play on Saturday, September 30.

	W	L	GB
Minnesota Twins	91	69	–
Detroit Tigers	89	69	1
Boston Red Sox	90	70	1
Chicago White Sox	89	71	2
California Angels	82	75	7½
Cleveland Indians	75	85	16
Baltimore Orioles	74	85	16½
Washington Senators	74	85	16½
New York Yankees	70	90	21
Kansas City Athletics	62	97	28½

The Twins had Thursday off before traveling to Boston for the season-ending two-game series over the weekend. While team officials were busy with the final details of preparing the mailing of World Series tickets to lucky lottery winners, the team's clubhouse was almost deserted.

Dean Chance and Jim Kaat, who would start the two weekend games, came in and worked out. They were the only ones. The rest of the players enjoyed a day away from baseball.

Cal Ermer discussed the upcoming series with a reporter. He was trying to relax at the beginning of two consecutive off days. Ermer had developed dark circles around his eyes making him look downtrodden. He admitted that he was so nervous that he could not sleep more than three or four hours each night.[1]

His coach Billy Martin was in worse shape. He reportedly stayed up all night staring blankly at the television even when the programming ended and was replaced by a test pattern.[2]

On Friday before leaving for the airport, the Twins met to vote on whom would receive World Series shares. These shares would go to players on all teams that finished in the top four places of each league. The *Detroit News* published the World Series shares from 1966. For winning the World Series, each Oriole received $11,683. The second-place Twins each got $2,200. The Tigers in third and the White Sox in fourth received $1,500 and $712 each respectively.[3]

League rules required a full share be awarded to all players on the roster on June 30. Players traded within the league after that date were not eligible for any portion of a share. Only players meeting this criterion were allowed to vote on shares. The money was substantial for the players, sometimes much more than their entire salary. So, these votes were important. Often there were strong feelings about the inclusion, exclusion or size of a fractional share given to coaches, trainers or players with the club for only part of a season.

After winning the pennant in 1948 Eddie Stanky and Alvin Dark famously led Braves players in denying a World Series share to manager Billy Southworth. Commissioner Happy Chandler intervened to give Southworth a full share.[4] In 1966, Braves players refused a share to fired manager Bobby Bragan. This so offended Commissioner Eckert that he now required the manager of each team to run the meeting.

Initially the Twins players voted departed manager Sam Mele a small partial share. Then the anti–Mele players led by Jim Kaat and Ted Uhlaender insisted that the players vote either a full share or no share for Mele. Bob Allison loudly joined the anti–Mele forces.

The meeting became so acrimonious that the players asked Ermer to leave and he did.[5] Kaat and Allison were the most outspoken and probably most articulate players on the team. Kaat believed that Mele "was taking too much credit for the good and none of the blame for the bad."[6] The debate was emotional and heated. In the second vote, players voted Mele no share.

The outcome did little to smooth the players' feelings. After the vote, Dean Chance yelled at his teammates, "I'm ashamed of you."[7] To players not emotionally engaged in the dispute, the vote against Mele was just another round in the rift between Billy Martin and Johnny Sain. Al Worthington confided to reporters after players left the meeting, "This is a terrible thing to do."[8] Two players who claimed to support Mele—Zoilo Versalles and Tony Oliva—did not attend the meeting. They were among 12 players who eventually volunteered to pay a portion of Mele's share from their own pockets.[9]

Although the Twins were later castigated as cheapskates, the vote had little to do with the money. The players overwhelmingly voted an entire share to a trust fund for Walter Bond's children. Bond, who had been new to the team and barely known by most players, had started the season with the Twins. He played in only ten games before being cut in May. On September 14 he died from leukemia in a Houston hospital.

The flight to Boston was uneventful. Cal Griffith fidgeted, already anxious about the next day's game. Like a proud parent showing off a baby he pointed to the dozing Harmon Killebrew and bragged, "He is as relaxed as a puppy."[10] Al Worthington spent most of the flight signing special baseball cards he had printed with a religious message on the back.[11]

The Twins arrived to a Boston deluged with rain. Puddles filled streets and in many places were inches deep, overflowing the curbs. Forecasters predicted more rain throughout the weekend.[12] Schedules for finishing the season in case of postponements were drawn up by league president Joe Cronin whose office was in Boston. With the likely need for a playoff, the weather might cause the start of the World Series to be delayed until the following weekend, or later.

On the short drive from the airport to their hotel, the Twins bus driver became lost. A few of the Twins did not hide their frustration at the delay. In response, the driver made some derogatory comments about the Twins in his thick Boston accent. Sherry Robertson, the Twins director of minor league operations who was also Cal Griffith's brother, had a few hot words with the driver before everyone settled down and the bus eventually arrived at the hotel.[13]

The next day, the Twins' bus arrived at Fenway Park without incident. The players were confident. If they won both games, they would win the pennant outright unless Detroit won all four games with the Angels. Even if they lost a game, the pressure would be on Detroit to win three of its games with the tough Angels to force a playoff.

The biggest reason for the Twins' confidence was their starting pitcher, Jim Kaat. An immense lefthander, he looked even bigger staring down from the mound. Opponents referred to him as hulking.[14] This physique only reinforced his reputation as an intense competitor who wanted to dominate every batter.

His personality fit Johnny Sain's basic pitching strategy of challenging hitters by throwing strikes. Kaat liked throwing his fastball, which tailed away from right-handed batters. To keep batters from crowding the plate to reach it, he threw his slider to the inside of the plate. Like Chance, Kaat had a long, slow wind up.[15] Unlike Chance, Kaat had trained himself from boyhood to field his position exceptionally well. By the time his pitch reached the batter, Kaat was set and prepared. Just before leaving Minnesota for Boston, Kaat had received a long-awaited box of new baseball gloves. Unfortunately, they were all made for a left hand.[16] Kaat pitched with his left hand.

After a horrible beginning to the year and a slump in August, Kaat had become one of the league's best pitchers in September. He had regained the form that made him the best pitcher in the American League in 1966. While many players were questioned about the negative effects of the pennant race tension, Kaat claimed that the extra adrenalin made him a better pitcher.[17] Whatever motivated him, Kaat had won seven games with a 1.57 ERA during the month. In seven starts, he had six complete games. In the last days of the race, Kaat had emerged as the pitcher who could carry the Twins on his shoulders.

Kaat would oppose Red Sox starter Jose Santiago. He had been anxious since he was named this game's starter by Dick Williams. For the first time he took sleeping pills so that he could sleep at nights. Santiago was one of the few major league Puerto Rican players. His first full year in the major leagues was 1966 when he started 28 games and was one of the better pitchers on a weak Red Sox team. His 1967 season under Dick Williams had been a little rockier. After poor starts in May caused his ERA to balloon to over 6.00, the Red Sox tried to trade him.[18] There was no interest. He spent a couple of months as a reliever. Although he made five starts in August and September, he was still used mostly as a reliever. In the beginning of September he had been hit in the eye while shagging flies during batting practice in Washington. With the horror of Tony Conigliaro's injury seared into the team's memory, Santiago flew back to Boston for evaluation by eye specialists. They had cleared him two days later.

His complete game win over the Orioles in the second game of the doubleheader the past Friday apparently convinced Williams to start him in this do-or-die game.[19] If the Red Sox lost, it would be impossible for them to win the pennant or qualify for a playoff. By one measure Santiago's arm was relatively fresh. He had not yet thrown 140 innings. Kaat had already thrown over 260, including over 63 innings in September alone.

Beyond the stress on all the players during this momentous weekend, Santiago had an additional handicap. He had spent his career in obscurity. Even during this pennant race, he had been almost anonymous. Suddenly, with no real preparation, he had been thrust into the glaring spotlight. During the two off days leading up to the game he was interviewed more than during the rest of his career. Photographs show an almost bewildered expression as Santiago tentatively displayed a gap-toothed smile. While he might have enjoyed the novelty in the middle of the season, now every innocuous question reinforced the magnitude of his task.

Under the unaccustomed barrage of questions, Santiago revealed that his wife, Edna, provided his coaching. She would sit in the stands and let him know if he had made any changes to his delivery. The night before every game, the two of them would go through the opposing team's entire lineup. Edna kept detailed scorecards from all of his past starts. On these she noted every pitch that he had thrown and what the result had been. Proudly Santiago declared, "Now she is almost an expert."[20]

While Santiago slept under the influence of sleeping pills, Red Sox slugger Carl Yastrzemski was sleep-deprived. On Thursday evening, his son Mike had become painfully ill. Yastrzemski and his wife became convinced that Mike was suffering from appendicitis. Yastrzemski rushed him to the local hospital in the middle of the night. It proved a false alarm, but Yastrzemski spent the night comforting his son until he was discharged Friday morning.[21]

Big Jim Kaat was a dominant pitcher for the Twins during the season's final month. He started eight games, winning seven and completing six with a 1.51 ERA. Articulate and outspoken, Kaat's difficult relationship with parts of the team's field staff festered throughout the season. National Baseball Hall of Fame and Museum.

On Friday, while Yastrzemski was at Fenway Park working out, his household transformed. Yastrzemski owned a nice suburban house in a quiet neighborhood. As the day progressed it became jammed with friends and his family from Long Island who had come up to Boston for the big games. The crowded, noisy house exacerbated every tension. For the visitors, the night was a celebratory party that went on and on. No matter how much he wanted to sleep, Yastrzemski was the center of attention.

This did not change Yastrzemski's game-day routine. On Saturday he arrived at the ballpark early. Mentally, he used the extra time to prepare to hit. He had heard the weather forecast on the radio as he drove to the park. Now he walked to the top of Fenway Park to feel what the wind was actually doing high above the interference from the stands. There was a substantial breeze blowing toward right field. It would help turn any high fly to right into a home run.

Retreating to the isolation of the trainer's room, Yastrzemski planned his approach based on what he knew of Kaat, the fielders who would be behind him, and various in-game scenarios. One of Yastrzemski's biggest concerns before this game was Kaat's fielding ability. Kaat was a five-time Gold Glove winner. In Yastrzemski's mind, he made it almost impossible to hit the ball up the middle.[22]

After batting practice Yastrzemski took a nap. Ironically, he had never felt such a heightened focus.

It was during batting practice that Red Sox players learned from some disaffected Twins that Mele had been cut out of their World Series shares. Mele had worked for the Red Sox throughout the summer after his firing. He was a personable man. The Red Sox players knew him and liked him. Many were furious that the Twins' players would give him nothing.[23] This slight of Sam Mele may have helped focus the players' tension toward anger and aggression.

The Red Sox needed to be aggressive. Both Yastrzemski and his manager felt that the Red Sox had been defensive at the plate in their two losses to Cleveland. Yastrzemski believed that against two strike-throwing pitchers like Kaat and Dean Chance defensive batting would not be successful.[24]

The press had used the days off to build up the struggle between Yastrzemski and Harmon Killebrew to secure the home run crown. They entered the game tied with 43 home runs—only one other player had more than 30. Yastrzemski was also poised to win the Triple Crown, if he could best Killebrew. Both men claimed that winning the pennant was far more important than individual honors.

Before the Red Sox took the field for the game, Santiago approached Yastrzemski. He promised that he would not allow Killebrew to hit a home run off him during the game. Yastrzemski replied, "You make sure none of his go out and I'll make sure I hit one for you."[25]

The game drew politicians like bears to honey. The Red Sox provided prime tickets directly along the first baseline to many of these dignitaries. There were reportedly six governors in attendance.[26] Minnesota native Vice President Hubert Humphrey sat next to Massachusetts Senator Ted Kennedy. An assortment of state and city grandees seated next to and directly behind them could be seen desperately leaning to be included in the news photos. Massachusetts' other United States Senator, Ed Brooke, purchased his own tickets and sat in the right-field bleachers with his daughters Remi and Edwina. When asked he told reporters, "These are the best I could get."[27] Coincidentally, Brooke was the only one of the politicians who was African American.

Newsmen from around the country had been sent to cover this series. The buildup for the game was largely deserved. Never before had three teams in the American League entered the next-to-last day of the season with a chance to win the pennant. Two of those teams, the Red Sox and Twins, were about to begin a knockout series. They could not emerge tied for first place.

If it had not been for the novelty of four teams vying for the pennant, more fans would have noticed that the Red Sox and Twins had staged one of the closest two-team races ever. Neither team had been more than one game out of first place since August. They had been tied for 13 of the 29 days in September. It was fitting that the two teams would battle each other directly during the season's final two days.

Since the early part of the season, Red Sox bullpen coach Al Lakeman had performed the same ritual with pitchers before every start. He handed Santiago a brand new baseball after he finished his warm-up pitches and told him, "Give it back to me after nine."[28]

Despite an inauspicious forecast, the game began in unbroken sunlight. Fenway's ragged grass was not unusual for a major league field at the end of a long season. More noticeable were the effects of the heavy rains. Where the foul line extended into right field, it went through a clearly visible puddle. Players could be seen trying to remove mud where it clumped under their spikes. A single to right field in the first inning caused small splashes from the wet sod.

Santiago started the game like a pitcher with a lot to lose. His posture was stiff as he delivered each pitch; there was no bend to his back. His pitches were high, and some wild. He rushed from pitch to pitch as if eager to forget what he had just thrown.[29] Zoilo Versalles led off and singled. After Cesar Tovar flied out, Santiago walked Killebrew on four careful pitches. Tony Oliva made him pay by singling, which scored Versalles from second. Bob Allison singled hard to left field. Carl Yastrzemski came up with the ball and fired it in. Fearing Yastrzemski's arm, Billy Martin had to hold the slow-footed Killebrew at third. Santiago appeared completely overmatched.

The bases were loaded for Rod Carew with only one out. There was a pitcher already warming in the Red Sox bullpen. Carew hit a soft line drive that Jerry Adair caught at third. The runners had to hold. Pitching to Ted Uhlaender, Santiago lost some of his control. With three balls on Uhlaender, Dick Williams decided that if Santiago walked him, or gave up a hit, he would have to replace him with Gary Bell.[30] Uhlaender hit the next pitch on the ground to Mike Andrews at second. He tossed it to George Scott to retire the side. Despite three singles and a walk, Santiago had escaped by yielding only one run. Surprisingly, he walked off the mound feeling confident. He believed that he had good stuff on his pitches.

Santiago may have been viewed as an inexperienced pitcher by most, but he had plenty of confidence and his teammates' respect. A demonstrative pitcher, he did not hesitate to reposition his outfielders or call out instructions to his infielders between pitches.

Both teams collected hits, but the pitchers settled in until Santiago came to bat in the bottom of the third. Santiago began the game batting .205, and was expected to be an easy out. Kaat came straight at him with fastballs. On a 1–2 pitch, Kaat felt a pop like the snapping of fingers in his left elbow.[31] Although he visibly winced while delivering each pitch, Kaat tenaciously battled through the eight-pitch at-bat until he struck Santiago out.

Kaat thought he might be hurt, but the pain was bearable. His catcher Jerry Zimmerman visited the mound and then returned to the plate to explain the situation to home plate umpire Jim Honochick. With Honochick and Cal Ermer at the mound, Kaat was allowed to take five warm-up pitches to assess his elbow.

He decided to continue. Trying to throw hard, he threw two low-velocity fastballs to Mike Andrews. He had neither control nor speed on his pitches. No matter how determined, he had to be taken from the game. Kaat always evinced great pride in the durability of his arm.[32] Like Lolich, he threw every day during the season to constantly strengthen it. Despite that regimen, in possibly his most important game of the season, it failed him.

This undermined the Twins at every level. Most had assumed that Kaat would pitch a complete game, possibly shutting out the Red Sox who had batted poorly in their two losses to the Indians. Now, Ermer had to go to his bullpen in which he had little confidence. Psychologically, the team felt a letdown. To win they would all have to raise their game. It was added pressure in a game already heavy with tension.

Jim Perry replaced Kaat, and was allowed to take as many warm-up pitches as needed on the mound.[33] He pitched well in the third and fourth innings.

Reggie Smith led off the Red Sox' fifth with a double to center. The aggressive Smith could be a dangerous baserunner. Only a few weeks earlier he had stolen five bases in one night against the Yankees. The Twins had to be aware of him at all times.

Williams pinch-hit the recently hot Dalton Jones for catcher Russ Gibson. Jones singled aided by a bad bounce. Perry struck out the next two batters. He seemed to have the third out when Adair hit a bloop pop into shallow center. Carew started back for it, but slipped and fell. Ermer later blamed the soaking rain from the previous day for making the infield dirt too soft for Carew's spikes.[34] Carew reached the ball only after it bounced on the outfield grass. Adair was safe and Smith scored.

Yastrzemski was the next batter. He approached the plate with runners on first and third. Perry got him to ground to the right side of the infield. Killebrew turned to his right and lunged toward the ball as it skipped past. Carew who was playing back near the outfield grass made an outstanding play to grab the ball before it skidded by for a single.

Perry never moved off the mound.

With no one covering first, Yastrzemski was safe and Jones scored the second run. It was the sort of inexplicably sloppy fielding play that had plagued the Twins all year. The next batter was Ken Harrelson who had been given the start after a week on the bench. He fouled out to end the inning, but the Red Sox led 2–1. Williams replaced Harrelson, who had already misplayed a fly ball into a triple, with Jose Tartabull.[35]

The Twins answered immediately. In the top of the sixth they collected two walks and two singles to score a run and leave the bases loaded with two outs.

Williams came to the mound to remove Santiago.

Santiago felt strong. Despite the rough inning, he was brimming with confidence. Throughout the past month, Williams had repeatedly shown a preference to stay with a pitcher rather than remove him at the first sign of trouble. He liked Santiago's attitude and left him on the mound to face Versalles. Santiago came in with a side arm curve that Versalles popped up to third to end the inning with the score tied 2–2. It was his best pitch of the game.[36]

Ermer had pinch-hit for Perry, so Ron Kline began the sixth. The first batter was George Scott who entered the game batting .303, the fourth best in the league. Kline was not foolhardy. His first pitch to Scott was low and outside. It did not matter. Scott blasted it five rows into the center-field seats to make the score 3–2. An out-of-town reporter felt compelled to describe the cheering, which he likened to over 90,000 fans celebrating a game-winning touchdown.[37] There was no baseball comparison. It was too loud for too long.

Santiago had possibly his best inning in the seventh. After numerous fouls, he struck out Killebrew for the second time in the game. Earlier after a called third strike, the mild-mannered Killebrew turned and barked at Honochick.[38] It was one of the few times in his long career that Killebrew disputed a called strike. Even his nerves were beginning to fray.

Killebrew was not the only one. The game had been tight from the beginning. There had been plenty of baserunners, which only added to the tension. To spectators as well as players, it seemed that every at-bat, maybe every pitch, might provide a turning point. Even the seasoned announcers working the game could not keep the strain out of their voices.

Kline was still on the mound for the Twins to start the seventh. With one out, Andrews started to swing at a Kline breaking pitch. He checked his swing, but connected with the ball. Andrews started sprinting for first as the ball dribbled onto the infield grass. Kline came off the mound to collect the ball, but Andrews beat the throw to first.

The next batter was Jerry Adair who already had a hit and an RBI. He topped the ball and it bounced weakly toward the mound. Kline grabbed it and started a double play with a good throw to Versalles at second. The ball bounced out of Versalles' glove for an error with both runners safe. The inning should have been over. Instead, the Red Sox had two baserunners.

In the Red Sox dugout Scott leaned over to Joe Foy and predicted that Yastrzemski would make the Twins pay for their poor fielding.[39] Ermer brought in the left-handed Jim Merritt to face the left-handed batting Yastrzemski. An overly baggy uniform accentuated Merritt's slim build. The crowd had been loud throughout the game. The roar was now described as intolerable—exceptional for a baseball game.[40] In this situation requiring a clutch performance, Boston's fans saw their star striding to the plate. The anxiety in all those hearts came pouring forth as incoherent noise.

Yastrzemski did not just step to the plate. He planted himself there, as if he owned it.[41] Merritt looked overmatched. Yastrzemski appeared to be in absolute control. He was looking for a high fastball and he was willing to wait for it.

On the defensive, Merritt pitched cautiously. His first three pitches were all near the edge of the strike zone, but Yastrzemski did not swing. Merritt's fourth pitch was poor, running the count to 3-1. This was a hitter's count. Merritt needed to throw a strike. The noise increased noticeably. It was painful. At the plate Yastrzemski always held his bat unusually high with his hands above his left ear. Normally, he wiggled the bat gently as he waited for each pitch to arrive.

For this pitch his bat was motionless.[42] Merritt threw his high fastball. There was no doubt when the bat met the ball. It landed in the visitors' bullpen beyond right field. The score was 6-2.

Santiago had thrown 120 pitches before he began the eighth by walking Bob Allison. Dick Williams removed him for Gary Bell. As Santiago took his slow walk from the mound to the dugout, the fans delivered an unrestrained standing ovation. He felt a surge of overwhelming emotion and for a moment feared that he would start crying on the field.[43] Keeping his eyes on the ground, Santiago put his hand to his cap's bill by way of acknowledgment before disappearing into the dugout.

While the pitching change was taking place, three fans made their way on to the field. Each ran to left field to congratulate Carl Yastrzemski by shaking his hand. Members of the small police detachment then escorted the intruders from the field.[44]

Bell finished the eighth and had two outs in the ninth when Tovar doubled. Killebrew was the next batter. Bell was prepared to pitch cautiously to him and yield a walk rather than give up a big hit. From the dugout, Dick Williams overruled him. He wanted Bell to challenge Killebrew by throwing strikes.[45]

Bell followed instructions and Killebrew homered. Bell then retired Tony Oliva to end the game 6–4.

The two sluggers had come through for their teams. Killebrew was 2 for 4 with a home run and two RBIs. Yastrzemski was 3 for 4 with a home run and four RBIs. They remained tied in their pursuit of the home run title. Their teams were now tied for first in their pursuit of the pennant.

In a seemingly empty gesture, a bitter Cal Ermer told reporters that he would fine Jim Perry for not covering first base.[46] A disgusted Perry had already told anyone who would listen that he was fining himself.[47]

After the players had left the field and headed to their clubhouses and after all the fans, delirious with the victory, had funneled through the exits and poured forth into the narrow city streets around Fenway Park, Zoilo Versalles sat at the home-plate end of the third-base dugout.[48] His big tinted glasses covered half his face. Only his mind moved. He thought about all the plays in the game. There were two in particular: his error and his popup with the bases loaded. He sat alone for a long time.

In the Red Sox clubhouse, Jose Santiago sat still flushed with victory and enjoying the attention that came with winning such a big game. A widely published photograph showed him kissing Yastrzemski on the cheek.[49] He confessed that while discussing the upcoming game with his wife during the previous evening, she had told him, "Honey, I think Oliva will give you trouble."

Not burdened by an enormous ego, Santiago had replied, "Honey, they all give me trouble."[50]

Among the throngs of newsmen in attendance was Jimmy Breslin, probably the country's most colorful columnist. Although based in New York, Breslin's column appeared in papers nationwide. If he traveled to cover an event, it was only because it was of interest throughout the country. He treated readers the next day with his assessment of this game: "From the start there was only one man on the field to watch. There were pitchers and fielders and umpires and there were hits and there were runs, but the whole game came down to Carl Yastrzemski."[51]

Chapter 26

"It was a dumb play"

American League standings before play on Saturday, September 30.

	W	L	GB
Minnesota Twins	91	69	–
Detroit Tigers	89	69	1
Boston Red Sox	90	70	1
Chicago White Sox	89	71	2
California Angels	82	75	7½
Cleveland Indians	75	85	16
Baltimore Orioles	74	85	16½
Washington Senators	74	85	16½
New York Yankees	70	90	21
Kansas City Athletics	62	97	28½

Despite two days of postponed games due to the foul weather, reporters stranded in Detroit still had to file stories with their papers. They grilled both managers hoping for insightful quotes. Mayo Smith blandly repeated his assertion, "We still need four for four against California."[1]

Bill Rigney had motivated his team through a successful series against the Twins. On Thursday, he took Smith's hope as a challenge. "There is no way the Tigers are going to sweep us," he bragged.[2] After Friday's game was postponed, that no longer seemed strong enough. He loudly confided to reporters that he had told his players, "We owe Detroit something."[3]

It was widely speculated that the delays would render the Tigers increasingly tight. Never one to forego a psychological advantage, Rigney piled on. Claiming that the delay had hurt the Tigers far more than his club he added, "I didn't have my big man Rick Reichardt in the lineup because of a sore left wrist. He may be able to play all the way now."[4] In midseason Rigney had benched Reichardt as his batting average plummeted. Since then, his average had risen almost .030. Reichardt had been out of Rigney's doghouse for over a month. He entered the weekend second on the team in both home runs and RBIs.

Rigney sent out George Brunet as the starting pitcher for the first game. At the beginning of the season, Brunet had been a Tigers killer registering his first two victories against them. His season had been as much of a roller coaster as that of the Angels. Early on he languished with a 1–9 record. As the Angels bats provided a little more support he posted a 6–1 record for a portion of the mid-season. That ended in August. He had not won since August 4. His pitching was not that bad. During one nine-start stretch he had an 0–5 record but a 2.03 ERA. Although Brunet's pudgy physique and legendary partying earned him a reputation as poorly conditioned, he was a workhorse.[5] His major league career started in 1956, but he still pitched a full season of winter baseball every year. Brunet had already faced over 1,000 batters in 247 innings. Although his arm was fine, he looked tired.

The Tigers should have been tight. Rigney was well aware of their struggles at the plate in New York and Washington earlier in the week. If they could be shut out by Al Downing and held to a single run by Mel Stottlemyre, then George Brunet might be able to hold them down, too.

This rosy scenario dissipated in the bottom of the first inning. Brunet walked Dick McAuliffe. He was still on first when Willie Horton came to bat with two outs. Horton blasted Brunet's fastball for his 18th home run.

The score was still 2–0 when Brunet took the mound in the second inning. He was less effective than he had been in the first inning. The first batter was Don Wert, who doubled. Eddie Mathews knocked him home with a single. The third batter also singled, leaving runners on first and second with none out. Mickey Lolich moved them along with a sacrifice before Dick Tracewski scored Mathews with a sacrifice fly. Brunet escaped the inning by inducing McAuliffe to ground weakly to first base.

Rigney could see that Brunet was not going to dominate the Tigers and pinch-hit for him in the top of the third. Like Stanky and Dark, Rigney believed that his role as a manager was to create favorable matchups for his players. Earlier in the season he had once sent five pinch-hitters to the plate in one inning; two of them batted for other pinch-hitters. The Angels scored seven runs that inning, but not everyone in Anaheim was happy with Rigney's maneuverings. One fan leaned into the dugout and "screamed nasty words" at Rigney for over-managing.[6]

In this game, Rigney used 16 players, but could never overcome this early deficit.

The game could not have gone better for Mayo Smith. Mickey Lolich pitched a complete game shutout. Only two Angels made it to second base.

Before the game, Lolich was fully aware of the magnitude of his situation. He was certain that this was the biggest game he had ever pitched. The team needed every win. One bad outing could ruin the Tigers season. Apparently lending Lolich public support, Smith added to the pressure by proclaiming, "He's my best pitcher and he's had enough rest now."[7] Smith should have been aware that his pitchers were not getting enough rest. This was Lolich's fourth start since September 19. He had a total of eight days' rest in that stretch, less than three per start.

Lolich had thrown three complete game shutouts in nine days—27 consecutive innings. In the last week of a pennant race that had seen the best pitchers in the American League lose critical games, his performances stood out.

The complete game was especially valuable for Smith who would need pitchers for three more games during the weekend. His problem was not that he wanted to save his best relievers for other games. Smith did not want to use any of his relievers. He had lost faith in them. Despite having hired the best pitching coach in baseball, Smith pointedly never consulted Johnny Sain about pitchers. There was never a consideration that Smith would ask Sain for advice about in-game moves. That was clearly the manager's prerogative. By the end of the season, though, it began to strike observers as odd that Smith would not even discuss the pitchers' readiness with Sain.[8]

Sain's methods focused on each pitcher's positive mental attitude. Smith's mentors in the 1940s and 1950s vented their displeasure at any player's shortcomings. It was received wisdom that beating players down made them tougher. Out of frustration Smith had announced that his bullpen was letting the whole team down. Smith was working at cross-purposes with his pitching coach and the results showed.

Smith was much happier with the Tigers batters who collected five runs on ten hits. Although Horton's home run made him the hero, eight of the starters had been on base.

Between the games, there was little about the Tigers' demeanor to suggest they had won.[9] Smith had repeatedly emphasized that they would need to win all four games against the Angels. The players knew that the Red Sox had defeated the Twins. The Tigers were officially in first place, .001 ahead of both the Red Sox and Twins. It meant little to the players trying to relax in the Tigers clubhouse. They had to win games. If they won their last three games, they would win the pennant outright. With the Twins loss, they finally had a small margin of comfort. Now if they lost one, they were still guaranteed to be in the playoff.

The Tigers started their 22-game winner Earl Wilson in the second game. He had enjoyed a luxurious four days of rest since his start against the Yankees.

Wilson had a 1–2 record against the Angels in 1967. He had pitched fairly well allowing only five earned runs in 24⅓ innings over three starts. That 1.85 ERA was well below his season ERA of 3.27. Having watched Lolich's performance, his teammates had every reason to be confident.

To oppose Wilson, Rigney was starting Jack Hamilton. In mid–September, Hamilton had pitched his best game of the season, holding the Yankees without an earned run for his entire 10-inning stint. Three days later he injured his arm throwing a wild pitch in the sixth inning. He finished the inning, but pitched only five more innings over the next two weeks. Hamilton's ERA had been 2.30 before he beaned Tony Conigliaro in August. Entering this game, it was 3.03.

From the beginning, it was not a competitive match. Hamilton was in pain every time he threw the ball and looked out of sync. He loaded the bases on a single and two walks, retiring only Al Kaline on a foul pop. After ⅓ of an inning Rigney replaced him with 38-year-old Curt Simmons. The Tigers scored three runs.

Jim Fregosi homered off Wilson in the third to make the score 3–1. The Angels scored again in the fourth on two singles and a passed ball, but Wilson was still strong. With the score 4–2 in the top of the sixth, Wilson walked Jimmie Hall. Mayo Smith pulled him and brought in Fred Lasher. It was as surprise move for a manager reluctant to use his bullpen.

Lasher pitched strongly, retiring six of seven batters he faced.

The Angels, by contrast, had already used six pitchers as they struggled to contain a Tigers attack that had already produced seven hits and seven walks. Despite the score, Rigney had no intention of just letting the game play out. Before the game was over, 20 Angels would play.

In the bottom of the seventh the Tigers took a 6–2 lead on Jim Northrup's home run. After the home run, the next two batters reached base. With Lasher due to bat, Smith faced a decision. His bench was almost full, as he had made only one substitution using Ray Oyler as a defensive replacement. There were some powerful hitters in the Tigers dugout including Norm Cash and Gates Brown.

On the other hand, Lasher was pitching well. He was well rested, having pitched only once since yielding Yastrzemski's home run on September 18. In his intervening appearance against the Senators, Lasher started by pitching two strong innings, facing the minimum of six batters. Then Smith had sent him out to pitch the ninth inning, a third inning of work. Lasher had allowed three of the four batters he faced to single. They all eventually scored and the Tigers lost. That was not the first time Lasher had been called on to pitch more than two innings. Despite twice throwing three or more shutout innings against the Twins, Lasher had been most effective in his short major league career when he pitched for two or fewer innings.

It was a critical moment. Maybe more important than Lasher's pitching history, was Smith's almost complete distrust of his relief pitchers.

Instead of a pinch-hitter, Smith allowed Lasher to bat. He struck out.

In the top of the eighth, Lasher gave up three singles, a walk and two runs without retiring a batter. As each batter came to the plate, Smith faced the same choice that he had had before the inning started. For three consecutive batters, Smith hoped and maybe prayed that somehow Lasher's sinker would induce a double-play groundball.[10] It never did.

Reluctantly, Smith brought in the left-handed Hank Aguirre with the score now 6–4. Runners stood on first and third with no outs. Rigney countered with right-handed Bubba Morton to pinch-hit for left-handed Roger Repoz. Morton hit a grounder back to Aguirre.

Running on contact from third base, Don Mincher was halfway down the baseline before he realized that the pitcher had fielded the ball. Everyone in Tiger Stadium could see that he would be an easy out at the plate. Bill Freehan yelled for the ball, but the bellowing sellout crowd drowned him out.[11] Aguirre never heard him and never looked toward Mincher. He threw to first and got one out while Mincher scored.

Only after he got the ball back from first baseman Eddie Mathews and started to walk to the mound did Aguirre realize his mistake. His shoulders slumped.

Aguirre walked Bob Rodgers before the procession of Tigers pitchers continued.

Bobby Knoop bounced a grounder to the next pitcher, Fred Gladding. He grabbed the ball, but it rolled out of his glove for an infield single, loading the bases. That was all for Gladding. Smith brought in John Hiller. He immediately yielded a single and the game-tying run. Two batters later Fregosi collected his second single of the inning and knocked in two more runs for the lead. When Hiller finally got the third out, the Angels led 8–6. Hiller's performance was reminiscent of the Tigers' Sunday loss to the Senators. In both games, Hiller allowed both tying and winning runs to score, but ended the day with a clean stat line and the loss pinned to one of his teammates.

The last six Tigers batters went meekly in order without getting a ball out of the infield.

There were plenty of failures during the Tigers meltdown in the top of the eighth starting with Smith's decision to send Lasher out for a third inning. Smith allowed the struggling Lasher to face four batters; Gladding could not field Knoop's groundball; Hiller allowed all three inherited runners to score. Smith remained oblivious to those missteps. After the game, he was vehement.[12] Aguirre's throw to first was the turning point in the game. It was inexcusable. Smith's phlegmatic stoicism had abandoned him. The weeks of tension had worn down and now shredded his self-control.

Aguirre sat on his stool ashen-faced, a cold sweat beaded on his skin. His hands shook noticeably and his eyes were glazed. After Smith's denunciation, reporters clumped at his locker. Aguirre could not believe what had happened: "I've made that play a thousand times. I should have looked Mincher back. It was a dumb play."[13]

On the other side of the room Hiller sat alone, head buried in hands. No one bothered him.[14]

The Tigers, who had not been able to enjoy their victory in the first game, were now despondent. Another late-inning lead had slipped away. Four of the Tigers last five losses had seen them turn a late-inning lead into a loss. Whether the problem was physical or mental, it appeared that they lacked the will to close games out. No lead was safe. They were 5–5 in their last ten games, but could have been 9–1 and preparing for the World Series. The Tigers played to their reputation of not being able to win a game to stay on top of the standings. To observers outside of Detroit, the problem was clear. The team lacked heart.[15]

The dark mood made it feel as if the Tigers had just lost their hold on the pennant. Even the recently chipper Al Kaline had no comment. The reality was not that bad. With two wins on Sunday, the Tigers would be in a playoff for the pennant.

If the players were disappointed, their fans were beyond frustration.

A big part of that might have been the largely negative coverage in the city's two papers. After this doubleheader split, the *Detroit Free Press* devoted less than five paragraphs to the win and focused almost exclusively on each mistake that led to the loss.[16] The rival *Detroit News* split their coverage similarly.[17] By contrast, the *Boston Globe* describing the Red Sox doubleheader split with the Orioles only six days earlier, dismissed the team's humiliating 10–0 loss in less than a paragraph. Virtually the entire, lengthy story trumpeted the Red Sox' victory.[18]

The Tigers' position was clear when Sunday dawned. If they won both games, they would be in a three-game playoff for the pennant with the last two games played in Detroit. If they lost either game of the doubleheader, their season was over.

Joe Sparma started the first game for the Tigers against Angel Clyde Wright. The Tigers had had the same four primary starters for the entire season, and Sparma had been one of them. He had thrown over 200 innings and had a 3.72 ERA. Despite Eddie Stanky's disparagement, Sparma was remarkably consistent. His ERA had remained virtually unchanged since the end of May. Sparma was rested. He had not pitched for a full week. Originally he had been scheduled for the Thursday game against the Angels. The rainouts and his manager's strategies had pushed his start behind Lolich's and Wilson's.

While not complaining, Sparma was a bit apprehensive. He admitted that sitting for the extra days gave him too much time to think about the importance of the game.[19] Sparma was a heavy smoker and had spent most of the week at the mercy of his nerves chain smoking.

That was not Wright's concern. He would be making only his fourth start since mid-July. Both Angels starters on Saturday had been knocked around in the first inning. He was determined to avoid that fate. While Wright was already 26, this was only his second partial season in the major leagues. He had been brought up to the Angels in June as a starter, but had spent much of the season in the bullpen. He had pitched well in September including a complete game win over the Orioles at the beginning of the month.

Even though the Angels were eliminated from the pennant race, this game on the season's last day suddenly gained importance for both the team and Wright. Although the pressure was on the Tigers, it did not look that way when the game started. Eager to avoid a bad first inning, Wright pitched tentatively.

Dick Tracewski led off with a single. Two batters later Willie Horton hit his second first-inning home run of the weekend. The score was 2–0. After two more singles, Wright finally got the third out.

Don Mincher led off the Angels' second inning with a home run to make it 2–1. Wright steadied himself in the bottom of the second. Then he watched as his teammates loaded the bases with no outs and yet still failed to score in a long inning. Wright got the first two batters out in the third before center fielder Roger Repoz allowed Horton's fly ball to get away from him for a two-base error. Three unearned runs scored before Wright was pulled from the game. He was the Angels' third consecutive starter who failed to make it through the third inning. The inning ended with the Tigers ahead 5–1.

Although the Angels scored three more runs on another two home runs, the Tigers cruised to a 6–4 win. Fred Gladding who had faced only one batter the day before, closed out the last two innings after Sparma yielded Mincher's second home run.

Despite plenty of scoring, the game was over in only two hours and 24 minutes. The game in Boston was still underway. With the win, the Tigers had equaled the records of the Twins and the Red Sox. The American League was, on the last day of the season, again in a three-way tie.

The Tigers knew two things as they retreated to their clubhouse between games. One of the teams playing in Boston would win that game. If the Tigers wanted to continue their season they would also have to win to create a tie and advance to a playoff series.

Chapter 27

"Surprised the hell out of me"

American League standings before play on Sunday, October 1.

	W	L	GB
Boston Red Sox	91	70	–
Minnesota Twins	91	70	–
Detroit Tigers	90	70	½
Chicago White Sox	89	72	2
California Angels	83	76	7
Baltimore Orioles	75	85	15½
Washington Senators	75	85	15½
Cleveland Indians	75	86	16
New York Yankees	71	90	20
Kansas City Athletics	62	98	28½

The Red Sox and Twins entered the final day of the season tied for first place with the Tigers a half-game behind. The Red Sox–Twins game would knock the loser out of the pennant race. The winner would win the pennant, unless the Tigers won both of their games. In that case, they would qualify for a playoff series with the Tigers and the pennant race would continue.

The benchmark for close multiple team pennant races had long been the 1908 season. In the American League that year, the Detroit Tigers held a half-game lead over Chicago and Cleveland with only three days left in the season. On the same day the National League race featured three teams within one game of the lead. The National League teams entered the final day of the season with the Cubs and Giants tied, a half-game ahead of the Pirates who had finished their season a few days earlier. In a make-up of a disputed tie game earlier in the season, the Cubs would beat the Giants 4–2 to win the pennant. Heading into the last day of the season, 1967 promised an even more exciting finish.

After two months of pennant race, the magnitude of this game did not sneak up on any of the players. After Saturday's loss Dean Chance told reporters, "This has to be the biggest game I have ever pitched. I hope I can meet the challenge."[1] The Twins had plenty of confidence in Chance. In 1967 he had a 4–1 record against the Red Sox including his rain-shortened perfect game. Pitching in Boston's Fenway Park he had allowed only two runs in 18 innings. Chance had always succeeded in big moments. He wanted the ball. Angels manager Bill Rigney volunteered, "If I had to go with somebody to win one game, I'd go with the big guy [Chance] even if he had only five minutes to rest."[2]

The other pillar of the Twins was oddly overlooked. Harmon Killebrew was having an outstanding year at the plate. Everyone knew he was tied with Yastrzemski for first in home runs. And that appeared to be all there was to Killebrew: he hit home runs. It was easy to dismiss his RBI total, second in the league, as merely a result of his home runs. His total was 20 RBIs in front of Frank Robinson in third place.

Maybe more surprising, he was second to Yastrzemski in runs scored. He had earned by far the most walks in the league. He was third in both on-base percentage and slugging percentage. While Yastrzemski's season was trumpeted around the nation, Killebrew's barely drew notice. Even his team's hometown newspapers seemed blissfully unaware that he contributed anything more than home runs.

As the pennant race ground relentlessly through its last two weeks, Killebrew elevated his play to meet the challenge. Since mid–September he was batting .462 with a .543 on-base percentage. He was averaging more than one RBI per game, and scoring almost a run per game. Like Yastrzemski, Killebrew had shown that he thrived in pressure situations.

Unless he hit a home run, Killebrew's retiring demeanor and reluctance to talk to reporters made it easier to overlook his stellar play. The lack of attention was not without benefits. After each loss, Killebrew could dress undisturbed and disappear to a quiet dinner watching television in his hotel room. Yastrzemski had to explain his team's failings to an ever-growing herd of clamoring reporters.

Even with the thrill of the pennant race, Yastrzemski had limits. Exhausted after the big win and having missed a night of sleep, he had difficulty playing the host. He knew that the quiet and sleep he needed would elude him amidst the throng in his house. Saturday evening he and his wife left their house and guests to check into a nearby hotel. He slept soundly, but awoke before dawn. He got up and walked the resort's 18-hole golf course while the sun rose.[3] He was thinking about Dean Chance and his sinking fastball.

There was another Red Sox player who spent the night before this home game in a hotel. Jim Lonborg had struggled pitching at Fenway over the last half of the season. In his past 10 starts there he was 4–4, but in six of those starts he had given up four or more earned runs. On the road, he was 6–2. His perceived pitching woes at home had been publicly discussed, analyzed and dissected in Boston for weeks.

Lonborg was determined to eliminate everything that might keep him from success. He confessed, "I actually started to become superstitious about [not winning at Fenway]. Can you imagine a college graduate being superstitious?"[4] Without telling anyone, he packed a bag just like he would for a road trip. Even though he had a car, he called a taxi. He checked into a hotel and ate dinner at its restaurant. His routine was as if he was in a different city.

Earlier in the week Lonborg sought out the best pitcher of the 1960s, the recently retired Sandy Koufax who was in Boston to broadcast the games. Koufax told him that before each start he would go through the opponent's lineup. He would visualize himself pitching to each batter, watching as he got each batter out. Just as he had listened closely to some of the best professors in the world at Stanford, Lonborg spent the evening following Koufax's advice. Player by player he visualized himself retiring the Twins lineup.[5]

The more frugal Dick Williams spent the weekend sleeping on his couch. He was displaced by an influx of family and friends. Although his children were sent to spend the nights with friends, there were still not enough beds in Williams' household.

The season's most anticipated game would be played in an unfortunate venue. Boston's Fenway Park had been built in 1912 and most recently renovated in the 1940s. While half the league's stadiums were more than 35 years old, there was no disputing that Fenway was the least viable as a ballpark. After decades of neglect, it was smelly and decrepit—the frequent butt of jokes both in Boston and throughout the country.[6] Its seating capacity of only 33,500, the smallest in the American League, was derided as inadequate. Kansas City had the only other stadium in the league that could seat fewer than 40,000; it was losing its team.

Tom Yawkey had spent most of the summer wrangling with city and state officials over a number of proposals for a new, publicly funded stadium. While the tax money was of little concern, outside of the public's view politicians fought bloody turf battles trying to control the greatest amount of patronage. Despite a multitude of grandiose plans located at various sites, nothing specific had been taken to either the city government or state legislature. As the pennant race intensified, public discourse on the new stadium plans disappeared.

The Sunday game was scheduled to start at 1:00. The Red Sox announced attendance at 35,780. Many felt that this substantially under-reported the people actually in the old park. Some estimated as many as 10,000 fans standing during the game.[7] Papers the next day included numerous accounts of fans slipping into Fenway.[8] Keeping unticketed fans out was a new and unanticipated problem. More than 45,000 people may have attended the game. A small stadium packed more than 30 percent over its capacity may help explain observers' amazement at the unprecedented levels of noise during the game.

Other fans were more creative in finding locations to view the game. A teenager climbed partway up the foul pole on top of the 37-foot wall in Fenway Park's left field. He hung there on the home run side. Umpires halted the game while the teenager moved out of fair territory. Photographs show billboards overlooking Fenway Park loaded with fans. Farther away, the three-year-old Prudential Tower, reputedly the tallest building in the world outside of New York City, had an observation deck equipped with coin-operated binoculars. Although it was about three-quarters of a mile from home plate, the building's 750-foot height gave spectators a view of most of the field including the entire infield. Even this location was crowded.[9]

Fans throughout greater Boston were passionately attached to the outcome of this game. McCarthy's Tavern in the gritty Charlestown neighborhood of Boston had the game on its small color television. More than 60 patrons crowded to see and hear every pitch in the monumental game. An uncontrollable fire broke out in the back of the building. The fire department was summoned, arrived with sirens blaring and eventually extinguished the blaze. Throughout it all, the bar's customers remained seated riveted to the action on the television.[10]

Before the game started the vibe inside Fenway Park was more like a rally for the Red Sox and less like a baseball game. When Jim Lonborg walked in from the bullpen after his warm-ups, the crowd gave him a standing ovation. This lasted so long that it delayed the playing of the national anthem.

In the top of the first inning, Lonborg retired the first two batters before walking Killebrew. Dick Williams had been clear before the game that he wanted to keep the ball away from Killebrew. This was a safe time to walk him. Tony Oliva was the next batter. He had hit safely in nine of his last 10 games.

He hit a ball off the wall in left-center field. Killebrew got a good start off first and sprinted around second watching the ball go between the two outfielders. About halfway to third he was beginning to slow when he saw Billy Martin, the third-base coach, frantically waving him on. Killebrew dutifully picked up his pace.[11]

Oliva arrived easily at second with a stand-up double. The throw from center fielder Reggie Smith came through to first baseman George Scott, standing on the diamond's grass. Scott caught the ball cleanly and turned.

He paused as if he could not believe the sight of Killebrew chugging halfway down the third baseline. It looked like an easy out, but Scott delayed.

When Scott finally threw the ball, it was wild dragging catcher Russ Gibson well up the third baseline. Gibson corralled the ball but lost it again when Killebrew slid past him. Killebrew scored; Oliva ended up on third base; Scott earned an error. Lonborg retired Allison on a hard-hit fly to left ending the inning, but the Twins had a 1–0 lead.

In the top of the third, Lonborg retired the first two batters before facing Cesar Tovar. Influenced by a month of accolades, Red Sox announcers started by describing Tovar as "hitting .267." That, apparently, was not exceptional enough, so they amended it to, "a strong .267." While his was only the fourth-best batting average among Twins regulars, Tovar was in the top 20 in the American League. He was just two spots above Red Sox rookie second baseman Mike Andrews, whose .263 was not strong enough to earn him a spot in the day's starting lineup.

Lonborg approached him carefully and walked him. For all of his lapses, Tovar's speed made him a constant threat on the bases. The Red Sox believed that he would always choose the more aggressive base-running option.

With Tovar on base, Lonborg went to work on Killebrew. Killebrew tagged one of his fastballs through the infield toward left-center. Yastrzemski sprinted over and reached down for the bouncing ball. He felt that he had to rush to get the ball out of his hand and keep Tovar from going into third. The ball went under his glove. On the error, Tovar scored and Killebrew continued to second. This was the second Twins run scored as a direct result of their out-of-the-ordinary aggressiveness. Here were two examples of their base-running reputation pressuring fielders into uncharacteristic mistakes.

Yastrzemski returned to left field furious with himself for allowing the run to score.[12] He determined to make up for the mistake. After intentionally walking Oliva, Lonborg struck out Allison to end the inning.

The Twins were ahead 2–0 on two unearned runs. Throughout the season's last month, the Red Sox, especially their infield, had avoided the costly errors that plagued the other contenders. Today they had lost that edge.

Dean Chance continued to dominate inning after inning. The Red Sox had four hits, including two by Yastrzemski, but they could never advance a baserunner. In the fifth, Chance retired the side quickly and in order. In this big game he was at his best. He had already induced two double plays. Behind him, his fielders were performing flawlessly. Through five innings he had thrown only 39 pitches. Chance was in control.

There were more than 125 sportswriters at the game; one writer estimated that there were as many as 600 in the expanded press box. When they filed their stories to papers in Chicago, Los Angeles or Kansas City they almost all tried to describe the fans' noise. Even with their team losing and struggling against the Twins ace, the fans in the stands never stopped yelling their encouragement. This game was played in an unfamiliar din.[13]

Lonborg would be leading off the sixth inning for the Red Sox. He had singled in his first at-bat. Chance had thrown him a sinking fastball right down the center of the plate. Lonborg had gotten his bat in front of the ball and blooped it into short center field. Lonborg was not a good batter, typical for a pitcher. After his first at-bat he decided that Chance was not going to waste any pitches on him.[14] Especially with the bases empty, he was going to throw strikes and challenge Lonborg to hit them.

While Lonborg hit like a pitcher, he ran like an athlete. He believed that he was one of the fastest players on the Red Sox.[15] As he walked to the plate confident that Chance would throw him strikes, he wondered about his batting approach. Gazing out at the Twins infield he noticed that Tovar was playing deep at third base.[16] He was almost on the outfield grass.

Lonborg decided a strong bunt down the third baseline would be his best opportunity to get on base. Chance had a big follow through on his pitches that normally carried him toward the first baseline. To help keep the Twins complacent, Lonborg took an enormous warm-up swing.

Chance came in with his first pitch, a strike as Lonborg expected. Lonborg squared and met it with his bat, bunting it sharply down the third baseline. Lonborg sprinted for first. Even before he arrived, he could see Killebrew relax and step off the bag. He was safe. The bunt had gone about 50 feet. When Tovar finally reached it, he fumbled the ball trying to pick it up. There was no throw. It was not even close.

The fans exploded. There was more cheering for this bunt single than there had been for Yastrzemski's home run the day before. While the home run was heroic, this was stunningly unexpected. The cheering continued; it never really stopped.

In the Red Sox dugout, Lonborg's teammates jumped around and yelled as if he had hit a walk-off home run.[17] There was no attempt to contain their youthful enthusiasm. Dick Williams said that the bunt "surprised the hell out of me. Shocked the living shit out of the Twins."[18]

The Twins were quite a sight. Billy Martin was in front of the dugout with the veins standing out from his thin neck and small eyes bulging as he screamed at Tovar. Cal Ermer joined him and vented his frustration by dramatically gesturing while he yelled ineffectively at his players into the torrential noise cascading from the stands.

In the third, Lonborg had led off with a single. The Twins had greeted that with a business-as-usual response. The apparent result here was the same: Lonborg stood on first. His bunt was different. It had somehow unhinged the Twins psyche. They were supposed to be the team that was aggressive both offensively and defensively. The bunt exposed them as overly conservative and slow. Ermer's, and especially Martin's, frustrated reactions had not helped. The Twins fielders were now mentally on the defensive. In response to the ranting from their dugout, they were keenly attuned to the need to play aggressively.

While Jerry Adair approached the plate, the infielders stood almost as if wondering what to do next. Lonborg's bunt had embarrassed them. Hoping for a groundball that they could turn into a double play, they all moved closer to the plate. Tovar and Carew were almost on the infield grass.

Adair was batting leadoff for only the fifth time all season. Although he was batting .291 on the Red Sox, his lack of speed made him an odd choice. He had already bounced into a double play. Chance continued his aggressive pitching, going right after Adair with a first-pitch fastball. Adair lined it past the drawn-in Carew and into center field. Ted Uhlaender sprinted in to collect the ball holding Lonborg at second.

Third baseman Dalton Jones strode to the plate. He looked down to his third-base coach and saw the bunt sign.[19] Chance's first pitch to him was a fastball outside and low. Jones got his bat on the ball, but fouled it off. He again peered down to third. This time the third-base coach gave him the sign to swing away.[20] Jones expected another outside fastball.

Tovar was eager to atone for Lonborg's single. Martin's disapproving screams were still fresh in his mind. Martin demanded aggressiveness. Tovar knew that neither Adair nor Jones was fast. If he could get to Jones' bunt quickly, there was a good chance that they could turn a double play. Tovar made a decision that should both placate Martin and redeem his poor positioning on Lonborg's bunt.

He was standing near third at the edge of the infield grass when Chance began his long, slow windup. Tovar started sprinting in, anticipating the bunt. To assure that he would be turning toward second base as he fielded the bunt, Tovar was in the basepath, hugging the foul line. He was about halfway down the line when Chance's sinking fastball arrived at the plate.[21] Jones slapped at it just trying to make contact. His bat connected and the ball skittered on the infield grass bouncing past the surprised Tovar.

If he had still been in position, it would have been an ideal double play ball. Instead, it kept bouncing into left field. Just four pitches into the inning and the Red Sox had the bases loaded with no outs. Most worrying for the Twins, the next batter was Carl Yastrzemski. He already had two hits in the game. Chance could not walk him because that would force home a run.

Cal Ermer stood alone on the top step of the dugout. His arms were crossed and his shoulders slumped. His bench players and Billy Martin had abandoned him. They were clumped in the shadows at the far end of the dugout. Only first-base coach Jim Lemon and pitching coach Early Wynn stood behind him down in the dugout.[22] The despairing frown on Ermer's face can hardly have been encouraging for his players on the field. The unceasing noise became oppressive, seeming to slow the Twins.

Yastrzemski approached the plate with plenty of respect for Chance's pitching. Although a home run would dramatically alter the game, Chance's sinking pitches made that difficult. Instead he decided to try to get the ball over the infielders and into the outfield. He would shorten his swing and attempt to just make contact. He planned to wait for Chance's trademark slider. The count was 2–1 when he got his pitch and punched the ball into center.[23] Fearing his power, Uhlaender had been playing deep. By the time he got the ball in, both Lonborg and Adair had scored. On the throw, Jones went to third.

The score was tied 2–2 and Fenway Park was bedlam.[24]

Ken Harrelson was the next batter. His batting had been largely disappointing since he joined the Red Sox, but Dick Williams had inserted him as the cleanup hitter in this most important game. So far, he had grounded out and then flied out. Despite those results, he felt great. Harrelson arrived confidently at the plate, convinced that he would hit a home run.[25] The roaring crowd stoked his emotional energy. This was the moment he had dreamed about since he signed with the Red Sox.

Chance was still pitching effectively, if less aggressively. The count went back and forth until it stood at 3–2. Harrelson bit on Chance's sinking fastball and topped it with a huge swing. Described as a Baltimore chopper, the ball bounded high toward the left side of second base. Zoilo Versalles had to wait for it to descend before easily collecting it.[26]

Not fearing a pick-off attempt, Yastrzemski had taken a big lead from first base and gotten a good jump. Versalles probably would not have beaten him to second, although he could have easily thrown out Harrelson.[27]

Neither play would prevent the runner on third base from scoring the go-ahead run. Versalles knew this was a likely turning point in the game. It required a big play to stop the Red Sox momentum and their rally. For three years he had been coached to take the aggressive choice in the field. He had seen this rally start with Tovar's timidity. Not afraid of the pressure-filled moment, Versalles was determined to make a game-changing play.[28] He threw home. The throw was on target, but not close to arriving in time. Jones scored, running across the plate.

The Red Sox now led 3–2 with runners on first and second, and no outs. Even after the cheering might have stopped, it continued. Jose Tartabull came in to run for Harrelson. Ermer decided to replace Chance who had failed to get any of the five batters in the inning out.

The bullpens at Fenway Park were located in right field. An orange golf cart emerged from an overhead door in center field to pick up the reliever and speed him to the infield. Al Forrester, the driver, was waiting on the warning track when Al Worthington walked through the gate from the bullpen. Forrester never talked to his passengers. Once Worthington was seated, Forrester pushed the accelerator down to get to the infield as fast as the golf cart could go. He drove along the warning track, toward the Red Sox' first-base dugout.

Worthington knew about the golf cart. Many ballparks used them. He had been in this one before, but it only further discombobulated him. Like all of the Twins, he was shocked by Chance's rapid downfall on a series of unlikely or lightly hit balls. Three of the five hits should have been infield outs. The mind-numbing noise also unsettled him. This was not the same pressure that he remembered from the World Series two years earlier. While there had been plenty of fans at those games, they had behaved normally. Desperate to describe the scene as Worthington entered the game, one Minneapolis columnist compared the noise to test day at an anvil factory.

Worthington prayed every time he entered a game. He preferred to walk from the bullpen to the mound. He could control his pace. The extra time allowed the prayer to settle him. Forrester stopped the golf cart before Worthington had even begun. Worthington stepped out of the cart and began repeating, "Lord, help me do my best. Help me keep calm."[29] With his eyes on the ground while he prayed, Worthington walked slowly apparently not eager to take the mound.

Giving him the ball, Ermer emphasized the importance of keeping his pitches down. Worthington was facing George Scott. He was all too aware that Scott had hit a home run the previous day. His first pitch bounced in front of home plate and skidded past Jerry Zimmerman to the backstop. The runners advanced to second and third.

Worthington settled down enough to get Scott to swing at two pitches making the count 1-2. The mound felt strange to Worthington.[30] He could not get comfortable. It was as if the noise or the pressure had resulted in a partial loss of coordination. Each of his pitches had been unexpectedly low. Instead of focusing on making great pitches, Worthington was mentally reviewing his basic mechanics.

That only made things worse. He bounced the next pitch past Zimmerman. Yastrzemski ran home, making the score 4-2. Worthington struck out Scott for the first out of the inning, but then walked Rico Petrocelli. With runners on first and third Reggie Smith hit a groundball to Killebrew. It eluded Killebrew's glove but managed to bounce off his shin and rebound about 15 feet, landing in foul territory.[31] While Smith sprinted safely to first, Tartabull scored the inning's fifth run. The next two batters hit the ball to Rod Carew at second base and the inning mercifully ended for the Twins.

Despite their World Series experience and the familiarity with pressure-packed games that it should have given them, the Twins crumbled in the middle of this sudden-death game. Worthington's two wild pitches, Killebrew's error and a selection of poor fielding decisions turned a 2–0 lead into a 5–2 disadvantage. The callow Red Sox took every opportunity.

As the Red Sox took the field to start the seventh inning, organist John Kiley played a familiar selection from the well-known musical *Gigi*.[32] Most of the fans in the stands would know the celebratory lyrics to the chorus of "The Night They Invented Champagne."

Lonborg retired the side in the seventh. The Red Sox loaded the bases with no outs in the bottom of the inning off Jim Roland, but Mudcat Grant induced a double play and then struck out Scott.

The Twins were far from giving up. Rich Reese batted for Versalles and singled to start the eighth. Tovar hit a grounder to the first-base side of second. Jerry Adair fielded the ball, tagged Reese running by, and threw to first. Running hard and trying to break up the double play, Reese crashed into Adair severely spiking him. This was no scratch. Adair was taken from the game with blood pouring down his leg. A thunderous standing ovation accompanied him off the field of play.[33] It would take seven stitches to close the deep wound.

Despite the collision, Adair's throw had been good, so there were two outs. Rookie Mike Andrews replaced Adair.

Killebrew was the next batter and he was not to be denied. He singled to right. It was his second hit of the game. He had been on base every at-bat. Tony Oliva approached the plate. He was a unique problem for every pitcher. Most dangerous hitters had an excellent sense of the strike zone and only swung at strikes. Oliva swung at bad pitches and had made a career by hitting them. He had an exceptionally large idea of the strike zone.[34] There was no safe place to throw a pitch to him. Lonborg would not give in. Oliva was determined to hit and he collected another single to right. Going on contact, Killebrew sprinted easily to third.

Bob Allison strode to the plate. He was 0 for 3, having stranded four baserunners in the game. Lonborg pitched confidently. He was not afraid of Allison and had already struck him out twice. Allison remembered his hard-hit fly ball in the first inning, convinced he could connect again. He arrived at the plate assuming he would hit just as Killebrew and Oliva had. For much of his career in Minnesota Allison had been known as "Mr. Clutch," or, when that was not superlative enough, as "Mr. Double Clutch."[35] He was confident that this was his moment.

Allison was right. He pulled a fastball bounding down the left-field line, just fair. The ball headed to Fenway's left-field corner. The box seats along the extended third-base foul line are angled so that they more or less face the pitcher's mound. The sidewall containing them is constructed only a couple of feet from the foul line and runs parallel to it. The wall's top rises with the rows of seats until it meets the famous Green Monster far above the field.

Allison sprinted from the box. He knew Killebrew would score easily from third. He wondered if Oliva would test Yastrzemski's arm and try to score all the way from first. As a left fielder, Allison knew that Yastrzemski's priority was to hold Oliva at third. The tin-covered left-field wall was notorious for its irregular surface that produced erratic bounces. Allison was mentally ready to continue to third if the ball eluded Yastrzemski.

As he sprinted down the line, he could see first-base coach Bob Lemon waving him to second.[36] Allison focused on first base, so that he would touch it without breaking stride. As he rounded toward second, he lifted his head and saw shortstop Rico Petrocelli on the edge of the outfield grass near the left-field foul line. He was positioned as a cutoff man if Yastrzemski's throw had to go home. Allison was digging for second when he peeked at Yastrzemski in the extreme left-field corner.

Yastrzemski had sprinted from the moment the ball had been hit. He was determined to get to the ball before it reached the left-field wall. Yastrzemski believed that Oliva's banged-up knees might slow him slightly. Allison's hit had been hard and he guessed that the Twins would not challenge his arm. He guessed correctly. With two outs in the eighth inning of a pennant-deciding game and the tying run headed toward second Billy Martin lost his aggressiveness. He held Oliva at third.

It did not matter. Yastrzemski had already decided what he would do. On the dead run, he reached across his body to grab the bouncing ball just before it reached the left-field wall. Pivoting before he crashed into the sidewall, he planted his right foot against the base of that wall. Pushing off, he threw the ball as hard as he could to second.

From the left-field corner, the throw to second was about 230 feet. Yastrzemski's throw was as flat as a hard-hit line drive. The startled Allison was out by ten feet. Andrews was the largest second baseman in the game at 6'3" and 200 pounds. He was the rare middle infielder whom Allison could not easily overpower. Knowing that Andrews was a rookie, Allison tried to fool him with a hook slide. It did not work. Andrews tagged him for the third out.

On that incredible throw, the comeback was over. For the second time in the game, the Twins stood stunned. Martin remained near the third baseline with his mouth open, gasping for air like a cartoon fish out of water. Indeed, the deafening cheers seemed to remove the oxygen from the Twins air.

The Red Sox still led 5–3.

The Twins had one more chance when they batted in the top of the ninth. Lonborg was still pitching. Uhlaender's grounder took an odd bounce and hit

Petrocelli in the face. By the time Jones recovered the ball Uhlaender was safe on first. Rod Carew came to the plate as potentially the tying run.

He grounded into a double play. Lonborg needed just one more out.

Ermer pinch-hit Rich Rollins for catcher Russ Nixon. Rollins wore large clear-framed glasses that made his ears stick out.[37] He looked more like a graduate student in engineering than a baseball player. One almost expected his uniform to have a breast pocket with pocket protector and slide rule. Rollins popped up Lonborg's pitch. Shortstop Rico Petrocelli backed under it and caught it on the outfield grass for the final out.

Ecstatic fans, "including girls,"[38] immediately stormed the field. Thousands packed the infield with miraculous speed. It was a joyous scene made more emotional by its utter improbability only a few months earlier. Lonborg was hoisted on to the shoulders of delirious fans. His glove and hat quickly disappeared. Then hands started ripping at his jersey, spikes, and socks. There was a frenzy with some fans simply trying to touch him while others maniacally tried to procure a souvenir. Lonborg was shouting for help as the mass supporting him drifted toward right field. In his mind an injury was suddenly likely.[39]

This was not an overreaction. From the stands, it was clear that Lonborg's safety was in jeopardy. It was 15 long minutes before a small police detail rescued the now partially clad Lonborg near the center-field door for the golf cart. From there the six policemen ran with Lonborg inside a protective ring pushing aside the relentless fans.[40]

Other players had scurried toward the safety of the dugout and the runway to the clubhouse. Faced with the out-of-control crowd, Yastrzemski sprinted from left field to the much closer Twins dugout and through it. It took Jose Tartabull 15 minutes to make it into the clubhouse from right field.[41]

Even the most jaded reporters high above the melee in the press box agreed that they had never seen such a mob after a sporting event.[42] From the safety of the clubhouse Elston Howard said, "I won a lot of pennants in New York, but we never had a crowd go this crazy. I thought it was wonderful."[43]

After the players disappeared, the fans turned their joyous destructiveness to the field. Bases disappeared immediately. More diligent fans began trying to dig up home plate. The iconic outfield scoreboard was attacked. Numbers and team names were torn from their slots. Some filled their pockets with dirt from the mound. Others fell to their knees and began ripping at the sod.

After about half an hour of fruitless loudspeaker announcements, the grounds crew turned on the sprinkler system.[44] The crowd calmed and happily streamed out of the stadium. The streets around Fenway Park and the nearby Kenmore Square were jammed with revelers. Some families had spent the whole game there listening on their radios, others streamed in for the impromptu celebration.[45] Chants and cheers reverberated off the buildings.

Closer to downtown Boston, the bells in the carillon of the venerable Park Street Church pealed the melody to "The Impossible Dream" joyfully into the evening. It was an additional sign that the young baseball team was helping the city shed its long-established dowdy image.

The next day, an entire first section story with multiple photographs was necessary to describe the unusual appearance at the game of Dorrie Nollman. Described as a 20-year-old female fan studying at Framingham State to be a teacher, Nollman wore a complete Red Sox uniform to the game. For reasons that were apparently obvious to readers of the *Boston Record American*, she hid the uniform under a trench coat until the seventh inning. Then she felt confident to shed the coat and lead cheers in her section of the bleachers, "complete with uniform and earrings."[46]

The two-game series brought out the best in the teams' biggest stars. Jim Lonborg pitched a complete game and contributed a hit that was arguably the turning point. Carl Yastrzemski entered the series as the object of an entire city's exorbitantly high expectations. He did not disappoint. He was seven for eight with a home run, six RBIs and two runs scored. And he sealed the final game by throwing out Bob Allison.

With the Twins losses, Harmon Killebrew's batting performance was ignored. He was four for six with three walks. With a home run, he knocked in two runs and scored three times. Even Dean Chance who took the loss was undone more by the indifferent positioning of his infield than poor pitching.

Chapter 28

The Last Game

The American League standings after the final Red Sox–Twins game on October 1.

	W	L	GB
Boston Red Sox	92	70	–
Detroit Tigers	91	70	½
Minnesota Twins	91	71	1
Chicago White Sox	89	73	3
California Angels	83	77	8
Baltimore Orioles	76	85	15½
Washington Senators	76	85	15½
Cleveland Indians	75	87	17
New York Yankees	72	90	20
Kansas City Athletics	62	99	29½

The Tigers were more upbeat between their doubleheader games on Sunday than they had been on Saturday. They were tired, but a successful finish to the season was within their grasp. In all three games, the Tigers had pounded Angels pitching. Their batters were in a groove.

While all pitchers on both teams had pitched, except for the two starters in the final game, the Tigers were aware of a couple of advantages—big advantages. The first was that the Angels relievers had pitched 20 innings in two days while the Tigers bullpen had thrown only six.

The biggest advantage was between the starters for the final game. Angels rookie Rickey Clark would be starting on three days' rest. Clark had had a good rookie season, but the Tigers would start Denny McLain. He had been one of the league's best pitchers for three years. McLain would not be merely well rested. After a two-week layoff, his arm would be fresh. No one worried about a little discomfort as he landed on his injured toes with every pitch. He had assured his teammates that his arm felt great after throwing a bullpen session on Friday. The Tigers' weakness was their bullpen. A fresh McLain should be able to throw a complete game and keep the relievers out of the game. If there was any concern with McLain, it was the first inning. All season that had been his toughest inning.

Many of the Tigers were not that interested in the final innings of the Red Sox–Twins game because they had to win to tie either team. If anything, they were wondering which city they would be flying to. Either way, the Tigers would be the away team for the first playoff game.

Once the game started, all the exhaustion left the players. Adrenalin took over. A World Series berth and potentially a big payday hinged on the outcome.

McLain started the game with swagger. He cruised through the first four batters, primed for an efficient game. The fifth batter was Rick Reichardt, Bill Rigney's new "big man." Reichardt took McLain deep and the game was 1-0 for the Angels. While disappointing to the Detroit fans who quieted in the stands, it was not unexpected. McLain had spent most of the season leading the league in home runs allowed. After Reichardt's blast, he reclaimed that dubious honor.

McLain retired the next two batters to finish the second inning strong.

In the Tigers second, Eddie Mathews led off with a double. Jim Northrup followed with a home run giving the Tigers the lead. By the time the inning ended, Clark was finished and the Tigers were ahead 3-1. The Tigers were playing with the confidence of a team that knows it will win.

The Angels refused to fold. Bobby Knoop led off the third inning with a single to right. Even though it was only the third inning, Rigney sent Jay Johnstone up to pinch-hit for the pitcher. Johnstone came through with another single, putting runners on first and second with no outs. With his team's season on the line, the pressure was now on McLain. The inning's third batter was the left-handed Roger Repoz. He drilled one of McLain's pitches right at Eddie Mathews playing first. Mathews easily doubled Johnstone off first. There were two outs and suddenly McLain was poised to escape the inning.

With a runner on second, Jim Fregosi brought his .288 batting average to the plate and increased it by pounding a double, scoring Knoop. McLain's inability to close out the inning frustrated Smith. This game seemed too big for him. Smith was not going to lose the game because of a pitcher who lacked confidence. Don Mincher was the next batter. He had hit two home runs in the opening game. McLain had already yielded one home run in the game. Smith decided not to trust McLain with a suddenly hot power hitter. He went to the bullpen. It was as if, after Lolich's complete game on Saturday, Smith was determined to emulate Eddie Stanky by removing his starting pitcher at the first sign of trouble.

Far from throwing a complete game as his teammates expected, McLain could not even finish the third inning. As his replacement, John Hiller, threw warm-up pitches, McLain trudged to the dugout and the confidence ebbed from the Tigers he left behind. Despite having the lead and a 17-game winner on the mound, Smith had panicked. He had turned the team's fate over to its weakest link, the relief pitchers.

Changing pitchers did nothing to slow Mincher down. On Hiller's first pitch, he hit his third home run of the day. The Angels were back in the lead 4–3.

Rigney brought a new pitcher into the game for the bottom of the inning. Jim McGlothlin had thrown two innings of scoreless relief the day before. He retired the heart of the Tigers order, Kaline, Horton, and Mathews without a ball leaving the infield.

The top of the fourth inning was even worse for the Tigers. An ineffective parade of four pitchers gave up two walks, two hits, a hit batsman, a stolen base and three runs. Although the particulars were different, the inning felt like a repeat of the eighth inning in Saturday's second game. When it was over, the Angels possessed a 7–3 lead. The Angels added another run in the fifth. With two out, the run in and a runner on first, Bobby Knoop punched a pop into foul ground on the first-base side. Eddie Mathews, playing first in this game, had to move quickly to try to make the play. There were no new fences like the one in Chicago, but a crowd of photographers had been allowed onto this part of the field for the monumental game. Mathews tripped over one slow-moving photographer just as he made the catch for the third out. His disgust at being behind 8–3 flared and he fired the ball at the photographer's feet. The Detroit fans booed long and loudly.[1]

For a team so coolly professional, the Tigers were susceptible to extraordinarily comprehensive losses in confidence. McGlothlin pitched to the minimum of nine batters in the next three innings taking an 8–3 lead into the bottom of the seventh.

During the top of the seventh inning with the Tigers in the field, a few fans climbed out of the stands. A couple went over to individual players and shook their hands. Another one ran the bases with an ineffective security detail in pursuit. These intrusions continued for the rest of the game. All told, as many as 50 fans spent time on the field interrupting play. By the end of the game, police had arrested 12.[2]

Less bold Tigers fans kept up a continual barrage of garbage. For their safety, the Angels relievers had to leave their bullpen.[3] They warmed up by throwing next to the foul line. If Bill Rigney had allowed any players to waver in their determination to win, this abuse from the Tigers fans steeled them.

In Boston the Red Sox players had started listening to the game on the only radio available. There was an AM set which belonged to the trainer that pulled in a scratchy signal from Detroit. Only four players could fit in the trainer's room, so they relayed the action of the early innings out to the rest of the team in the clubhouse.[4]

Most of the team continued a joyful celebration in the clubhouse: many used their shaving cream to lather teammates' heads.[5] A few sprayed beer or dumped it over someone's head, but most were content to drink. Mindful that a Detroit victory would force a playoff the following day, Williams alerted Lee Stange that he would be the starter and warned him to restrain his celebrations.[6] The atmosphere was relaxed. Reporters had plenty of time to interview players between the updates.

While players, manager Dick Williams, and owner Tom Yawkey gleefully celebrated, Tony Conigliaro sat on a bench and cried.[7] While happy for his teammates, he was devastated that he could not contribute to the final victory.

By the middle of the game a large console radio was brought into the clubhouse and the entire team listened quietly as McGlothlin methodically mowed down one Tiger batter after another.

The players' wives and families were not allowed in the clubhouse. They congregated upstairs in the Red Sox offices at Fenway Park and listened to the game in the offices of general manager Dick O'Connell.[8]

In the seventh, the Tigers finally broke through against McGlothlin. With runners on second and third, Dick McAuliffe punched a single over McGlothlin and into center. Both runners scored closing the gap to 8–5. Rigney brought in his star reliever Minnie Rojas who induced pinch-hitter Gates Brown to fly out, ending the inning.

Pat Dobson, the Tigers' seventh pitcher of the game, lasted just two batters after entering the game in the top of the eighth. Mickey Lolich relieved him with one out and a runner on second. The fans gave him a lengthy standing ovation. Lolich had thrown a complete game on Saturday, his third complete game shutout of the week.

Lolich faced five batters. He retired all five, striking out three. Far from feeling the pressure, Lolich had never looked more confident and in command.

Rojas cruised through the eighth inning. He was still on the mound to start the bottom of the ninth.

Bill Freehan was the Tigers' first batter. He had caught all 36 innings of the two doubleheaders. That was physically brutal, especially at the end of the long season and its stressful pennant race. Mentally he had coped with the carousel of relief pitchers, 12 pitching changes in the two days. Each pitcher had idiosyncratic preferences and strengths that Freehan had to try to match with the specific Angels batter at the plate. Freehan should have been exhausted, but he was so focused on the game that he did not realize it. His entire season had come down to these final three outs.

Whatever Eddie Stanky's motivations were for promoting Freehan as league MVP back in August, Freehan had believed Stanky's assessment. In Freehan's mind, an MVP would get a big hit in a critical game situation. Mentally toughened and psychologically prepared for this moment, he doubled off Rojas.

Rojas walked the next batter and suddenly the Tigers had the tying run at the plate with none out. Lenny Green was announced as the pinch-hitter for Lolich.

In the Detroit bullpen, Earl Wilson was warming to pitch the 10th inning and beyond if necessary.

In Boston, the Red Sox clubhouse became tense. An inning earlier, it had seemed as if the pennant was theirs. That happy assumption was replaced by doubt. The carefree, almost giddy chitchat was gone. Sitting at his locker, Stange would chain smoke through the inning.[9] Each player stared into space trying to visualize the scene described by the announcers. It was clear that Rigney was doing everything in his power to win the game. The Red Sox believed that he had as many as four relievers warming to be ready for what could be the final outs of the season. When Rigney walked to the mound to replace the tiring Rojas, the room became absolutely silent as players held their breath to hear the name of the incoming pitcher.

In what seemed like a psychological ploy to the players in Boston, Rigney summoned George Brunet from the bullpen. Earlier in the season he had been a Tigers killer. That was no longer the case. The Tigers had beaten him in August. Just the day before, they had pummeled him for four earned runs in two innings.

The left-handed Brunet entered the game with runners on first and second with no outs. Smith immediately countered by sending rookie catcher Jim Price up to pinch-hit for Green who batted lefty. Price was the 23rd Tiger to enter the game. Smith could be confident that no one could criticize him for inaction in this game.

Brunet induced Price to fly out to left for the first out of the inning. The runners had to hold.

Leadoff batter Dick McAuliffe was next. He had already been on base three times in the game and collected three RBIs. McAuliffe had channeled all of his usually out-sized intensity and somehow increased it. He was determined to single-handedly propel the Tigers to victory and a playoff if necessary.

McAuliffe had hit 22 home runs during the season, so he was a threat to tie the game if Brunet threw just one bad pitch. McAuliffe did not have to try for a big hit. He just needed to get on base. The Tigers big hitters could then come to bat and drive in some runs.

Convinced by Tigers radio announcers who tried to assure their hometown listeners with the fact that McAuliffe had grounded into only one double play all season, the Red Sox players began to assume that McAuliffe would hit safely. The man they feared was Al Kaline who was the second batter after McAuliffe. How, they wondered, would Rigney handle that situation? Kaline already had two hits in the game. Like McAuliffe, he was playing his best in this must-win game.

Kaline was desperate to bat again. He had waited 15 major league seasons for a moment like this. Despite its many lows, Kaline had reveled in the excitement of the pennant race. There was nothing he wanted more than to have his team's season rely on his at-bat in the bottom of the ninth inning in the last regular-season game of the year.[10]

While Kaline waited, the pressure was on Brunet. He had faced McAuliffe many times in their careers. The two at-bats the day before were fresh in his mind. He had walked McAuliffe in the first inning. In the second inning he had fooled McAuliffe with a curve, getting him to ground out to first.

Rigney positioned his infielders to get an out. He did not care if the Tigers scored one run or two, as long as his team got two outs before they scored three. There were no feints to hold Freehan on second, so he took a long lead. On a single, he would almost certainly score. McAuliffe swung at Brunet's first curve, grounding to Knoop at second. Knoop tossed to Fregosi who had an easy relay to Mincher at first for the double play.

Suddenly and surprisingly, the season and the pennant race were over. There would be no playoff games.

In the Tigers clubhouse, the players sat with the empty feeling of a golden chance somehow missed. Some repeated to themselves as much as to quizzing reporters, "So close. So close." As the crushing defeat settled on them, many cried.[11] Mayo Smith was described as shaken, his face a shade of gray. After talking to reporters, Smith was seen on the phone with his wife, tears streaming down his face.[12]

Kaline, who may have become tired of reading each day about how the Tigers failed, said, "We have nothing to be ashamed of. We did the best we could."[13] This may have been a condemnation of the relief pitchers, Smith, or both. Kaline was well aware that Smith had blamed the relief pitchers for earlier losses, but he had inexplicably put the team's fate in their hands repeatedly during this crucial weekend. The Tigers had pounded Angels pitching, but somehow had lost two of the four games. It would frustrate even the most team-oriented veteran.

Long after the game, Tigers general manager Jim Campbell sought out Rigney outside the Angels clubhouse door. Campbell congratulated him for the spirit and resilience with which his team had played.[14]

The next morning Pete Waldmeir delivered the Tigers' eulogy in the *Detroit News*: "The Detroit Tigers, who had been trying for weeks to lose the American League baseball championship, finally got the job done."[15]

In the Red Sox clubhouse, the joy of winning the pennant was heightened by the sudden release of nervous tension. Dick Williams hugged his young son who had spent part of the summer as the team's ballboy and mascot. "Don't ever forget this," he whispered.[16] Players shook bottles of beer and sprayed each other, then posed, hugging and smiling without restraint for photographers.

The Red Sox were effusive in their praise for Rigney. Yastrzemski prominently credited Rigney's in-game maneuvers and motivation of his players for helping deliver the pennant to Boston.[17]

While the Red Sox players enjoyed another round of celebration in their clubhouse, outside on the streets of Boston thousands of fans chanted, "We're number one." That chant would continue for hours.[18]

The 1967 World Series

The final standings of the American League.

	W	L	GB
Boston Red Sox	92	70	–
Detroit Tigers	91	71	1
Minnesota Twins	91	71	1
Chicago White Sox	89	73	3
California Angels	84	77	7½
Baltimore Orioles	76	85	15½
Washington Senators	76	85	15½
Cleveland Indians	75	87	17
New York Yankees	72	90	20
Kansas City Athletics	62	99	29½

Sportswriters stranded in Boston waiting for the World Series filed reports disparaging the excessive celebration of the Boston papers on the day after the pennant was clinched.[1, 2]

The tabloid *Record American* broke out its largest typeface for the word "Champs!" and filled the rest of the front page with the two socks of the Red Sox logo. The first piece of non–Red Sox news appeared on page five. It could have been written a day, or even a month earlier running under the headline "Cardinal in Favor of Celibacy."

The *Herald Traveler* acknowledged the rest of the world with a small offering at the bottom of the front page. The editors devoted the space above the fold to a team photo under the headline, "Pennant is Ours."

The *Globe*'s front page was all Red Sox. In a small, boxed note its editors wrote, "If you think we've flipped over the Red Sox ... well, we have and some regular *Globe* features do not appear today." In fact, the paper included a few wire service stories but they were buried obscurely in page after page of Red Sox coverage and congratulatory ads.

The typesetting at all three papers showed a giddy inattention to detail.

Game One

The Red Sox and their opponents, the St. Louis Cardinals, had two days off before the World Series began in Boston on Wednesday.

Red Sox reliever Bill Landis was called away to military duty during the last week of the season. Additionally, the Red Sox had two pitchers on their World Series roster who were injured. The commissioner granted them exemptions for each of the three players. Rookie catcher Russ Gibson, who had spent the mid-part of the season back in the minors, was allowed to replace Landis. Rookie pitcher Gary Waslewski replaced Bucky Brandon. The Cardinals were reputed to be weak against lefty pitching. Sparky Lyle was the only left-handed Red Sox pitcher but he was the other injured pitcher. The Red Sox replaced him with Ken Brett, a left-hander who had been an end-of-the-season call-up from Class AA. Only two weeks earlier, Brett had turned 19. He had pitched two major league innings.

Dick Williams named Jose Santiago his Game One starter. Santiago would oppose the Cardinals ace, Bob Gibson. Gibson had missed seven weeks of the season with a broken leg, but had returned at the beginning of September and had started five games since then. One of the best pitchers in the National League, Gibson was at full strength entering the World Series. This was clearly a mismatch.

Indeed, observers outside of Boston noted that the entire series substantially favored the Cardinals. Comparing the field players at each position, the Red Sox were superior only with Yastrzemski in left field and Petrocelli at shortstop. Even these advantages were small. The Cardinals left fielder was Lou Brock, an All-Star who led the National League in runs scored and stolen bases while batting .299. The Cardinals pitchers earned an even bigger edge. Gibson was better than Lonborg. Behind Gibson were three more high-quality starters and effective relievers in the bullpen. The Red Sox did not seem to have any other good starting pitchers. Except in Boston, it was obvious that the Cardinals would win. They were 5–1 favorites in Las Vegas.

Both Red Schoendienst and some of his players appeared much more concerned with the fact that Fenway Park's small capacity would cut into their World Series winnings than with playing the Red Sox.[3]

Hardened by the long, stressful pennant race, Red Sox players retained the aggressively competitive edge that all of the American League contenders had displayed. The Cardinals were more relaxed—confidently professional.

Despite the combative natures of the two managers, some players still retained a certain collegiality. In this context, it did not seem unusual that during the evening before the first game, Jose Santiago had dinner with Cardinals first baseman Orlando Cepeda. Cepeda was the Cardinals slugger and favored to become the National League MVP. This dinner was not random. The two were described as childhood friends from Ponce, Puerto Rico. While Cepeda had been a star for years, Santiago had appeared from nowhere in the last week of the season.

Dick Williams considered Cepeda's batting as a key to the series. Just as he had instructed all of his pitchers to walk Killebrew rather than give him a ball that he might hit for a home run, Williams warned his pitchers from challenging Cepeda in this series.[4]

Santiago started Game One looking much more confident than he had three days earlier against the Twins. Despite that, the Cardinals had plenty of baserunners. Santiago escaped a jam in the first by inducing Cepeda to ground into a double play. In the third Brock singled and moved to third on Curt Flood's double. He scored on Roger Maris' groundout. Santiago closed the inning by inducing both Cepeda and third baseman Mike Shannon to pop out.

Gibson was even more overpowering. Although he yielded a George Scott single in the second, he was having little trouble with the Red Sox batters when he struck out Russ Gibson to start the bottom of the third. He had no reason to respect Santiago as a batter. To the surprise of everyone in Fenway Park, Santiago homered on a Gibson curve. It was his second career home run and evened the score 1–1.

In the fourth, the speedy Julian Javier tried to score from second base on Brock's single to left field. Yastrzemski fielded the bounding ball while sprinting toward the infield. His throw carried to catcher Russ Gibson on the fly and Gibson tagged out the sliding Javier. Through the sixth inning both teams had baserunners but could not score. Santiago was holding his own. In the top of the seventh, Brock hit his fourth single in four at-bats. Schoendienst signaled that he should not attempt to steal. Ignoring the sign, Brock stole second, his second stolen base of the game.[5] He moved to third on one groundout and then scored on another. Although he allowed a baserunner in each of the last three innings, Gibson closed the Red Sox down. The Cardinals won 2–1.

Gibson had thrown 117 pitches, allowing only six hits while holding Yastrzemski hitless. Before the game the Cardinals had allowed that Yastrzemski was a fine player, but possibly overrated because he played in such a weak league.[6] Even though he threw out Javier, Schoendienst felt it was because of the short left field at Fenway Park. "He'd better not play that shallow in St. Louis. If one gets by him it'll be for all four."[7]

After the game, Yastrzemski returned to the field for batting practice, hitting 150 pitches. Harrelson and Petrocelli joined him. Back in the clubhouse, a reporter from a National League city asked if he had World Series jitters. Yastrzemski replied, "Apparently you did not watch the last two months of the American League pennant race. After that, this is a fun game—like playing stickball in the street."[8] Cardinals players took great offense at this remark, which somehow seemed to demean them and the august World Series.

Game Two

Jim Lonborg would start the second game for the Red Sox. His father, a professor at Cal Poly in San Luis Obispo, was given leave without pay to see his son pitch. Before the game, Lonborg ate dinner with his ex-teammate Dennis Bennett. Bennett had spent part of the season pitching for the Mets and gave Lonborg a rundown on the Cardinals batters.[9] Before going to bed in a Boston hotel Lonborg continued his newfound practice of visualizing himself retiring each of the Cardinals batters.

Lonborg was a mystery to the Cardinals from the beginning of the game. He had a high kick in his delivery, bringing his left knee almost to his chin before pushing forward to deliver each pitch. With his long right arm if he varied his release point even a little, the ball arrived at a dramatically different angle.

Inning after inning, Lonborg retired every Cardinal batter who stepped to the plate. One of baseball's many unwritten rules is that players do not speak with a pitcher who is in the middle of a perfect game. There was no chance of that in the Red Sox dugout. Lonborg could not shut up, talking with everyone between the innings.

Lonborg pitched a perfect game until he walked Curt Flood in the seventh. Flood would later claim that the last two balls looked like strikes to him.[10] Flood did not seem pleased as he trotted head down to first base, refusing the proffered hand of first-base coach Dick Sisler.

Javier broke up his no-hitter in the eighth with a hard-hit double. Watching the ball rocket into the outfield, Lonborg felt like he had been stabbed. What an out-of-town newspaper disparaged as "slightly hysterical fans"[11] gave Lonborg a prolonged standing ovation that continued into pinch-hitter Bobby Tolan's at-bat. Flood and Javier were the only two Cardinals baserunners. Lonborg completed the game throwing only 95 pitches. It was the fourth one-hitter in World Series history.

Before the game Schoendienst told reporters that Yastrzemski would get no special treatment, "We'll challenge him."[12] The Red Sox won 5–0 behind ten hits including two Yastrzemski home runs. He led off the fourth sending a Dick Hughes pitch into the right-field stands. In the seventh with two men on base left-hander Joe Hoerner was brought in to face Yastrzemski. On a 2-2 pitch, Yastrzemski's home run landed slightly deeper in the right-field stands. After the game Yastrzemski said, "I am living a dream."[13]

It suddenly did not seem like much of a dream to the Cardinals. A number of them assured reporters that there were plenty of pitchers in the National League who were better than Lonborg.[14] Their problems at the plate were because of the horrible hitting background at Fenway Park. They were eager to return to St. Louis where the size and shape of the field were major league.

Schoendienst who shared Stanky's enjoyment of stirring the pot dismissed Yastrzemski as "a plain good hitter."[15] As far as Lonborg went, Schoendienst announced, "We could have gotten him in trouble."[16]

Game Three

There was a day off as the teams traveled to St. Louis. Despite his insistence at the end of the season that he did not care about the World Series, Eddie Stanky was in St. Louis and highly visible for the games. Schoendienst was a Stanky disciple. Stanky had benched himself while player/manager of the Cardinals to make the young Schoendienst the starting second baseman. Most of Stanky's career between his managing jobs had been with the Cardinals organization.

It was not surprising that Schoendienst, Brock and other players began complaining loudly to the press about Lonborg's inside pitches. It had worked well for Stanky's White Sox who had come to dominate the Red Sox by the end of the season.

The Cardinals expected a big crowd. Before the game, they stocked Busch Stadium with six tons of hot dogs, 500 half-barrels of beer and another 6,000 cases of bottled beer, 5,000 pounds of popcorn, and another 5,000 pounds of hamburger.[17] They needed all of it. The largest crowd in St. Louis history, 54,575, enjoyed the game.

Despite the fact that the new Busch Stadium was a beautifully modern facility, wire service reports stated that the field was "pockmarked," in worse shape than the playing surface in Boston.[18]

After the second game Curt Flood assured reporters, "We're going to get Yastrzemski."[19] Starting pitcher Nelson Briles backed Flood up. He started by throwing a pitch at Yastrzemski and hitting him. It was a successful strategy. Yastrzemski went 0 for 3. The Cardinals pounded Gary Bell for three runs in two innings and continued for a 5–2 win.

There were few offensive highlights for the Red Sox. Starting at third base, Dalton Jones had three hits. Reggie Smith had two including a solo home run.

Apparently believing Schoendienst's claim that Yastrzemski did not have a dangerous arm, Javier tried for second on his single to left. Yastrzemski threw him out again.

Game Four

In the fourth game, the Cardinals brought back Bob Gibson. In papers across the country, it was noted that Gibson had not pitched with only three days' rest all year.[20] Many had expected Schoendienst to start his young left-hander, Steve Carlton. Despite pitching on such short rest, Gibson took the ball and shut out the Red Sox. After the game Gibson confided to reporters, "This time I had to force myself. It's not easy" pitching with only three days' rest.[21]

Santiago, who was apparently pitching with a regular amount of rest, did not fare as well. The Cardinals lit him up for four runs in the first inning on their way to an easy 6–0 win.

After two such dominating performances Red Schoendienst bubbled with confidence, "I look for it to end tomorrow. I don't think we'll have to make the trip back to Boston."[22]

Game Five

Dick Williams made wholesale changes to his starting lineup. Mike Andrews, Ken Harrelson, and Joe Foy replaced Jerry Adair, Jose Tartabull, and Dalton Jones. Elston Howard had already replaced Russ Gibson behind the plate.

Jim Lonborg would be the Game Five starter for the Red Sox. The Cardinals' complaints about his inside pitching were so effective that headlines in neutral cities referred to this as "The Beanball Series."[23] In the entire series, a Red Sox pitcher never hit a Cardinal batter. Although the Cardinals' legacy as whiners is probably related to these complaints, they had a solid tactical reason. It is possible that they expected their comments to limit Lonborg's effectiveness by taking away his inside fastball.

While the Cardinals pretended to be upset with Lonborg's pitching, Lonborg was furious after Cardinals batters dismissed his performance in Game Two as merely a matter of a poor hitting background. He started the game as an angry pitcher, deliberately meaner than he had been for any other game in 1967.[24]

Lonborg made another change that had nothing to do with the Cardinals complaints or excuses. In Fenway Park's small field, Lonborg had relied heavily on his breaking pitches. He was afraid that the Cardinals could too easily hit a home run if they connected with his fastball. He used the inside fastball primarily to keep the Cardinals hitters off the plate and away from his outside pitches. Lonborg felt that Busch Stadium's much larger playing field dimensions allowed him to throw his fastball to all parts of the plate. Cardinals batters who had seen mostly breaking balls in Game Two, never quite caught up to the idea that Lonborg was throwing fastballs.

The Cardinals started Steve Carlton who pitched six strong innings, allowing only an unearned run in the third.

Lonborg allowed just two hits through eight innings and the Red Sox held a 1-0 lead going into the top of the ninth. The Red Sox loaded the bases with no outs. Elston Howard hit a soft bloop to short right field. Right fielder Roger Maris faked as if he was going to be able to catch the ball as he sprinted in. George Scott retreated to third base, tagging up. Starting on second, the more aggressive Reggie Smith jogged two-thirds of the way to third base before turning to watch Maris close on the ball.

As the ball landed in shallow right field near the foul line, Scott took off sprinting trying to beat the short throw. Smith took a peek ahead of him to locate Scott and the Cardinals fielders. He did not want to run into an out. When he looked back, he saw Maris on the ground and concluded that the ball had bounced past him.[25] He sprinted for home, going through the third-base coach's stop sign.

Maris was on the ground as a result of the follow-through on his adrenalin-laced throw to the plate. Scott's speed allowed him to easily run across the plate as the throw came in high to catcher Tim McCarver.

McCarver dropped the ball.

He acted surprised that Smith would try to score on such a shallow hit. After picking up the ball, he ineffectively kicked at the sliding Smith as if to block him, instead of diving to tag him out. Smith was safe giving the Red Sox a 3-0 lead.

In the bottom of the ninth Maris homered, his second hit of the game. The final score was 3-1. Lonborg had given up just four hits in two complete games. This was believed to be a World Series record for consecutive starts.

After the game, the Red Sox dressed and left directly for their charter flight home. The New England area was besieged by heavy rain and there was a real danger that Boston's Logan Airport might have to close down later.

The Cardinals departure was delayed by over four hours. The players were so certain of their victory over Lonborg that none of them packed travel bags. Each had to return home, pack, and then recongregate. Legend has it that the Cardinals flight was the last into Logan before it temporarily closed because of water on the runways. A slightly later departure and the Cardinals would have had a long bus ride to Boston from New York City or Albany.

A lengthy discussion of knockdown pitches had provided a constant subtext while the series was in St. Louis.[26] Some opined that the Red Sox' only chance was through brinksmanship. The inside pitch was clearly part of this inelegant repertoire. To this point Roger Maris told reporters that he had "never" seen a knockdown pitch in a World Series game.[27] It was an odd claim for someone who had played in World Series games with the Yankees that included 14 hit batsmen.

In the knockdown dispute, Bob Gibson seemed to come to Lonborg's defense, "The average person gets the wrong idea about knocking a guy down. You brush him back to keep him from leaning over the plate—not to hit him."[28]

Game Six

The Cardinals now led the series 3–2 as it moved back to Boston. It had been a pitchers' series. The Red Sox were batting .206 and the Cardinals only a little better at .210. The Cardinals remained huge favorites. After their last two wins, it was easy to believe that they had decisively won every game Lonborg did not start.

While the teams waited for the sixth game to start, news spread through the nation's newspapers that Che Guevara, a firebrand Marxist revolutionary who had been prominent in the Cuban Revolution, had been killed in a firefight with Bolivian rangers.

Dick Williams gave reporters something else to write about by naming Gary Waslewski his starting pitcher for Game Six. A rookie, the 6'4" Waslewski's career record was 2–2. He had been sent down to the minors twice during the season, compiling an unimpressive 5–6 record there. His last start had been more than a month earlier against a team from Syracuse. It was widely reported that no pitcher had ever started a World Series game with fewer career wins.[29] He may also have been the only World Series starter who would not receive a full World Series share. As the season was ending but before he was added to the World Series roster, his teammates had voted him a quarter share. Waslewski told some reporters that he hoped a good performance in Game Six would earn him an increase to a half-share.[30]

In response to the general disparagement of his decision, Dick Williams insisted, "This is no gamble."[31] He was not exactly backed by his pitching coach Sal Maglie, who told reporters, "[Waslewski] has a good arm, but … who knows? I can't figure him out."[32]

Unknown to the Cardinals, back in July Waslewski had been so erratic in his warm-ups before a scheduled start that his catcher Mike Ryan had warned Williams before the game started. Waslewski walked the first two batters on eight pitches. Thanks to the warning, Williams had a pitcher warmed up. Waslewski was replaced after his first two pitches to the third batter were balls.[33]

Before this game, Schoendienst gave his team a pep talk. Maybe he was not as confident as he claimed when they took the field against an unknown rookie. The Cardinals had no scouting report on Waslewski.

Dick Williams did not talk to his team. "All our men know the situation," he said.[34]

Waslewski had two days to think about his start. He was so anxious during warm-ups it felt like his stomach was boiling.[35] He hoped that he would settle down once he stood on the mound and could focus on the game. Instead, his arm went numb from the excitement.[36] It was not the best sensation when facing leadoff batter Lou Brock who was 8 for 12 in the series when not facing Lonborg.

Waslewski struck Brock out. For the second half of the season, Red Sox fans had reveled in an inferiority complex about their overachieving team. Seeing an inexperienced, apparently mediocre rookie dispatch Brock who seemed to be the Cardinals' best player stoked their enthusiasm. The noise began.

Waslewski was not the only starter whose nerves gave him an upset stomach. Hughes had pitched well in his first start in Game Two making it into the sixth inning. He did not fare well in this start. Petrocelli homered in the second, giving the Red Sox a 1–0 lead. During the regular season, Petrocelli's wife had attended many home games. For this World Series game, she was not in attendance to see her husband hit the home run. She could not find a babysitter for their three young sons, so she stayed home and watched the game on TV.

The Cardinals struck back with four hits and two runs against Waslewski in the top of the third. Williams displayed what seemed like foolish patience leaving Waslewski in the game despite this barrage. Behind 2–1, Williams let Waslewski lead off in the bottom of the inning.

In the fourth, Hughes yielded solo home runs to Yastrzemski, Smith, and Petrocelli. Schoendienst pulled him from the game despite his belief that Hughes was pitching well. He would later say that he could not understand how the Red Sox hit Hughes' pitches.[37] It was believed to be the first time in World Series history that three players had hit home runs in one half-inning. The Red Sox now led 4–2.

In the bottom of the fifth, Nelson Briles entered the game for the Cardinals. Waslewski was the first batter and hit Briles' pitch over Fenway Park's tall left-field wall, just foul. Briles hit him on the elbow with his next pitch.

By the seventh, John Wyatt had replaced the tiring Waslewski. With one out, he walked pinch-hitter Bobby Tolan. Brock was the next batter. He had already collected a hit, a stolen base and a run. Wyatt tried to pitch carefully to him. Brock responded with a two-run home run to tie the game 4–4.

In the bottom of the seventh with the crowd cheering like they had in the Minnesota series, the Red Sox sent ten batters to the plate. Four Cardinals pitchers gave up six hits and four runs. It was 8-4 when Elston Howard grounded out with the bases loaded.

Gary Bell gave up three hits and a walk, but pitched two scoreless innings to finish the game. The teams had used a World Series record of 11 pitchers.

Game Seven

In Boston, the main story leading to the final game was that Lonborg would be pitching on only two days' rest. He had not pitched well in the season's final week against Cleveland with only two days between starts. Lonborg confidently proclaimed that a strong mind could overcome a tired body.[38] He planned to limit his warm-up pitches to save his arm for the game.[39]

In the rest of the country, Lonborg's short rest was a side story compared to the fact that Gibson would be pitching for the second straight start on only three days' rest. Many writers echoed the genuine concern that this might be more than a pitcher should be asked to endure.[40]

Outside of Boston, newspaper readers would have no way of knowing that this would be Lonborg's eighth start since September 12. He made six of those starts on three days' rest and the other two with only two days' rest. (Gibson had also started a game on September 12. This would be his sixth start since then.)

Like all of the World Series games, this was sold out. The ticket lottery assured that most of the fans at the game were fans, not the wealthy buying from well-connected ticket brokers. One mother arrived to view the game with her four young children. Anticipating the ecstatic chaos that a victory might bring, she tied a large tag to each with the child's name, address, and home telephone number.[41]

For the first time in the series, Red Schoendienst did not give his players a pre-game pep talk.

Both pitchers started strong, but Lonborg made the first mistake. In the third inning, Dal Maxvill tripled and was driven home on a Curt Flood single. After Roger Maris singled, Lonborg threw a wild pitch allowing Flood to score.

It was still 2–0 in the top of the fifth. Bob Gibson homered off Lonborg to make the score 3–0. Brock collected his first hit of the game and then stole second. On a ball four to Flood, Brock stole third. He scored on a sacrifice fly making the score 4–0.

In the bottom of the inning George Scott tripled and scored on Javier's throwing error. It was the first hit for the Red Sox. The reprieve was short-lived. Williams sent Lonborg out for the sixth inning. The first two batters reached base, although one was the result of a Joe Foy error.

Williams visited the mound intending to replace the obviously tiring Lonborg. Lonborg convinced him that Javier would probably be trying a sacrifice bunt. Lonborg was convinced that he could prevent that. Williams left him in.

Javier hit the second home run of the game off Lonborg. Lonborg rallied to retire three of the next four batters. The game was almost certainly out of reach. Fans realized that Lonborg would likely be replaced by a pinch-hitter in the bottom of the inning. As Lonborg trudged from the mound to the dugout his season finished, the fans at Fenway gave him a long, loud standing ovation.

Maglie would later strongly criticize Williams for leaving the tiring Lonborg in the game.[42] During the preceding weeks, Williams had repeatedly left starting pitchers in games too long. It had been successful much more often than not. Williams did not have confidence in his bullpen and stayed away from it.

The Red Sox scored a run in the eighth to make the final score 7–2. Gibson allowed only three hits, another masterful outing. In 27 innings the slugging Red Sox scored only three times against him. His performance was one of the best in World Series history—a clear choice to be named World Series MVP.

Lou Brock had an MVP-worthy series. He set a World Series record with seven stolen bases, padding his stats with one in the ninth inning of Game Seven. He batted .414 with a .452 on-base percentage (OBP), scoring eight runs and hitting a home run. The Red Sox were never able to cope with his base running. He was constantly on base—a threat to steal.

Yastrzemski also carried his team: He batted .400 with an OBP of .500. With three home runs and two doubles his slugging percentage was .840. Both players made great catches in the field, although Yastrzemski also threw out two runners.

After the game, the Red Sox clubhouse had a predictable gloom. It lacked the devastated disappointment that the White Sox, Twins, and Tigers displayed after losing their chance at the pennant. Williams and owner Tom Yawkey were both quoted celebrating the team's success in unexpectedly winning the pennant and reaching the final game of the World Series.

Some of the Cardinals seemed to reap little joy from their victory. A few, like underperformers McCarver and Cepeda, used their post-game interviews to denigrate the Red Sox rather than celebrate their own triumph. One columnist wrote, "The Cardinals won with a minimum of grace and sportsmanship."[43]

The team's manager reinforced this enduring image. In a nationally broadcast network interview immediately after the game, Harry Caray asked the Cardinals manager, "You must have something to say about the courageous Red Sox."

Red Schoendienst replied, "I think they were pretty lucky."[44]

Epilogue: After 1967

The Cleveland Indians fired **Joe Adcock** on the last day of the season in 1967. He never coached or managed in the major leagues again. The Indians immediately named his successor, Alvin Dark.

Traded by the White Sox after the 1967 season, **Tommie Agee** was a critical component of the 1969 Amazin' Mets. In the World Series victory over the Baltimore Orioles, his exceptional fielding was decisive.

A reliever for his entire 11-year career, **Jack Aker** compiled 124 saves for six different teams. Despite his desire to be traded, Aker played the 1968 season for Charlie Finley's Oakland A's.

Bob Allison retired from the Twins after they lost in the 1970 playoffs. He hit 256 home runs and gathered 796 RBIs during his 13-year career. He hit 216 doubles.

Attendance in 1967: The American League drew 11,376,923 fans, a record. The Boston Red Sox drew 1,727,832 fans, a franchise record and more than double their attendance in 1966. In the next 50 years, the Red Sox would never again host fewer than 1,000,000 fans in a season. On the other hand, the White Sox had their lowest attendance since 1958. It was the second of what would become six consecutive seasons where their attendance failed to reach 1,000,000. Despite the mid-season riots, the Detroit Tigers drew 1,447,143 fans, the most since 1961 and the sixth highest in franchise history. The Minnesota Twins set a franchise record for attendance dating to 1901. The California Angels had the second highest attendance in their short history. It was a benchmark that would not be passed for another decade. Even the lowly Senators set a franchise attendance record. They had the largest season attendance in Washington since 1948.

Red Sox pitcher **Gary Bell**, who was signed to his initial contract by Indians scout Rawmeat Rogers, spent part of his last season pitching again for Sal Maglie on the Seattle Pilots in 1969. He finished his career with 233 starts and 121 wins. One more start and two more regular-season wins than Maglie who had dismissively predicted his early demise.

Rookie reliever **Ken Brett**, who had pitched in only one major league game before being added to the Red Sox World Series roster, pitched in two World Series games holding the Cardinals hitless. At that point in his career, he may have been the first pitcher ever to pitch in twice as many World Series games as regular season games. He had a 14-year career with one All-Star appearance.

Gates Brown spent most of his 13-year career as a feared pinch hitter. He usually entered games after the seventh inning and would often eat a hot dog with other bench players in the middle innings. In one game he had just started eating when manager Mayo Smith unexpectedly ordered him to hit. Knowing the hot dog would disappear if he left it on the bench, Brown tucked it inside his uniform. He hit the ball into the gap and had to slide headfirst into second for a double. The entire Tigers bench broke up when he stood up with his uniform covered in ketchup and mustard. Smith fined him.[1]

George Brunet's major league career spanned 16 seasons with nine teams. In 1967 he led the American League with 19 losses. He led the league again in 1968 becoming the second pitcher to achieve that in consecutive years during the 1960s. Ten years earlier Pedro Ramos had led the league in losses for an amazing four consecutive seasons.

Brunet was still pitching effectively in the Mexican League at age 49. That year he set the Mexican League career record with 55 complete game shutouts.[2]

Smoky Burgess retired after the 1967 season with 145 career pinch hits, the most in major league history.

A first ballot Hall of Famer, **Rod Carew** was American League Rookie of the Year in 1967. A seven-time batting champion, he was the 1977 MVP when he batted .388. Carew stole home seven times in 1969.

Twins catcher Jerry Zimmerman was throwing batting practice one day. Carew yelled, "I could hit you blindfolded." Zimmerman accepted the challenge. Carew tied a towel over his eyes. Unannounced, Zimmerman threw his first pitch. Guessing, Carew swung.

He hit it.[3]

Cisco Carlos finished the 1967 season 2–0 with a 0.86 ERA. He never regained that dominance, winning only nine more games over three years.

When **Norm Cash**'s career ended in the middle of the 1974 season after the Tigers released him, he was believed to have been the last major league player to bat without wearing a batting helmet.[4] A four-time All Star, he had a 17-year career hitting 377 home runs.

Dean Chance won the Comeback Player of the Year in 1967. He held out in a contract dispute for much of spring training in 1969. Reportedly a player who did little offseason conditioning, he hurt his back pitching soon after signing his contract. His career ended two seasons and three teams later. He won 128 games with two 20-win seasons and two All-Star game starts. Chance retired with a career batting average of .066.

Tony Conigliaro missed the entire 1968 season following his beaning. He came back and played two full seasons and parts of two others despite frequent setbacks with his damaged eye. In 1970 he hit 36 home runs—one for every 15.5 at bats—against major league pitching with only one fully functioning eye.

Charlie Finley rehired **Alvin Dark** again before the 1974 season. Dark led the Oakland A's to a World Series championship that season. Dark was fired after the A's failed in the playoffs the following season. He won 994 games as a manager.

When he managed pitcher Gaylord Perry in the early 1960s, Dark watched Perry's awkward swing and pronounced, "A man will land on the moon before he hits a home run." On July 20, 1969, about 30 minutes after Neil Armstrong and Buzz Aldrin landed on the moon in *Eagle*, Perry hit his first career home run off the Dodgers' Claude Osteen.[5]

Cal Ermer, who played in just one major league game, had only one major league managing opportunity. After the Twins stumbled to a seventh place finish in 1968, Ermer was fired and replaced by Billy Martin.

Along with Angel (formerly Anaheim) Stadium, which was opened in 1966, **Fenway Park** is the only American League venue from 1967 still in major league use. Since the end of the Yawkeys' control, the stadium has been cleaned, revitalized and expanded. Although still Spartan by current standards, it now seems quaint rather than dilapidated. To emphasize this, it has been branded as America's Most Beloved Ballpark.

Even observers trying to be positive have trouble complimenting **Charlie Finley** for anything beyond his promotion and marketing innovations. Dick Williams would say that he enjoyed managing the A's in the 1970s because it was the only time that his players hated someone more than they hated him. Almost everyone in baseball associated with Finley developed at least a strong dislike for him.

Overlooked is Finley's single-minded, patient development of elite players. In 1973, six years after this 1967 season, his A's won the second of three consecutive World Series—a dynasty equaled by only one other franchise in the history of major league baseball. Six of the eight starting field players were on the Athletics or in their farm system in 1967, as were five of the eight pitchers used. Between those homegrown players there were three Hall of Famers, three Cy Young Award winners, three MVPs and only two who were never All Stars.

Reports at the time treat Finley's ownership of the A's dynasty as an unfortunate accident. He is arguably the most underrated owner of all time.

Joe Foy was the Red Sox fulltime third baseman in 1968, but his batting average dropped to .225. His fielding and conditioning remained issues. He played for three more teams before being cut by the Senators in 1971 ending his career when he was only 28.

Bill Freehan had a dominant year in 1968 when he finished second in the MVP voting and the Tigers won the World Series. He was an eight-time All Star and five-time Gold Glove winner. He led the league in being hit by pitches three times and hit exactly 200 home runs in his career.

At the ceremony when **Calvin Griffith** officially sold the Minnesota Twins in 1984, he cried. He once said, "I love baseball so goddamn much—it's like dessert."[6]

When **Jack Hamilton** visited Boston with the Angels during the 1968 season, he not only used an alias but also stayed at a different hotel than the rest of the team. He never recovered from his arm injury at the end of the 1967 season. He pitched half a season for the Angels in 1968 and 43 increasingly unsuccessful innings for the Indians and White Sox in 1969. Many believed that his loss of effectiveness was due to timidity after the Conigliaro beaning. Hamilton always denied this explanation.

In 1967 **Ron Hansen** played 1,357 innings while leading the American League in both assists and double plays turned. He was traded to the Senators during the offseason. In 1968 he completed an unassisted triple play.

Ken Harrelson had his career year in 1968. Playing in right field, he led the league with 109 RBIs, while hitting 35 home runs. His ebullient personality made him a celebrity in Boston. With Tony Conigliaro's return, Harrelson was moved to first base in 1969. In a surprise move, he was traded to Cleveland after 10 games. After that season he played in only 69 games before his career ended.

Gil Hodges managed the Amazin' Mets of 1969 to 100 wins and a World Series championship. He was named major league manager of the year. As a manager his lifetime winning percentage was .467.

In 1968 **Joe Horlen** started the season struggling with arm issues and lost his first five starts. He finished the season with 35 starts and a 2.37 ERA, which was eighth in the American League. His record, typically, was only 12–14 for the woeful White Sox. He won a World Series with the Oakland A's in 1972, his last year in the majors. His career record was 116–117 with a 3.11 ERA.

Tony Horton was the starting first baseman for the Indians until his sudden and mysterious departure from the team during the 1971 season. He never returned to baseball.

Immediately after the 1967 season ended, **Willie Horton** underwent surgery for his damaged Achilles tendon. He played another nine years with the Tigers before concluding his career as a designated hitter for the Rangers, Indians, A's, Blue Jays and Mariners. He remained enormously popular in Detroit. A three-time All Star, he finished his career with 325 home runs.

In the 17 seasons that he managed without Johnny Sain as his pitching coach, **Ralph Houk** had a losing record and never led a team to the postseason.

Bruce Howard pitched in 23 games for Baltimore and Washington in 1968. Despite a few great outings, he was increasingly ineffective. He spent a final year in the minors before retiring at 26.

Tommy John is probably the most well-known American League pitcher from the 1967 season—his name permanently attached to a surgical procedure, ulnar collateral ligament reconstruction or Tommy John surgery. Dr. Frank Jobe successfully performed the procedure on John in 1974. He had a 26-year career and pitched in three World Series. A four-time All Star, he ended his career with 288 wins.

Dalton Jones retired with 55 pinch hits, a Red Sox career record.[7]

After a 25-year career, **Jim Kaat** retired as a 16-time Gold Glove winner. Later in his career Kaat developed a short wind-up accentuated by an ultra-quick tempo. His catchers would sometimes signal the next pitch while returning the ball to the mound so Kaat could immediately begin his wind-up.

Al Kaline concluded his 22-year Tigers career with 3,007 hits and 399 home runs. A 1968 World Series champion, he was a first-ballot Hall of Famer. Kaline never played a game in the minor leagues.

The 1969 American League MVP, **Harmon Killebrew** retired after the 1975 season with 573 home runs, fifth on the career list and just ten behind his contemporary Frank Robinson. He won six home run titles and was 11 times an All Star. Oddly for such a poor fielder, Killebrew was the first player to be selected as an All Star at three different positions.

Always considerate, in his Hall of Fame induction speech Killebrew thanked each one of his major league managers by name, except one. He omitted the abrasive Billy Martin who managed the Twins during Killebrew's MVP year.

Despite his demands to be traded, **Lew Krausse** spent two more years pitching for Charlie Finley and the Oakland A's. He never realized his potential, although he was a full-time major league pitcher for 6 seasons in a career that spanned 14 years.

It was eventually revealed that the August 3 airplane incident started when players taped a slip of paper to the air vent over sleeping radio broadcaster Monte Moore. He awoke startled and looked around in panic trying to find the source of the noise. The perpetrators enjoyed a good laugh at his expense.[8] When Al Dark refused to discipline the players, Moore apparently took his complaint to Charlie Finley. This may have started the butterfly effect for the now immensely powerful MLB Players Association.

Mickey Lolich was a great big-game pitcher. In addition to finishing the 1967 season with 28⅔ scoreless innings, he won three complete games in the 1968 World Series. His only other playoff appearances were in 1972 when he pitched nine scoreless innings in one game before losing in the tenth. In his second start he allowed one run in nine full innings, getting a no-decision.

He retired with an American League–best 2,679 strikeouts for a lefty. He had 41 shutouts and 217 wins in a 16-year career. Despite being a fastball pitcher, in 1971 he threw a surreal 376 innings—a post-deadball era record at the time. He never suffered from serious arm troubles.

In the sixth inning of Game Seven of the 1968 World Series, Lolich picked off the game's two most feared base-stealers—Lou Brock and Curt Flood—from first base. In the midst of this pivotal inning Bill Freehan visited the mound to give his whole team a chance to take a deep breath and settle down. He asked Lolich, "Anything I can do for you?"

"Yeah, can you get me a couple of hamburgers between innings?"[9]

In addition to hit by pitches, in 1967 **Jim Lonborg** led the league in wins and strikeouts, winning the Cy Young Award. In an accident that is a byword in Boston for terrible judgment, he blew out his left knee in a skiing mishap before the 1968 season. He pitched four more largely disappointing years for the Red Sox, but continued his career until 1979, winning 157 games.

After the seventh World Series game, Lonborg was asked about the mental strain. He replied, "It has to be physical. That's why I'm soaking my arm now. If it was mental, I'd be soaking my head."[10]

Dick Williams fired **Sal Maglie** after the 1967 season. Maglie coached for one more major league season, 1969 with the Seattle Pilots. Jim Bouton chronicled that year in *Ball Four* portraying Maglie as a second-guessing buffoon.

Billy Martin became a manager in 1969 with the Twins. That otherwise successful season was marred when he punched out one of his pitchers, Dave Boswell, in an alley fight outside a Detroit bar. Martin remained an inspirational motivator, but with a short managerial shelf life. His career was a less successful version of Dick Williams', but frequently disrupted by Martin's temper and fighting. He won 1,253 games, two pennants and one World Series with five teams over eight full and an amazing eight partial seasons.

After a 17-year career, **Eddie Mathews** retired as a world champion after his 1968 season with the Tigers. He started over 2,100 games at third base and finished with 512 home runs. He was elected to the Hall of Fame in 1978.

An All Star in 1967, **Dick McAuliffe** played in Detroit for 14 seasons before finishing his career in Boston.

In 1968 **Denny McLain** had a 1.96 ERA while pitching 28 complete games. He won 31 games, the Cy Young and MVP awards. Never a big game pitcher, McLain lost twice to Bob Gibson in the World Series. After the second outing, when he failed to complete the third inning, he told his teammates that he would not pitch again for them in the World Series. Mayo Smith and Johnny Sain pulled his psyche back together and he started Game Six. The Tigers scored 12 runs in the first three innings. With the pressure off, McLain pitched a complete game shutout on two days rest. He won 24 games and the Cy Young again in 1969. In five seasons he had won 108 games while throwing over 1,380 innings. He was 25. He won only 17 more games, throwing his last major league pitch when he was 28.

He once wrote of a teammate, "[His] trouble is that he was blessed with a million-dollar arm and a ten-cent brain. He's a good competitor, but deep down he's a spoiled brat."[11] It is a description that might apply more accurately to McLain.

Despite his .546 winning percentage, **Sam Mele** never managed or coached again. Teams may have questioned his motivation. He told the *Chicago Tribune* that he wanted to manage again because, "I have nearly 18 years of pension time and I'd like to get a complete 20."[12] Mele completed his career working in a variety of scouting and front office positions for the Boston Red Sox.

The Minnesota Twins and Minnesota Vikings moved out of **Metropolitan Stadium** after their 1981 seasons. It was razed in early 1985. In the Mall of America, which was built on the site, there is a bronze replica of the Met's home plate. 520 feet away and high off the ground, bolted to the face of a massive white wall hangs a single red bleacher seat. This commemorates Harmon Killebrew's home run into the second deck on June 3, 1967, the longest in the history of Metropolitan Stadium.

His teammates voted **Don Mincher** the Angels' team MVP in 1967 and that was before he hit three home runs on the last day of the season. He won a World Series with the 1972 A's—his last major league appearance. He retired having played in exactly 1,400 games and hitting exactly 200 home runs during 13 seasons.

Rick Monday played in 19 major league seasons, amassing over 1,600 hits. He was a two-time All Star.

From 1964 through 1971 **Tony Oliva** was, with Frank Robinson, one of the most consistently dominating all-around hitters in baseball. In those seven years, he won three batting crowns, led the league in hits five times and doubles four times. He seemed headed for the Hall of Fame before recurring knee injuries prematurely ended his career. He retired with 220 home runs and 947 RBIs.

Gary Peters hurt his back pinch hitting in May 1968, but still started 25 games that year. Traded to the Red Sox in 1970, he confided to Carl Yastrzemski that Stanky told his 1967 pitching staff to drill Yastrzemski any time they had a chance.[13] Peters completed more than a quarter of his 286 career starts, throwing 23 shutouts. He retired with 19 home runs and 102 RBIs. Baseball historian Bill James claimed that Peters was the only pitcher in major league history to be intentionally walked three times.[14]

A slugger for a shortstop, **Rico Petrocelli** hit 40 home runs in 1969. A two-time All Star, he spent his lengthy career in Boston. He finished with 210 home runs and a .970 fielding percentage.

Ken Poulsen spent about two weeks with the Red Sox in July before returning to the minors. He played in five games, doubling in his last at bat. He never returned to the major leagues. He married Vicki Swaton after the 1967 season.

The 1967 season was an unmistakable watershed for the **Red Sox**. Before that, they were largely irrelevant in Boston, where politicians had spent more than a decade ignoring owner Tom Yawkey's threats to move if they would not approve a new stadium. After 1967, the franchise was a jewel for the entire New England region. Fans arrived in droves to pay the highest ticket prices in the major leagues.

The year of the pitcher, 1968, was **Rick Reichardt**'s career season. That year he hit 21 home runs and drove in 73 runs. He retired after one at bat in 1974.

Although he managed during 18 seasons over 21 years, **Bill Rigney** took only one team to the postseason. In 1970, he improved Billy Martin's Twins by one game in the regular season. Like Martin's team, the Orioles swept them in the first round of the playoffs. As a manager, Rigney won 1,239 games.

Reporters in 1967 referred to the Angels' catcher almost exclusively as **Bob Rodgers**. He would later manage for most of 13 major league seasons and be known as "Buck Rodgers." Rodgers batted only .219 in 1967 and his playing time diminished rapidly after that.

On June 10, 1967, **Billy Rohr** headed to Camp Drum to fulfill his Reserve commitment with the 351st Medical Unit. When his two weeks were over, the Red Sox, preferring his replacement, optioned him to AAA Toronto. He would pitch just one more major league inning in 1967. In 1968 he pitched 18 innings for the Indians and his career was over.

In just his second major league season, **Minnie Rojas** led the league in saves and finished second in appearances in 1967. He never recovered from being Bill Rigney's workhorse. In July 1968 with an ERA persistently over 4.00, his major league career ended.

John Sain spent 18 years as a successful major league pitching coach. His strong personality and unusual techniques limited his major league employment opportunities despite the long list of pitchers who had career years under his tutelage.

The first Latin pitcher ever to start the first game of the World Series, **Jose Santiago** started 1968 9–4 with a 2.25 ERA and was named to the All-Star team. Elbow tendonitis derailed his season in July. He never fully recovered and his career ended in 1970 with only 34 wins. His 2.000 slugging percentage may be a career record against Bob Gibson.

Later in his career when he was more secure in his position as a major leaguer, **George Scott** was known for his uplifting presence in a clubhouse. An increasingly burly man, Scott wore a necklace while playing in the 1970s. When asked what was on the necklace he replied, "The teeth of opposing pitchers."[15] An eight-time Gold Glove winner, Scott led the American League in home runs and RBIs in 1975.

Mayo Smith's Tigers won the American League pennant by 12 games and then the World Series in 1968. He managed the Tigers for only two years after that season.

A seven-time All Star and Gold Glove winner, **Reggie Smith** finished his 17-year career with 314 home runs and a batting average of .287. After the first six games of the 1967 season, he never again played second base.

Before the 1968 season, the rules prohibiting **spitballs** were re-written in an attempt to stop what was seen as a rapid increase in their use during the mid–1960s.

The White Sox convinced **Eddie Stanky** to resign after starting the 1968 season 34–45. He never worked in professional baseball again with one bizarre exception. The Texas Rangers hired him in June 1977 to replace fired manager Frank Lucchesi. After winning his first major league game in almost 10 years, Stanky called Rangers owner Bob Short from the airport just before flying out of town. He quit.

In an interview with sports talk radio pioneer Art Rust, Jr., during the mid–1970s, Rust twice pressed Stanky to name the great players from the 1948 Braves team. Stanky came up with ten names pointedly leaving his roommate, fellow middle infielder and longtime friend Al Dark off the list. Rust gave Stanky an opportunity to set the record straight about Stanky's petition before Jackie Robinson's rookie season. Stanky, who was well aware how mores had changed, declined.[16]

Cesar Tovar played in a major league record 164 regular season games in 1967—the Twins had two ties. He would receive a single MVP first place vote from *Minneapolis Star* writer Max Nichols after the 1967 season. It deprived Yastrzemski of a unanimous selection and was greeted with disbelief, if not dismay.

In a publicity stunt at the end of the disappointing 1968 season, Tovar became the second player in MLB history to play all nine positions in a single game. He struck out Reggie Jackson.

The **Twins starting pitchers** finished the season with 58 complete games. Dean Chance led the league with 18; Jim Kaat threw 13 including six in September. Jim Merritt and Dave Boswell each had 11. Jim Perry threw three and Mudcat Grant contributed two. In the National League, pitchers for the San Francisco Giants had 64 complete games.

No one knew why **Zoilo Versalles** had such a brief span of excellence. It was accepted that he lied about his age and that he was a year older than he claimed. Fellow Cuban Tony Oliva felt that Versalles might have been as many as four years older. He was plagued after 1964 with chronic back problems that proved intractable. There are also rumors that he paid little attention to dosage amounts on his prescription painkillers.[17] After his disappointing 1967 season, Versalles was traded with Mudcat Grant to the Los Angeles Dodgers. His batting average slumped to .196 with the Dodgers. His career ended when the Braves released him after the 1971 season.

Pete Ward retired after the 1970 season having been ejected from only one game in his career. In the middle of the 1967 pennant race, newspapers nationwide showed Eddie Stanky tackling him and then holding him on the ground to keep him from assaulting an umpire.

Hoyt Wilhelm is one of a select group of major leaguers to hit a home run in his first at bat. He is the only one in that group to never hit another home run in a 21-year career. The Dodgers cut him for the final time in 1972 just five days shy of his 50th birthday. Wilhelm had a career ERA of 2.52 and was the first pitcher to have over 1,000 appearances. He was the first relief pitcher elected to the Hall of Fame.

The Boston Red Sox fired **Dick Williams** just before the end of the 1969 season. His abrasive manner was no longer motivating the players. This complaint was repeated throughout his managerial career. He managed Oakland to two World Series titles and took San Diego to its first World Series appearance. In his 21 seasons, he won 1,571 games. Inducted into the Hall of Fame in 2008, some historians consider him among the ten best managers in MLB history.[18]

Although he may have pitched better the year before, 1967 was **Earl Wilson**'s career year. Despite 22 wins, he did not receive any Cy Young Award votes. He was the third pitcher in the MVP voting. Wilson finished his 121-win career with some of the best power-hitting statistics of any pitcher: 35 home runs and 111 RBIs.

From 1971 to 1975 **Wilbur Wood** had one of the best five-year periods in modern baseball history winning 106 games for poor teams while throwing 99 complete games. He started 224 games, including 49 in one year and 48 the next. In 1972 he pitched 376 ⅔ innings—more than 27 percent of the team's total—the most by a pitcher since the deadball era. His left knee was shattered by a line drive in 1976, ending his effective career.

One afternoon during his prime, Wood shook off a signal from his catcher. The catcher started laughing so hard that the umpire called time out to find out why. The catcher said, "I don't know what he wants. We don't have any other signals."[19]

Al Worthington's 14-year major league career concluded at age 40 when the Twins released him after the 1969 season. He appeared in over 600 games, winning 75 and saving 110. He remains the only pitcher in the modern era to start his career with two complete game shutouts.

Although he had been an All Star in 1964, 1967 was the best season of **John Wyatt**'s career. He finished with 20 saves, 10 wins and an ERA of 2.60. The next year he pitched only 49 innings for three teams. Oakland released him in May 1969 ending his career.

The 1967 American League MVP, **Carl Yastrzemski**'s season was arguably the best by a field player in the 1960s. In the context of a grueling pennant race, Yastrzemski's final month is unmatched. He batted .417 with nine home runs and 26 RBIs. He was on base in every single game and scored 22 runs. He threw out four runners and intimidated many others.

Yastrzemski played his entire 23-year career for the Red Sox. He was the first American Leaguer to retire with more than 3,000 hits and more than 400 home runs. He is a first-ballot Hall of Famer.

Tom Yawkey died in 1976 beloved in Boston for his generosity. The Veterans Committee voted Yawkey into the Hall of Fame in 1980. His plaque, after noting his futility while owning the Red Sox for over four decades and never winning a World Series, lauds him as a benefactor. Coincidentally, his widow became a director of the museum, donating a new wing.

Chapter Notes

Prologue

1. Bill James, *The New Bill James Historical Baseball Abstract* (New York: Free Press, 2001), 507.
2. Alvin Dark with John Underwood, *When in Doubt, Fire the Manager: My Life and Times in Baseball* (New York: E.P. Dutton, 1980), 17.
3. Danny Peary, ed., *Cult Baseball Players: The Greats, the Flakes, the Weird and the Wonderful* (New York: Fireside, 1990), 42.
4. Dark, *When in Doubt*, 17.
5. Thomas Kiernan, *The Miracle at Coogan's Bluff* (New York: Thomas Y. Crowell, 1975), 34.
6. Dark, *When in Doubt*, 47.
7. Kiernan, *Miracle*, 33.
8. Jonathan Eig, *Opening Day: The Story of Jackie Robinson's First Season* (New York: Simon & Schuster, 2007), 42.
9. Eig, *Opening Day*, 87.
10. Eig, *Opening Day*, 75.
11. Mike Blake, *Baseball Chronicles: An Oral History of Baseball Through the Decades* (Cincinnati: Betterway, 1994), 140.
12. Dark, *When in Doubt*, 47–48.

Chapter 1

1. *Baseball Digest*, April 1967.
2. "Rising Dynasty for the Birds?" *Sports Illustrated*, April 17, 1967, 72.
3. Dick Williams and Bill Plaschke, *No More Mr. Nice Guy: A Life of Hardball* (San Diego: Harcourt Brace Jovanovich, 1990), 50.
4. Williams and Plaschke, *Mr. Nice Guy*, 63.
5. Ron Anderson, *Long Taters: A Baseball Biography of George "Boomer" Scott* (Jefferson, NC: McFarland, 2012), 91.
6. Anderson, *Long Taters*, 54.
7. Unidentified, undated newspaper clipping in Rico Petrocelli folder at Giamatti Research Center, Cooperstown, NY.
8. Rico Petrocelli and Chaz Scoggins, *Rico Petrocelli's Tales from the Impossible Dream Red Sox* (Champaign, IL: Sports Publishing, 2007), 114.
9. *Boston Globe*, April 4, 1967.
10. *Boston Globe*, April 8, 1967.
11. *Chicago Sun-Times*, April 4, 1967.
12. *Chicago Tribune*, April 10, 1967.
13. *Boston Globe*, April 12, 1967.
14. *Boston Herald*, April 15, 1967.
15. Steven Krasner, *Play Ball Like the Hall of Famers* (Atlanta: Peachtree, 2005), 201.
16. Bill Nowlin and Dan Desrochers, *The 1967 Impossible Dream Red Sox: Pandemonium on the Field* (Cambridge: Rounder, 2007), 209.
17. *Boston Herald*, April 16, 1967.
18. Williams and Plaschke, *Mr. Nice Guy*, 87–88.

Chapter 2

1. *Chicago Sun-Times*, April 25, 1967.
2. Jim Hawkins, *Al Kaline: The Biography of a Tigers Icon* (Chicago: Triumph, 2010), 10, 71, 73.

3. Hawkins, *Al Kaline*, 212.
4. Hawkins, *Al Kaline*, 138.
5. Hawkins, *Al Kaline*, 164.
6. *Detroit News*, April 11, 1967.
7. *Detroit News*, May 12, 1967.
8. Bill James, *The New Bill James Historical Baseball Abstract* (New York: Free Press, 2001), 559.
9. Mark Pattison and David Raglin, eds., *Sock It to 'Em Tigers: The Incredible Story of the 1968 Detroit Tigers* (Hanover, MA: Maple Street Press, 2008), 23.
10. George Cantor, *The Tigers of '68: Baseball's Last Real Champions* (Dallas: Taylor, 1997), 39.
11. Pattison and Raglin, *Tigers*, 22.
12. *Detroit News*, April 11, 1967.
13. Bill Freehan, *Behind the Mask: An Inside Baseball Diary*, ed. Steve Gelman and Dick Schaap (New York: Popular Press, 1970), 15.
14. Hal Butler, *Al Kaline and the Detroit Tigers* (Chicago: Henry Regnery, 1973), 104–105.
15. Ron Fimrite, "Detroit Tigers Catcher Bill Freehan April 14, 1969," *Sports Illustrated*, July 28, 1997, 10.
16. Freehan, *Mask*, 52.
17. *Detroit News*, April 3, 1967.
18. Freehan, *Mask*, 27.
19. *Detroit News*, April 21, 1967.
20. *Detroit News*, April 21, 1967.
21. Freehan, *Mask*, 75–76.
22. *Detroit News*, May 4, 1967.
23. *Detroit News*, May 4, 1967.
24. *Detroit News*, May 4, 1967.

Chapter 3

1. "Rising Dynasty for the Birds?" *Sports Illustrated*, April 17, 1967, 70.
2. *St. Paul Pioneer Press*, July 19, 1967.
3. Hal Butler, *The Bob Allison Story* (New York: Julian Messner, 1967), 58.
4. Butler, *Allison*, 83.
5. Wayne J. Anderson, *Harmon Killebrew: Baseball's Superstar* (Salt Lake City: Deseret Book, 1971), 192–193.
6. Jim Thielman, *Cool of the Evening* (Minneapolis: Kirk House, 2005), 140.
7. Butler, *Allison*, 42–44.
8. *Minneapolis Tribune*, May 17, 1967.
9. Thielman, *Evening*, 145.
10. George Vass, *The Game I'll Never Forget* (Evanston, IL: Baseball Digest, Century Publishing, 1999), 49.
11. *Chicago Sun-Times*, April 9, 1967.
12. *Minneapolis Star*, May 20, 1967.
13. *Minneapolis Star*, May 17, 1967.
14. *Minneapolis Tribune*, May 28, 1967.
15. Butler, *Allison*, 47.
16. *Minneapolis Star*, May 29, 1967.

Chapter 4

1. Tony Conigliaro with Jack Zanger, *Seeing It Through: The Story of a Comeback* (New York: Macmillan, 1970), 144–146.
2. Frank Deford, "Not Much to Do but Eat, Sleep and Play Baseball," *Sports Illustrated*, August 3, 1964, 50.
3. Bill Reynolds, *Lost Summer* (New York: Warner, 1992), 153.
4. David Cataneo, *Tony C: The Triumph and Tragedy of Tony Conigliaro* (Nashville: Rutledge Hill, 1997), 230.
5. Conigliaro, *Comeback*, 166.
6. Conigliaro, *Comeback*, 173.
7. Reynolds, *Summer*, 25–26.
8. Cataneo, *Tony C*, 75.
9. Cataneo, *Tony C*, 6.
10. Cataneo, *Tony C*, 5.
11. Cataneo, *Tony C*, 72–73.
12. Conigliaro, *Comeback*, 186–187.
13. Center of Military History, *American Military History* (Washington, D.C.: Center of Military History, United States Army, 1989), 612–618.
14. Richard B. Crossland and James T. Currie, *Twice the Citizen: A History of the United States Army Reserve, 1908-1983* (Washington, D.C.: Office of the Chief, Army Reserve, 1984), 197.
15. Cataneo, *Tony C*, 89–90.
16. *Boston Globe*, May 12, 1967.
17. *Boston Globe*, June 3, 1967.

Chapter 5

1. *Minneapolis Tribune*, May 26, 1967.
2. Billy Martin and Peter Golenbock, *Number 1* (New York: Delacorte, 1980), 190.
3. *World Champion Baltimore Orioles 1967 Press/Radio/Television Guide*, 19.
4. Ron Luciano and David Fisher, *The Umpire Strikes Back* (New York: Bantam, 1982), 59.
5. *Minneapolis Tribune*, June 5, 1967.

6. *Minneapolis Tribune*, June 5, 1967.
7. *Minneapolis Tribune*, June 6, 1967.
8. Eric Hammel, *Six Days in June: How Israel Won the 1967 Arab-Israeli War* (New York: Charles Scribner's Sons, 1992), 57–60, 107.
9. Robert Stephens, *Nasser: A Political Biography* (New York: Simon & Schuster, 1971), 494–497.
10. David Anderson, ed., *Quotations from Chairman Calvin* (Stillwater, MN: Brick Alley Books, 1984).
11. Dean Urdahl, *Touching Bases with Our Memories: The Players Who Made the Minnesota Twins: 1961 to 2001* (St. Cloud, MN: North Star Press of St. Cloud, 2001), 317.
12. Steve Aschburner, *The Good, the Bad, and the Ugly: Minnesota Twins: Heart-Pounding, Jaw-Dropping, and Gut-Wrenching Moments from Minnesota Twins History* (Chicago: Triumph, 2008), 38, 115.
13. Gary Smith, "A Lingering Vestige of Yesterday," *Sports Illustrated*, April 4, 1983, 112.
14. Urdahl, *Touching Bases*, 171.
15. *Minneapolis Star*, September 7, 1967.
16. *Minneapolis Tribune*, May 21, 1967.
17. *Minneapolis Tribune*, September 21, 1967.
18. *Minneapolis Tribune*, June 10, 1967.
19. "They Said It," *Sports Illustrated*, June 19, 1967, 12.

Chapter 6

1. *Chicago Daily News*, April 22, 1967.
2. *Chicago Sun-Times*, April 8, 1967.
3. *Chicago Daily News*, March 29, 1967.
4. Mark Liptak, "Flashing Back with Gary Peters," www.whitesoxinteractive.com.
5. Joe Jares, "Yoweee, Chicago!" *Sports Illustrated*, July 10, 1967, 16.
6. *Chicago Tribune*, June 15, 1967.
7. Liptak, "Gary Peters."
8. *Boston Globe*, September 5, 1967.
9. *Chicago Tribune*, May 26, 1967.
10. *Chicago Tribune*, June 10, 1967.
11. *Boston Traveler*, July 5, 1967.
12. *Boston Herald*, June 12, 1967.
13. *Minneapolis Star*, June 13, 1967.
14. *Minneapolis Star*, June 13, 1967.
15. Liptak, "Gary Peters."
16. *Chicago Sun-Times*, April 19, 1967.
17. *Chicago Tribune*, June 7, 1967.
18. *Boston Globe*, June 7, 1967.
19. Jim Prime with Bill Nowlin, *Tales from the Red Sox Dugout* (Champaign, IL: Sports Publishing, 2000), 155.
20. *Chicago Tribune*, June 16, 1967.
21. *Chicago Tribune*, June 16, 1967.
22. *Chicago Tribune*, June 16, 1967.
23. *Boston Herald*, June 16, 1967.
24. David Cataneo, *Tony C: The Triumph and Tragedy of Tony Conigliaro* (Nashville: Rutledge Hill, 1997), 98.
25. Mark Mulvoy, "Virtue Is Rewarded," *Sports Illustrated*, August 21, 1967, 17.
26. *Boston Globe*, June 16, 1967.
27. *Boston Herald*, June 16, 1967.
28. *Boston Globe*, June 17, 1967.
29. Jares, "Yoweee," 16.
30. *Chicago Tribune*, June 17, 1967.

Chapter 7

1. William Craig, "Don't Dig in on Gentleman Jim," *The Saturday Evening Post*, September 9, 1967, 72.
2. Craig, "Gentleman Jim," 72.
3. Craig, "Gentleman Jim," 72.
4. Bill Nowlin and Dan Desrochers, *The 1967 Impossible Dream Red Sox: Pandemonium on the Field* (Cambridge: Rounder, 2007), 179.
5. Mark Mulvoy, "Virtue Is Rewarded," *Sports Illustrated*, August 21, 1967, 17.
6. Craig, "Gentleman Jim," 72.
7. *Boston Globe*, June 14, 1967.
8. *Minneapolis Star*, August 10, 1967.
9. Nowlin and Desrochers, *Red Sox*, 232.
10. Sal Maglie and Robert Boyle, "Baseball Is a Tough Business," *Sports Illustrated*, April 15, 1968, 80.
11. Jim Bouton and Leonard Shecter, *Ball Four Plus Ball Five* (New York: Stein and Day, 1981), 67.
12. *Boston Globe*, July 7, 1967.
13. *Boston Globe*, April 2, 1967.
14. *Chicago Tribune*, June 22, 1967.
15. *Boston Globe*, June 22, 1967.
16. *Boston Globe*, July 3, 1967.
17. Nowlin and Desrochers, *Red Sox*, 232.
18. Nowlin and Desrochers, *Red Sox*, 232.

Chapter 8

1. *Chicago Tribune*, June 27, 1967.
2. Joe Jares, "Yoweee, Chicago!" *Sports Illustrated*, July 10, 1967, 16.

3. *Chicago Tribune*, June 28, 1967.
4. Danny Peary, ed., *Cult Baseball Players: The Greats, the Flakes, the Weird and the Wonderful* (New York: Fireside, 1990), 200.
5. *Detroit Free Press*, July 2, 1967.
6. *Detroit Free Press*, September 23, 1967.
7. Milton J. Shapiro, *Heroes of the Bullpen: Baseball's Greatest Relief Pitchers* (New York: Julian Messner, 1967), 97.
8. Bill Libby, *Star Pitchers of the Major Leagues* (New York: Random House, 1971), 96.
9. *Los Angeles Herald Examiner*, July 19, 1967.
10. Shapiro, *Heroes*, 98.
11. Libby, *Star Pitchers*, 103.
12. George Vass, *The Game I'll Never Forget* (Evanston, IL: Baseball Digest, Century Publishing, 1999), 133.
13. *The Sporting News*, August 5, 1967.
14. *Chicago Sun-Times*, April 23, 1967.
15. Ron Fimrite, "Wilbur's Knuckler Is Alive and Swell," *Sports Illustrated*, June 4, 1973, 26.
16. *Chicago Tribune*, July 3, 1967.
17. *Chicago Tribune*, June 18, 1967.
18. *Chicago Tribune*, July 19, 1967.
19. Jim Bouton, and Leonard Shecter, *Ball Four Plus Ball Five* (New York: Stein and Day, 1981), 211.
20. *Chicago Tribune*, July 19, 1967.
21. Gary Smith, "Diamond Cutters the Bossards, Baseball's First Family of Groundskeeping," *Sports Illustrated*, September 21, 1998, 103.
22. *Los Angeles Herald Examiner*, July 15, 1967.
23. *Minneapolis Star*, June 8, 1967.
24. *Detroit Free Press*, July 5, 1967.
25. Bill Nowlin and Dan Desrochers, *The 1967 Impossible Dream Red Sox: Pandemonium on the Field* (Cambridge: Rounder, 2007), 91.
26. Ross Newhan, *The Anaheim Angels* (New York: Hyperion, 2000), 101.

Chapter 9

1. *Chicago Tribune*, July 8, 1967.
2. Herman Weiskopf, "The Infamous Spitter," *Sports Illustrated*, July 31, 1967, 12–17.
3. Tony Conigliaro with Jack Zanger, *Seeing It Through: The Story of a Comeback* (New York: Macmillan, 1970), 176.
4. *Detroit Free Press*, July 7, 1967.
5. *Boston Herald*, July 8, 1967.
6. *Detroit News*, July 8, 1967.
7. Mark Pattison and David Raglin, eds., *Sock It to 'Em Tigers: The Incredible Story of the 1968 Detroit Tigers* (Hanover, MA: Maple Street Press, 2008), 155.
8. Pattison and Raglin, *Tigers*, 155.
9. Dick Williams and Bill Plaschke, *No More Mr. Nice Guy: A Life of Hardball* (San Diego: Harcourt Brace Jovanovich, 1990), 90.
10. Dan Gutman, *It Ain't Cheatin' If You Don't Get Caught* (New York: Penguin, 1990), 21.
11. Rico Petrocelli and Chaz Scoggins, *Rico Petrocelli's Tales from the Impossible Dream Red Sox* (Champaign, IL: Sports Publishing, 2007), 71.
12. Carl Yastrzemski and Gerald Eskenazi, *Yaz: Baseball, the Wall and Me* (New York: Doubleday, 1990), 128.
13. Raymond Sinibaldi, *1967 Red Sox: The Impossible Dream Season* (Charleston, SC: Arcadia Publishing, 2014), 47.
14. *Boston Herald Traveler*, July 27, 1967.
15. *Detroit News*, April 4, 1967.
16. Weiskopf, "Spitter," 13.
17. *Detroit News*, May 11, 1967.
18. *Detroit News*, July 8, 1967.
19. *Detroit News*, July 17, 1967.
20. *Detroit News*, July 15, 1967.
21. *Boston Herald Traveler*, July 17, 1967.
22. *Detroit Free Press*, July 17, 1967.
23. *Detroit Free Press*, July 18, 1967.
24. *Detroit Free Press*, July 23, 1967.
25. *Boston Herald*, July 8, 1967.
26. *Boston Herald Traveler*, July 24, 1967.
27. *Boston Herald Traveler*, July 19, 1967.
28. Hal Butler, *Al Kaline and the Detroit Tigers* (Chicago: Henry Regnery, 1973), 178.

Chapter 10

1. *Los Angeles Herald Examiner*, July 16, 1967.
2. *Los Angeles Herald Examiner*, July 18, 1967.
3. *St. Paul Pioneer Press*, July 26, 1967.
4. *Minneapolis Tribune*, July 24, 1967.
5. *Minneapolis Tribune*, May 28, June 2, 1967.

6. Peter Golenbock, *Wild, High and Tight: The Life and Death of Billy Martin* (New York: St. Martin's, 1994), 183.
7. Golenbock, *Billy Martin*, 20.
8. Golenbock, *Billy Martin*, 20–21.
9. Golenbock, *Billy Martin*, 21.
10. Golenbock, *Billy Martin*, 36–46.
11. Golenbock, *Billy Martin*, 48.
12. Golenbock, *Billy Martin*, 96.
13. Todd Masters, *The 1972 Detroit Tigers: Billy Martin and the Half-Game Champs* (Jefferson, NC: McFarland, 2012), 20.
14. Billy Martin and Peter Golenbock, *Number 1* (New York: Delacorte, 1980), 187.
15. Jerry Izenberg, *Great Latin Sports Figures* (Garden City, NY: Doubleday, 1976), 77–78.
16. James Terzian, *The Kid from Cuba: Zoilo Versalles* (Garden City, NY: Doubleday, 1967), 12–30.
17. *Chicago Sun-Times*, March 18, 1967.
18. Jim Kaat with Phil Pepe, *Still Pitching: Musings from the Mound and Microphone* (Chicago: Triumph, 2003), 44.
19. Izenberg, *Latin Sports Figures*, 81.
20. Jim Thielman, *Cool of the Evening* (Minneapolis: Kirk House, 2005), 93.
21. *Chicago Sun-Times*, March 18, 1967.
22. Thielman, *Evening*, 29.
23. *Minneapolis Star*, September 30, 1967.
24. Terzian, *Versalles*, 75–76.
25. Izenberg, *Latin Sports Figures*, 85.
26. Golenbock, *Billy Martin*, 158–159.
27. Terzian, *Versalles*, 102–104.
28. Izenberg, *Latin Sports Figures*, 84.
29. *Minneapolis Tribune*, July 20, 1967.
30. *Boston Globe*, July 17, 1967.
31. Dick Williams and Bill Plaschke, *No More Mr. Nice Guy: A Life of Hardball* (San Diego: Harcourt Brace Jovanovich, 1990), 92.
32. *Boston Herald Traveler*, July 24, 1967.
33. *Boston Herald Traveler*, July 24, 1967.

Chapter 11

1. *Detroit News*, July 24, 1967.
2. Kerner Commission, *Report of the National Advisory Commission on Civil Disorders* (Washington, D.C.: U.S. Government Printing Office, 1968).
3. Jim Hawkins, *Al Kaline: The Biography of a Tigers Icon* (Chicago: Triumph, 2010), 141.

4. Mark Pattison and David Raglin, eds., *Sock It to 'Em Tigers: The Incredible Story of the 1968 Detroit Tigers* (Hanover, MA: Maple Street Press, 2008), 68.
5. Hal Butler, *The Willie Horton Story* (New York: Julian Messner, 1970), 89.
6. George Cantor, *The Tigers of '68: Baseball's Last Real Champions* (Dallas: Taylor, 1997), 5–6.
7. Cantor, *Tigers*, 6.
8. *Detroit News*, July 24, 1967.
9. *Detroit Free Press*, July 25, 1967.
10. Cyrus Vance, *Final Report of Cyrus R. Vance Special Assistant to the Secretary of Defense Concerning the Detroit Riots* (http://www.lbjlib.utexas.edu/johnson/archives.hom/oralhistory.hom/Vance-C/Detroit Report.asp), Section IV.
11. *Detroit Free Press*, July 26, 1967.
12. *Detroit Free Press*, July 26, 1967.
13. *Detroit News*, July 26, 1967.
14. *Detroit Free Press*, September 3, 1967.
15. Kerner Commission, *Report*.
16. *Boston Herald Traveler*, July 28, 1967.
17. *Detroit Free Press*, July 1, 1967.
18. *Detroit News*, July 31, 1967.
19. *Detroit News*, July 30, 1967.

Chapter 12

1. *Chicago Sun-Times*, March 19, 1967.
2. *Chicago Tribune*, March 20, 1967.
3. *Minneapolis Star*, August 11, 1967.
4. *Detroit Free Press*, July 31, 1967.
5. *Minneapolis Tribune*, June 12, 1967.
6. Tony Oliva with Bob Fowler, *Tony O! The Trials and Triumphs of Tony Oliva* (New York: Hawthorn, 1973), 116.
7. Oliva, *Tony O*, 38.
8. Oliva, *Tony O*, 106.
9. Oliva, *Tony O*, 113.
10. *St. Paul Pioneer Press*, July 14, 1967.
11. *Los Angeles Herald Examiner*, August 13, 1967.
12. *St. Paul Pioneer Press*, July 2, 1967.
13. *Los Angeles Herald Examiner*, September 23, 1967.
14. *Boston Globe*, August 5, 1967.
15. Mark Kram, "Take the Boy Out of the Country," *Sports Illustrated*, March 8, 1965, 41.
16. Kram, "Boy," 42.
17. Kram, "Boy," 42.
18. Maury Allen, *Bo: Pitching and Wooing* (New York: Dial Press, 1973), 104.

19. Edward Kiersh, *Where Have You Gone, Vince DiMaggio?* (New York: Bantam, 1983), 269.
20. *Chicago Tribune*, April 24, 1967.
21. *Boston Globe*, July 2, 1967.
22. Bob Showers, *The Twins at the Met* (Edina, MN: Beaver's Pond Press, 2009), 108.
23. *Minneapolis Tribune*, July 29, 1967.
24. *Los Angeles Herald Examiner*, July 24, 1967.
25. *Boston Herald Traveler*, July 31, 1967.
26. *St. Paul Pioneer Press*, August 7, 1967.

Chapter 13

1. *Detroit Free Press*, August 6, 1967.
2. Jim Kaat with Phil Pepe, *Still Pitching: Musings from the Mound and Microphone* (Chicago: Triumph, 2003), 46.
3. Fay Vincent, *We Would Have Played for Nothing: Baseball Stars of the 1950s and 1960s Talk About the Game They Loved* (New York: Simon & Schuster, 2008), 201.
4. Wayne J. Anderson, *Harmon Killebrew: Baseball's Superstar* (Salt Lake City: Deseret Book, 1971), 66–67.
5. Hal Butler, *The Harmon Killebrew Story* (New York: Julian Messner, 1966), 23–25.
6. Butler, *Killebrew*, 32.
7. Butler, *Killebrew*, 32.
8. Butler, *Killebrew*, 35.
9. Anderson, *Killebrew*, 153.
10. Butler, *Killebrew*, 53.
11. Butler, *Killebrew*, 50–56.
12. Butler, *Killebrew*, 57.
13. *Minneapolis Tribune*, August 8, 1967; *St. Paul Pioneer Press*, August 9, 1967.
14. *St. Paul Pioneer Press*, August 10, 1967.
15. *Minneapolis Tribune*, August 4, 1967.
16. *Minneapolis Tribune*, August 9, 1967.
17. Mike Mandel, *SF Giants: An Oral History* (Santa Cruz, CA: Mandel, 1979), 24.
18. Mandel, *Giants*, 25.
19. Mandel, *Giants*, 27.
20. Rico Petrocelli and Chaz Scoggins, *Rico Petrocelli's Tales from the Impossible Dream Red Sox* (Champaign, IL: Sports Publishing, 2007), 130–31.
21. *Chicago Sun-Times*, March 29, 1967.
22. *Minneapolis Star*, May 22, 1967.
23. Butler, *Killebrew*, 128.
24. Butler, *Killebrew*, 141.
25. *Chicago Tribune*, August 19, 1967.
26. Ron Anderson, *Long Taters: A Baseball Biography of George "Boomer" Scott* (Jefferson, NC: McFarland, 2012), 115.
27. *Minneapolis Star*, September 15, 1967.
28. *Los Angeles Herald Examiner*, July 19, 1967.
29. *Boston Herald Traveler*, August 14, 1967.
30. *The Sporting News*, August 12, 1967.
31. *Minneapolis Tribune*, August 14, 1967.
32. *Minneapolis Tribune*, August 14, 1967.
33. *Los Angeles Herald Examiner*, August 11, 1967.
34. *Los Angeles Herald Examiner*, August 11, 1967.

Chapter 14

1. *Los Angeles Herald Examiner*, August 5, 1967.
2. *Minneapolis Tribune*, August 7, 1967.
3. *Minneapolis Tribune*, August 4, 1967.
4. *Detroit Free Press*, August 15, 1967.
5. David Cataneo, *Tony C: The Triumph and Tragedy of Tony Conigliaro* (Nashville: Rutledge Hill, 1997), 105.
6. Cataneo, *Tony C*, 105.
7. Tony Conigliaro with Jack Zanger, *Seeing It Through: The Story of a Comeback* (New York: Macmillan, 1970), 194.
8. Cataneo, *Tony C*, 96.
9. Curry Kirkpatrick, "Baseball Week," *Sports Illustrated*, August 28, 1967, 81.
10. Cataneo, *Tony C*, 106.
11. Cataneo, *Tony C*, 108.
12. Rico Petrocelli and Chaz Scoggins, *Rico Petrocelli's Tales from the Impossible Dream Red Sox* (Champaign, IL: Sports Publishing, 2007), 137.
13. James D. Szalontai, *Close Shave: The Life and Times of Baseball's Sal Maglie* (Jefferson, NC: McFarland, 2002), 366.
14. Jim Bouton and Leonard Shecter, *Ball Four Plus Ball Five* (New York: Stein and Day, 1981), 78.

Chapter 15

1. Alvin Dark and John Underwood, *When in Doubt, Fire the Manager: My Life and Times in Baseball* (New York: E.P. Dutton, 1980), 131.
2. Dark and Underwood, *When in Doubt*, 2.

3. Dark and Underwood, *When in Doubt*, 16.
4. Leonard Koppett, *The Man in the Dugout* (New York: Crown, 1993), 254.
5. Alvin Dark and John Underwood, "Rhubarbs, Hassles and Other Hazards," *Sports Illustrated*, May 13, 1967, 47.
6. *The Sporting News*, June 24, 1967.
7. *Chicago Tribune*, July 22, 1967.
8. *Minneapolis Star*, September 28, 1967.
9. *Chicago Sun-Times*, April 11, 1967.
10. *Detroit News*, April 16, 1967.
11. Ken Harrelson with Al Hirshberg, *Hawk* (New York: Viking, 1969), 138–40.
12. Harrelson with Hirshberg, *Hawk*, 143–45.
13. Harrelson with Hirshberg, *Hawk*, 145–47.
14. Harrelson with Hirshberg, *Hawk*, 147.
15. *Kansas City Star*, August 19, 1967.
16. *Kansas City Star*, August 20, 1967.
17. Harrelson with Hirshberg, *Hawk*, 184.
18. Dark and Underwood, *When in Doubt*, 132.
19. *Kansas City Star*, August 21, 1967.
20. *Kansas City Star*, August 21, 1967.
21. *Kansas City Star*, August 21, 1967.
22. Dark and Underwood, *When in Doubt*, 133.
23. Harrelson with Hirshberg, *Hawk*, 186.
24. *Kansas City Star*, August 21, 1967.
25. *Kansas City Times*, August 22, 1967.
26. Harrelson with Hirshberg, *Hawk*, 194.
27. Jim Prime with Bill Nowlin, *Tales from the Red Sox Dugout* (Champaign, IL: Sports Publishing, 2000), 54–5.
28. Harrelson with Hirshberg, *Hawk*, 203.
29. *Boston Globe*, August 29, 1967.
30. Harrelson with Hirshberg, *Hawk*, 102.
31. *Chicago Daily News*, August 30, 1967.

Chapter 16

1. *Minneapolis Star*, August 23, 1967.
2. *Detroit News*, September 2, 1967.
3. *Chicago Sun-Times*, April 2, 1967.
4. *Chicago Sun-Times*, April 5, 1967.
5. *Chicago Daily News*, March 21, 1967.
6. *Chicago Sun-Times*, April 5, 1967.
7. *Chicago Sun-Times*, April 5, 1967.
8. *Chicago Daily News*, April 1, 1967.
9. *Chicago Tribune*, August 17, 1967.
10. *Chicago Tribune*, August 17, 1967.
11. *Chicago Tribune*, August 17, 1967.
12. Eddie Stanky with William Leggett, "Better from the Neck Up," *Sports Illustrated*, August 28, 1967, 18–23.
13. *Boston Record American*, August 26, 1967.
14. *Minneapolis Tribune*, August 25, 1967.
15. Bob Vanderberg, *Sox, from Lane and Fain to Zisk and Fisk* (Chicago: Chicago Review Press, 1982), 94.
16. Richard C. Lindberg, *Total White Sox: The Definitive Encyclopedia of the Chicago White Sox* (Chicago: Triumph, 2011), 79.
17. Lee Heiman, Dave Weiner, and Bill Gutman, *When the Cheering Stops: Ex–Major Leaguers Talk About Their Game and Their Lives* (New York: Macmillan, 1990) 286.
18. Mark Liptak, *Flashing Back with Joe Horlen*, Whitesoxinteractive.com.
19. *Chicago Tribune*, August 30, 1967.
20. *Chicago Tribune*, August 26, 1967.
21. *Chicago Tribune*, August 26, 1967.
22. *Chicago Tribune*, September 19, 1967.
23. *Minneapolis Star*, August 26, 1967.
24. *Boston Globe*, August 27, 1967.
25. *Boston Herald Traveler*, August 3, 1967.
26. *Kansas City Star*, August 10, 1967.
27. Carl Yastrzemski and Gerald Eskenazi, *Yaz: Baseball, the Wall and Me* (New York: Doubleday, 1990), 152.
28. *Boston Herald Traveler*, August 28, 1967.
29. *Boston Globe*, August 28, 1967.
30. *Chicago Tribune*, August 28, 1967.
31. *Boston Record American*, August 28, 1967.
32. *Chicago Tribune*, August 28, 1967.
33. *Boston Globe*, August 28, 1967.
34. *Chicago Tribune*, August 28, 1967.
35. *The Sporting News*, July 29, 1967.
36. *Chicago Daily News*, August 28, 1967.

Chapter 17

1. *Boston Herald Traveler*, September 2, 1967.
2. *Boston Globe*, August 30, 1967.
3. *Boston Herald Traveler*, September 5, 1967.
4. *Boston Herald Traveler*, September 1, 1967.
5. The NHL franchise was officially the

Chicago Black Hawks in 1967. Currently, they are the Chicago Blackhawks.
6. *Chicago Sun-Times*, March 13, 1967.
7. *Chicago Sun-Times*, April 7, 1967.
8. *Chicago Tribune*, September 2, 1967.
9. *Chicago Daily News*, September 2, 1967.
10. *Chicago Tribune*, August 20, 1967.
11. *Chicago Tribune*, June 1, 1967.
12. *Chicago Tribune*, September 3, 1967.
13. *Boston Herald Traveler*, September 4, 1967.
14. *Chicago Tribune*, September 4, 1967.
15. *Kansas City Times*, August 28, 1967.
16. *Detroit Free Press*, September 3, 1967.
17. *Detroit Free Press*, September 6, 1967.
18. *Detroit News*, September 4, 1967.
19. *The Sporting News*, September 23, 1967.
20. *Minneapolis Tribune*, September 2, 1967.
21. *Detroit Free Press*, September 7, 1967.

Chapter 18

1. Eddie Stanky with William Leggett, "Better from the Neck Up," *Sports Illustrated*, August 28, 1967, 20.
2. William Leggett, "Those Big Tiger Muscles," *Sports Illustrated*, June 5, 1967, 26.
3. Jim Hawkins, *Al Kaline: The Biography of a Tigers Icon* (Chicago: Triumph, 2010), 138.
4. Mark Pattison and David Raglin, eds., *Sock It to 'Em Tigers: The Incredible Story of the 1968 Detroit Tigers* (Hanover, MA: Maple Street Press, 2008), 194.
5. *Chicago Sun-Times*, March 13, 1967.
6. *Chicago Tribune*, September 8, 1967.
7. *Minneapolis Star*, August 22, 1967.
8. *Chicago Tribune*, September 12, 1967.
9. *Chicago Sun-Times*, September 18, 1967.
10. *Detroit News*, September 8, 1967.
11. Stanky with Leggett, 21.
12. *Chicago Sun-Times*, September 9, 1967.
13. *Chicago Sun-Times*, September 9, 1967.
14. *Chicago Tribune*, June 4, 1967.
15. *Detroit News*, September 9, 1967.
16. *Detroit News*, September 10, 1967.
17. *Detroit News*, September 10, 1967.
18. *Detroit Free Press*, September 10, 1967.
19. *Detroit Free Press*, September 10, 1967.
20. *Chicago Sun-Times*, September 10, 1967.
21. *Chicago Sun-Times*, September 10, 1967.
22. Dan Helpingstine, *Chicago White Sox: 1959 and Beyond* (Charleston, SC: Arcadia Publishing, 2004), 21.
23. *Chicago Tribune*, September 10, 1967.
24. Mark Liptak, "Flashing Back with Joe Horlen," www.whitesoxinteractive.com.
25. Lew Freedman, *Game of My Life: White Sox* (Champaign, IL: Sports Publishing, 2008), 54.
26. *Chicago Tribune*, June 20, 1967.
27. *Chicago Tribune*, June 20, 1967.
28. *Chicago Tribune*, June 20, 1967.
29. *Minneapolis Star*, June 9, 1967.
30. *Chicago Tribune*, March 24, 1967.
31. *The Sporting News*, July 29, 1967.
32. Liptak, "Joe Horlen."
33. *Chicago Sun-Times*, September 11, 1967.
34. Stanky with Leggett, 20.
35. *Kansas City Times*, August 28, 1967.
36. Freedman, *White Sox*, 55.
37. *Chicago Sun-Times*, September 20, 1967; *The Sporting News*, September 30, 1967.
38. *Chicago Daily News*, September 9, 1967.
39. *Boston Globe*, September 19, 1967.
40. Liptak, "Joe Horlen."
41. *Chicago Tribune*, September 15, 1967.
42. *Chicago Sun-Times*, September 19, 1967.

Chapter 19

1. *Chicago Daily News*, September 12, 1967.
2. *Minneapolis Tribune*, August 25, 1967.
3. *Chicago Tribune*, September 13, 1967.
4. *Detroit Free Press*, September 12, 1967.
5. *Detroit Free Press*, September 15, 1967.
6. *Detroit Free Press*, September 30, 1967.
7. *Detroit Free Press*, September 3, 1967.
8. *St. Paul Pioneer Press*, September 12, 1967.
9. *St. Paul Pioneer Press*, September 15, 1967.
10. *St. Paul Pioneer Press*, September 22, 1967.
11. *St. Paul Pioneer Press*, September 13, 1967.

12. *St. Paul Pioneer Press*, September 14, 1967.
13. *Minneapolis Star*, September 12, 1967.
14. *Chicago Daily News*, March 28, 1967.
15. *Kansas City Times*, September 14, 1967.
16. *Boston Herald Traveler*, September 16, 1967.
17. *Detroit News*, September 10, 1967.
18. *Boston Record American*, August 31, 1967.
19. *Boston Globe*, September 21, 1967.
20. Howard Bryant, *Shut Out: A Story of Race and Baseball in Boston* (New York: Routledge, 2002), 3.
21. Bryant, *Race and Baseball*, 31–32, 45–46.
22. Bryant, *Race and Baseball*, 54.
23. *Detroit News*, April 12, 1967.
24. Bryant, *Race and Baseball*, 77.
25. Bryant, *Race and Baseball*, 77–80.
26. Jim Prime with Bill Nowlin, *Tales from the Red Sox Dugout* (Champaign, IL: Sports Publishing, 2000), 10.
27. Bryant, *Race and Baseball*, 78–79.
28. *The Sporting News*, September 30, 1967.
29. *Detroit News*, May 2, 1967.
30. *The Sporting News*, September 9, 1967.
31. *Detroit News*, April 18, 1967
32. Jim Thielman, *Cool of the Evening* (Minneapolis: Kirk House, 2005), 51.
33. Thielman, *Evening*, 51.
34. Bill Freehan, *Behind the Mask: An Inside Baseball Diary*, edited by Steve Gelman and Dick Schaap (New York: Popular Press, 1970), 189–90.
35. Jim Kaat with Phil Pepe, *Still Pitching: Musings from the Mound and Microphone* (Chicago: Triumph, 2003), 56.
36. Freehan, *Mask*, 190.
37. *Detroit News*, September 9, 1967.
38. *Minneapolis Star*, August 19, 1967.
39. *Detroit News*, April 8, 1967.
40. *Detroit News*, April 19, 1967.
41. Jim Bouton and Leonard Shecter, *Ball Four Plus Ball Five* (New York: Stein and Day, 1981), 190–91.
42. *Chicago Sun-Times*, September 17, 1967.
43. Eddie Stanky with William Leggett, "Better from the Neck Up," *Sports Illustrated*, August 28, 1967, 20.
44. *St. Paul Pioneer Press*, September 25, 1967.
45. *Detroit News*, September 26, 1967.
46. *Los Angeles Herald Examiner*, September 25, 1967.
47. *St. Paul Pioneer Press*, September 6, 1967.
48. *Minneapolis Star*, August 31, 1967.

Chapter 20

1. *Minneapolis Tribune*, September 18, 1967.
2. Bill Reynolds, *Lost Summer* (New York: Warner, 1992), 205.
3. *Minneapolis Tribune*, September 3, 1967.
4. *Boston Globe*, September 19, 1967.
5. *Chicago Sun-Times*, September 18, 1967.
6. David Cataneo, *Tony C: The Triumph and Tragedy of Tony Conigliaro* (Nashville: Rutledge Hill, 1997), 99.
7. *Boston Globe*, September 19, 1967.
8. *Boston Globe*, September 19, 1967.
9. *Boston Globe*, September 19, 1967.
10. *Detroit Free Press*, September 19, 1967.
11. Carl Yastrzemski with Al Hirshberg, *Yaz* (New York: Viking, 1968), 94–97.
12. Yastrzemski with Hirshberg, *Yaz*, 104–06.
13. Yastrzemski with Hirshberg, *Yaz*, 142.
14. *Boston Globe*, June 27, 1967.
15. *Boston Herald Traveler*, July 30, 1967.
16. *Boston Herald Traveler*, July 28, 1967.
17. Yastrzemski with Hirshberg, *Yaz*, 106.
18. *Detroit News*, September 18, 1967.
19. *Boston Globe*, September 19, 1967.
20. *Boston Globe*, September 21, 1967.
21. *Detroit Free Press*, September 20, 1967.
22. *Boston Globe*, September 20, 1967.
23. *Boston Globe*, September 20, 1967.
24. *Detroit News*, September 20, 1967.

Chapter 21

1. *Detroit News*, September 20, 1967.
2. *Detroit Free Press*, September 21, 1967.
3. Mark Pattison and David Raglin, eds., *Sock It to 'Em Tigers: The Incredible Story of the 1968 Detroit Tigers* (Hanover, MA: Maple Street Press, 2008), 110.
4. Pattison and Raglin, *Tigers*, 111.
5. Denny McLain and David Diles, *Nobody's Perfect* (New York: Dial Press, 1975), 3.

6. George Cantor, *The Tigers of '68: Baseball's Last Real Champions* (Dallas: Taylor, 1997), 14.
7. Dave Klein, *Tom Seaver, Dave McNally, Ferguson Jenkins, Mickey Lolich* (New York: Grosset & Dunlap, 1974), 142–43.
8. McLain and Diles, *Perfect*, 85.
9. Denny McLain and Mike Nahrstedt, *Strikeout* (St. Louis: Sporting News, 1988), 57.
10. McLain and Nahrstedt, *Strikeout*, 58.
11. Morton Sharnik, "Downfall of a Hero," *Sports Illustrated*, February 23, 1970, 20–1.
12. *Detroit Free Press*, September 29, 1967.
13. McLain and Nahrstedt, *Strikeout*, 59–60.
14. *Boston Record American*, September 22, 1967.
15. *Detroit Free Press*, September 22, 1967.
16. *Minneapolis Tribune*, September 22, 1967.
17. *Chicago Tribune*, March 6, 1967.
18. *Chicago Tribune*, March 22, 1967.
19. *Chicago Sun-Times*, September 23, 1967.
20. Joe Falls, "I Throw Lefthanded but Think Upside Down," *Sport*, March, 1965, 90.
21. Bill Freehan, *Behind the Mask: An Inside Baseball Diary*, edited by Steve Gelman and Dick Schaap (New York: Popular Press, 1970), 49–50.
22. Pattison and Raglin, *Tigers*, 85–86.
23. Hugh Bernreuter, "Durable Lefty and Detroit Tigers Hero Mickey Lolich," *The Saginaw News*, June 15, 2010.
24. Steve Kornacki, "Detroit Tigers 1968 World Series MVP Mickey Lolich," mlive.com/tigers, March 16, 2011.
25. Freehan, *Mask*, 49.
26. Tom E. Mahl, *The Spitball Knuckleball Book: How They Were Thrown, Those Who Threw Them* (Elyria, OH: Trick Pitch Press, 2009), 223.
27. *Detroit Free Press*, September 22, 1967.
28. *Detroit News*, September 25, 1967.

Chapter 22

1. *Boston Herald Traveler*, September 24, 1967.
2. *St. Paul Pioneer Press*, September 25, 1967.
3. *Los Angeles Herald Examiner*, September 25, 1967.
4. *Boston Globe*, September 25, 1967.
5. *Boston Globe*, September 25, 1967.
6. *Kansas City Star*, September 25, 1967.
7. *Boston Globe*, September 10, 1967.
8. *Boston Herald Traveler*, August 8, 1967.
9. *Boston Globe*, September 26, 1967.
10. *Boston Record American*, August 29, 1967.
11. *Boston Globe*, October 10, 1967.
12. *Boston Globe*, September 25, 1967.
13. *Kansas City Star*, August 10, 1967.
14. *Boston Globe*, September 25, 1967.
15. *Boston Globe*, September 25, 1967.
16. *Detroit Free Press*, September 25, 1967.
17. *Chicago Sun-Times*, September 17, 1967.
18. *Minneapolis Tribune*, August 30, 1967.
19. *Kansas City Star*, September 15, 1967.
20. *Chicago Sun-Times*, September 20, 1967.
21. *Chicago Daily News*, September 22, 1967.
22. Bill Freehan, *Behind the Mask: An Inside Baseball Diary*, edited by Steve Gelman and Dick Schaap (New York: Popular Press, 1970), 75.
23. *Chicago Daily News*, September 25, 1967.
24. Richard C. Lindberg, *Total White Sox: The Definitive Encyclopedia of the Chicago White Sox* (Chicago: Triumph, 2011), 244.
25. *Chicago Daily News*, September 26, 1967.
26. *Chicago Daily News*, September 26, 1967.
27. *Detroit News*, September 25, 1967.

Chapter 23

1. *Detroit News*, September 25, 1967.
2. *Chicago Daily News*, September 26, 1967.
3. *Detroit Free Press*, September 26, 1967.
4. *Boston Globe*, September 26, 1967.
5. *Minneapolis Tribune*, September 26, 1967.
6. *Los Angeles Herald Examiner*, September 26, 1967.
7. *Detroit News*, September 26, 1967.
8. *Boston Herald Traveler*, September 26, 1967.

9. *Boston Record American*, September 26, 1967.
10. *Minneapolis Tribune*, September 28, 1967.
11. *Detroit News*, September 28, 1967.
12. *Boston Globe*, September 26, 1967.
13. *St. Paul Pioneer Press*, September 19, 1967.
14. *Los Angeles Herald Examiner*, September 27, 1967.
15. *Detroit News*, September 27, 1967.
16. Fay Vincent, *We Would Have Played for Nothing: Baseball Stars of the 1950s and 1960s Talk About the Game They Loved* (New York: Simon & Schuster, 2008), 215.
17. *Los Angeles Herald Examiner*, September 27, 1967.
18. *Chicago Daily News*, September 29, 1967.
19. Rico Petrocelli and Chaz Scoggins, *Rico Petrocelli's Tales from the Impossible Dream Red Sox* (Champaign, IL: Sports Publishing, 2007), 161.
20. *Minneapolis Tribune*, September 27, 1967.
21. *Boston Herald Traveler*, September 27, 1967.
22. *Detroit Free Press*, September 27, 1967.
23. *Chicago Daily News*, September 27, 1967.
24. *Detroit Free Press*, September 27, 1967.
25. *Boston Herald Traveler*, September 28, 1967.
26. *Chicago Daily News*, September 27, 1967.
27. *Kansas City Times*, September 26, 1967.

Chapter 24

1. *Boston Globe*, September 28, 1967.
2. *Boston Herald Traveler*, September 28, 1967.
3. *Chicago Daily News*, September 28, 1967.
4. *Chicago Tribune*, September 28, 1967.
5. *Chicago Daily News*, September 28, 1967.
6. *Minneapolis Tribune*, September 28, 1967.
7. *Los Angeles Herald Examiner*, September 26, 1967.
8. *Chicago Sun-Times*, September 28, 1967.
9. *Minneapolis Tribune*, September 28, 1967.
10. *Los Angeles Herald Examiner*, September 28, 1967.
11. *Minneapolis Tribune*, September 28, 1967.
12. *Minneapolis Tribune*, September 25, 1967.
13. *Chicago Tribune*, September 28, 1967.
14. *Chicago Tribune*, September 26, 1967.
15. Dick Williams and Bill Plaschke, *No More Mr. Nice Guy: A Life of Hardball* (San Diego: Harcourt Brace Jovanovich, 1990), 99.
16. *Minneapolis Star*, September 28, 1967.
17. *Chicago Daily News*, March 28, 1967 and September 22, 1967; *Chicago Tribune*, September 8, 1967.
18. *Chicago Tribune*, September 28, 1967.
19. *Boston Globe*, September 26, 1967.
20. *Los Angeles Herald Examiner*, September 25, 1967.
21. Richard C. Lindberg, *Total White Sox: The Definitive Encyclopedia of the Chicago White Sox* (Chicago: Triumph, 2011), 384.
22. Dan Helpingstine, *Through Hope and Despair: A Fan's Memories of the Chicago White Sox 1967-1997* ([S.I.: s.n.], 2001), 13.
23. *Chicago Daily News*, September 28, 1967.
24. *Minneapolis Star*, September 28, 1967.
25. *Kansas City Times*, September 29, 1967.
26. *Chicago Tribune*, September 29, 1967.
27. *Chicago Daily News*, September 28, 1967.
28. *Minneapolis Tribune*, September 29, 1967.
29. *Detroit News*, September 28, 1967.
30. *Detroit News*, September 29, 1967.
31. *Chicago Sun-Tribune*, September 30, 1967.
32. *Chicago Daily News*, September 30, 1967.
33. *Chicago Sun-Tribune*, September 30, 1967.
34. *Chicago Daily News*, September 30, 1967.
35. *Chicago Tribune*, September 30, 1967.
36. Bill Reynolds, *Lost Summer* (New York: Warner, 1992), 214-15.
37. *Chicago Daily News*, September 30, 1967.
38. *Detroit News*, September 30, 1967.
39. *Chicago Sun-Times*, October 2, 1967.

Chapter 25

1. *St. Paul Pioneer Press*, September 29, 1967.
2. *St. Paul Pioneer Press*, September 29, 1967.
3. *Detroit News*, September 27, 1967.
4. *St. Paul Pioneer Press*, October 1, 1967.
5. *Minneapolis Tribune*, October 4, 1967.
6. Steve Aschburner, *The Good, the Bad, and the Ugly: Minnesota Twins: Heart-Pounding, Jaw-Dropping, and Gut-Wrenching Moments from Minnesota Twins History* (Chicago: Triumph, 2008), 28.
7. William Leggett, "A Wild Finale—And It's Boston!" *Sports Illustrated*, October 9, 1967, 34.
8. *Minneapolis Tribune*, October 2, 1967.
9. *Minneapolis Star*, October 2, 1967.
10. *Minneapolis Tribune*, October 2, 1967.
11. *Minneapolis Tribune*, October 2, 1967.
12. *Boston Record American*, September 30, 1967.
13. *Minneapolis Tribune*, October 2, 1967.
14. *Minneapolis Star*, September 10, 1967.
15. Jim Kaat with Phil Pepe, *Still Pitching: Musings from the Mound and Microphone* (Chicago: Triumph, 2003), 195.
16. *St. Paul Pioneer Press*, September 27, 1967.
17. *Minneapolis Tribune*, September 23, 1967.
18. Raymond Sinibaldi, *1967 Red Sox: The Impossible Dream Season* (Charleston, SC: Arcadia Publishing, 2014), 28.
19. *Boston Globe*, September 29, 1967.
20. *Boston Globe*, September 30, 1967.
21. *Boston Record American*, September 30, 1967.
22. *Boston Globe*, September 30, 1967.
23. *Minneapolis Tribune*, October 4, 1967.
24. *Boston Globe*, September 29, 1967.
25. *Boston Globe*, October 1, 1967.
26. *Detroit News*, October 1, 1967.
27. *Boston Herald Traveler*, October 1, 1967.
28. Will McDonough, "Red Sox Surge Due to Pitching," *Boston Globe*, July 5, 1967.
29. *Boston Globe*, October 1, 1967.
30. *Boston Sunday Advertiser*, October 1, 1967.
31. *St. Paul Pioneer Press*, October 1, 1967.
32. Kaat with Pepe, *Still Pitching*, 31.
33. *St. Paul Pioneer Press*, October 1, 1967.
34. *Minneapolis Tribune*, October 1, 1967.
35. *Boston Globe*, October 1, 1967.
36. *Boston Globe*, October 1, 1967.
37. *St. Paul Pioneer Press*, October 1, 1967.
38. *Boston Globe*, October 1, 1967.
39. *St. Paul Pioneer Press*, October 1, 1967.
40. *Boston Herald Traveler*, October 1, 1967.
41. *Boston Herald Traveler*, October 1, 1967.
42. *Boston Herald Traveler*, October 1, 1967.
43. *Boston Herald Traveler*, October 1, 1967.
44. *Chicago Tribune*, October 1, 1967.
45. Bill Reynolds, *Lost Summer* (New York: Warner, 1992), 220.
46. *Chicago Sun-Times*, October 1, 1967.
47. *St. Paul Pioneer Press*, October 1, 1967.
48. *Boston Globe*, October 1, 1967.
49. *Boston Globe*, October 1, 1967.
50. *Boston Herald Traveler*, October 1, 1967.
51. *Boston Herald Traveler*, October 1, 1967.

Chapter 26

1. *Chicago Daily News*, September 27, 1967.
2. *Minneapolis Star*, September 28, 1967.
3. *Detroit News*, September 28, 1967.
4. *Detroit News*, September 29, 1967.
5. *The Sporting News*, June 29, 1967.
6. *Los Angeles Herald Examiner*, August 8, 1967.
7. *Los Angeles Herald Tribune*, October 1, 1967.
8. *Detroit News*, October 2, 1967.
9. *Detroit Free Press*, October 1, 1967.
10. *Detroit News*, October 1, 1967.
11. *Detroit News*, October 1, 1967.
12. *Detroit Free Press*, October 1, 1967.
13. *Detroit Free Press*, October 1, 1967.
14. *Detroit Free Press*, October 1, 1967.
15. *Kansas City Star*, August 29, 1967.
16. *Detroit Free Press*, October 1, 1967.
17. *Detroit News*, October 1, 1967.
18. *Boston Globe*, September 23, 1967.
19. *Detroit Free Press*, September 29, 1967.

Chapter 27

1. *Minneapolis Tribune*, October 1, 1967.

2. *Minneapolis Star*, September 28, 1967.
3. Bill Reynolds, *Lost Summer* (New York: Warner, 1992), 220.
4. *Boston Herald Traveler*, October 2, 1967.
5. *Boston Herald Traveler*, October 6, 1967.
6. *Los Angeles Herald Examiner*, October 3, 1967.
7. *Chicago Tribune*, October 4, 1967.
8. *Boston Globe*, October 2, 1967.
9. *Boston Record American*, October 2, 1967.
10. *Boston Record American*, October 2, 1967.
11. *Boston Globe*, October 2, 1967.
12. Carl Yastrzemski and Gerald Eskenazi, *Yaz: Baseball, the Wall and Me* (New York: Doubleday, 1990), 181.
13. *Chicago Daily News*, October 2, 1967.
14. *Boston Globe*, October 2, 1967.
15. *Boston Globe*, October 2, 1967.
16. Bill Nowlin and Dan Desrochers, *The 1967 Impossible Dream Red Sox: Pandemonium on the Field* (Cambridge: Rounder, 2007), 181.
17. Rico Petrocelli and Chaz Scoggins, *Rico Petrocelli's Tales from the Impossible Dream Red Sox* (Champaign, IL: Sports Publishing, 2007), 173.
18. Dick Williams and Bill Plaschke, *No More Mr. Nice Guy: A Life of Hardball* (San Diego: Harcourt Brace Jovanovich, 1990), 101.
19. *Boston Globe*, October 2, 1967.
20. *Boston Globe*, October 2, 1967.
21. *Boston Herald Traveler*, October 2, 1967.
22. *St. Paul Pioneer Press*, October 2, 1967.
23. George Vass, *The Game I'll Never Forget* (Evanston, IL: Baseball Digest, Century Publishing, 1999), 113.
24. *St. Paul Pioneer Press*, October 2, 1967.
25. *Boston Globe*, October 2, 1967.
26. *Boston Herald Traveler*, October 2, 1967.
27. Reynolds, *Lost Summer*, 226.
28. *Boston Herald Traveler*, October 2, 1967.
29. James C. Hefley, *Play Ball! True Stories of Faith in Action* (Grand Rapids: Zondervan Books, 1974), 80.
30. *St. Paul Pioneer Press*, October 2, 1967.
31. *Boston Herald Traveler*, October 2, 1967.
32. *Boston Globe*, October 2, 1967.
33. *Boston Record American*, October 2, 1967.
34. Jim Thielman, *Cool of the Evening* (Minneapolis: Kirk House, 2005), 152.
35. Hal Butler, *The Bob Allison Story* (New York: Julian Messner, 1967), 103.
36. *St. Paul Pioneer Press*, October 2, 1967.
37. Bob Showers, *The Twins at the Met* (Edina, MN: Beaver's Pond Press, 2009), 152.
38. *Boston Globe*, October 2, 1967.
39. *Boston Record American*, October 2, 1967.
40. *Boston Herald Traveler*, October 2, 1967.
41. *Boston Herald Traveler*, October 2, 1967.
42. *Boston Record American*, October 2, 1967.
43. *Boston Herald Traveler*, October 2, 1967.
44. *Chicago Daily News*, October 2, 1967.
45. *Boston Record American*, October 2, 1967.
46. *Boston Record American*, October 2, 1967.

Chapter 28

1. George Cantor, *The Tigers of '68: Baseball's Last Real Champions* (Dallas: Taylor, 1997), 11.
2. *Detroit News*, October 2, 1967.
3. *Los Angeles Herald Examiner*, October 2, 1967.
4. Rico Petrocelli and Chaz Scoggins, *Rico Petrocelli's Tales from the Impossible Dream Red Sox* (Champaign, IL: Sports Publishing, 2007), 177.
5. Bill Reynolds, *Lost Summer* (New York: Warner, 1992), 230.
6. *Boston Herald Traveler*, October 2, 1967.
7. Reynolds, *Lost Summer*, 230.
8. *Boston Record American*, October 2, 1967.
9. *Boston Herald Traveler*, October 2, 1967.
10. *Los Angeles Herald Tribune*, October 2, 1967.
11. Cantor, *Tigers*, 12.

12. *Detroit Free Press*, October 3, 1967.
13. *Detroit Free Press*, October 2, 1967.
14. *Los Angeles Herald Examiner*, October 2, 1967.
15. *Detroit News*, October 2, 1967.
16. Cantor, *Tigers*, 12.
17. *Chicago Sun-Times*, October 2, 1967.
18. *Boston Record American*, October 2, 1967.

The 1967 World Series

1. *Chicago Sun-Times*, October 3, 1967.
2. William Leggett, "Aftermath of a Bittersweet World Series," *Sports Illustrated*, October 23, 1967, 62–63.
3. *Chicago Sun-Times*, October 3, 1967.
4. *Minneapolis Star*, October 4, 1967.
5. *Los Angeles Herald Examiner*, October 5, 1967.
6. *Chicago Sun-Times*, October 4, 1967.
7. *Minneapolis Star*, October 5, 1967.
8. *St. Paul Pioneer Press*, October 5, 1967.
9. *Boston Herald Traveler*, October 6, 1967.
10. *Chicago Tribune*, October 6, 1967.
11. *Los Angeles Herald Examiner*, October 6, 1967.
12. *Chicago Sun-Times*, October 4, 1967.
13. *Boston Herald Traveler*, October 6, 1967.
14. *Los Angeles Herald Examiner*, October 6, 1967.
15. *Los Angeles Herald Examiner*, October 7, 1967.
16. *Los Angeles Herald Examiner*, October 6, 1967.
17. *Los Angeles Herald Examiner*, October 6, 1967.
18. *Los Angeles Herald Examiner*, October 8, 1967.
19. *Los Angeles Herald Examiner*, October 8, 1967.
20. *Chicago Sun-Times*, October 8, 1967.
21. *Los Angeles Herald Examiner*, October 9, 1967.
22. *Chicago Sun-Times*, October 9, 1967.
23. *Los Angeles Herald Examiner*, October 8, 1967.
24. *Boston Globe*, October 10, 1967.
25. *Boston Herald Traveler*, October 10, 1967.
26. William Leggett, "El Birdos Fly High," *Sports Illustrated*, October 16, 1967, 26–29.
27. *Los Angeles Herald Examiner*, October 9, 1967.
28. *Chicago Tribune*, October 8, 1967.
29. *Chicago Sun-Times*, October 11, 1967.
30. *Los Angeles Herald Examiner*, October 11, 1967.
31. *Minneapolis Star*, October 10, 1967.
32. *Chicago Tribune*, October 11, 1967.
33. *Boston Herald Traveler*, July 16, 1967. *Boston Globe*, July 16, 1967.
34. *Los Angeles Herald Examiner*, October 12, 1967.
35. Bill Nowlin and Dan Desrochers, *The 1967 Impossible Dream Red Sox: Pandemonium on the Field* (Cambridge: Rounder, 2007), 234.
36. *Boston Herald Traveler*, October 12, 1967.
37. *Los Angeles Herald Examiner*, October 12, 1967.
38. *Boston Herald Traveler*, October 12, 1967.
39. *Boston Herald Traveler*, October 13, 1967.
40. *Chicago Sun-Times*, October 10, 1967.
41. *Boston Herald Traveler*, October 13, 1967.
42. Sal Maglie and Robert H. Boyle, "Baseball Is a Tough Business," *Sports Illustrated*, April 15, 1968, 80.
43. *Boston Herald Traveler*, October 13, 1967.
44. *Boston Herald Traveler*, October 13, 1967.

Epilogue: After 1967

1. Seth Swirsky, *Something to Write Home About: Great Baseball Memories in Letters to a Fan* (New York: Crown, 2003), 12.
2. Unidentified, undated newspaper clipping in George Brunet folder at Giamatti Research Center, Cooperstown, NY.
3. Bob Showers, *The Twins at the Met* (Edina, MN: Beaver's Pond Press, 2009), 172.
4. Unidentified, undated newspaper clipping in Norm Cash folder at Giamatti Research Center, Cooperstown, NY.
5. Swirsky, *Write Home*.
6. David Anderson, ed., *Quotations from Chairman Calvin* (Stillwater, MN: Brick Alley Books, 1984).
7. Raymond Sinibaldi, *1967 Red Sox:*

The Impossible Dream Season (Charleston, SC: Arcadia Publishing, 2014), 82.

8. *Boston Herald Traveler*, September 14, 1967.

9. Bill James, *The New Bill James Historical Baseball Abstract* (New York: Free Press, 2001), 899.

10. Jim Prime with Bill Nowlin, *Tales from the Red Sox Dugout* (Champaign, IL: Sports Publishing, 2000), 67.

11. Denny McLain and David Diles, *Nobody's Perfect* (New York: Dial Press, 1975), 67.

12. *Chicago Tribune*, August 15, 1967.

13. Peter Gammons, "Yaz's Most Memorable Games," *Baseball Digest*, September 1981, 18–22.

14. Bill James, *The New Bill James Historical Baseball Abstract* (New York: Free Press, 2001), 858.

15. Ron Luciano and David Fisher, *The Umpire Strikes Back* (New York: Bantam, 1982), 138.

16. Art Rust, Jr., with Michael Marley, *Legends: Conversations with Baseball Greats* (New York: McGraw-Hill, 1989), 84.

17. Daniel R. Levitt, "The Late 1960s Twins" (SABR, node 3953).

18. James, *Baseball Abstract*, 149.

19. Ron Luciano and David Fisher, *The Umpire Strikes Back* (New York: Bantam, 1982), 120.

Bibliography

Books

Abu-Lughod, Ibrahim. *The Arab-Israeli Confrontation of June 1967: An Arab Perspective.* Evanston: Northwestern University Press, 1970.

Allen, Maury. *Baseball: The Lives Behind the Seams.* New York: Macmillan, 1990.

_____. *Bo: Pitching and Wooing.* New York: Dial Press, 1973.

Anderson, David, ed. *Quotations from Chairman Calvin.* Stillwater, MN: Brick Alley, 1984.

Anderson, Ron. *Long Taters: A Baseball Biography of George "Boomer" Scott.* Jefferson, NC: McFarland, 2012.

Anderson, Wayne J. *Harmon Killebrew: Baseball's Superstar.* Salt Lake City: Deseret Book, 1971.

Appel, Marty. *Yesterday's Heroes: Revisiting the Old-time Baseball Stars.* New York: William Morrow, 1988.

Aschburner, Steve. *The Good, the Bad, and the Ugly: Minnesota Twins: Heart-Pounding, Jaw-Dropping, and Gut-Wrenching Moments from Minnesota Twins History.* Chicago: Triumph, 2008.

_____. *Harmon Killebrew: Ultimate Slugger.* Chicago: Triumph, 2012.

Blake, Mike. *Baseball Chronicles: An Oral History of Baseball through the Decades.* Cincinnati: Betterway, 1994.

Bouton, Jim, with Leonard Shecter. *Ball Four Plus Ball Five.* New York: Stein and Day, 1981.

Bryant, Howard. *Shut Out: A Story of Race and Baseball in Boston.* New York: Routledge, 2002.

Burke, Larry. *The Baseball Chronicles: A Decade-by-Decade History of the All-American Pastime.* New York: Smithmark, 1995.

Burkett, B.G., and Glenna Whitley. *Stolen Valor: How the Vietnam Generation Was Robbed of its Heroes and its History.* Dallas: Verity Press, 1998.

Butler, Hal. *Al Kaline and the Detroit Tigers.* Chicago: Henry Regnery, 1973.

_____. *The Bob Allison Story.* New York: Julian Messner, 1967.

_____. *The Harmon Killebrew Story.* New York: Julian Messner, 1966.

_____. *The Willie Horton Story.* New York: Julian Messner, 1970.

Cantor, George. *The Tigers of '68: Baseball's Last Real Champions.* Dallas: Taylor, 1997.

Carter, Dan T. *The Politics of Rage: George Wallace.* New York: Simon & Schuster, 1995.

Cataneo, David. *Tony C: The Triumph and Tragedy of Tony Conigliaro.* Nashville: Rutledge Hill, 1997.

Center of Military History. *American Military History.* Washington, D.C.: Center of Military History, United States Army, 1989.

Conigliaro, Tony, with Jack Zanger. *Seeing It Through: The Story of a Comeback.* New York: Macmillan, 1970.

Crossland, Richard B., and James T. Currie. *Twice the Citizen: A History of the United States Army Reserve, 1908–1983.* Washington, D.C: Office of the Chief, Army Reserve, 1984.

Danver, Steven L. *Revolts, Protests, Demonstrations, and Rebellions in American History: An Encyclopedia, Volume 3.* Santa Barbara, CA: ABC-CLIO, 2011.

Dark, Alvin, with John Underwood. *When in Doubt, Fire the Manager: My Life and Times in Baseball.* New York: E.P. Dutton, 1980.

Decker, Duane. *Good Field, No Hit.* New York: William Morrow, 1947.

Durocher, Leo, with Ed Linn. *Nice Guys Finish Last.* New York: Simon & Schuster, 1975.

Eig, Jonathan. *Opening Day: The Story of Jackie Robinson's First Season.* New York: Simon & Schuster, 2007.

Fine, Sidney. *Violence in the Model City: The Cavanagh Administration, Race Relations, and the Detroit Riots of 1967.* Ann Arbor: University of Michigan Press, 1989.

Freedman, Lew. *Game of My Life: White Sox.* Champaign, IL: Sports Publishing, 2008.

_____. *Latino Baseball Legends: An Encyclopedia.* Santa Barbara, CA: Greenwood, 2010.

Freedman, Lew, and Billy Pierce. *"Then Ozzie Said to Harold...": The Best Chicago White Sox Stories Ever Told.* Chicago: Triumph, 2008.

Freehan, Bill. *Behind the Mask: An Inside Baseball Diary.* Edited by Steve Gelman and Dick Schaap. New York: Popular Press, 1970.

Gallen, David. *The Baseball Chronicles.* New York: Carroll & Graf, 1991.

Golenbock, Peter. *Wild, High and Tight: The Life and Death of Billy Martin.* New York: St. Martin's, 1994.

Gonzales, Mark. *The Good, the Bad and the Ugly Chicago White Sox: Heart-Pounding, Jaw-Dropping and Gut-Wrenching Moments from Chicago White Sox History.* Chicago: Triumph, 2009.

Gutman, Dan. *It Ain't Cheatin' If You Don't Get Caught.* New York: Penguin, 1990.

Hammel, Eric. *Six Days in June: How Israel Won the 1967 Arab-Israeli War.* New York: Charles Scribner's Sons, 1992.

Harrelson, Ken, with Al Hirshberg. *Hawk.* New York: Viking, 1969.

Hawkins, Jim. *Al Kaline: The Biography of a Tigers Icon.* Chicago: Triumph, 2010.

Hefley, James C. *Play Ball! True Stories of Faith in Action.* Grand Rapids: Zondervan, 1974.

Heikal, Mohamed Hassanein. *The Cairo Documents: The Inside Story of Nasser and His Relationship with World Leaders, Rebels, and Statesmen.* Garden City, NY: Doubleday, 1973.

Heiman, Lee, Dave Weiner, and Bill Gutman. *When the Cheering Stops: Ex-Major Leaguers Talk about Their Game and Their Lives.* New York: Macmillan, 1990.

Helpingstine, Dan. *Chicago White Sox: 1959 and Beyond.* Charleston, SC: Arcadia, 2004.

_____. *Through Hope and Despair: A Fan's Memories of the Chicago White Sox 1967–1997.* [S.I.: s.n.], 2001.

Hillstrom, Kevin. *Vietnam War: Almanac.* Detroit: UXL, 2001.

_____. *Vietnam War: Primary Sources.* Detroit: UXL, 2001.

Holtzman, Jerome. *The Jerome Holtzman Reader.* Chicago: Triumph, 2003.

Hussein of Jordan, Vick Vance, and Pierre Lauer. *Hussein of Jordan: My "War" with Israel.* New York: William Morrow, 1969.

Izenberg, Jerry. *Great Latin Sports Figures.* Garden City, NY: Doubleday, 1976.

James, Bill. *The Bill James Guide to Baseball Managers from 1870 to Today.* New York: Scribner's, 1997.

_____. *The New Bill James Historical Baseball Abstract.* New York: Free Press, 2001.

John, Tommy, and Sally John, with Joe Musser. *The Tommy John Story.* Old Tappan, NJ: Fleming H. Revell, 1978.

Kaat, Jim, with Phil Pepe. *Still Pitching: Musings from the Mound and Microphone.* Chicago: Triumph, 2003.

Kelley, Brent. *The Case For: Those Overlooked by the Baseball Hall of Fame.* Jefferson, NC: McFarland, 1992.

Kennedy, Kostya. *56: Joe DiMaggio and the Last Magic Number in Sports.* New York: Sports Illustrated, 2011.

Kerner Commission. *Report of the National Advisory Commission on Civil Disorders.* Washington, D.C.: U.S. Government Printing Office, 1968.

Kerr, Jon. *Calvin: Baseball's Last Dinosaur.* Dubuque: Wm. C. Brown, 1991.

Kiernan, Thomas. *The Miracle at Coogan's Bluff.* New York: Thomas Y. Crowell, 1975.

Kiersh, Edward. *Where Have You Gone, Vince DiMaggio?* New York: Bantam, 1983.

Klein, Dave. *Tom Seaver, Dave McNally, Ferguson Jenkins, Mickey Lolich.* New York: Grosset & Dunlap, 1974.

Koppett, Leonard. *A Thinking Man's Guide to Baseball.* New York: E.P. Dutton, 1967.

———. *The Man in the Dugout.* New York: Crown, 1993.

Krasner, Steven. *Play Ball Like the Hall of Famers.* Atlanta: Peachtree, 2005.

Kuenster, John. *At Home and Away: 33 Years of Baseball Essays.* Jefferson, NC: McFarland, 2003.

Libby, Bill. *Star Pitchers of the Major Leagues.* New York: Random House, 1971.

Lindberg, Richard C. *Stealing First in a Two-Team Town: The White Sox from Comiskey to Reinsdorf.* Champaign, IL: Sagamore, 1994.

———. *Total White Sox: The Definitive Encyclopedia of the Chicago White Sox.* Chicago: Triumph, 2011.

Linkugel, Wil A., and Edward J. Pappas. *They Tasted Glory: Among the Missing at the Baseball Hall of Fame.* Jefferson, NC: McFarland, 1998.

Luciano, Ron, and David Fisher. *The Umpire Strikes Back.* New York: Bantam, 1982.

Mahl, Tom E. *The Spitball Knuckleball Book: How They Were Thrown, Those Who Threw Them.* Elyria, OH: Trick Pitch, 2009.

Mandel, Mike. *SF Giants: An Oral History.* Santa Cruz, CA: Mandel, 1979.

Marino, John. *Pitchers of Perfection: The Cy Young Award Winners.* New York: MetroBooks, 1996.

Martin, Billy, and Peter Golenbeck. *Number 1.* New York: Delacorte, 1980.

Masters, Todd. *The 1972 Detroit Tigers: Billy Martin and the Half-Game Champs.* Jefferson, NC: McFarland, 2012.

McLain, Denny, and David Diles. *Nobody's Perfect.* New York: Dial Press, 1975.

McLain, Denny, and Mike Nahrstedt. *Strikeout.* St Louis: Sporting News, 1988.

McNamara, Robert. *Argument Without End: In Search of Answers to the Vietnam Tragedy.* New York: Public Affairs, 1999.

Moffi, Larry. *This Side of Cooperstown.* Iowa City: University of Iowa Press, 1996.

Nabokov, Peter. *Tijerina and the Courthouse Raid.* Albuquerque: University of New Mexico Press, 1969.

Newhan, Ross. *The Anaheim Angels.* New York: Hyperion, 2000.

Nowlin, Bill, and Dan Desrochers. *The 1967 Impossible Dream Red Sox: Pandemonium on the Field.* Cambridge: Rounder, 2007.

Oliva, Tony, with Bob Fowler. *Tony O! The Trials and Triumphs of Tony Oliva.* New York: Hawthorn, 1973.

Oren, Michael B. *Six Days of War: June 1967 and the Making of the Modern Middle East.* New York: Oxford University Press, 2002.

Pattison, Mark, and David Raglin, eds. *Sock It To 'Em Tigers: The Incredible Story of the 1968 Detroit Tigers.* Hanover, MA: Maple Street Press, 2008.

Peary, Danny, ed. *Cult Baseball Players: The Greats, the Flakes, the Weird and the Wonderful.* New York: Fireside, 1990.

Pennington, Bill. *Billy Martin: Baseball's Flawed Genius.* Boston: Houghton Mifflin Harcourt, 2015.

Petrocelli, Rico, and Scoggins, Chaz. *Rico Petrocelli's Tales from the Impossible Dream Red Sox.* Champaign, IL: Sports Publishing, 2007.

Powers, Thomas. *Vietnam: The War at Home.* New York: Grossman, 1973.

Prime, Jim, with Bill Nowlin. *Tales from the Red Sox Dugout.* Champaign, IL: Sports Publishing, 2000.

Reynolds, Bill. *Lost Summer.* New York: Warner, 1992.

Roberts, Russell. *100 Baseball Legends Who Shaped Sports History.* San Mateo, CA: Bluewood, 2003.

Roeper, Richard. *Sox and the City: A Fan's Love Affair with the White Sox from the Heartbreak of '67 to the Wizards of Oz.* Chicago: Chicago Review Press, 2006.

Rust, Art, Jr., with Michael Marley. *Legends: Conversations with Baseball Greats.* New York: McGraw-Hill, 1989.

Schoor, Gene. *Billy Martin.* Garden City, NY: Doubleday, 1980.

Shapiro, Milton J. *Heroes of the Bullpen: Baseball's Greatest Relief Pitchers.* New York: Julian Messner, 1967.

Showers, Bob. *The Twins at the Met.* Edina, MN: Beaver's Pond, 2009.

Sinibaldi, Raymond. *1967 Red Sox: The Impossible Dream Season.* Charleston, SC: Arcadia, 2014.

Skipper, John C. *Umpires: Classic Baseball*

Stories from the Men Who Made the Calls. Jefferson, NC: McFarland, 1997.
Spatz, Lyle, ed. *The Team That Forever Changed Baseball and America: The 1947 Brooklyn Dodgers*. Lincoln: University of Nebraska Press, 2012.
Stephens, Robert. *Nasser: A Political Biography*. New York: Simon & Schuster, 1971.
Swirsky, Seth. *Something to Write Home About: Great Baseball Memories in Letters to a Fan*. New York: Crown, 2003.
Szalontai, James D. *Close Shave: The Life and Times of Baseball's Sal Maglie*. Jefferson, NC: McFarland, 2002.
Terzian, James. *The Kid from Cuba: Zoilo Versalles*. Garden City, NY: Doubleday, 1967.
Thielman, Jim. *Cool of the Evening*. Minneapolis: Kirk House, 2005.
Urdahl, Dean. *Touching Bases with Our Memories: The Players Who Made the Minnesota Twins: 1961 to 2001*. St. Cloud, MN: North Star Press of St. Cloud, 2001.
Vance, Cyrus. *Final Report of Cyrus R. Vance Special Assistant to the Secretary of Defense Concerning the Detroit Riots*. http://www.lbjlib.utexas.edu/johnson/archives.hom/oralhistory.hom/Vance-C/Detroit Report.asp.
Vanderberg, Bob. *Sox, From Lane and Fain to Zisk and Fisk*. Chicago: Chicago Review Press, 1982.
Vass, George. *The Game I'll Never Forget*. Evanston, IL: Baseball Digest, 1999.
Vincent, Fay. *We Would Have Played For Nothing: Baseball Stars of the 1950s and 1960s Talk About the Game They Loved*. New York: Simon & Schuster, 2008.
Waldman, Frank. *Famous American Athletes of Today*. Boston: L.C. Page, 1949.
Wilbert, Warren N. *Rookies Rated: Baseball's Finest Freshman Seasons*. Jefferson, NC: McFarland, 2000.
Williams, Dick, and Bill Plaschke. *No More Mr. Nice Guy: A Life of Hardball*. San Diego: Harcourt Brace Jovanovich, 1990.
Yastrzemski, Carl, with Al Hirshberg. *Yaz*. New York: Viking, 1968.
Yastrzemski, Carl, and Gerald Eskenazi. *Yaz: Baseball, the Wall and Me*. New York: Doubleday, 1990.
Young, A.S. "Doc." *The Mets from Mobile: Cleon Jones and Tommie Agee*. New York: Harcourt, Brace & World, 1970.

SABR Biographies

In addition to the many SABR biographies incorporated in books above, the following Biography Project profiles were consulted.

Joe Adcock
Tommie Agee
Luke Appling
Ray Berres
Curt Blefary
Ossie Bluege
Dave Boswell
Nelson Briles
Lou Brock
Gates Brown
Smoky Burgess
Joe Cambria
Bert Campaneris
Rod Carew
Norm Cash
Danny Cater
Joe Christopher
Rocky Colavito
Leo Durocher
Curt Flood
Bob Gibson
Pumpsie Green
Fred Haney
Joe Haynes
Billy Herman
Gil Hodges
Joe Horlen
Tony Horton
Willie Horton
Frank Howard
Jim Kaat
Don Mincher
Gary Peters
Jim Piersall
Johnny Sain
Andy Seminick
Curt Simmons
Joe Sparma
Eddie Stanky
Al Weis
Hoyt Wilhelm

Periodical Articles

Astor, Gerald. "Rick (The Ripper) Reichardt: California's Super Angel." *Look*, July 25, 1967, 66–68.
Bernreuter, Hugh. "Durable Lefty and De-

troit Tigers Hero Mickey Lolich." *The Saginaw News*, June 15, 2010.
Bock, Hal. "Expansion Leftovers." *Los Angeles Times*, November 15, 1992.
Craig, William. "Don't Dig In On Gentleman Jim." *The Saturday Evening Post*, September 9, 1967, 70–73.
Dark, Alvin, and John Underwood. "Rhubarbs, Hassles and Other Hazards." *Sports Illustrated*, May 13, 1967, 47.
Falls, Joe. "I Throw Lefthanded but Think Upside Down." *Sport*, March, 1965, 90.
Fimrite, Ron. "Wilbur's Knuckler is Alive and Swell." *Sports Illustrated*, June 4, 1973, 26.
Gammons, Peter. "Yaz's Most Memorable Games." *Baseball Digest*, September 1981, 18–22.
Jares, Joe. "Yoweee, Chicago!" *Sports Illustrated*, July 10, 1967, 16.
Kirkpatrick, Curry. "Baseball Week." *Sports Illustrated*, August 28, 1967, 81.
Kornacki, Steve. "Detroit Tigers 1968 World Series MVP Mickey Lolich." mlive.com/tigers, March 16, 2011.
Kram, Mark. "Take the Boy out of the Country." *Sports Illustrated*, March 8, 1965, 41.
Leggett, William. "Aftermath of a Bittersweet World Series." *Sports Illustrated*, October 23, 1967, 62–63.
———. "El Birdos Fly High." *Sports Illustrated*, October 16, 1967, 26–29.
———. "Those Big Tiger Muscles." *Sports Illustrated*, June 5, 1967, 26.
———. "A Wild Finale—and It's Boston!" *Sports Illustrated*, October 9, 1967, 34.
Liptak, Mark. "Flashing Back with Gary Peters." Whitesoxinteractive.com.
———. "Flashing Back with Joe Horlen." Whitesoxinteractive.com.
———. "Flashing Back with Walt Williams." Whitesoxinteractive.com.
Maglie, Sal, and Robert Boyle. "Baseball Is a Tough Business." *Sports Illustrated*, April 15, 1968, 80.
Mulvoy, Mark. "Virtue Is Rewarded." *Sports Illustrated*, August 21, 1967, 17.
Newhan, Ross. "Those Were the Days." *Los Angeles Times*, June 16, 1967.
"Rising Dynasty for the Birds?" *Sports Illustrated*, April 17, 1967, 72.
Sharnik, Morton. "Downfall of a Hero." *Sports Illustrated*, February 23, 1970, 18.

Smith, Gary. "Diamond Cutters—The Bossards, Baseball's First Family of Groundskeeping." *Sports Illustrated*, September 21, 1998, 103.
———. "A Lingering Vestige of Yesterday." *Sports Illustrated*, April 4, 1983, 112.
Stanky, Eddie, with William Leggett. "Better from the Neck Up." *Sports Illustrated*, August 28, 1967, 18–23.
Terrell, Roy. "Part 1: Sal Maglie on the Art of Pitching." *Sports Illustrated*, March 17, 1958.
"They Said It." *Sports Illustrated*, June 13, 1966, 22.
"They Said It." *Sports Illustrated*, June 19, 1967, 12.
Weiskopf, Herman. "The Infamous Spitter." *Sports Illustrated*, July 31, 1967, 12–17.
World Champion Baltimore Orioles 1967 Press/Radio/Television Guide.

The following periodicals were consulted for some or all of the 1967 season:

Baseball Digest
Boston Globe
Boston Herald
Boston Herald Traveler
Boston Record American
Boston Sunday Advertiser
Boston Traveler
Chicago Daily News
Chicago Sun-Times
Chicago Tribune
Detroit Free Press
Detroit News
Kansas City Star
Kansas City Times
Los Angeles Herald Examiner
Minneapolis Star
Minneapolis Tribune
St. Paul Pioneer Press
The Sporting News
Sports Illustrated

Websites

The following were used as the primary references for statistics and game summaries.
www.baseball-reference.com
www.retrosheet.org

Index

Numbers in **_bold italics_** indicate pages with illustrations

Aaron, Henry 137
ABC 52
Adair, Jerry 45, 60, 73, 75–76, 80, 144, 212, 231–233, 249–250, 252, 268
Adcock, Joe 13, 104, 129, 209, 213, 275
Agee, Tommie 20, 29, 54, 74, 76, 150, 162, 217–218, 275
Aguirre, Hank 240–241
Air Force, United States 43
Aker, Jack 23, 130–132, 275
Albany, New York 270
Aldrin, Buzz 277
Alexander, Pete 109
Ali, Muhammad 44–45
All Star 51, 77, 92, 94, 98, 115, 120, 133, 161, 180–181, 183, 208, 264, 276–279, 281–283; AAA All-Star team 168; Game 25, 83, 85, 87, 121, 182, 277
Allen, Hank 222–223
Allison, Bob 31–38, **_32_**, 48, 51, 83, 87, 101, 104, 137, 166, 173, 196, 207–208, 226, 231, 234, 247, 252–253, 255, 275
Allyn, Arthur 130
Almendares (baseball team) 34
Alston, Walter 46
Alvis, Max 174
Amer, Abdel Hakim 49
American League 1, 3, 5, 13, 19, 25, 28, 37, 42, 48, 51, 58, 60–61, 65, 71–72, 74–75, 77, 92, 95, 98, 105, 107, 121, 137, 139, 145, 153, 160, 163, 165, 167–168, 179, 182, 190–192, 201, 203–204, 207, 210, 220, 222, 228, 230, 238, 242–243, 245, 247, 262, 264, 266, 275–280, 282, 285; see also standings
Anaheim, California 86, 117, 123, 177, 187, 237

Anaheim Stadium 87, 277
Andrews, Mike 118, 178, 183, 231–233, 247, 252–253, 268
Angels see California Angels
Appling, Luke 215, 218–219
Armstrong, Neil 277
Army, United States 42–43, 151
Army Reserve 43–45, 63, 199
Athletics see Kansas City Athletics
Atkinson, Freddie 44
Atlanta, Georgia 137
Atlanta Braves see Boston Braves
Atlanta Falcons 198
Azcue, Joe 212–213

Baltimore, Maryland 99, 100, 132, 133; fans 58; grounds crew 100, 198
Baltimore Colts 198
Baltimore Orioles 14, 24–25, 27–28, 30, 40, 45, 53, 58, 69–70, 72–73, 76, 99, 108, 111, 120, 160–161, 164–165, 173, 175–176, 192, 197–199, 226, 228, 241–242, 275, 279, 282; see also standings
Bando, Sal 217–218
Barber, Steve 24
Baseball Digest 15
Bauer, Hank 13, 77, 108
beanball 4, 41, 67, 81, 122, 124–125, 134, 136, 139, 268
Bell, Gary 66, 123, 145, 184, 199, 209, 231, 234–235, 267, 272, 275
Bennett, Dennis 170, 266
Berde, Gene 181
Berkeley, California 89
Berres, Ray 55, 139

309

Index

Berry, Ken 58, 59, 60, 70, 76, 143, 145, 158, 216–217, 219
Birmingham, Alabama 116,
Black Muslims 44
Blefary, Curt 198
Bluege, Ossie 113, 115
Bond, Walter 226
Bossard, Gene 75, 156
Boston, Massachusetts 5, 10, 15, 18–20, 39–40, 42, 45, 61–63, 65–66, 74–75, 77, 85, 94, 100–101, 107, 117–118, 123, 134–135, 137, 147–148, 155, 168, 175, 178, 182, 203, 212, 225, 227, 229, 242, 245, 255, 259–260, 263–264, 267–270, 272, 278, 280–282, 285; fans 42, 59–60, 94, 119, 123–124, 148, 150, 168, 177–178, 180, 206, 213, 234–235, 246–248, 252, 254–255, 262, 266, 271–273, 275, 282; newspapers/sportswriters 15, 19–20, 59, 62, 150, 178–179, 246, 263
Boston Braves 11, 126, 137, 226, 282; Atlanta Braves 133–134, 284; Milwaukee Braves 155
Boston Celtics 20
Boston Edison 147
Boston Globe 15, 60, 109, 146, 177, 219, 241, 263
Boston Herald Traveler (includes *Boston Herald* and *Boston Traveler*) 58, 80, 119, 206, 263
Boston Record American 206, 255, 263
Boston Red Sox 1, 3–4, 13–15, 17, 19–20, 23, 38–42, 45–46, 57, 59–60, 62–67, 75–77, 80–81, 83–85, 87, 94, 101, 103, 107–108, 110, 117–119, 122–125, 133–134, 136–137, 140, 142–143, 145–152, 167–171, 173, 175–176, 178–180, 182–183, 186, 189–192, 197–200, 203, 206, 208–209, 211–212, 214–216, 220, 223, 228–235, 238, 241–253, 255, 257, 259–276, 278–282, 284–285; team MVP 44, 169; *see also* standings
Boston Symphony Orchestra 65
Boswell, Dave 30, 108, 115, 166, 177, 196, 205, 207, 280, 284
Bouton, Jim 172, 280
Boyer, Ken 104–105, 120, 141, 149–150, 156, 162, 165, 202, 215, 218–219, 222
Bragan, Bobby 226
Branca, Ralph 13
Brandon, Bucky 197, 200, 264
Braves *see* Boston Braves
Breslin, Jimmy 235
Brett, Ken 264, 276
Brewer, Jim 167
Briles, Nelson 267, 271–272
Brock, Lou 264–265, 267, 271–273, 280
Brooke, Ed 230
Brooklyn, New York 67, 116; fans 116
Brooklyn Dodgers 7, 10–12, 16–17, 67, 116–117, 127, 168; Los Angeles Dodgers 35, 119, 197, 277, 284

Brown, Gates 83, 154, 187, 239, 259, 276
Brunet, George 48, 82, 237, 260–261, 276
Buffalo, New York 96
Buford, Don 28–29, 104, 218–219, 222
Bull, General Odd 49
Burgess, Smoky 191, 218, 276
Busch Stadium 267, 269
Buzhardt, John 60

Cabin, Charles 52
Cairo, Illinois 96
Cal Poly San Luis Obispo 266
California 40, 64, 77, 109, 119, 167
California Angels 1, 14, 30, 38, 48, 58, 62, 75, 77, 81–83, 86–88, 93–94, 101, 107, 109–111, 119–120, 123, 125, 133, 136, 152, 167, 177, 187, 205–208, 210, 214, 221–222, 227, 236–242, 244, 256–258, 260–262, 275, 278, 282; fans 83, 87, 119, 237, 275; *see also* standings
Cambria, Papa Joe 91
Cambridge, Maryland 100
Cambridge, Massachusetts 124
Camilli, Doug 200
Campanella, Roy 68
Campaneris, Bert 37, 167
Campbell, Jim 105, 151, 182, 262
Cantor, George 112, 190
Caray, Harry 274
Cardenal, Jose 110, 123
Carew, Rod 35–36, 51, 75, 87–88, 92, 108, 151, 176, 207, 214, 231–232, 249, 251, 254, 276
Carlos, Cisco 142–143, 148–149, 162, 177, 202, 276
Carlton, Steve 268–269
Cash, Norm 24, 26, 151, 155, 158, 179, 195, 221, 239, 276
Castro, Fidel 34, 92, 179–180
Causey, Wayne 175, 191, 218
Cepeda, Orlando 265, 274
Chance, Dean 30, 37, 68, 78–80, 93, 100, 107–111, 119–120, 137, 140, 146, 152, 159, 165–166, 174–175, 186, 196–197, 205, 207, 213–214, 219–220, 225–227, 230, 244, 247–251, 255, 276, 284
Chandler, Happy 121, 226
Chapman, Ben 11
Chapman, Roy 124
Charlotte (A, AA and AAA baseball teams) 50, 91, 105, 114, 142
Chattanooga (AA baseball team) 33, 50, 114, 115
Chicago, Illinois 10, 45, 56, 59, 61, 78, 100, 113, 120, 126, 130, 144, 157, 160, 167, 176–177, 215, 220–221, 258; fans 61, 74, 146, 161, 163–164, 214–215, 275; newspapers 139, 142, 149, 156, 158, 160–161, 163, 191, 247
Chicago Cubs 74, 104, 141, 191, 243

Index

Chicago Daily News 139, 149, 203, 208, 224
Chicago Sun-Times 36, 59, 157, 224
Chicago Tribune 58, 69, 74–75, 77–78, 156, 158, 214, 281
Chicago White Sox 1, 3, 5, 14, 19–20, 28–29, 36–38, 45, 53–61, 67–71, 73–76, 78–79, 83, 85–89, 94, 101–105, 111–112, 115, 117, 119–120, 130, 133, 136–142, 144–145, 147–150, 152, 156–168, 173–177, 182, 187–188, 190–192, 195, 200–203, 206, 210–211, 214–219, 222–224, 226, 243, 267, 273, 275, 278; Hitless Wonders 224; *see also* standings
Christopher, Joe 170
Clark, Rickey 82, 214, 220, 256–257
Clary, Ellis 91
Clay, Cassius *see* Ali, Muhammad
Cleveland, Ohio 45, 100, 104, 146, 174, 191
Cleveland Indians 13, 50, 66, 68, 72, 77, 94, 101, 111, 129, 164–165, 190–191, 201, 203, 209, 212–213, 216, 230, 232, 243, 272, 275, 278–279; *see also* standings
Colavito, Rocky 25, 104–105, 141, 149, 156–157, 165, 167, 175, 215, 217–219
Comiskey Park *see* White Sox Park
Conigliaro, Sal 40, 45
Conigliaro, Tony 4, 18, 21, 39–45, 60, 79–80, 84–85, 122, 134, 136, 259, 277–278; beaning 123–125, 136, 210, 228, 239, 278
Cooperstown, New York 99
Cronin, Joe 51, 61, 182, 191, 201, 227
Cuba 33–34, 51, 91–92, 105, 113, 179
Culver, George 77
Cy Young Award 37, 63, 109, 159, 204, 219, 277, 280–281, 284

Dark, Alvin 9, 11, 13–14, 58, 77, 88, 126–128, 130–132, 143–144, 157, 200, 215, 226, 237, 275, 277, 278, 283
Demeter, Don 151, 170
Denver (AAA baseball team) 52
Detroit, Michigan 27–28, 151–152, 155, 165, 170, 178, 182–183, 187, 189, 193, 221, 236, 241, 259, 279–280; fans 25–26, 62, 95–97, 99, 101, 105, 152, 154, 165, 177, 183, 194, 241, 257–259, 275; media 25, 29, 58, 62, 101, 154, 261; riots 95–101, 194
Detroit Free Press 71, 84, 112, 183, 188, 190, 241
Detroit News 26, 80, 83, 129, 138, 157, 204, 224, 226, 241, 262
Detroit Tigers 1, 3–5, 13–14, 23–29, 36, 38, 45, 53, 58, 61–62, 64, 68, 70, 74, 76, 80–81, 83–85, 95, 97–102, 105–107, 120, 133–134, 137–140, 147, 150–158, 161–164, 167–173, 175–176, 178, 182–195, 200, 204–205, 208, 210, 220–222, 226–227, 236–237–243, 256–262, 273, 275–276, 278–279, 282; *see also* standings

Dobson, Chuck 215, 218, 220
Dobson, Pat 138, 259
Dodgers *see* Brooklyn Dodgers
Donaldson, John 216, 219
Downing, Al 205, 237
Dressen, Charlie 16–17, 24–25, 90, 98, 189
Durocher, Leo 9–13, 58, 70–72, 82, 127, 128

Ebbets Field 12, 116
Eckert, William 226
Ed Sullivan Show 21
Egypt 49
Elliott, Bob 11
Elmira (D baseball team) 91
Elson, Bob 158
Epstein, Mike 160
Erie, Pennsylvania 96
Ermer, Cal 33, 52–53, 78, 89, 105, 107–108, 110, 116, 152, 166–167, 173–176, 196–197, 205–208, 225–226, 232–235, 248–251, 254, 277
Etchebarren, Andy 69
Evanston (AAA baseball team) 142

Farrell, Kerby 78
Feller, Bob 188
Fenway Park 19, 41–42, 60, 63, 118, 123–124, 178, 180, 184, 227, 229, 231, 235, 244, 245–246, 250, 252, 254, 259, 264–265, 267, 269, 272, 277
Fetzer, John 184–5
Finley, Charlie 128–133, 200–201, 215, 275, 277–280; mule Charlie O 129–130
Fisher, Eddie 73
Flaherty, Red 61
Flint, Michigan 100, 189
Flood, Curt 265–267, 272–273, 280
Florida 41, 106, 169, 180, 223
Ford, Whitey 20, 79, 159, 179
Forrester, Al 250–251
Fort Dix, New Jersey 43
Fort Drum, New York 45
Foy, Joe 19, 60, 66, 67, 94, 117, 234, 268, 273, 278
Framingham State College 255
Freehan, Bill 23, 27–29, 74, 80, 83, 100, 122, 137, 155, 158, 162, 171, 173, 183, 188, 194, 240, 259–261, 278, 280
Fregosi, Jim 88, 124, 207, 239–240, 257, 261
Frick, Ford 12
Froelich, Eddie 56

Georgia 110
Giants *see* New York Giants
Gibson, Bob 264–265, 268, 270, 272–273, 281, 283
Gibson, Russ 20–21, 80, 183–184, 232, 247, 264–265, 268

312   Index

Gigi 252
Giles, Warren 121
Gladding, Fred 203, 240, 242
Gleason, Bill 161, 163, 224
Gold Glove 21, 25, 27, 29, 92–93, 104, 106, 180, 230, 278–279, 283
Golenbeck, Peter 89
Gosger, Jim 216–217, 219
Grand Rapids, Michigan 100
Grant, Jim "Mudcat" 30, 37, 47, 107, 115–116, 205, 252, 284
Green, Jerry 224
Green, Lenny 221, 260
Green, Pumpsie 168
Greenville, Mississippi 8, 84
Griffith, Calvin 34–36, 46–47, 50–52, 90, 92, 115–117, 120–121, 165, 173–174, 197, 201, 207, 227, 278
Griffith, Clark 50–51, 113
Griffith Haynes, Thelma 50
Griffith Stadium 31, 34
Grimm, Charlie 104
Grissom, Marv 71, 73, 139, 160–161
Guard *see* National Guard
Guevara, Che 270
Gutteridge, Don 29

Hacker, Warren 159
Hall, Jimmie 30–31, 172, 214, 239
Hall of Fame 51, 56, 109, 126, 172, 188, 276–277, 279–281, 284–285
Hamilton, Jack 81–83, 93, 123–125, 239, 278
Haney, Fred 82, 108–109
Haney, Larry 198
Hansen, Ron 54–55, 76, 79, 149–150, 158, 216, 218, 222, 278
Harrelson, Ken 129–135, 165, 176–177, 183, 198, 200, 215, 219, 233, 250, 266, 268, 278
Harris, Bucky 113, 168
Harwell, Ernie 97
Havana, Cuba 34, 91
Havana Sugar Kings 179
Hayes, Woody 162
Haynes, Joe 51
Held, Woodie 88
Hengan, Bill 36
Herman, Billy 18–19, 64, 170, 180–181
Hershberger, Mike 216, 219
Hiller, John 200, 222, 240–241, 258
Higgins, Pinky 66, 168–169
Hodges, Gil 13–14, 82, 129, 278
Hoerner, Joe 267
Holdrege (D baseball team) 55
home run 4, 13, 26–27, 29, 31–32, 35–36, 41–42, 44–45, 48, 50, 57, 66–67, 70, 79, 83, 93, 97–98, 104, 106–107, 113–116, 118, 122, 127, 134–135, 137, 143, 148–149, 164, 167, 172, 178–179, 181, 183–184, 186–188, 190–192, 196, 198, 207–208, 230, 233–235, 237–239, 242, 244, 248, 250–251, 255, 257–258, 265, 267–268, 271–273, 276–278, 283, 285
Honochick, Jim 232–233
Horlen, Joe 41, 56, 61, 68, 70, 79, 94, 102, 118, 141, 150, 156, 158–163, **159**, 166–167, 173, 177, 201, 215, 218–220, 222, 224, 278
Horton, Tony 40, 191, 278
Horton, Willie 24, 27, 81, 83, 95, **97**, 98, 137–138, 150, 155, 158, 173, 187, 221, 237–238, 242, 258, 279
Houk, Ralph 14, 21, 171–172, 279
Houston Astros 137
Howard, Bruce 83, 138–141, 160, 188, 224, 279
Howard, Elston 21, 79, 111, 145–146, 165, 254, 268–269, 272
Howard, Frank 103, 167, 222
Howser, Dick 67
Hughes, Dick 267, 271
Humphrey, Vice President Hubert 140, 174, 230
Hunter, Billy 70,
Hunter, Jim "Catfish" 219–220
Hurley, Eddie 79

"Impossible Dream" 60, 179, 255
Indiana 128
Indianapolis (AAA baseball team) 115, 138
Indianapolis, Indiana 115
Indians *see* Cleveland Indians
International League 17
Israel 48–49, 53
Izquierdo, Hank 137

Javier, Julian 265–266, 268, 273
Jethroe, Sam 168
John, Tommy 56, 61, 86, 138, 150, 156, 159–160, 167, 174, 177, 187, 222–224, 279
Johnson, President Lyndon 42–43, 49, 77, 99, 142, 174, 203
Johnstone, Jay 257
Jones, Dalton 59, 77, 85, 179, 183–184, 209, 212, 232–233, 249–250, 254, 268, 279
Jones, Sheldon 12
Josephson, Duane 37, 76, 103–104, 145, 219
Jurges, Billy 19

Kaat, Jim 30, 35, 37, 47, 53, 68, 101, 106, 116, 119, 137–138, 160, 166, 175, 177, 192, 197, 205, 207–208, 225–230, **229**, 279, 284; injuries 208, 232
Kaese, Harold 146
Kaline, Al 25–28, 80–81, 83–85, 101, 106, 137, 154–156, 158, 170, 183–184, 187, 205, 215, 221, 239, 241, 258, 261, 279
Kansas City, Missouri 37, 75, 86, 128, 129,

133, 144, 151, 157, 173, 177, 201, 210, 215, 220, 245; fans 37, 130, 201, 215, 218; newspapers 247
Kansas City Athletics 14, 23, 36–38, 53, 57, 62, 80–81, 85, 107, 126, 128–129, 131–133, 144, 152–153, 167, 171, 187, 190, 201, 206, 210, 214–219, 223, 277; *see also* standings
Kansas City Star 131
Kell, George 100, 168, 195
Kennedy, Jacqueline 21
Kennedy, Ted 230
Kenworthy, Dick 104
Key West, Florida 91
Kiernan, Thomas 9
Kiley, John 252
Killebrew, Elaine 115
Killebrew, Harmon 30, 32–33, 35, 48, 51, 68, 87–88, 93, 101, 106–107, 112–115, **114**, 118, 138, 166, 173–175, 190, 196–197, 207–208, 214, 227, 230–235, 244, 246–247-248, 251–253, 255, 265, 279, 281
King, Jim 69
Klages, Fred 145
Kline, Ron 115–117, 214, 233
Knoop, Bobby 207, 240, 257–258, 261
Knoxville (baseball team) 143
knuckleball 59, 71–74, 79, 85, 217
Korince, George 26
Koslo, Dave 11
Koufax, Sandy 35, 37, 109, 159, 245
Krausse, Lew 131, 200–201, 218, 279
KSTP 221
Kubiak, Ted 219

Lakeman, Al 231
Lakeville, Massachusetts 122
Landis, Bill 184, 264
Landis, Jim 134
Lane, Ray 97
Las Vegas (odds) 264
Lasher, Fred 137, 152, 178, 200, 203, 239–240
The Last Battle 224
Lavagetto, Cookie 34, 46, 51, 114
Lefebvre, Jim 35
Lemon, Jim 47, 115, 249, 253
Lentz, George 33
Leonard, Dutch 71
Lindblad, Paul 218
Locker, Bob 29, 70–71, 74, 162, 177, 187, 202–203, 219
Lockman, Whitey 12
Logan Airport 94, 269
Lolich, Mickey 23, 27, 95, 98–99, 102, 137–138, 154, 157, 183, 187, 192–195, **193**, 210, 222, 232, 237–239, 241, 257, 259–260, 280
Lonborg, Jim 20, 57, 62–68, **63**, 100, 108, 110, 120, 124–125, 142–143, 145, 150, 175, 183,

186, 199, 208, 212–213, 220, 245–250, 252–255, 264, 266–269, 271–273, 280
Long Island, New York 134, 22
Lopez, Al 56, 117
Lopez, Marcelino 82
Los Angeles, California 87, 109, 120; newspapers 247
Los Angeles Dodgers *see* Brooklyn Dodgers
Los Angeles Herald Examiner 87
Lucchesi, Frank 283
Lumpe, Jerry 155, 221
Lyle, Sparky 84, 264
Lynn, Massachusetts 40, 45

Maglie, Sal 11–12, 65–68, 124, 170, 270, 273, 275–276, 280
Major League Baseball Players Association 28, 60, 131, 155, 200–201, 280
Mantle, Mickey 21, 67, 109, 210
Marianao, Cuba 91
Marine Reserves 108
Marines, United States 43, 108, 151
Maris, Roger 265, 269–270, 272
Marshall, Mike 80, 95, 122, 203
Marshall, Thurgood 142
Martin, Billy 47, 52, 89–93, 138, 167, 172, 174, 225–226, 231, 246, 248–249, 253, 277, 279–280, 282
Martin, J.C. 59, 70, 163, 216–217, 219
Mathews, Eddie 137–138, 151, 154–156, 158, 162, 165, 184, 210, 221, 237, 240, 257–258, 280; injury 165, 187
Mauch, Gene 180
Maxvill, Dal 272
Maye, Lee 190
Mays, Willie 168
McAuliffe, Dick 26, 64, 83, 137, 155, 175, 200, 210, 237, 259–261, 281
McCarthy, Joe 46–47
McCarver, Tim 269, 274
McCraw, Tommy 20, 57, 59, 69, 76, 157, 177, 192, 218–219, 222–223
McDonough, Will 109
McDowell, Sam 202
McGlothlin, Jim 82, 87, 136, 207, 258–259
McLain, Denny 23, 27, 29, 58, 102, 138, 162, 172, 178, 187–190, 256–258, 281; injury 187, 189, 222
McMahon, Don 45, 74, 76, 202–203, 216–217
McNamara, Robert 43
McNertney, Jerry 75
Mele, Sam 14, 32, 36–37, 46–52, 78, 89, 105, 107, 226, 230, 281
Memorial Stadium (Baltimore) 100, 198
Merritt, Jim 47, 88, 108, 116, 119, 138, 166–167, 205, 214, 234, 284

Metropolitan Stadium (Minnesota) 36, 48, 50–51, 120, 152, 196, 207, 281
Mexican League 80, 276
Michigan State University 80
Miller, Marvin 60
Milwaukee, Wisconsin 137, 165, 201
Milwaukee Braves *see* Boston Braves
Mincher, Don 30–31, 101, 213, 240–242, 257–258, 261, 281
Minneapolis Millers (AAA baseball team) 179–180
Minneapolis Star 36–38, 283
Minneapolis Tribune 48–49, 51
Minnesota (state and Minneapolis/St. Paul metropolitan area) 35–36, 46, 48, 51–52, 67, 91–92, 100, 109–110, 119, 129, 151, 155, 165, 173, 196, 207–208, 252; fans 30, 36, 47–48, 51, 83, 112, 140, 167, 174, 177, 207, 275; newspapers/sportswriters 35–36, 52, 120, 167, 174
Minnesota Twins 1, 3, 14, 30, 31, 35–38, 45, 47–52, 62, 67, 75–76, 78, 79, 83, 87–94, 100–101, 103–111, 113, 115–117, 120, 123, 133, 137–138, 140, 146–147, 151–153, 161, 165–168, 172–174, 176–177, 190–192, 195–197, 199, 203–208, 211, 213–215, 220–221, 223, 225–228, 230–234, 236, 238–239, 242–245, 247–255, 257, 265, 272–273, 275–282, 285; *see also* standings
Mobile, Alabama 142
Monday, Rick 57, 216–219, 281
Moore, Monte 131, 279–280
Morehead, Dave 170
Morning Sun, Iowa 82
Morton, Bubba 208, 240
Mueller, Don 13
Municipal Stadium (Cleveland) 190
Municipal Stadium (Kansas City) 151
MVP (Most Valuable Player). American League 21, 25, 31, 51, 92, 93, 133, 173, 174, 260, 276–279, 281, 283–285; Boston Red Sox 44, 169; California Angels 281; Minnesota Twins 173, 174, 214; National League 104, 265; World Series 273

Napp, Larry 61
Naragon, Hal 47
Nash, Jim 107
Nason, Jerry 219
Nasser, President Gamal 49
National Guard 43–44, 86, 96, 98–99, 194
National League 9, 12–13, 24, 74, 81, 104, 107, 117, 121, 127, 155, 182, 207, 243, 264, 266–267, 284
Navy, United States 43
NBC 84, 121, 223
Nelson, Roger 191, 217

New York 168
New York, New York 10, 20, 35, 66–67, 116–117, 134, 148, 201, 204, 210, 237, 246, 270; fans 21, 58, 254; newspapers 156
New York Giants 11–13, 58, 65–66, 71–72, 116, 127, 128, 243; San Francisco Giants 117, 284
New York Mets 81–82, 266, 275, 278
New York Yankees 13–14, 20, 36, 47, 57–58, 61, 66–67, 72, 81, 85, 90, 95, 100, 109, 111, 134, 140, 147, 159, 168, 171–172, 179, 186, 191–192, 196, 204–205, 210, 232, 235, 238–239, 270; *see also* standings
Newark, New Jersey 96
Newcombe, Don 12–13
Nichols, Max 283
"The Night They Invented Champagne" 252
Nightingale, Dave 139
Nitschke, Ray 198
Nixon, Russ 254
Nollman, Dorrie 255
North Carolina 74, 77
Northrup, Jim 27, 80, 137, 155, 183, 187–188, 239, 257
Northwestern High School (Detroit) 98

Oakland, California 201
Oakland A's 275, 277–279, 281, 284–285
Oakland Oaks 89–90
O'Boynick, Paul 131
O'Connell, Dick 134, 259
Ohio State University 162
Oklahoma City, Oklahoma 151
Oklahoma State University 158
Oliva, Tony 31, 35–36, 87, 105–108, **106**, 110, 166, 174, 176, 190, 196, 226, 231, 235, 246–247, 252–253, 281, 284
Ollom, Jim 116
Oregon 113, 115
Orioles *see* Baltimore Orioles
Ortega, Phil 223
Osteen, Claude 277
Osterman, Larry 100
Oyler, Ray 24, 26, 74, 184, 221, 239

Pacific Coast League 89
Paige, Satchel 193
Pascual, Camilo 47
Paul, Gabe 104
Payette, Idaho 113
Pearson, Albie 34–35
Penney, Ed 122
Pepitone, Joe 67, 80–81, 168
Perry, Gaylord 277
Perry, Jim 107, 116, 166, 205, 232–233, 235, 284
Pesky, Johnny 114
Peters, Gary 29, 54–57, **56**, 59, 61, 74, 78, 94,

142–143, 145–146, 149, 156–158, 160, 167, 176, 191, 202, 215–216, 220, 222, 224, 282
Petrocelli, Rico 18–19, 63, 67, 76–77, 85, 124, 183, 209, 212, 251, 253–254, 264, 266, 271, 282
Philadelphia, Pennsylvania 8, 10
Philadelphia Phillies 11–12, 81
Phoenix, Arizona 100
Pittsburgh Pirates 73–74, 243
Plainfield, New Jersey 96
Players Association *see* Major League Baseball Players Association
players' union *see* Major League Baseball Players Association
playoff 182
Polo Grounds 12
Ponce, Puerto Rico 265
Poulsen, Ken 77, 282
Powell, Boog 69, 175
Price, Jim 26, 260
Prudential Tower 246
Pucci, Emilio 129
Puerto Rico 55, 98, 162, 228; *see also* Ponce, Puerto Rico

Ramos, Pedro 276
Raytown, Missouri 173
Red Sox *see* Boston Red Sox
Reese, Rich 252
Reichardt, Rick 177, 187, 236–237, 257, 282
Repoz, Roger 240, 242, 257
Reseda, California 87
Reserve *see* Army Reserve
Resinger, Grover 54, 202
Revere, Massachusetts 39
Richards, Paul 134
Richert, Pete 161
Rickey, Branch 7, 10, 17
Rigney, Bill 12–14, 58, 77, 82, 87, 117, 123, 125, 203, 205–207, 214, 236–237, 239–240, 244, 257–262, 282
Riley, Don 30
Rizzuto, Phil 13
Robertson, Billy 51
Robertson, Jimmy 51
Robertson, Sherry 51, 227
Robinson, Brooks 69, 198
Robinson, Frank 69–70, 106, 198, 244, 279, 281
Robinson, Jackie 10–11, 168, 283
Rochester, New York 100
Rockefeller, Nelson 168
Rodgers, Bob 75, 87, 109, 124–125, 208, 214, 240, 282
Rodgers, Buck *see* Rodgers, Bob
Rodriguez, Aurelio 214
Rogers, Rawmeat 275

Rohr, Billy 20–21, 282
Rojas, Minnie 203, 259–260, 282
Roland, Jim 116, 252
Rollins, Rich 37, 83, 105, 173, 176, 208, 254
Romano, John 139
Romney, Governor George 98
Roof, Phil 144
Rookie of the Year 55, 106, 126, 168, 276
Rubio, Jorge 82
Rudi, Joe 216, 218
Rusk, Dean 203
Russell, Bill 20
Rust, Art, Jr. 283
Ryan, Cornelius 224
Ryan, Mike 124, 144, 271

Saginaw, Michigan 100
Sain, John 25, 27, 47, 80, 138, 161–162, 171–172, 188, 193–194, 222, 226–227, 238, 279, 281–282
St. Louis, Missouri 16, 167, 265, 267, 270
St. Louis Cardinals 16, 72, 104, 167, 203, 264–274, 276
St. Mary's High School 40, 44
St. Paul Pioneer Press 30
Salerno, Al 78
San Diego, California 108
San Diego Padres 284
San Francisco Giants *see* New York Giants
Sancta Maria Hospital 124–125
Sanford, Jack 82
Santiago, Edna 228–229, 235
Santiago, Jose 184, 192, 209, 228–235, 264–265, 268, 283
Scheffing, Bob 27
Scheinblum, Richie 191
Schoendienst, Red 203, 264–268, 271–272, 274
Scott, George 17–19, 45, 59, 80, 84–85, 117–119, 123, 143, 145, 147, 183, 198, 212, 222, 231, 233–234, 246–247, 251–252, 265, 269, 273, 283
Seattle, Washington 201
Seattle Pilots 276, 280
Seminick, Andy 11–12
Senators *see* Washington Senators
Shannon, Mike 265
Short, Ed 75, 104, 133, 163
Shotten, Burt 16
Siebern, Norm 183–184
Siebert, Sonny 220
Simmons, Curt 239
Sisler, Dick 266
Skaff, Frank 24
Skowron, Moose 101
Smith, Mayo 13–14, 24–27, 80, 83–84, 102, 138, 151–152, 155–158, 162–163, 172, 178,

182–183, 187, 195, 200, 203–205, 210, 221–222, 236–240, 257, 260–261, 276, 281–283
Smith, Red 200, 205
Smith, Reggie 19–20, 59, 80, 94, 123, 134, 143–144, 184, 186, 199, 209, 213, 232, 246, 251, 268–269, 271, 283; Sanchin stance 144
Soar, Hank 190
South Bend, Indiana 100
South Carolina 129, 130
Southworth, Billy 126–127, 226
Sparma, Joe 27, 80, 84, 138–139, 161–162, 173, 186, 200, 222, 241
spitball 4, 79–82, 110, 124, 283
Spoelstra, Watson 28, 83–84
The Sporting News 128, 161, 200
Sports Illustrated 15, 30, 79, 81, 140, 154, 161, 173
spring training 10, 13, 17–19, 24–26, 28–29, 31, 34–35, 41–43, 51–52, 54–55, 64, 73, 76, 82, 90, 93, 95, 98, 103, 106, 114–115, 118, 122, 138–139, 158, 168–170, 180–181, 188
Springstead, Marty 146
Stafford, Bill 144
standings 15, 23, 30, 39, 46, 53, 62, 69, 78, 86, 95, 103, 112, 121, 126, 136, 147, 154, 164, 176, 186, 190, 196, 204, 206, 212, 221, 225, 236, 243, 256, 263
Stanford University 20, 62–63, 245
Stange, Lee 183, 197–198, 259–260
Stanky, Eddie 5, 7–14, 16, 19–20, 23, 29, 53–61, 69–70, 73–77, 79, 81, 85, 88–89, 101, 103–104, 112, 118–119, 125–128, 136, 138–146, **141**, 148–150, 154–158, 161–165, 167, 173, 177, 182, 188, 191–192, 201–203, 215–217, 219–224, 226, 237, 241, 258, 260, 267, 283–284; dog Go-Go 144
Stanley, Mickey 27–28, 74, 152, 170
Stengel, Casey 89–90, 171
Stephenson, Jerry 178, 192
Stottlemyre, Mel 210, 237
Stroud, Ed 76, 175, 200
Stuart, Dick 41, 170
Sullivan, Haywood 133
Supreme Court 44
Swaton, Vicki 77, 282
Swift, Bob 24
Syracuse (AAA baseball team) 270
Syria 49, 53

Tampa, Florida 96
Tartabull, Jose 145, 170, 233, 250–251, 254, 268
Terry, Ralph 172
Texas Rangers 279, 283
Thant, U 49
Thompson, Hank 12
Thomson, Bobby 13, 60

Tiant, Luis 191, 209
Tiger Stadium 48, 101, 120, 172, 175, 178, 194, 240
Tigers *see* Detroit Tigers
Tillman, Bob 81
Tillotson, Thad 66–67
Tolan, Bobby 266, 272
Toronto (AAA baseball team) 17, 67, 282
Tovar, Cesar 31, 36, 87, 173–175, 207, 214, 231, 234, 247–250, 252, 283–284
Tracewski, Dick 26, 155, 237, 242
Tresh, Tom 21
Triandos, Gus 72
Triple Crown 133, 182, 230
Turner, Jim 171
Twiggy (supermodel) 119
Twins *see* Minnesota Twins

Uhlaender, Ted 31, 101, 108, 152, 207, 226, 231, 249–250, 253–254
United Nations 49
University of Kansas 32–33
University of Michigan 27
University of Minnesota 196
University of Utah 196

Valdivielso, Jose 92
Valentine, Bill 123–124, 216
Valentine, Fred 222–223
Veeck, Bill 36, 173, 201
Venezuela 34, 64
Versalles, Zoilo 31, 37, 47, 51, 79, 88, 90–93, 167, 173–174, 206, 214, 226, 231, 233–235, 250, 252, 284
Vietnam 1, 42, 43–45, 49, 77; North Vietnam 191

Wagner, Leon 104
Waldmelr, Pete 26, 129, 157, 262
Walker, Dixie 10–11
Ward, Pete 29, 57, 76, 104, 149–151, 158, 164, 175, 215–216, 284
Washington, DC 31, 50–51, 58, 126, 131, 166, 174, 187, 189, 192, 204, 237; fans 275; sportswriters 58, 166
Washington Redskins 33
Washington Senators (post-1960 team) 14, 31, 36, 58–59, 61, 82, 103, 111, 115–116, 126, 129, 132, 165, 167, 173, 176, 200–201, 206, 221–224, 239–240, 275, 278–279; *see also* standings
Washington Senators (pre-1961 team) 31, 33–34, 50–51, 91, 105, 106, 113–115; fans 34, 51
Waslewski, Gary 67–68, 80, 264, 270–272
Waukegan, Illinois 100
Weaver, Jim 207
Webster, Ramon 219

Weis, Al 70, 220
Wert, Don 137, 155, 237
WGN 215
White Sox *see* Chicago White Sox
White Sox Park 56, 61, 75, 130, 140, 156, 214, 223–224
Wickersham, Dave 151, 162, 203
Wilhelm, Hoyt 70–74, **72**, 145, 159, 162, 191, 203, 217, 284
Wilhite, Nick 82
Williams, Dick 13–14, **16**, 17–22, 41, 61, 66–67, 81, 85, 94, 117–120, 123, 142–145, 148, 150, 175–178, 181, 183–184, 190, 192, 197–200, 209, 212, 215, 228, 231–234, 245–246, 248, 250, 259, 262, 264–265, 268, 270–271, 273, 277, 280, 284
Williams, Ted 17–18, 42, 122, 144, 168, 180–181
Williams, Walt 76, 150
Wilson, Earl 23–24, 27, 68, 137–138, 152–153, 168–172, **169**, 175, 183, 187, 192, 194, 204, 222, 238–239, 241, 260, 284; Cloud Nine 169–170
Winston-Salem (A baseball team) 77
WMAQ 177, 215
Wood, Wilbur 59, 73, 74, 85, 142, 191, 203, 217, 219, 284–285
World Series 3, 11, 13, 25, 35, 47, 50, 58, 60, 88, 90, 117–118, 121, 127, 133, 155, 168, 171–172, 177, 182, 197, 199, 201–202, 205, 208, 222, 224, 227, 241, 251, 257, 275–285; Caribbean World Series 34; Junior World Series 179; money/share 177, 199, 226, 230, 264, 270; 1967 World Series games 263–274; tickets 182, 225, 272
World War II 42–43, 71
Worthington, Al 36, 50, 79, 115–117, 137, 167, 175, 197, 226–227, 251, 285
Wright, Clyde 241–242
WTCN 221
Wyatt, John 60, 80–81, 109, 122, 143, 145, 170, 175, 198, 272, 285
Wynn, Early 249

Yankee Stadium 20–21, 58, 66, 135
Yankees *see* New York Yankees
Yastrzemski, Carl 15, 17–18, 21, 41, 59–60, 65, 84–85, 94, 101, 122, 123, 134–135, 142, 144–145, 148, 151, 161, 168, 178–183, **179**, 186, 190, 198, 208–209, 229–235, 239, 244, 247–251, 253–255, 262, 264–268, 271, 273, 282–283, 285; Carl Yastrzemski Night 134
Yastrzemski, Mike 229
Yawkey, Tom 60, 66, 111, 123–124, 134, 168–169, 180, 184, 245, 259, 274, 282, 285
Yost, Eddie 114–115

Zimmerman, Jerry 101, 214, 232, 251, 276

www.ingramcontent.com/pod-product-compliance
Ingram Content Group UK Ltd.
Pitfield, Milton Keynes, MK11 3LW, UK
UKHW041923140426
5217IPUK00014B/295